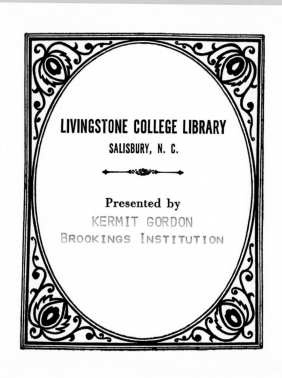

BUREAUCRATIC POLITICS
and FOREIGN POLICY

Morton H. Halperin

with the assistance of
Priscilla Clapp *and* Arnold Kanter

THE BROOKINGS INSTITUTION
Washington, D.C.

Library of Congress Cataloging in Publication Data:

Halperin, Morton H
  Bureaucratic politics and foreign policy.
  Bibliography: p.
  1. United States—Foreign relations administration.
I. Clapp, Priscilla, joint author.   II. Kanter, Arnold, joint author.
III. Title.
JX1706.A4 1974   353.008'92   73-22384
ISBN 0-8157-3408-5
ISBN 0-8157-3407-7 (pbk.)

In memory of
JOHN T. MCNAUGHTON

THE BROOKINGS INSTITUTION is an independent organization devoted to nonpartisan research, education, and publication in economics, government, foreign policy, and the social sciences generally. Its principal purposes are to aid in the development of sound public policies and to promote public understanding of issues of national importance.

The Institution was founded on December 8, 1927, to merge the activities of the Institute for Government Research, founded in 1916, the Institute of Economics, founded in 1922, and the Robert Brookings Graduate School of Economics and Government, founded in 1924.

The Board of Trustees is responsible for the general administration of the Institution, while the immediate direction of the policies, program, and staff is vested in the President, assisted by an advisory committee of the officers and staff. The by-laws of the Institution state, "It is the function of the Trustees to make possible the conduct of scientific research, and publication, under the most favorable conditions, and to safeguard the independence of the research staff in the pursuit of their studies and in the publication of the results of such studies. It is not a part of their function to determine, control, or influence the conduct of particular investigations or the conclusions reached."

The President bears final responsibility for the decision to publish a manuscript as a Brookings book or staff paper. In reaching his judgment on the competence, accuracy, and objectivity of each study, the President is advised by the director of the appropriate research program and weighs the views of a panel of expert outside readers who report to him in confidence on the quality of the work. Publication of a work signifies that it is deemed to be a competent treatment worthy of public consideration; such publication does not imply endorsement of conclusions or recommendations contained in the study.

The Institution maintains its position of neutrality on issues of public policy in order to safeguard the intellectual freedom of the staff. Hence interpretations or conclusions in Brookings publications should be understood to be solely those of the author or authors and should not be attributed to the Institution, to its trustees, officers, or other staff members, or to the organizations that support its research.

Foreword

A natural assumption is that governments—including that of the United States—tailor their national security decisions to what is happening abroad or what they hope to achieve abroad. The truth is apparently more complicated. The decisions and actions of governments result from the interplay among executive and legislative organizations, public and private interests, and, of course, personalities. This interplay becomes a determinant of foreign policy no less than events abroad or at home.

It has become increasingly clear, therefore, that policy prescriptions must take account of the process from which government policy emerges. This book is a study of that decision process within the U.S. government, particularly as it relates to national security affairs.

The book is arranged in three major parts. The first identifies the participants in national security decisions and seeks to explain the interests they represent. The second describes the manner in which policy positions are advanced and defended. The third relates policy decisions to their implementation, a process that has often been underemphasized in decision-making studies. In the final chapter, the author offers his views of the relevance of this type of analysis to policy making.

Morton H. Halperin came to Brookings directly from the environment he describes in this book. From 1966 to 1969 he was deputy assistant secretary for political-military planning and arms control in the Office of the Assistant Secretary of Defense for International Security Affairs. In January 1969, he joined the National Security Council as a senior staff member for planning. During the six years before he entered government service, Mr. Halperin was an assistant professor of government at Harvard University and a research associate at the Harvard Center for International Affairs. He has been a Brookings senior fellow since late 1969.

The Institution wishes to acknowledge the valuable assistance of the study group formed to advise Mr. Halperin as this book was written. Its members (with their affiliations at the time they participated) were: Richard E. Neustadt of Harvard University, chairman; Robert Bowie of Harvard University, chairman in Mr. Neustadt's absence; Graham T. Allison of Harvard University; Francis M. Bator of Harvard University; William Beecher of the *New York Times*; Henry Brandon of the *Sunday Times* of London; Joseph Califano of the firm of Williams, Connolly, and Califano; Irving M. Destler of the Brookings Institution; Elizabeth B. Drew of the *Atlantic Monthly*; Leslie H. Gelb of the Brookings Institution; Edward K. Hamilton, Deputy Mayor of New York City; Arnold Kanter of the Brookings Institution; Herbert Kaufman of the Brookings Institution; Ernest May of Harvard University; Jonathan Moore of the Department of State; Henry Owen of the Brookings Institution; Benjamin Read of the Woodrow Wilson International Center for Scholars; Chalmers M. Roberts of the *Washington Post*; Thomas C. Schelling of Harvard University; Warner Schilling of Columbia University; Charles L. Schultze of the Brookings Institution; Philip H. Trezise of the State Department; and Richard H. Ullman of Princeton University. The group met twice in Washington to review the manuscript, and each member gave generously of his time throughout the project.

The manuscript was edited by Robert Erwin; the index was prepared by Helen B. Eisenhart.

The views advanced in this book are those of the author and should not be ascribed to the trustees, officers, or other staff members of the Brookings Institution.

KERMIT GORDON
President

October 1973
Washington, D.C.

Preface

The purpose of this book is easy to state but difficult to accomplish. My aim is to give the reader a feel for the process by which decisions are made and actions taken by the American government in the field of national security. In writing I have, of course, been influenced by my own experience as Deputy Assistant Secretary of Defense (1966–69) and as a member of the staff of the National Security Council (1969), but this book is in no sense autobiographical. The cases used in the book are all from the published works of others and, mainly, from the memoirs of those who served in the national security bureaucracy in the postwar period. Indeed, in doing the research for this book I have examined all such memoirs of which I am aware, and they are listed in the bibliography along with the other sources examined.

Although all of the examples are from the United States in the postwar period, I believe that a substantial portion of the book is also relevant to other countries and other periods. Some readers have suggested to me that much of what is described is no different from the behavior of domestic agencies, state and local governments, and large business firms. Without rejecting this view, I would be satisfied if the reader came away feeling that he had a better understanding of how national security policy emerged from Washington. I consider briefly in the concluding chapter the policy implications of the approach presented.

The reader will find a number of long quotations. They are meant to be read. In many cases they are illuminating descriptions of events by a participant; in a few cases they are analyses of key issues stated clearly and succinctly. Readers of successive drafts have reported that the quotes are extremely interesting. To repeat: read them.

I have been writing this book on and off for a long time and in the process have accumulated a number of obligations. More of this book than I care to acknowledge was taught to me by two of my professors: Warner

Schilling (under whom I studied at Columbia College in 1956–57) and H. Bradford Westerfield (Yale University, 1958–59). My interest in the subject was rekindled by the formation at Harvard in 1966 of the "May Group" which met from time to time to discuss the role of bureaucracy in the making of national security policy. I learned much from the members of that group, which included Graham T. Allison, Joseph L. Bower, Fred C. Iklé, William W. Kaufman, Andrew W. Marshall, Ernest R. May, Richard E. Neustadt, Don K. Price, and Henry S. Rowen.

In July 1966 I went to work in the government, intending to stay for one year as a "participant-observer"; I stayed for more than three but quickly lost my status as "observer." I did, however, learn much about how the bureaucracy functions and about the obligations and responsibilities of a middle-level in-and-outer. My greatest debt is to the late John T. McNaughton, in memory of whom this book is dedicated. McNaughton was killed tragically in an airplane disaster in August 1967 just as he was preparing to move from his post as Assistant Secretary of Defense for International Security Affairs to become Secretary of the Navy. From McNaughton I learned much about how to operate effectively while maintaining one's integrity and concentrating on important issues.

I learned also from the two men who served as Secretary of Defense while I was in the Pentagon—Robert S. McNamara and Clark Clifford— from my two other bosses Paul C. Warnke and Henry A. Kissinger, and from numerous colleagues in the federal government, among them Philip Farley, Leslie C. Gelb, Haakon Lindjord, Winston Lord, Richard C. Steadman, Frederick C. Wyle, and Adam Yarmolinsky.

In September 1969 I came to the Brookings Institution to write this book. From the first day to the end, through an almost endless series of outlines, drafts, and redrafts, Arnold Kanter read every word that I produced and provided detailed comments. Many of the ideas in this book resulted from discussions between us and from his written comments on my drafts. In the latter stages of the project Priscilla Clapp worked to bring cohesion and clarity to the manuscript and played a major role in shaping its final structure. Whatever lack of clarity remains in the ideas presented here is attributable in large part to my stubborn refusal to accept all of their suggestions.

During the course of writing, many others commented on parts or all of my manuscript. I am indebted to the members of my study group, listed in the Foreword, and in particular to Richard Neustadt, its chairman, and Robert R. Bowie, who chaired the final meeting of the group.

I also benefited from discussion of portions of my manuscript at sessions of the May Group and from discussions at a conference on bureaucracy and foreign policy held at the RAND Corporation in the summer of 1972. I am also grateful to Chalmers Roberts and Alexander George for a careful reading of the entire manuscript and for numerous helpful comments. Ann Corbett typed and retyped the drafts with unfailing good humor and with a sharp eye for what did not make sense.

Ina, my wife, provided strong support and encouragement throughout, as well as bringing a critical perspective to bear on the manuscript.

M. H. H.

Contents

xvii

CHAPTER ONE

The ABM Puzzle: An Introduction to Politics inside Government

On September 18, 1967, Secretary of Defense Robert S. McNamara rose to deliver an address on "The Dynamics of Nuclear Strategy" to a meeting of the United Press International Editors and Publishers in San Francisco. He stressed that neither the United States nor the Soviet Union had increased their security in any way by deploying strategic nuclear weapons, and he suggested that the United States had bought many more weapons than it needed only because of a groundless fear that the Russians would step up their arms production. Having sketched this general background, McNamara turned to a subject which was then in the headlines—namely, the possibility of American deployment of an antiballistic missile (ABM) system.

He pointed out that the United States had substantially improved its technological capability. But he emphasized that even an advanced ABM system could easily be defeated if the Soviet Union simply fired more offensive warheads or dummy warheads than there were defensive missiles capable of dealing with them. Proceeding with this line of argument, he asserted:

Were we to deploy a heavy ABM system throughout the United States, the Soviets would clearly be strongly motivated so to increase their offensive capability as to cancel out our defensive advantage.

It is futile for each of us to spend $4 billion, $40 billion, or $400 billion—and at the end of all the spending, and at the end of all the deployment, and at the end of all the effort, to be relatively at the same point of balance on the security scale that we are now.[1]

---

1. McNamara, "The Dynamics of Nuclear Strategy," p. 448.

The notes in our book pinpoint for the reader where in the sources the passages we quote are located and the episodes we cite are described. For this purpose, an author's

Until then the Johnson administration had been resisting substantial pressure in refusing to deploy an ABM.

The Secretary of Defense, however, did not conclude his statement here. Rather he took another tack. He argued that it was important to distinguish between an anti-Russian ABM and an ABM system designed to defend the United States against emerging Chinese nuclear capability. Reviewing the arguments in favor of a deployment against China, he announced, "We have decided to go forward with this Chinese-oriented ABM deployment; and we will begin actual production of such a system at the end of this year."[2]

Before concluding, McNamara returned to his earlier theme:

There is a kind of mad momentum intrinsic to the development of all new nuclear weaponry. If a weapon system works—and works well—there is strong pressure from many directions to procure and deploy the weapon out of all proportion to the prudent level required.

The danger of deploying this relatively light and reliable Chinese-oriented ABM system is going to be that pressures will develop to expand it into a heavy Soviet-oriented ABM system.

We must resist that temptation firmly, not because we can for a moment afford to relax our vigilance against a possible Soviet first strike, but precisely because our greatest deterrent against such a strike is not a massive, costly, but highly penetrable ABM shield, but rather a fully credible offensive assured destruction capability.

The so-called heavy ABM shield—at the present state of technology—

---

name, the title or short title of a source, and a page number or similar designation suffice.

The sources in full are identified in the Bibliography, which begins on p. 317. There the reader will find three sections, each alphabetized within itself. Section A of the Bibliography is a comprehensive list of the memoirs written by men involved in the making of U.S. foreign policy during the postwar period. Section B, likewise focused upon participants in the policy process, lists a number of interviews conducted, recorded, and transcribed by the John F. Kennedy Library. Section C—for "non memoirs"—lists all other sources consulted by us, whether quoted or not.

Since the source referred to here in this first note, "The Dynamics of Nuclear Strategy," is an address rather than a memoir or an interview, it is entered under the author's name (Robert S. McNamara) in Section C. In that entry the title of the periodical that printed the complete address is given (*Department of State Bulletin*), along with the date of issue (October 9, 1967).

More than one source may come from the same author, and his respective writings may fall into more than one category. Mr. McNamara, for example, is also listed in Section A, as the author of *The Essence of Security*.

2. Ibid., p. 450.

would in effect be no adequate shield at all against a Soviet attack but rather a strong inducement for the Soviets to vastly increase their own offensive forces. That, as I have pointed out, would make it necessary for us to respond in turn; and so the arms race would rush hopelessly on to no sensible purpose on either side.[3]

Why had Robert McNamara used a speech which was largely anti-ABM in tone and substance to announce an ABM deployment? Some Washington reporters speculated that he had been overruled at the last minute; what was meant by him to be an anti-ABM speech had been converted by others in the administration into a vehicle for announcing an ABM deployment. Others argued that the speech should be taken at face value: the administration had come to the conclusion that an ABM against Russia was not desirable but that one against China was necessary.

Those in the audience and in the country who had followed the issue wondered how the Secretary's speech related to the annual budget message delivered by President Lyndon Johnson in January 1967. The President had asked for funds to deploy an ABM system but had stated that he would defer a decision to start construction pending an effort to begin strategic arms limitation talks with the Russians. At that time the President was vague about the purpose of the ballistic missile defense but stated that the funds might be used to deploy an ABM "for such purposes as defense of our offensive weapons systems."[4] McNamara, in his speech, had briefly mentioned the defense of Minuteman missiles only as a possible add-on to the ABM deployment against China.

The purpose for which the administration was deploying its ABM system was further clouded in the coming weeks. The Joint Chiefs of Staff and leading senators, including Richard Russell, Chairman of the Senate Armed Services Committee, described the ABM deployment as the beginning of a large anti-Russian system, even though McNamara had warned against attempting one. McNamara himself continued to describe the system as a defense against China; the President said nothing.

As the first steps toward deployment were made, it appeared that the initial construction was no different from what it would have been if the purpose were to protect American cities against a large Russian attack.

These puzzles have usually prompted an all-inclusive question which is assumed to have a single answer: Why did the United States decide to

3. Ibid.
4. Lyndon B. Johnson, *Public Papers of the Presidents of the United States, 1967,* Bk. I, p. 48.

deploy an anti-Chinese ABM system in the fall of 1967? In trying to explain foreign policy decisions, most observers assume that decision makers are motivated by a single set of national security images and foreign policy goals. Supposedly decisions reflect these goals alone, and actions are presumed to flow directly from the decisions. Thus "explanation" consists of identifying the interests of the nation as seen by the leaders and showing how they determine the decisions and actions of the government. Graham Allison has argued persuasively that this type of analysis is the pervasive form of explanation for foreign policy actions of the United States and other governments.[5]

With this approach, the explanation offered for the American decision to deploy an ABM against China would be that the American government decided that its interests in the Far East required a Chinese-oriented ABM system but that a system against the Soviet Union made no sense because of the technological difficulty of building a system against a sophisticated military opponent.

Sometimes such explanations are sufficient; they provide all that anyone needs to know or wants to know when his interest in an issue is limited. Often such explanations are the best that can be constructed, given the data available. This is true not only of the decisions and actions of foreign governments, particularly ones with a closed decision system, but also, unfortunately, of many contemporary American decisions. In cases where someone seeks more detailed and satisfactory answers, such explanations are highly inadequate. They often require positing a very unusual set of interests to explain decisions and actions. In the case of the ABM, one would have to conjure up a set of interests that explain why different officials of the American government made conflicting statements about whether or not a large ABM system against the Soviet Union was a good idea and whether or not the system to be deployed would be a first step toward an anti-Russian system.

There is no question that the reality is different. The actions of the American government related to foreign policy result from the interests and behavior of many different groups and individuals in American society. Domestic politics in the United States, public attitudes, and the international environment all help to shape decisions and actions. Senators, congressmen, and interest groups are involved to varying degrees, depending on the issue. The relevant departments of the federal bureau-

5. See Allison, *Essence of Decision*.

cracy are involved, as is the President, at least on major issues. The participants, while sharing some images of the international scene, see the world in very different ways. Each wants the government to do different things, and each struggles to secure the decisions and actions he thinks best.

Here we focus only on part of this process—that involving the bureaucracy and the President as he deals with the bureaucracy. Bureaucracy, as the term is used here, refers to civilian career officials and political appointees, as well as to military officers. For some issues, distinctions between these groups need to be made—and will be made—but most of what we have to say about the interests and maneuvers of the bureaucracy applies to career officials, political appointees, and military officers alike. Our attention is directed primarily to political and military rather than economic issues.

Other cases besides the ABM episode are used in the following chapters to illustrate our propositions. These cases are drawn mainly from the memoirs of those who have served in the federal bureaucracy, and the rest come from the published works of analysts of governmental decision making. No cases have been worked up from accounts that we believe to be erroneous, but it should be noted that we have relied on the approximate accuracy of the authors' reports; we have not researched the cases independently. We do not purport to be writing history. Our aim is to illustrate through elements of the historical record certain propositions about how politics *within a government* influence decisions and actions ostensibly directed outward.

Because of the dominant concern with security issues in most postwar memoirs, the decision to rely on those writings rather than interviews as a basis for this book has compounded its bias toward military and security issues as distinct from economic issues, technological issues, and so forth. However, our propositions about bureaucratic behavior would probably also be applicable to economic issues, although a book that focused on them would undoubtedly give more attention to Congress and to outside interest groups.

Since our goal is to describe the national security decision process, particularly that part of it where organizational or personal interests are brought to bear on the issue at hand, we begin with a discussion of participants. Who is involved? What interests do they have? How do these interests affect their stands on particular issues?

Part I deals with these questions, concentrating on those parts of the bureaucracy concerned with political-military affairs: namely, the White

House, the State Department, and the Defense Department. The role of shared images about what the national security requires is followed by a discussion of organizational and presidential interests. A final chapter explores the factors that determine how a participant develops a stand on an issue.

Part II considers the process by which participants and organizations struggle to bring about the decisions that they want. It considers how issues arise and are shaped by the rules of the game. The degree to which participants plan their maneuvers is considered; this is followed by a discussion of information and arguments and the process by which presidential decisions are made. Finally, Part II explores sources of power in the bureaucracy and the kinds of decisions that emerge. The focus is on issues that work their way up through the bureaucracy, ultimately requiring a decision by the President.

Part III turns to the generally ignored question of what happens after the government makes a decision. Here we trace the process by which presidential decisions become governmental actions. The reader will have to keep in mind that the events described in each section often occur simultaneously or in quick succession.

At the end of the book, in Part IV, we return to the ABM case, to show how the approach used throughout provides a framework for considering these four puzzles that arose with regard to the ABM decisions:

1. Why, in January 1967, did President Johnson ask Congress to appropriate the funds to deploy an ABM system but state that he would defer a decision to initiate the deployment pending an effort to get the Soviets to engage in talks on limiting the arms race?

2. Why was the decision to deploy an ABM announced at the end of a speech whose main purpose was to explain why an ABM defense against the Soviet Union was impossible and undesirable?

3. Why did Secretary of Defense McNamara describe the system as one directed against China, while the Joint Chiefs of Staff and senior senators described it as a first step toward a full-scale defense against the Soviet Union?

4. Why was the system authorized for deployment one which was designed and deployed as if its intent was to protect American cities against a large Russian attack?

The purpose of this analysis—of the book as a whole—is to help the reader understand how decisions are made and to predict likely courses of behavior. The book provides only part of the answer, however, since it focuses only on that part of the decisionmaking process which involves the bureaucracy and the relation between the bureaucracy and the President. The role of the Congress and public opinion is not treated in depth. Furthermore, not every national security decision becomes subject to the pulling and hauling described in the following chapters. The book seeks to explain elements of the foreign policy decision process that, for one reason or another, are often overlooked or at least not taken into account systematically. The concluding chapter suggests that the analysis has important implications for U.S. foreign policy. In the end, the reader will have to judge for himself the utility of the approach.

PART ONE

Interests and Participants

CHAPTER TWO

National Security Interests

When participants share a set of global images, these will decisively shape stands taken on particular issues. From the onset of the cold war until quite recently, a majority of American officials (as well as the American public) have held a set of widely shared images.

Shared Images

The shared images of the postwar period may be summarized as follows, in the language employed at the time.[1]

1. The preeminent feature of international politics is the conflict between Communism and the Free World.

2. Every nation that falls to Communism increases the power of the Communist bloc in its struggle with the Free World.

3. The surest simple guide to U.S. interests in foreign policy is opposition to Communism.

4. Russian intentions toward Western Europe are essentially expansionist. So, too, are Chinese intentions in Asia.

5. The main source of unrest, disorder, subversion, and civil war in underdeveloped areas is Communist influence and support.

6. The United States—and only the United States—has the power, ability, responsibility, and right to defend the Free World and maintain international order. The rest of the Free World must contribute as much as possible to the U.S. effort to defend against aggression.

7. The United States has an obligation to aid any Free People resisting Communism at home or abroad.

1. This list draws heavily on Graham Allison's "Cool It: The Foreign Policy of Young America," pp. 144–60. In particular it relies on his chart of what he calls "Axioms of the Postwar Era." See also Ernest R. May, "The Nature of Foreign Policy: The Calculated versus the Axiomatic," pp. 666–67.

8. Peace is indivisible. Therefore collective defense is necessary. The new international order is based primarily on U.S. assumption of responsibility for other states' security, in support of which the United States must show itself ready to resist aggression. Thus any expansion of Communist influence must be resisted.

9. Concessions made under pressure constitute appeasement which only whets the appetite of aggressors.

10. Coalition governments are inevitably taken over by the Communists.

11. The Third World really matters, because (a) it is the battleground between Communism and the Free World; (b) Western capital will generate economic development and political stability with a minimum of violence; and (c) instability is the great threat to progress in the Third World.

12. The United States can play an important role in inducing European integration, which will solve the German problem.

13. Military strength is the primary route to national security.

14. The United States must maintain military superiority over the Soviet Union, including the ability to destroy the Soviet Union after a Soviet first strike.

15. Nuclear war would be a great disaster and must be avoided.

16. U.S. prosperity depends on the economic health of other developed nations, a favorable U.S. balance of payments, and the preservation of the American gold supply.

The list is admittedly oversimplified and is not intended to imply that all perceptions of national security are naive. It is meant to illustrate the sort of common denominator from which more refined perceptions of national security derive. Naturally not every participant in the United States government in the postwar era has fully accepted each one of these shared images.

Regional Images

The change of attitudes toward Europe over the past decade can serve to illustrate the role of more specific images.

Several different images of what the trend of European developments is and what the U.S. should be seeking to accomplish in Europe have competed for the allegiance of those in the foreign policy community within the United States. During the 1960s U.S. European policy tended to be dominated by a set of images held by "Europeanists," who saw Europe as moving inevitably toward a unification based on the ideas of Jean Monnet and believed that this unification was vital to U.S. security. This view was held by most of the leaders of the Kennedy administration, particularly George Ball, the Under Secretary of State, who was given wide autonomy in European policy.

With Ball's departure, with the coming to office of President Johnson (who had a less definite image of U.S.-European relations than did President Kennedy), and with increasing irritation over the policies of French President Charles de Gaulle, there was a gradual diffusion of responsibility for policy toward Europe to the point where no single set of images prevailed. The State Department Bureau of European Affairs, supported by Under Secretary of State for Political Affairs Eugene Rostow, held to the Europeanist point of view. In the White House and the Pentagon, however, European unification was no longer seen as especially likely or as crucially important. Here various officials and advisers emphasized the management of particular problems among European states and between Washington and particular European capitals.

The change of administrations in 1968 led to a clear articulation of a new image of U.S.-European relations. In large part this reflected the views of Henry Kissinger (the President's Assistant for National Security Affairs) and of President Nixon himself. The new image emphasized that Europe's future evolution was uncertain and that European unification was a matter for the Europeans to determine and not a vital security interest of the United States. It emphasized the need for close cooperative relations with all European countries, whether or not this appeared to hinder efforts at European unification or NATO military integration.

These changes in the U.S. image of where Europe was going, what the effect of U.S. policy would be, and what would serve U.S. interests were not closely correlated with changes in the reality of U.S.-European relations or of European politics; nor were they correlated with changes in national mood. They reflect, almost entirely, changes in personnel, who brought with them a different set of images that came to dominate policy in a particular area.

Shifting Images

The example provided above brings us to a discussion of the ways in which images may shift. In some cases, as we have seen, something as routine as a change in personnel may cause a set of shared images to shift. In other cases, events in the outside world may bring about fundamental changes in the way American society looks at the world, as occurred in the late 1960s, partly in relation to the Vietnam War.

Changes in personnel are more likely to affect images of American policy toward particular regions. In such cases, the set of shared images guiding policy is likely to be held by a relatively small number of individuals whose concerns society as a whole is hardly aware of. Here, changes in personnel can make an enormous difference. Shifts such as those noted for European policy have also taken place in regard to Latin America and East Asia.

It sometimes happens that images are shared widely within the bureaucracy and among those currently in senior government positions but not within American society as a whole. In this situation, the introduction of new participants from outside government (and outside the usual channels of recruitment) might bring about changes in shared images. Bill Moyers has in fact prescribed just such a change in American policy:

The best thing that could happen to this country's foreign policy would be for the next President to appoint to the State Department a team of men beholden to no orthodox liturgy—to no liturgy, period—of foreign policy. What a horrible thing to do to the custodial bureaucracy—to have newcomers running our foreign policy—but I think the establishment would survive. Certainly the country would. It would do our foreign policy good to have a new beginning free of yesterday's cant. But that would require some men from other than traditional molds.[2]

However, it is rare for the images shared within the government to diverge radically from those in the society as a whole, and the appointment of individuals who cannot accept the broader images shared within the bureaucracy is probably equally rare. Moreover, the socialization process within the government is such that individuals who come in with doubts about, or in ignorance of, particular aspects of the set of shared images prevalent in the bureaucracy frequently find themselves quickly coming to support them.

Dramatic changes in the outside world, either at home or abroad, may become so sharp that they intrude upon the perceptions of even those with fixed ideas of foreign policy, leading to changes in shared images. At the same time, the changes in reality that occur at home can affect beliefs

---

2. "Bill Moyers Talks about the War and LBJ," pp. 270–71.

about what the public will stand for or what the public will demand, an important part of the set of shared images shaping policy in the United States. Arguments about public mood play a role in internal debate about foreign policy proposals and shift with reality as that reality becomes manifest. In addition, images of the outside world held by government officials bear some relation to the set of shared images held by the larger foreign policy community and by the electorate at large. If the gap becomes too large, the political cost of maintaining a policy dependent on these images will come to appear excessive. Thus, as changes in national mood lead to changes in the images of the world held by the population at large, these changes come to be reflected within the bureaucracy. The causes of such changes in national mood are complex and varied and lie beyond the scope of this study. However, it is important to recognize that changes in national mood do affect changes in the images shared by the bureaucracy. This may well be the most important way in which general public attitudes affect foreign policy in the United States, although the time it takes the bureaucracy to respond can be substantial.

On some occasions, events in the outside world force changes in images. For example, the proposition that ideology would prevent the Soviet Union and Communist China from ever thinking of each other as potential military opponents was widely accepted within the American government throughout much of the postwar period, but is no longer a tenable proposition. Very few changes in the world are such as to produce unambiguous evidence of the need to alter images immediately. Most events can be interpreted various ways, and their effect on U.S. interests and the way in which the world operates is difficult to assess. Gradually, changes in international reality do bring about changes in the set of shared images within the American government, but the effect is rarely direct and immediate. In some cases, images may change even though reality does not, or reality may change substantially without bringing about any change in the beliefs of officials.

A proposed course of action that can be shown to be unambiguously necessary to preserve a shared objective will be agreed to by all. However, this is a very rare event. Widely shared images often do lead to agreement on basic objectives and therefore to the exclusion of certain conceivable courses of action. Thus, confronted with a developing Russian intercontinental ballistic missile (ICBM) capability and the initial deployment of a Soviet ABM system, no one suggested that the United States need not be concerned at all and could sit back and permit the Soviet Union to gain strategic superiority. Nor did anyone openly argue that the United States needed to build a large ABM system so it would be in a position to carry out, at a time of its own choosing, a strategic nuclear attack against the Soviet Union. In the early and mid-1960s, the debate within the government about ABM was carried out in the context of a shared belief that American strategic superiority was necessary as "insurance" and that it could and would be maintained. Some, including McNamara, no longer accepted the value of superiority, but they had to argue as if they did.

Clues to National Security Interests

There is always great uncertainty about what is going on in the world and what the effects of alternative courses of action would be. The way an individual copes with this uncertainty is affected by his background—the personal experiences, intellectual baggage, and psychological needs he brings with him—as well as by his position in the bureaucracy.

Each participant, depending on where he sits, will see a somewhat different face of an issue, because his perception of the issue will be heavily shaded by his particular concerns. What is primarily a budget issue to one participant will be an issue of relations with a foreign government to a second and of relations with Congress to a third. Those in the Defense Department and the Budget Bureau concerned with limiting military spending tended to view the ABM as a budget issue. Scientists in the Pentagon and in the so-called defense industry felt ABM deployment would maintain the technological superiority of the United States. Officials in the Arms Control and Disarmament Agency viewed the issue in terms of possible arms control agreements with the Soviet Union. Foreign Service officers in the West European division of the State Department were concerned with the effect of ABM deployment on our relations with European allies and on the cohesion of NATO. Participants sensitive to the President's relations with senior congressional leaders who supported the ABM saw the issue in terms of future dealings with Congress. Secretary of Defense McNamara assessed ABM deployment in terms of decreasing spending for strategic forces and increasing the prospects for arms control arrangements with the Soviet Union. Army officials saw the issue in terms of the size of the Army budget and maintaining an Army role in strategic nuclear deterrence. The President, sitting at the top, saw the issue in terms of his own sense of what national security required, of his relations with McNamara and military and congressional leaders, and of his own desires to keep spending down and to reach agreement with the Soviet Union.

Thus each participant may focus on a different face of the issue and sense different dangers and/or opportunities. For budget officials, preventing large expenditures was most important, and the rationale given for any system or the way decisions were communicated to foreign governments were matters of relative indifference. For State Department officials, the cost of the ABM was not important, for the funds did not come from the State Department budget; but the way the issue was communicated to our allies and to the Soviet Union was a matter of great concern. Where an individual sits in the process determines in large part the faces of the issue that he sees and helps to determine the stakes that he sees involved and hence the stand that he takes. We thus need to identify briefly who the main participants are before considering how their personal experience, background, and official position may affect their concept of interests, the face of the issue they see, and the stands they take.

Participants

The President stands at the center of the foreign policy process in the United States. His role and influence over decisions are qualitatively different from those of any other participant. In any foreign policy decision widely believed at the time to be important, the President will almost always be the principal figure determining the *general* direction of actions. Thus it was President Johnson who made the final decision that the United States should deploy an ABM system.

Furthermore, the President serves as the surrogate for the national interest. Many senior participants look to the President as to a blueprint for clues to the national security. His perception and judgment of what is in the national interest are dominant in the system. A strong President—with a clear sense of direction and leadership—can have a very strong influence on the images shared by bureaucratic participants, by Congress, and by the public.

Although the President is the principal decision maker on important foreign policy matters, he does not act alone. He is surrounded by a large number of participants with whom he consults, partly at his pleasure and partly by obligation. These other participants are arrayed around the President at varying distances determined by the probability that they will be consulted by him. For convenience, those participants whom he regularly consults will be called "senior" participants, and those who have access to the President only very infrequently or only through some senior participant will be called "junior" participants. It is important to note that whether a particular participant is senior or junior is only imperfectly related to the formal hierarchy of organization.

Whom the President consults depends in large part on the nature of the issue. Regardless of who is President, Cabinet officers and heads of relevant agencies will be consulted from time to time because of their formal responsibilities and access to information. Law and custom dictate that the Cabinet officers involved in foreign policy issues will almost always include both the Secretary of State and the Secretary of Defense, and in economic matters the Secretary of the Treasury will be called upon. The Joint Chiefs of Staff are consulted particularly on military budget issues and matters concerning the possible use of force. The Director of Central Intelligence will be consulted when information about foreign governments, particularly hostile ones, is viewed as critical.

These officials will routinely be influenced by their subordinates with whom they in turn consult. The Secretary of State usually depends most heavily on the regional Assistant Secretary most directly concerned. Bureaus with specialized responsibilities such as policy planning, political-military affairs, and economic affairs will also be involved, as will the Secretary's principal assistants, the Deputy Secretary, the Under Secretaries, and the Deputy Under Secretaries.

On national security issues related to foreign policy the Secretary of Defense is likely to consult with the military services, with his Deputy, and with the Assistant Secretary for International Security Affairs. Particularly on budget matters, he will also consult with the Assistant Secretaries responsible for systems analysis and research and development. The Chairman of the Joint Chiefs of Staff and his colleagues the service Chiefs of Staff will be supported by their aides as well as by the staff of each service. The Director of Central Intelligence will join with his colleagues from State and Defense to produce formal National Intelligence Estimates. The Director will also consult with his current intelligence and scientific intelligence staffs and, where covert operations are involved, with his "program" staff. In many cases, military commanders in the field and American ambassadors and their staffs are involved. Officials from agencies such as AID, USIA, Agriculture, and Commerce may become involved in economic decisions.

Others who may be consulted, depending on the particular President and his preferences, include members of the White House staff—specialists on national security or foreign policy, as well as political advisers, speech writers, and managers of the legislative program of the President. President Eisenhower relied less on such advisers than did other postwar Presidents; President Johnson drew on them less for defense budget issues than general foreign policy matters; President Richard Nixon relied for several years on his Assistant for National Security Affairs.

Some of these participants are career officials. Others are "in-and-outers" who come from careers outside the government for limited periods of government service. Often these participants are lawyers, bankers, businessmen, or experts from universities or foundations. Although not formally members of the national security bureaucracy, individuals outside the executive branch are frequently consulted by the President and have significant influence on decisions. Some congressmen and senators are senior participants in the sense that they are routinely contacted by the President for advice and support. These legislators are most often chairmen or high-ranking members of the congressional committees with direct responsibility for national security affairs (e.g., Armed Services, Foreign Relations, Appropriations, Atomic Energy), and they have discretionary power over the federal budget. To the extent that the Congress represents the focus of the President's domestic political concerns, influential congressmen and senators will be important participants regardless of their direct legislative responsibilities for national security policy.

In some cases, Congress has taken the initiative itself to direct foreign policy decisions within the bureaucracy, especially with regard to foreign economic and military assistance. Because the legislative branch enjoys certain rights to control the operations of the executive branch, from time to time the exercise of these rights has a very direct effect on either the outcome of a particular decision or the decision-making process itself.

In 1973, for example, Congress voted to cut off funds for the bombing of Cambodia, thereby making it exceedingly difficult for the administration to continue the policy it was following at the time.

Finally, Congress serves as an important forum for the discussion of national interests and the shared images by which they are determined. On both ABM and Vietnam, Congress has played a major role in weighing the arguments and making vital decisions on funding. In 1967, congressmen applied major pressure for an ABM deployment, whereas in 1969 Congress came within one vote of denying its deployment—contrary to the wishes (and beliefs) of the President; and at least the broader national security debate over ABM was aired in committee hearings.

Sometimes individuals outside government are participants in the national security policy process. Ostensibly private citizens who are the close personal confidants of the President are included in this category. Private interest groups, such as defense contractors affected by foreign policy decisions, will seek influence. Such groups may be consulted by the President from time to time and are routinely involved by means of their contacts with the Congress. Other outsiders may be formally invited to participate in the process, usually for limited periods of time and with narrowly defined responsibilities. The various presidential commissions and study groups are examples.[3]

Determining Stands

With this brief listing of participants, we come back to the question of how each of the participants determines what stands are in the national interest. Given the intellectual difficulty of dealing with uncertainty, it is surprising that participants do have strongly held positions on particular issues. In part, this may be the result of what has been called the "51–49 principle." That is, a participant who judges an issue to be very close and who only with some difficulty comes down on one side or the other by a very narrow margin nevertheless feels obliged to advocate his position as if he believed it 100 percent. He recognizes that, if he shows great uncertainty, his views will not be taken seriously.

However, participants usually do not see issues as arbitrary, and they tend to find strong grounds to favor one position. Participants often employ two different techniques to simplify the problem of determining what is in the national interest: (1) they employ techniques for choosing among options less rigorous than those required by an analytic model, and (2) they equate a desirable state of the world beyond the borders of the United States with a desirable state of the world at home. That is, they come to determine the national security of the United States in terms of the health and well-being of the organization to which they belong, the political and other interests of the President, or their own personal interests, all of which are discussed in the following chapters.

3. Readers unfamiliar with the formal structure of the foreign policy process may wish to consult a standard work in the subject, such as Burton M. Sapin, *The Making of United States Foreign Policy*.

Whether they look directly to events in the outside world or to organizational, presidential, or personal interests as a surrogate for national security interests, participants will need a means of monitoring for threats and judging how to respond to them. We consider first the use of analytic techniques and then turn to a consideration of what John Steinbruner has called cognitive processes.

ANALYSIS

A "rational" approach assumes that an individual seeking to determine what is in the national interest of the United States would list a series of objectives and attempt to put them in hierarchical order; next he would examine a series of alternatives available to the United States and consider the cost and gains of each alternative in relation to the hierarchy of objectives. He would then search for additional information which would reduce the range of uncertainty and permit him to calculate what position was indeed good for the country. Armed with this analysis, he would take a particular stand on an issue but would be ready to change his position if he could obtain additional information or better calculations.

Such a mode of thinking, applied directly to national security interests, no doubt does seem logical to many of the participants. Where an analysis or a set of arguments substantially reduces the range of uncertainty, unambiguously pointing to the desirability of a particular stand, that position is likely to be adopted by most, if not all, participants. However, the making of such calculations involves an enormous cost in time and intellectual resources. Seldom does a participant, in fact, engage in such a search to determine what is in the national interest. Problems are too difficult, and time is short. Even if a participant looks to organizational, presidential, or personal interests as a means of determining what is in the national interest, analytic processes are likely to prove to be too cumbersome. Thus, whatever the source of clues to interests, individuals are likely to use shortcuts in place of an analytic model.

COGNITIVE PROCESSES

To save himself time-consuming analysis, a participant will focus, as John Steinbruner has suggested, on a few variables and develop a set of programmed responses to changes in any one of these variables.[4] Events in

---

4. Steinbruner, *Decisions under Complexity*, Chap. 4.

the outside world are screened in such a way as to filter out variables that would expose him to uncertainty. Moreover, participants tend to respond to changes in each variable separately, producing fragmented responses to each change. Steinbruner finds that an individual can deal with uncertainty in the outside world by using several standard techniques:

1. *Use of pat images and arguments by analogy.* Frequently individuals attempt to determine which previous event, either in international politics or in their own personal experience, most closely relates to the event at hand, and then they seek to reason by analogy. Thus the impulse to avoid another Munich played a major role in shaping the reaction of many government officials to the Vietnam situation.

2. *Inferences of transformation.* This technique, commonly known as "wishful thinking," involves the assumption that, if a problem is recognized, eventually it will somehow be solved, in a manner that one cannot specify. Thus one need not worry about that problem, but can focus on others.

3. *Inferences of impossibility.* Using this technique, a participant rules out one particular option by arguing that a critical premise on which it depends is, in fact, impossible.

4. *Negative images.* Through this technique, a possible option is ruled out by predicting dire consequences following from the implementation of this possibility. Opponents of ABM deployment argued that any decision to deploy an ABM system would inevitably lead to a very large system and eliminate the prospects for any negotiations with the Soviet Union.

Using these techniques, uncertainty is resolved by certainty in support of a particular position. The processes described by Steinbruner suggest three typical patterns of thinking by which an individual relates his interests to stands. Each pattern seems to be typical of a particular set of interests. (1) Those who focus directly on national security interests are likely to exhibit ideological thinking. (2) Those who focus on organizational interests will reflect grooved thinking. (3) Presidential interests are frequently reflected in uncommitted thinking. Each of these is explained and discussed in turn.

Ideological thinking is characterized by a very abstract and extensive belief pattern which is internally consistent and tends to be extremely stable. Generally, the belief pattern is characterized by emphasis on a single value (say, fighting communism or seeking disarmament) which tends to be pursued independently of reality as others may perceive it. Officials who hold to such a pattern are frequently known as "theologians" within the government, and in Anthony Downs' terms are "zealots."[5] Individuals whose position is characterized by ideological thinking use various techniques, such as the selective perception of information, to maintain their views in face of conflicting information. Because of the consistency of their position, they are able to act quickly and with confidence when others see ambiguity or are uncertain as to how to behave.

Ideological thinking generally characterizes in-and-outers who enter the government with strong commitments in a particular area. For in-and-outers and "regulars" alike, commitments often arise out of the first professional contact with an issue or from a seminal event in their past. For example, President Nixon's view of the Cuban regime seems to have been strongly affected by his long conversation with Fidel Castro during Castro's visit to the United States during the Eisenhower administration.

Ideological thinking also tends to characterize staff men who have had a long period of involvement in a particular area and become committed to a doctrine such as European unification. It may be exhibited by military officers or bureau chiefs in small interacting groups who commit themselves to a particular ideology that enhances the importance of the activity in which they are engaged.

Those whose approach is dominated by ideological thinking tend to see all issues in terms of a particular value, to disregard conflicting information and roadblocks, and to press hard for the particular solution which would support the dominant variable.

Participants who exhibit *grooved thinking* tend to focus on a few key variables and to have a programmed response to those particular variables. They are confronted by a repeated need to respond to particular events and do so by breaking a complex problem into its parts and responding in a programmed way to each variable. Often such individuals see national security in terms of organizational interests. For example, a State Department official responsible for maintaining good relations with an American ally is likely to focus on reports from the foreign office of that country and statements by the country's leaders. When signals from these sources suggest that there is a problem, he will respond with certain programmed responses, such as sending the ambassador to talk to the prime minister or requesting that a statement of reassurance be issued in Washington. He

5. Downs, *Inside Bureaucracy*, p. 88.

will tend to ignore signals for which he has no set response, such as the statements of newly risen opposition spokesmen or evidence of growing political or economic unrest.

This pattern of thought is typical of career officials, particularly at relatively low levels, who need to act constantly and become accustomed to regularized patterns of behavior. Many low-ranking Army officials, perhaps even senior officials, responded to the ABM in this way. They monitored Russian activities and typically responded to a Russian deployment by arguing that the United States needed to match that deployment. They also responded to Russia's increased offensive capability by arguing that the United States needed to add a direct defense specifically to deal with that offensive capability. Grooved thinking tends to produce routine responses to changes perceived one by one, and it ignores larger factors that might render the response inappropriate.

Uncommitted thinking characterizes those officials who must deal with generalized concepts, who are habitually confronted with uncertainty, and who tap a variety of information channels urging the importance of different problems and advocating different solutions to problems. Exposed to alternative patterns of belief designed to bring order to great uncertainties, individuals exhibiting uncommitted thinking will adopt different patterns at different times for the same problem. This will appear to outsiders to be oscillation, because the uncommitted thinker will seek freedom of maneuver by avoiding the integration of problems that appear to others to be closely related.

This pattern of thought often characterizes the President, who in dealing with a particular problem will have little weight of past experience and little firsthand knowledge. Issues tend to come to him and his closest associates in an abstract or generalized form, and pressure will be brought from many sides. The White House tends to relate each theory to its sponsors and to appeal to the allegiance of as many groups as possible.

President Johnson's behavior in dealing with the question of the ABM suggests the pattern of uncommitted thinking. Secretary of Defense McNamara attempted to get him to see the issue in terms of the danger of stimulating the arms race and of vastly increasing military expenditures. McNamara argued that the ABM was unnecessary and would increase the risk of nuclear war. Senior military officers and leading congressional figures, by contrast, attempted to have Johnson see the issue in terms of the importance of maintaining American strategic nuclear superiority. Since each of these views appeared sensible in its own terms, Johnson moved back and forth between support of the ABM and opposition to it. He probably never made a firm judgment of his own as to which of the two views being presented to him was correct. Rather, he responded to short-run pressures in an effort to keep the participants from breaking out and denouncing the decision that he must make. The President's behavior appeared to be a form of oscillation because his decision was characterized by uncommitted thinking in an effort to find a consensus which would satisfy all of those putting pressure on him.

When a persuasive case is made that a certain stand is required by, or ruled out by, the interests of the United States, most participants will agree to the decision. Indeed, much of what goes on in the government involves efforts to analyze an issue from the point of view of shared images and to persuade others that the requirements of national security, flowing from those shared images, require that a particular stand be taken. However, what is in fact in the national interest is often elusive despite shared images, and participants frequently find it difficult to develop a stand simply by focusing on national security directly. In such cases they will often look to organizational and presidential interests and explore these in light of their personal interests.

CHAPTER THREE

Organizational Interests

To the extent that participants come to equate national security with the interests of their organization, what stands do they tend to take, and how do these relate to organizational interests? Do organizations always seek to grow larger and do more things? This chapter attempts to specify in detail the organizational interests of the Defense Department, the State Department, the CIA, and their components.

Missions, Capabilities, and Influence

Most organizations have a mission to perform, either overseas or at home, and some organizations need to maintain expensive capabilities in order to perform their missions effectively. All organizations seek influence.

Organizations are formally charged with specific *missions*. Some of these can be accomplished entirely at home (such as maintaining good relations with Congress); others require actions abroad (such as deterring a Soviet attack on the United States).

Participants in a policy decision examine any proposal to gauge whether or not it would help their particular organization carry out its missions. For example, in examining ABM, the Budget Bureau and the Comptroller's Office in the Pentagon were concerned with how it would affect their ability to keep down the military budget. State Department officials were concerned with the impact of deployment on relations with European allies and with the Soviet Union.

The missions of some organizations in the national security field encourage them to maintain substantial and expensive *capabilities* which may be employed abroad. The armed services, for example, are responsible for creating very expensive military forces. Organizations with expensive capabilities will see the face of an issue which affects their ability to maintain what they view as the necessary capability for a variety of actions.

Organizations with expensive capabilities will be particularly concerned about budget decisions and about the budgeting implications of policy decisions. Organizations with missions but low-cost capabilities will be relatively unconcerned about the budget implications but highly concerned over the immediate implications of specific policy decisions. This is an important difference between the armed services and the State Department. The case of ABM illustrates this point. For the Army ABM meant a bigger budget and a greater role in strategic warfare. State Department officials, on the other hand, cared much less about costs and capabilities than about how the decision would affect relations with allies and potential adversaries. The fact that an ABM system might cost several billion dollars while an alternative way of reassuring allies might cost very little does not affect State Department interests, since State neither pays the costs nor operates the capabilities.

All organizations seek to have *influence* in order to pursue their other objectives. Those that have large operational capabilities seek influence on decisions, in part, to maintain the capability to perform their mission. Some organizations—the Office of International Security Affairs in the Office of the Secretary of Defense, for instance, and the policy planning staff in the State Department—have neither large capabilities nor stable, clearly defined missions. Their *organizational* goal tends to be that of gaining influence in pursuit of ideological concerns. Individuals on these staffs share with their counterparts in other organizations the belief that they can best judge the nation's security interests. One way or another, pursuit of influence is felt to be in the national interest. Not only is influence necessary to protect the organization's other objectives, but senior members of the organization are considered by its junior members to be peculiarly qualified to advise the President on what is in the national interest.

Stands on issues are affected by the desire to maintain influence. This could lead to support for certain policies which will require greater reliance on the organization. Participants prefer courses of action which will require information from them or which they will be asked to implement. They recognize that they will gain in influence if such decisions are made. The desire for influence can also lead organizations to avoid opposing a particular policy in the belief that to do so would reduce their influence on other issues. To develop a reputation for losing reduces a group's standing with other groups.

Organizational Essence

Organizations have considerable freedom in defining their missions and the capabilities they need to pursue these missions. The organization's *essence* is the view held by the dominant group in the organization of what the missions and capabilities should be. Related to this are convictions about what kinds of people with what expertise, experience, and knowledge should be members of the organization.

Career officials generally have a clear notion of what the essence of their organization is or should be. In some organizations the same view of the essence is shared by all those in the same promotion and career structure. In other cases there will be differences of view. The differences may concern the particulars of a broader agreed essence or may reflect struggles for dominance. In either case there are often conflicts among subgroups within a single career structure to define the essence of the organization. Struggles over essence and the results for some of the major national security organizations are discussed below.

Air Force

Since its inception as a separate service in the early postwar period, the dominant view within the Air Force has been that its essence is the flying of combat airplanes designed for the delivery of nuclear weapons against targets in the Soviet Union.[1] More recently, this has been challenged by Air Force proponents of ICBMs.

The most serious internal challenge to this definition of the role of the Air Force has come from those officers involved in Tactical Air Command (TAC). Some officers in this group have argued that providing combat air support for the ground forces is an equally important mission. Others assigned to TAC have taken the line that their group can prosper only if it emulates the Strategic Air Command (SAC) by developing an

---

1. For an excellent description of the Air Force's push for autonomy and choice of the strategic delivery of nuclear weapons by air as its prime mission, see Perry McCoy Smith, *The Air Force Plans for Peace, 1943–1945*, esp. pp. 23–25, 97.

overseas theater-based nuclear delivery capability, what Alain C. Enthoven and K. Wayne Smith have described as a "junior SAC."[2]

TAC officers seeking to enhance the role of their command have had a difficult problem. On the one hand they have been obliged to pay lip service to the formal missions for TAC, and on the other hand they have been tempted to seek to develop capabilities for the role seen as the essence of the Air Force—namely, the combat delivery of nuclear weapons against the Soviet Union. This dilemma shaped the arguments used by the Air Force in an effort to get a new tactical airplane at first called the TFX and in a later version named the F-111. The officer largely responsible for the design of TAC, General F. F. Everest, argued that the TFX was essential to meet the three missions of his command, which were to maintain air superiority, to disrupt enemy supply lines, and to supply close air support. However, the political scientist Robert J. Art in a careful study of the TFX decision reports that General Everest's underlying motives were, in fact, quite different:

These three missions represented TAC's dogma, to which Everest had to pay lip service. It appears, however, that he was interested primarily in having his new aircraft penetrate enemy defenses at a low level at supersonic speeds while carrying nuclear weapons. The reason Everest wanted such an aircraft is self-evident. In the late 1950's American military doctrine still concentrated primarily on maintaining a strategic nuclear retaliatory capability in order to ensure that deterrence was a credible posture. Under such a doctrine, TAC, as well as the Army, suffered from a relative lack of funds. The Air Force received a large share of the military budget; but within that service, the Strategic Air Command (SAC) received the preponderant portion of those funds. By trying to acquire a nuclear capability for TAC and by thus providing it with an ability to deliver nuclear weapons in a way that SAC's B-52 bombers could not (by low level, supersonic interdiction), Everest attempted to protect the present identity of and future role for TAC. (The Army did exactly the same thing when it stressed that the United States lacked an ability to fight limited conventional wars. It too used doctrinal arguments as a means of protecting its service identity and share of defense funds.)[3]

The most successful challenge to the Air Force definition of its essence arose because of the development of ICBMs. However, until fairly recently (when those concerned with missiles developed some influence

2. Enthoven and Smith, *How Much Is Enough?* p. 9.
3. Art, *The TFX Decision*, p. 16.

within the Air Force) the impetus for development of missiles came largely from outside the Air Force and was bitterly resisted by officers who continued to give highest priority to the development of combat aircraft. Herbert F. York, former Director of Defense Research Engineering, reports on the resistance within the Air Force to the decision by the Defense Department to give highest priority to the development of ballistic missiles, following the Soviet Union's successful testing of an ICBM and the launching of Sputnik:

General Curtis E. LeMay, the man with the cigar, was the commander of the Strategic Air Command (SAC) at the time. As I recall his personal view of the priorities, he placed the B-52H first (it was then called the B-52 Squared) and the B-70 second (it was then called the WS-110). The nuclear airplane (ANP) was somewhere in the middle of his short list, and the long-range missiles were at the bottom. He and other leading Air Force generals managed to make it clear to the contractor that they personally considered the B-70 to be at least as important as the ICBMs, whatever the official priorities might be, and they ordered first flight by the end of 1961.[4]

Sitting in silos just cannot compare to flying bombers.

The high priority given by the Air Force to maintaining its strategic bomber role is shown not only by its resistance to ICBMs but also by its continuing campaign for a nuclear airplane, its advocacy of the B-70 and then the B-1 as a follow-on to the B-52, and its effort in every way possible to extend the flying effectiveness of the B-52.[5] It was this concern that made the Skybolt issue of such critical importance to the Air Force. Skybolt was designed as a missile that would enable bombers to fly toward the Soviet Union and then fire missiles which could penetrate Soviet defenses. In the face of the growing Soviet air defense capability, bombers without missiles were considered too vulnerable. While some argued that Skybolt was no different from an ICBM, in the Air Force view the difference was that Skybolt would be delivered from an airplane, thus enabling Air Force officers to continue their preferred role. The Air Force would continue to have a large intercontinental bomber fleet which was more important to it than the actual mechanism by which the bombs would be dropped.

In the 1960s, with the growing emphasis on non-nuclear forces and in-

---

4. York, *Race to Oblivion: A Participant's View of the Arms Race*, p. 53.
5. See ibid., pp. 60–74; W. Henry Lambright, *Shooting Down the Nuclear Plane*, p. 10.

creased recognition of inhibitions against using nuclear weapons, the Air Force was forced to choose between continued reliance on nuclear delivery and its ability to play the dominant role as the deliverer of other kinds of weapons against enemy targets. After considerable initial resistance the Air Force finally came around to accepting a non-nuclear role, recognizing that this was the way to maintain its dominance in delivery of weapons by air.[6]

The part of the Air Force that has been least effective in challenging the dominant role of SAC is the Military Airlift Command (MAC), charged with movement of men and materiel primarily for the Army. In the evaluation of possible alternatives to relieve the blockade of Berlin in 1948 the Air Force bitterly resisted the airlift concept because it would use up all of the planes believed to be necessary for the combat role of the Air Force.[7] After the successful airlift the Air Force failed to exploit this success to enhance its prestige, and the reasons for not capitalizing on the episode related to the top officers' view of the essence of the service, as explained by Paul Y. Hammond:

Why did the Air Force thus fail fully to exploit the public relations value of the notable achievement of air power in the Berlin airlift? And why did the extraordinary and unexpected experience of the airlift have so little effect upon the developing dispute over roles and missions? Any answers to these questions must be wholly speculative, but some seem possible. The airlift was a freight-carrying operation which served to demonstrate the importance of air transport. But the Air Force has been paring its transport facilities to a minimum in order to maximize its strategic bombing forces. Supporters of strategic air power, the predominant strategic doctrine in the Air Force, might have viewed the airlift as a potential threat to the primary mission of the Air Force, and feared that airlift publicity would only give substance to the charges which had often been voiced in Army circles that the Air Force was neglecting its duty to provide air transport for Army troops. This answer to the first question suggests an answer to the second. Since the airlift was more relevant to Air Force–Army relations than to Air Force–Navy relations, and since the latter were the ones which were currently raising the inter-service issue of roles and missions, the airlift had no direct relationship to the aviation controversy then developing. Moreover, as has been indicated, boasting about the airlift

6. Theodore C. Sorensen, *Kennedy*, p. 588.
7. Robert Murphy, *Diplomat among Warriors*, p. 318.

could have been shared by the British and even the Navy. Sharing of aviation responsibilities was not what the Air Force was trying to enlarge.[8]

Years later in the mid-1960s the Air Force did accept procurement of a large number of C-5A troop-carrying airplanes, but only because the move was forced on it by civilians. When given their own way, the priorities of the Air Force officers have always been clear. Hammond recalls a classic decision made in 1949:

The Senior Officers Board of the Air Force had convened in late December to consider in closed sessions the procurement program of the Air Force in the light of (1) the existing situation in aircraft development in the Air Force, particularly the greatly improved performance of the B-36, and (2) the President's stand on the budget. Anticipating the severe cuts in existing and future force strength which the President was determined to make, the Board decided to concentrate the limited resources of the Air Force upon strategic bombing aircraft (i.e., long-range and heavy bombers), in order to make sure that the Air Force could at least fulfill what they regarded as its first responsibility, retaliatory capability. It recommended to the Secretary of the Air Force on January 6 that the procurement of medium bombers (B-45, RB-49), troop transports (C-125), and a new version of the F-86 jet fighter (F-93) be cut back and the money thus saved transferred to purchasing B-36's and B-50's.[9]

To sum up, in taking stands on many strategy and policy questions the Air Force has been guided by the effort to protect its role in the strategic delivery of weapons by air.

Navy

Naval officers agree on the general proposition that the essence of the Navy is to maintain combat ships whose primary mission must be to control the seas against potential enemies. Unlike the Air Force, with SAC usually dominating the other commands, the Navy has been affected by serious dispute among three groups: naval flyers (the brown shoe Navy) emphasize carrier-based air units; seapower advocates (the black shoe Navy) stress the surface Navy; submariners focus on attack submarines. In recent years a fourth group has come to be identified with the Polaris submarines. No senior naval officers see the essence of the Navy as in-

8. Hammond, "Super Carriers and B-36 Bombers," p. 485.
9. Ibid., pp. 489–90.

volved in transport, and this function has received relatively little attention.

In the early postwar period, the Navy's struggle was to maintain its capability despite a tight budget and the rise of the Air Force. Naval aviators were locked in a struggle with the Air Force over the relative role of super-carriers and B-36 bombers and, within the Navy, over the relative role to be accorded to carriers in contrast with submarines and conventional ships. Though the carrier admirals argued in debate with the Air Force that the carriers could do a better job of firing nuclear weapons against targets in the Soviet Union, their primary interest was in targets connected with naval warfare such as submarine bases and air bases of planes directed at sea operations. Within the Navy, the struggle was about which kind of force could best carry out the role of dominating the seas. The victory of the carrier admirals was signified by the offer of the Navy to scrap many ships then currently under construction if in return the relatively modest naval budget in the late 1940s might be used to construct super-carriers for the delivery of nuclear weapons.[10] Such thinking has continued to play a large role in Navy calculations, leading to emphasis on aircraft carriers and their missions long after many outside observers concluded that carriers had been rendered obsolete by developments in Soviet naval capabilities.

The most serious challenge to the dominant role of the aircraft carriers came from the proposals first developed by small groups within the Navy to develop a submarine missile-launching capability. Superficially the two roles were the same, since both the carriers and the submarines armed with Polaris missiles could deliver nuclear weapons against the Soviet Union. However, the Polaris missiles, besides being "unpiloted," were primarily directed at the destruction of Soviet cities and played only a very limited role in control of the seas. Thus the carrier advocates in their opposition to Polaris, which would deprive them of aircraft, had the support of much of the rest of the Navy.

Senator Henry M. Jackson reports on his frustration in seeking to win support for the Polaris program within the Navy:

I was interested in this program from the very outset, going back many, many years. I found that in trying to get the Navy to do something about it, I ran headlong into the competition within the Navy for requirements in

10. Ibid., p. 470.

connection with their day-to-day operational needs, whether it was anti-submarine warfare or limited war requirements; whatever it was . . . , I was told that this strategic system would just eat away and erode their limited funds. . . . The result was that Polaris was not pushed hard until Sputnik came along.[11]

When the program passed from the R&D stage to that of procurement, the Navy's resistance once again was aroused because of the large amount of funds necessary to procure a substantial number of Polaris submarines. In approaching this problem, the Navy took the stand traditionally taken by the services when civilians seek to force on them programs that they view as contrary to the essence of their activity. As noted by Enthoven and Smith:

In its budget requests for fiscal years 1961 and 1962, the Navy budgeted for only three Polaris submarines in each year. One of the first things that President Kennedy and Secretary McNamara did when they came into office was to speed up the Polaris program and to authorize the building of ten Polaris submarines in each of these fiscal years. Nobody, to our knowledge, has since questioned the necessity or the wisdom of that action. But at the time, senior Navy officers, when confronted with arguments for increasing the Polaris program based on urgent national need replied: Polaris is a national program, not a Navy program. By this was meant: the Polaris mission is not a traditional Navy mission and therefore should not be financed out of the Navy's share of the defense budget.[12]

Army

Career Army officers agree that the essence of the Army is ground combat capability. They tend to deprive of funds those functions which they view as peripheral, such as advisory roles in Military Assistance Advisory Group (MAAG) missions, air defense, and the so-called "Green Beret" counterinsurgency forces.

In the 1950s, there was considerable dispute among career officers about the degree to which the Army should be organized primarily for nuclear warfare as opposed to conventional ground combat operations. In the early 1960s two battles raged. One, related to the conventional notion of the Army's mission, concerned the role of air mobility. The other con-

11. Senator Jackson, quoted in Michael H. Armacost, *The Politics of Weapons Innovation*, pp. 65–66.
12. Enthoven and Smith, *How Much Is Enough?* pp. 16–17 .

cerned the Green Berets: the most determined challenge to the Army's definition of its essence since the separation of the Air Force from the Army.

In the case of air mobility, the issue turned on the degree to which the Army should depend on helicopters as opposed to heavy tanks and artillery. Outside groups pressing for air mobility found considerable support within the Army, particularly from paratroopers, and were able eventually to prevail.

The effort to enhance the role of the Green Berets, though it had much more active high-level support, was considerably less successful. President Kennedy came into office believing that American security would be challenged by guerrilla forces against whom American power would have to be used in limited and quite special ways. He therefore began an effort to develop such a capability within the Army. This ran contrary to the Army's definition of its essence, which involved ground combat by organized regular divisional units, and the Army by and large was able to resist.

Advocates of air and missile defense within the Army have not proclaimed that the element of warfare that interests them should become the dominant form of Army activity. They have merely said that it deserves a partial role, and they have made headway with the argument that the money for air and missile defense would not come from the Army ground combat forces. According to them, the funds would otherwise be spent on equivalent programs of the other services. In the 1950s, faced with growing priority for strategic delivery systems, some Army officers sought to get the Army involved in the deployment of medium-range ballistic missiles. In the 1960s, Army efforts of this sort focused on ABMs. Although these Army programs failed to elicit the all-out commitment aroused by issues believed to affect the organizational essence of the service, there was some steam behind them. The Army, a more eclectic group with many long and differing historical traditions, does have greater tolerance for diverse groups even though its essence remains that of ground combat.

Central Intelligence Agency

CIA career officials are split into three groups according to their notion of what the essence of the agency ought to be. Each group has looked to senior officials in the agency for support of its own notions.

One group, reportedly headed by Richard Helms, director of the CIA during the Johnson and Nixon administrations, emphasizes intelligence collection. This group believes that the primary function of the CIA should be to conduct clandestine operations designed primarily to get information about potentially hostile governments. It also believes the CIA should be involved in limited clandestine efforts in foreign countries to support movements such as labor unions or political parties friendly to the United States.

In contrast, a second group, long headed by Richard Bissell, a former senior CIA official, believes that the CIA should actively intervene in events abroad. This group led the CIA during a period in which it was involved in relatively large-scale operations in Iran and in Guatemala, as well as embarking on the U-2 program and the Bay of Pigs invasion. CIA involvement in Laos and in Vietnam also represents the influence of this group's notion of what the agency's function ought to be.

Still a third group, with considerably less influence, emphasizes intelligence evaluation. It has often been said that the CIA gets 90 percent of its information from public sources, and a large part of its staff is involved in the evaluation of material received from both clandestine and public sources. Members of the third group believe that the conduct of operations jeopardizes the CIA's claim to impartiality and reduces its involvement in policy issues.

Foreign Service

In contrast to career officials in the military services and in the CIA, Foreign Service officers are agreed on the essence of their profession, as they would call it. The basic function of the State Department and hence of the Foreign Service is seen as political reporting about the activities of foreign governments that bear relevance to the United States, general representation of American interests abroad, and negotiation of specific issues when directed by the government.[13] Charles W. Thayer, a Foreign Service officer, notes approvingly the views traditionally held: *Secretary Cordell Hull once said he required four things of his ambassadors: to report what was going on; to represent the United States before foreign governments and publics; to negotiate United States government business; and to look after American lives and property.*[14]

13. John Ensor Harr, *The Professional Diplomat*, pp. 35–40, 43–44, 243–44; Smith Simpson, *Anatomy of the State Department*, p. 3; and Andrew M. Scott, "The Department of State: Formal Organization and Informal Culture," p. 3.

14. Thayer, *Diplomat*, p. 81.

Career Foreign Service officers view their enterprise as an elite organization composed of generalists, and they resist the introduction into the department of novel functions and of experts who might be needed to perform those functions. In the immediate postwar period, Foreign Service officers were appalled to discover that various agencies had been disbanded and their personnel assigned to the State Department. They were particularly concerned about the transfer of propaganda officials and intelligence analysts. Robert Murphy, a senior Foreign Service officer, commented on this:

Meanwhile, in Washington, the weakened Department of State suffered a postwar influx of manpower from unexpected sources, some of it dumped by President Truman and Secretary Byrnes from liquidated war agencies such as the Office of War Information, the Office of Strategic Services, and others. The new employees arrived—certainly not at the request of the Foreign Service—without qualification examination or security screening, and they created an awkward situation. . . . At the same time greatly increased responsibilities were heaped upon the State Department. Foreign Service officers, no longer limited to orthodox consular and diplomatic activities, were allocated to propaganda, intelligence, and military government, and became involved in many of the conflicts arising from Soviet expansion.[15]

State has continued to resist the transfer to it of such agencies as USIA and AID and in so doing has demonstrated that organizations may oppose expansion instead of seeking it. Still today career officials tend to take the operations of USIA and AID less seriously than traditional functions and to disparage efforts to give State direction and control over them. Only in recent years have career ambassadors, particularly in the field, come to be at all concerned about operations. Many Foreign Service officers resisted the policy ordained in the letter from President Kennedy to ambassadors instructing them that they would have operational control over all programs in their bailiwick, including at least some of those of the Central Intelligence Agency.[16] These officers feared that control over such programs might prove to be embarrassing and would prevent them from focusing on the important functions of reporting and negotiation. A retired Foreign Service officer, Ellis Briggs, expressed this point of view with regard to the functions of an ambassador:

In theory each ambassador is responsible for all government operations

15. Murphy, *Diplomat among Warriors*, pp. 451–52 (italics added).
16. Jackson Subcommittee, *Administration of National Security*, pp. 8–10.

conducted within his jurisdiction. *That is a good thing, but in practice it would be manifestly impossible for a chief of mission to accomplish, as ambassador, anything in the way of business with the government to which he is accredited, if in addition he tried personally to supervise all the programs operated in the name of the American government within his bailiwick. Liaison with other agencies is customarily delegated to the ambassador's overworked deputy, who in turn must rely on the senior members of the embassy staff, an appreciable part of whose time is devoted to preventing the representatives of other agencies, who invariably regard themselves as diplomats, from damaging the delicate machinery of international relations.*[17]

Career Foreign Service officers view the regional bureaus of the State Department—those dealing with Europe, East Asia, the Near East and South Asia, Africa and Latin America—as the heart of the State Department operations. They believe that the Assistant Secretaries for these regions should be career officials and should have flexibility in managing relations with the relevant countries. They resist the growth of functional bureaus such as those dealing with economics and political-military affairs, in part because such bureaus tend to be dominated by civil servants or in-and-outers rather than by Foreign Service officers. In the early postwar period, State Department officials saw a threat from non-regional bureaus, and the United Nations Bureau in particular worried them because of an influx of non-career officers who had been planning for the UN during the war. After a brief struggle, State's Foreign Service officers were able to confirm their dominance of the department and uphold the regional bureaus, particularly the Bureau of European Affairs.[18]

To the extent that they differ over missions, career diplomatic officials contest the relative priority to be given to different geographic areas. Subgroups within the department do not rally around particular kinds of missions, as in the case of the CIA, so much as they take sides over the relative attention to be given to improving relations with different parts of the world or, in the case of potential enemies, effectively opposing them. There is a West European group, a Soviet group, an "Arabist" group, and groups concerned primarily with African and Latin American affairs. Internal controversy consists of disputes among these groups over particular policy issues.

17. Briggs, *Farewell to Foggy Bottom: The Recollections of A Career Diplomat*, p. 166.
18. Martin Wishnatsky, "Symbolic Politics and the Origins of the Cold War," pp. 3–5.

Enhancement of Essence

An image of the essence of an organization shapes an organization's conception of its interests. The concern with essence is manifest in several ways. (1) An organization favors policies and strategies which its members believe will make the organization as they define it more important. For example, the Air Force some years ago favored the new look strategy which called for reliance on weapons of mass destruction, while the Army favored the strategy of flexible response which implied reliance on conventional ground forces. The State Department in the early postwar period, resisting efforts to rely on the UN and on economic cooperation if such efforts entailed reliance on experts outside the Foreign Service, fought for a policy which would involve direct bilateral diplomatic dealings with the Soviet Union and with the countries of Western Europe.

(2) An organization struggles hardest for the capabilities which it views as necessary to the essence of the organization. It seeks autonomy and funds to pursue the necessary capabilities and missions. Thus long after most experts had concluded that Skybolt was not technically feasible, the Air Force continued to seek the missile as a means of preserving the manned strategic bomber.

(3) An organization resists efforts to take away from it those functions viewed as part of its essence. It will seek to protect these functions by taking on additional functions if it believes that foregoing these added functions may ultimately jeopardize its sole control over the essence of its activities. The Navy and Air Force, for instance, insist on performing the troop transport role for the Army, and the Air Force rejects Army efforts to perform the close air support role. If the Army transported its own troops by sea, it might well build ships which would enable Army troops to come ashore firing—the (not previously discussed) essence of the Marine Corps' activity. In dread of such an "infringement," the Navy demanded that the Army's proposed fast-deployment logistics (FDL) ships be constructed in such a way that they cannot be used for amphibious operations. Failing to kill the medium-missile program, the Air Force, to cite another example, fought to take on the program itself because it feared that the Army would use the missiles as a foot in the door on the strategic deterrence mission.

(4) An organization is often indifferent to functions not seen as part of its essence or necessary to protect its essence. It tends not to initiate new activities or seek new capabilities even when technology makes them feasible. Thus the Air Force did not press for the adoption of intercon-

tinental ballistic missiles, and the program had to be forced on it from the outside. Similarly, career Foreign Service officers have not championed the use of such techniques as economic aid, propaganda, or military advisory missions. If assigned such functions, organizations will devote as few resources as they can to them. For example, the Air Force and the Navy have devoted limited resources to airlift and sealift techniques while insisting on performing the transport function. Ambitious career officers avoid serving in "unessential" activities. U.S. Army officers in Vietnam, for example, preferred leading troops in combat and serving on a combat staff over advisory assignments.

(5) Sometimes an organization attempts to push a growing function out of its domain entirely. It begrudges expenditures on anything but its chosen activity. It is chary of new personnel with new skills and interests who may seek to dilute or change the organization's essence. For example, the Army after World War II urged the creation of a separate Air Force in the belief that, if this were not done, flyers would come to dominate the Army, changing the conception of its role.[19] Similarly, Foreign Service officers resisted efforts to assign operational responsibility for aid, propaganda, and intelligence functions to the State Department.

In short, an organization will accept new functions only if it believes that to refuse to do so would be to jeopardize its position with senior officials or if it believes that the new function will bring in more funds and give the organization greatest scope to pursue its "own" activities. The military services describe functions not related to their essence as "national programs" rather than service programs and demand that the funding for them be counted outside their regular service budget. For many years, the Navy took this position in relation to the Polaris program, and the Army did so in relation to the ABM.

Roles and Missions

From what has been said so far, it follows that conflicts over roles and missions arise constantly in politics inside the government. Furthermore, fights over roles and missions are particularly acute when they impact on the essence of the contending organizations.

The three classic disputes which divided the military services in the

19. Perry Smith, *The Air Force Plans for Peace*, p. 19.

1940s and continue to divide them now are: (1) the struggle between the Navy and Air Force over naval aviation; (2) that between the Army and Air Force over combat support; and (3) that between the Army and Marines over Marine participation in ground combat operations. Two conflicts pitting the CIA against the older agencies have become equally familiar: (4) the struggle between the CIA and the military over control of combat operations; and (5) that among CIA, State, and the military over the domain of each in intelligence collection and evaluation. Because career officials feel so strongly about the essence of their respective organizations, the conflicts have been intense and have affected stands on issues as well as implementation of decisions. Each of the conflicts is discussed in turn.

Naval Aviation

The depth of feeling in the Navy and the Air Force about the role of naval aviation is reflected in Secretary of Defense James Forrestal's report of a conversation which he had with Air Force General Hoyt Vandenberg in 1948:

I remarked that there were these fundamental psychoses, both revolving around the use of air power:

  (1) *The Navy belief, very firmly held and deeply rooted, that the Air Force wants to get control of all aviation;*

  (2) *The corresponding psychosis of the Air Force that the Navy is trying to encroach upon the strategic air prerogatives of the Air Force.*[20]

The intensity of the dispute comes from the fact that each service sees its essence being threatened by the presumed intentions of the other. The Air Force fears that the Navy will seek to expand its air power until it performs a dominant part of the strategic offensive mission. On the other hand, the Navy fears that the Air Force seeks to take over the entire air mission, controlling all airplanes whether based at sea or on land or, at a minimum, all airplanes based on land, even those involving the function of control of the seas.[21]

Some naval aviators trace the fight back to 1925, when the Army Air

20. Walter Millis (ed.), with E. S. Duffield, *The Forrestal Diaries*, p. 466. Cited hereafter as *Forrestal Diaries*.

21. On the controversy between the Navy and the Air Force over air power, see ibid., pp. 222–26, 228–29; Demetrios Caraley, *The Politics of Military Unification*, pp. 79, 96; and Hammond, "Super Carriers and B-36 Bombers," pp. 488, 538–39.

Force group headed by General William A. Mitchell sought to take over complete control of all air forces. This conflict has raised its head intermittently since then.

In the postwar conflict over unification the Air Force sought to get control over all land-based air operations. This struggle was further exacerbated by the fact that naval air enthusiasts, having recently won the struggle for dominance within the Navy, were not prepared to yield anything to the Air Force. In the end, the controversy over naval aviation became the stumbling block to naval support for unification—support which was necessary to get congressional approval. The issue was finally compromised by President Truman's allowing the Navy authority over aircraft to be used in conjunction with all matters related to control of the sea.

The controversy was not over, however. In 1948, the Air Force argued for the absorption of all naval air into its forces, while the Navy went on the attack by criticizing the effectiveness of Air Force strategic bombers and arguing that super-carriers could more effectively perform the strategic bombing mission. This led to the famous revolt of the admirals: when the Navy was denied authority to build super-carriers, several admirals resigned and took their case to the public.

In the 1950s Navy aviation commanders and the Air Force quarreled about the proposed nuclear-powered airplane. The Air Force, originally uninterested in the project, began to be concerned when the Navy pressed for a nuclear-powered airplane which could fly off aircraft carriers and perform the strategic mission. From then on both services vied for the nuclear-powered airplane despite the increasing evidence that such an aircraft was simply not technologically feasible.[22]

This dispute arose again in connection with the TFX. The Air Force sought a plane which would carry only nuclear weapons and which could carry them over long distances. The Navy, on the contrary, sought a short-takeoff plane with limited range. Robert Art explains:

The Navy was so insistent because of its own perspectives. It had no real interest in seeing a plane built with such a long ferry range. If missiles had reduced the strategic and interdiction roles of aircraft, including naval aircraft, a plane that could fly across the Atlantic, nonstop, without refueling, and that could be deployed from semiprepared fields would be even more injurious to the Navy's interests: such a plane could only downgrade the role of the aircraft carrier. If it could fly over oceans, there would be no need to transport it over them. If it could operate from semiprepared fields,

22. Lambright, *Shooting Down the Nuclear Plane*, pp. 9, 13–14.

there would be less need for carriers to stand offshore to service it. On the other hand, the Missileer was the ideal aircraft for the Navy. It would protect the fleet, including the aircraft carriers, from an enemy air attack. It would thereby ensure the safety of aircraft like the F-4H, which were designed to perform tactical missions from aircraft carriers.

Each service thus saw its future threatened by the other's TFX design. The Air Force wanted to extend the life of the airplane. The Navy wanted to do the same for the aircraft carrier. Both knew that the TFX program was going to be costly. Each knew that the supply of defense funds was limited. Neither wanted its future programs jeopardized by those of the other. The result of these opposing perspectives was three months of interminable discussion, delay, and disagreement.[23]

The controversy has also affected combat operations. In Korea and especially in Vietnam the Navy sought as large a role as possible for carrier-based aircraft in an effort to demonstrate that carriers could operate as effectively, if not more effectively, than land-based air power. The Air Force, on the other hand, sought to restrict the role of the Navy (arguing that it could deliver weapons more effectively and more cheaply). This controversy probably led each service to exaggerate the effectiveness of its bombing in order to outshine the other. Neither service has any doubt that in the post-Vietnam period the other service will go after a larger share of the air mission. Inasmuch as both the Air Force and the Navy aviators see as their essence the flying of combat air missions, the conflict between them has been inevitable and has shaped a good deal of the overall rivalry between the two services. The conflict over missiles, discussed below, has been less intense because it has not touched the essence of either service.

Combat Air Support

In contrast to the Navy, which opposed reunification and favored the status quo, the Army was anxious in the late 1940s to divest itself of its air units in order to protect the essence of its ground combat mission. It was, therefore, in no position to argue very hard about its need to keep some air capability. Thus the Army came to depend on the Air Force not only for transport and interdiction but also for combat support—airplanes which fly in the immediate vicinity of a battle to give support to infantry.

In the 1950s, the Army began to have second thoughts about its deci-

23. Art, *The TFX Decision*, p. 46.

sion. It recognized that the Air Force was giving highest priority to strategic bombardment and therefore neglecting missions of concern to the Army. For the Army, autonomy (discussed below) was at stake, and for the Air Force a potential threat to its essence seemed to be developing. General Matthew B. Ridgway described the situation in the following terms in his memoirs:

There is an understandable opposition in the Air Force to the development of those types and the procurement of those number of aircraft for which the Army has so vital a need. The helicopter and the converti-plane do not now fit into the pattern of the Air Force's primary missions, or the limitations of its budget. Nor does the young airman want to fly the close-support and assault aircraft—the dive bombers, cargo ships, the transport planes that carry the paratroopers. He wants to fly jets, for that is where the glamour and the glory lies. And I don't find it in my heart to blame him.

But somebody must man these planes and the Army, of course, has considered seeking to relieve the Air Force of its unwanted burden. Plans have been advanced whereby the Army would develop its own specialized assault aircraft, and recruit and train its own pilots to fly them, and to a slight degree this has been done. If neither manpower nor dollars were to be considered, such an idea would be feasible. Since manpower and dollars both are very much to be considered, the prospect that the Army will be able to develop its own aviation in the near future is highly improbable.

Ridgway concluded:

I think perhaps there is a balance to be found somewhere, a reasonable compromise. Of one thing, though, I am sure. To do its job on the battlefield, to gain its objectives in the least time with the least loss of life, the Army must have the support of combat aircraft that can fly in any kind of weather, under all conditions incident to enemy interference, both in the air and from the ground, and deliver its bomb load, or its rockets, on target with the accuracy of a field gun. If the Air Force should develop such planes, we would be deeply pleased. If they continue to ignore our needs in this respect, we eventually will have to develop them ourselves.[24]

Toward the end of the fifties, the Army was pressing an all-out assault on the Air Force control of tactical air. After his retirement as Army Chief of Staff, General Maxwell D. Taylor made public the Army position:

24. Ridgway, *Soldier*, pp. 314–15.

Since 1947, the Army has been dependent upon the Air Force for tactical air support, tactical air lift, and for longe-range air transport. Throughout this period, the Army has been a dissatisfied customer, feeling that the Air Force has not fully discharged its obligations undertaken at the time of unification. The Air Force, having something which the Army wanted, has been in a position to put a price upon cooperation and to insist upon acquiescence in Air Force views on such controversial issues as air-ground support procedures, air resupply, and control of air space over the battlefield. As technical improvements in weapons and equipment offered the Army the possibility of escaping from dependence upon the Air Force, the latter has vigorously resisted these efforts and has succeeded in obtaining the support of the Secretary of Defense in imposing limitations on the size and weight of aircraft procured by the Army, on the ranges of Army missiles, and on the radius of Army activities in advance of the front line of combat.

As a result of the controversies arising from the dependence of the Army on the Air Force, the two services have been constantly at loggerheads. They have been unable to agree on a doctrine for cooperation in battle. They are at odds as to the adequacy of levels of Air Force support for the Army, and as to the suitability of types of Air Force equipment to furnish this support. Because of the very high performance of their airplanes, designed primarily to meet the needs of the air battle today, the Air Force is not equipped to discharge its responsibilities to the Army in ground combat. Having witnessed this unhappy state of affairs for over a decade, I am convinced that the Army must be freed from this tutelage and receive all the organic means habitually necessary for prompt and sustained combat on the ground. It should have its own organic tactical air support and tactical air lift, or rather the new weapons and equipment which will perform the functions presently comprehended under those two headings.

Special restrictions of size, weight, and in the case of weapons, of range should be abolished forever and the Army encouraged to exploit technology to the maximum to improve its weapons and equipment habitually necessary for prompt and sustained ground combat. It is essential to end the present fragmentation of the land force function, particularly at a time when the role of land forces should assume increased importance under the strategy of Flexible Response.[25]

In return, Taylor proposed that the Army cede the continental air de-

25. Taylor, *The Uncertain Trumpet*, pp. 168–70.

fense mission to the Air Force. Since this was a mission that neither considered part of its essence, Taylor was not giving up very much, nor would the Air Force see it as much of a compromise.

The Air Force was nevertheless in a bind. Unwilling to devote substantial resources to developments of tactical air power and unwilling to adapt itself to Army requirements for tactical air support, the Air Force found itself without a convincing rebuttal from the national viewpoint.

By the time of Vietnam, the Army was persuading others that it needed to develop its own combat air support. Secretary of Defense McNamara had been pushing air mobility, thereby getting the Army into helicopters to carry troops. Improvements in helicopter technology enabled the Army to begin using support helicopters for combat missions as well as troop transport and so to reduce dependence on the Air Force. Despite the increased attention the Air Force gave to tactical combat operations in response to the Army's encroachment, the Army emerged from the Vietnam War with more pilots than the Air Force and with even greater determination to develop its own organic air capability.

The Role of the Marines

The Marine Corps sees itself as an elite combat unit primarily designed for amphibious operations—that is, the landing of shiploads of armed men under combat conditions against a hostile force. Some Marine Corps officers would like to see their service also take on specialized ground combat operations not involving amphibious operations.

The conflict between the Marine Corps and the Army like that between the Navy and the Air Force goes to the essence of each service. The controversy about the definition of the functions of the Marines and the size of the Corps was a major issue in the unification battle of the late 1940s.

Some Marine Corps officers feared that the Army desired to integrate the Marines into the Army as a specialized unit. If nothing else, the Army sought to limit the Marine Corps to the role of auxiliary to the fleet, with the job of accompanying landing parties to protect Americans during disturbances in foreign countries and in wartime and of providing expeditionary forces to attack bases that were of exclusive interest to the Navy and that could be overcome by small combat units.[26] The principal area of

---

26. Caraley, *The Politics of Military Unification*, p. 67. See also *Forrestal Diaries*, pp. 224–25, and Hammond, "Super Carriers and B-36 Bombers," pp. 529–30.

contention then was large amphibious operations. The Marines argued that such operations were more clearly within their scope of activity, while the Army suggested that such operations should come under Army control.

In the mid-1950s the Army, struggling for a limited war strategy, feared that the Navy and the Marine Corps together would seek to take over this mission. The Marines could argue that they were the only integrated force containing its own sea transport and combat air capability and therefore the most effective unit for limited war operations. General Taylor spoke out:

As for the Marines, the Army acknowledges their potential contribution to limited-war situations occurring on or near the coast but resists vigorously any suggestion that the Marines should become a second Army and take over any part of the Army's role of prompt and sustained ground combat.[27]

During the Vietnam War, the Marines were assigned to general combat responsibilities and occupied the I Corps close to the demilitarized zone. In conducting operations in I Corps the Marines were seeking to demonstrate that they could more effectively carry out counterinsurgency operations. The Army, on the other hand, sought to show that Marines because of their independence could not be effectively fitted into an Army chain of command. This debate probably affected the Army unwillingness to adopt the strategy of combined action patrols pioneered by the Marine Corps and may also have affected the decision by General Westmoreland to assign the Marines the highly difficult task of defending the Khe Sanh base, close to the demilitarized zone.[28]

The Question of the CIA

The CIA frequently collides with the military services over the conduct of relatively large-scale covert operations and intelligence gathering programs. These operations go to the heart of the CIA mission as conceived by many of its career personnel and yet arouse the misgivings of the Pentagon about creating an alternative military capability. The debate is largely carried on behind closed doors but came out into the open in the controversies surrounding the Bay of Pigs invasion, the Cuban missile crisis, and U.S. actions in Indochina.

27. Taylor, *The Uncertain Trumpet*, p. 100.
28. William R. Corson, *The Betrayal*, pp. 77–80.

The CIA had responsibility for training the Cuban forces to be used in the Bay of Pigs invasion and for planning the military operations. The Joint Chiefs gave only cursory review to the plans and later were in a position to argue that the operations had been botched by the CIA. As a result, President Kennedy turned responsibility for such operations over to the Pentagon.[29]

In the opening days of the Cuban missile crisis, the military services, particularly the Air Force, challenged the CIA's control of U-2 flights over Cuba. As long as U-2s were used in relatively peaceful situations in which the likelihood of combat was small, the Air Force was more or less content to have the CIA manage the program. However, as the possibility of conflict heated up in the Caribbean, the U-2 forays began to look more and more to the Air Force like a separate air arm, and a campaign was mounted which ultimately succeeded in taking the function away from the CIA.

The dispute over U.S. operations in Indochina centered upon CIA influence over the Montagnards and other irregular forces in Laos and South Vietnam. Early in the 1960s, the military apparently succeeded in having the Special Forces take over arrangements with the Montagnards, but the CIA seems to have counteracted by gaining substantial influence over the Special Forces themselves.[30]

Other Conflicts

From time to time, new technological developments have produced other role and mission conflicts among the services, often overlapping with the ongoing disputes described above. In the early postwar period the development of nuclear weapons produced a fight as to whom these weapons would be assigned. The Air Force originally had a virtual monopoly on nuclear weapons. This control was first challenged successfully by the Navy on the grounds that its carriers could effectively deliver such weapons; later the Army introduced tactical nuclear weapons which would be supplied to ground forces.

The development of strategic missiles also produced controversy over roles and missions, although it lacked the intensity of the other fights because it did not go to the essence of any of the services. The Air Force, however, did see some infringement on its strategic primacy. It tried for a

29. Theodore Sorensen, *Kennedy*, p. 630.
30. Roger Hilsman, *To Move a Nation: The Politics of Foreign Policy in the Administration of John F. Kennedy*, p. 455.

while, but without success, to prevent the development of the Polaris submarine force (a program pushed by the civilian analysts and the scientists rather than by the Navy itself). The Air Force was more successful in resisting the Army's effort to enter into the strategic offensive realm through the development of medium-range missiles. For a time, both services had medium-range missile programs, but the Air Force was able to secure authority over the development of such weapons.[31]

All three services competed for a role in space exploration, with the Air Force first getting the upper hand and then losing status in regard to the newly created National Aeronautics and Space Administration (NASA) in 1957. The Air Force is now engaged in a conflict with NASA over the relative roles of the two agencies in the space program. It has also sought to recoup by infiltrating NASA itself with active duty Air Force officers.

Implications of Roles and Missions

The conflict over roles and missions, particularly as it relates to the essence of each agency's activity, produces several characteristic forms of behavior in the pursuit of organizational interest.

1. Disputes over roles and missions affect the information reported to senior officials.

For example, according to a former Air Force intelligence officer, both the Air Force and the Navy exaggerated the effectiveness of their bombing of North Vietnam. Both recognized that the postwar dispute over the Navy's bombing role would be affected by evaluation of their bombing operations in Vietnam. Each, believing (or fearing) that the other service would exaggerate, decided to emphasize the positive in order to protect its position.[32]

2. In implementing missions which they know to be coveted by another organization, organizations may bend over backward to avoid giving reason to increase their bureaucratic competitor's share of the responsibility.

Townsend Hoopes, who was then Under Secretary of the Air Force, reports that he saw this process at work in the Air Force request for an additional 17 tactical fighter squadrons as part of a proposed increase in American forces in Vietnam in March 1968 following the Tet offensive:

Moreover it was a matter of some delicacy in Army–Air Force relations because it touched the boundary line between the assigned roles and mis-

---

31. Armacost, *The Politics of Weapons Innovation*, p. 63.
32. Morris J. Blachman, "The Stupidity of Intelligence," pp. 271–79.

sions of the two Services. If the Air Force did not provide close air support in a ratio satisfactory to the Army, that would strengthen the Army's argument for developing its own means of close support. Already, through the development of helicopter gunships of increasing power, speed, and sophistication, the Army had pressed against that boundary.[33]

3. In periods of crisis, career officials calculate how alternative policies and patterns of action will affect future definitions of roles and missions.

Participants have learned over time that changes in roles and missions frequently occur during crises. Thus an organization concerned about its mission and desiring either to expand it or prevent others from expanding theirs at its cost will be particularly alert to both challenges and opportunities during a crisis. Because this phenomenon is widely understood, organizations must be on guard: they cannot trust other organizations not to take advantage of a crisis situation. Frequently, an organization whose functions were expanded during a crisis tries to argue that it has now established a precedent and should continue to perform the new function. Thus organizations seldom put forward options which might lead to changes in roles and missions to their detriment. If suggested by other participants, they may argue that such options are infeasible. Participants may also feel obliged to distort information reported to senior officials in order to guard against the danger that it will in the future affect roles and missions. Disputes over roles and missions also affect policy stands and the way policy decisions are implemented.

During the Cuban missile crisis, for example, both the CIA and the military services were concerned with how intelligence operations during the crisis would affect future definitions of roles and missions. A key episode is described by Graham Allison:

The ten-day delay between decision [to direct a special flight over western Cuba] and flight is another organizational story. At the October 4 meeting, where the decision to dispatch the flight over western Cuba was made, the State Department spelled out the consequences of the loss of a U-2 over Cuba in the strongest terms. The Defense Department took this opportunity to raise an issue important to its concerns. Given the increased danger that a U-2 would be downed, the pilots should be officers in uniform rather than CIA agents, so the Air Force should assume responsibility for U-2 flights over Cuba. To the contrary, the CIA argued that this was an

33. Hoopes, *The Limits of Intervention*, pp. 161–62.

intelligence operation and thus within the CIA's jurisdiction. Besides, CIA U-2s had been modified in certain ways that gave them advantages over Air Force U-2s in avoiding Soviet SAMs. Five days passed while the State Department pressed for less risky alternatives, and the Air Force (in Department of Defense guise) and the CIA engaged in territorial disputes. On October 9, COMOR [the Committee on Overhead Reconnaissance] approved a flight plan over San Cristobal, but, to the CIA's dismay, the Air Force rather than the CIA would take charge of the mission. At this point details become sketchy, but several members of the intelligence community have speculated that an Air Force pilot in an Air Force U-2 attempted a high altitude overflight on October 9 that "flamed out," i.e., lost power, and thus had to descend in order to restart its engine. A second round between Air Force and CIA followed, as a result of which Air Force pilots were trained to fly CIA U-2s. A successful overflight did not take place until October 14.[34]

Autonomy

Career officials of an organization believe that they are in a better position than others to determine what capabilities they should have and how they should best fulfill their mission. They attach very high priority to controlling their own resources so that these can be used to support the essence of the organization. They wish to be in a position to spend money allocated to them in the way they choose, to station their manpower as they choose, and to implement policy in their own fashion. They resist efforts by senior officials to get control of their activities.

In particular, priority is attached to maintaining control over budgets. Organizations are often prepared to accept less money with greater control rather than more money with less control. Even with the smaller funds they are able to protect the essence of their activities. The priority attached to autonomy is shown by the experiences of two recent Secretaries of Defense. Robert McNamara caused great consternation in the Pentagon in 1961 by instituting new decision procedures which reduced the autonomy of the services, despite the fact that he increased defense spending by $6 billion and did not directly seek to alter the roles and missions

34. Allison, *Essence of Decision,* pp. 122–23.

of the various services. Melvin P. Laird, in contrast, improved Pentagon morale in 1969 by increasing service autonomy in budget matters while reducing the defense budget by more than $4 billion.

Organizations also seek total operational control over the forces required to carry out a mission and are reluctant to undertake shared operations involving forces of other organizations. To avoid encroachment by other agencies, they seek to report directly to the President, in hopes that this will mean infrequent interference in their affairs. For example, the Office of Strategic Services pressed hard at the end of World War II for the creation of a Central Intelligence Agency which would no longer be subordinate to the Joint Chiefs of Staff but would report directly to the President.

The quest for autonomy also leads organizations to resist operations in which control must be shared with foreign governments. This leads the military services to seek bases under U.S. control and to resist integrated forces.

We have already mentioned that the quest for autonomy on the part of the military services affected the unification struggle in the late 1940s. The Air Force drive for existence as a separate service was fundamentally a quest for autonomy. Air Force doctrine and strategy were stated in terms which would justify autonomy.[35] The Navy resisted the unification plan precisely because it saw the plan as a threat to its autonomy. Fearing that the Air Force would use the integrated structure in an effort to dominate the other services, the Navy argued that the Secretary of Defense should be coordinator of the services and not have operational control over them. The Army was in a dilemma: it had to choose between autonomy for its operations by maintaining an integrated combat air arm or give this up in order to prevent the Air Force officers from coming to dominate the Army. It chose to "let the Air Force go" in order to maintain autonomy over its favored field of action—ground combat operations; since then it has been struggling to regain some air capability.

The State Department's quest for autonomy has led it to reject White House interference in its ongoing operations and to resist non-career ambassadors as well as special presidential envoys.

The quest for autonomy has a significant impact on the stands and actions of organizations. The following patterns show up repeatedly.

1. In negotiations among organizations about desirable actions, each

35. Perry Smith, *The Air Force Plans for Peace*, pp. 14, 27, 28.

prefers an agreement which leaves it free to pursue its own interests even if this appears to an outside observer to lead to an uncoordinated and hence inefficient policy. Thus both the Air Force and the Navy prefer the situation in which the Polaris missiles are controlled independently of the Air Force missiles and strategic bombers. Each service developed its own strategic doctrine and its own targeting. Both services, but especially the Navy, have resisted efforts to create an integrated command, and only with great reluctance did the Navy acquiesce in a joint strategic targeting organization set up under intense civilian pressure in the early 1960s. In Vietnam, the services conducted largely independent combat operations with each service getting a share of the target areas. Each preferred this to an overall plan that would limit its autonomy.

The State Department has frequently maintained its autonomy in the conduct of diplomatic negotiations and political relations with foreign governments by leaving the Treasury Department and the foreign aid agencies free to conduct their own bilateral negotiations and arrangements on trade and aid matters.

2. In devising options for senior officials, organizations tend to agree on proposals which exclude any joint operations and which leave each free to go its own way and continue to do what it prefers to do. As one keen student of the Washington bureaucracy has observed:

Over time, each agency has acquired certain "pet projects" which its senior officials promote. These are often carried out by one agency despite concern and even mid-level opposition from others, as part of a tacit trade-off: "We'll let you do your thing, and you let us do ours." Such deals, or "non-aggression treaties," are almost never explicit, but are nonetheless well understood by the participants. The results from such arrangements obviously vary. Sometimes programs are in direct conflict. Waste and duplication are frequent; lack of information about what one's colleagues are doing is common. These are all direct costs of the multi-agency system, which is too large and scattered to come under one driver.[36]

In budgetary negotiations, organizations most often seek a compromise by which subordinate officials are committed to set limits but are free to spend money within that limit.

3. In presenting policy proposals to senior officials, organizations typically indicate that the proposed course of action is infeasible unless they are given full freedom to carry it out. During the 1958 Quemoy crisis the

36. Richard Holbrooke, "The Machine That Fails," p. 70.

Joint Chiefs of Staff repeatedly pressed for freedom to use nuclear weapons on their own authority. They informed the President that they could guarantee to defend the offshore islands against the Chinese attack only if granted this autonomy.[37] In developing their preferred overseas base structure, the armed forces are particularly concerned with their freedom to conduct operations without the interference of allied governments. This leads them to insist upon the need for unambiguous U.S. control over bases, as they did in the case of the Trust Territories in the Pacific and for many years in the case of Okinawa. Where this is not feasible, the military press for bases in countries which they judge are unlikely to object to any operations they wish to conduct. This was apparently a major motive for the military's efforts to develop bases in Spain.[38]

4. Organizations seek to guard their autonomy by presenting to the President or Cabinet officials only a single option so that he cannot choose among options interfering with their preferred course of action. U. Alexis Johnson, for many years the senior State Department Foreign Service Officer, has said that he objected to President Kennedy's introduction of procedures that prevented the Secretary of State and the Secretary of Defense from conferring with each other and arriving at a consensus before meeting with the President.[39]

Organizational Morale

An organization functions effectively only if its personnel are highly motivated. They must believe that what they are doing makes a difference and promotes the national interest; that the organization's efforts are appreciated and that its role in the scheme of things is not diminishing (and preferably is increasing); and that the organization controls its own resources. Above all the career official must believe that there is room for advancement in the organization and that the organization is seeking to protect his opportunities for advancement. In order to keep open promotions to top positions, an organization resists efforts to contract the size

37. Dwight D. Eisenhower, *The White House Years* (Vol. II: *Waging Peace, 1956–1961*), p. 299. Cited hereafter as *Waging Peace*.

38. Theodore J. Lowi, "Bases in Spain," pp. 677–78.

39. U. Alexis Johnson, John F. Kennedy Library Oral History Interview, pp. 14–15. See also Arthur M. Schlesinger, Jr., *A Thousand Days: John F. Kennedy in the White House*, p. 557, and Scott, "The Department of State," p. 6.

of the organization (unless the contraction is necessary to protect the essence of its activities). It also strives to assure that top jobs are held primarily by career officials of its service. Thus the Foreign Service generally opposes the appointment of non-career ambassadors, although it has learned to accept some non-career appointees as inevitable. The military services struggle for the post of Chairman of the Joint Chiefs as well as positions which put their representatives in charge of integrated commands (such as the Commander-in-Chief in Europe and the Commander-in-Chief in the Pacific). They oppose efforts to close out functions which would mean a reduction in the number of senior personnel.

Career personnel are assigned so as to appear to give everyone a reasonable chance of promotion rather than to put people in the slots where they are likely to do the most good. Military officers compete for roles in what is seen as the essence of the services' activity rather than other functions where promotion is less likely. Thus the commander of the ill-fated *Pueblo* tells us of his great disappointment at being appointed commander of that ship rather than of a submarine.[40] So, too, Army officers compete for roles in combat organizations rather than advisory missions. Foreign Service officers seek assignments in political sections and on regional desks in the department rather than in economic sections or in specialized bureaus.

An organization resists functions which it believes may interfere with career patterns either by bringing in people who would not be eligible for the top spots or bringing in people who would, because of their senior rank, fill the top spots and foreclose advancement for others. Both of these considerations affected the Air Force's decision not to fight for the air defense mission at the time of the separation of the Air Force from the Army.[41]

Organizations also seek to maintain morale by laying down modes of conduct for their staff members which avoid conflict within the group. Andrew M. Scott reports, for example, a series of injunctions about how Foreign Service officers are to deal with each other: "Play the game, don't rock the boat, don't make waves, minimize risk taking."[42]

Organizations may also seek to maintain morale by seeking a homogeneous group of career officials. According to research cited by Harold

40. Lloyd M. Bucher, *Bucher: My Story*, pp. 2–3.
41. Perry Smith, *The Air Force Plans for Peace*, pp. 101–2.
42. Scott, "The Department of State," p. 4. See also Chris Argyris, *Some Causes of Organizational Ineffectiveness within the Department of State*, pp. 1–9.

Seidman, both the military services and the foreign service are relatively homogeneous although the two groups differ in terms of the area of the country from which they incline to draw their personnel.[43]

Because they have learned the vital importance of morale for the effective functioning of an organization, bureaucrats give close attention to the likely effects of any change of policy or patterns of action on the morale of the organization, and they shun changes which they feel will have a severe effect on morale. Even changes which would probably improve the organization's effectiveness in carrying out its mission may be resisted if officials believe that such actions would severely affect the morale of the organization. In particular, they will be concerned about the effects on the promotion patterns of the organization. Short-run accomplishment of goals and even increases in budgets take second place to the long-run health of the organization.

For example, almost every observer of U.S. operations in Vietnam concluded that extending the tour of duty of commissioned Army officers from one year to two or three years would substantially improve the U.S. military performance. Yet the Army refused to make this change. This is not because the Army differed with the assessment that there would be an improvement in effectiveness. Rather, the Army believed that there would be immediate adverse effects on morale if officers were sent to Vietnam either for an indefinite period or for a prolonged period such as three years; and, particularly in the early stages of the war, Army leaders felt that there would be long-range morale problems if only a small percentage of career Army officers had combat experience in Vietnam, since those officers who did would have an inside track on promotions. They believed it desirable not only for morale but also for improving the effectiveness of the service over the long run to give as many career officers as possible experience in Vietnam.[44]

Budgets

Career officials examine any proposal for its effect on the budget of their organization. All other things being equal, they prefer larger to

43. Seidman, *Politics, Position, and Power: The Dynamics of Federal Organization*, p. 113.
44. Adam Yarmolinsky, *The Military Establishment*, p. 20; Seymour M. Hersh, *My Lai 4: A Report on the Massacre and Its Aftermath*, p. 6.

smaller budgets and support policy changes which they believe will lead to larger budgets.

There is, however, a substantial asymmetry between the Department of Defense and the Department of State in regard to the impact of policy issues on budgets. The State Department budget is relatively small, and very few of the foreign policy matters with which the State Department deals have any direct effect on its budget. For the military services, most policy issues are likely to have important budgetary implications. For example, the ABM had no implications for the State Department budget, but it had very important consequences for the budget of the Army and the Defense Department as a whole.

An organization is usually quick to question whether a proposed change which generates a new function will in fact lead to a budget increase or merely add to its responsibilities without any corresponding increase in its budget. The calculation of whether or not a new function will lead to an increased budget depends in part upon the nature of the budget-making process. For example, during the 1950s the budgets for the military services were largely determined by allocating fixed percentages of an overall budgetary ceiling established by the President. In general, new responsibilities had to be financed out of existing budgetary levels. By contrast, during the 1960s there was at least no explicit budgetary ceiling. The budget was determined by the Secretary of Defense on the basis of functional categories and responsibilities. Thus the services believed that new functions tended to mean increased budget levels.

Whether a new function will lead to new funds, and hence should be desired, or to a reallocation of old funds, which may need to be resisted, depends in part also on whether the new function is seen as closely related to existing functions. For example, the Army was interested in acquiring responsibility for the deployment of medium-range ballistic missiles (MRBMs) in the 1950s, in part because this would give the Army a strategic nuclear role. The army hoped that this would justify altering the existing percentages so as to increase its share of the overall defense budget, since the existing allocation was based on the Army having no strategic function. On the other hand, the Air Force recognized that MRBM would simply be considered another strategic weapon and that it would be forced to finance development and deployment out of existing budget funds. Thus, in terms of budgetary interests, the Army sought the MRBM role, while the Air Force was reluctant to take it on. Concern with protecting its existing roles and missions, on the other hand, meant that if there was to be an MRBM program, the Air Force was determined to have it.

Organizations are vigilant not only about their absolute share of the budget but also about their relative share of a larger budget. This proposition applies particularly to each of the military services, although it may also apply to parts of the AID organization. They fear that once established levels change in an adverse direction, the trend may continue, leading to substantial reductions in the activities of a particular service, which could have substantial effects on morale.

As a precaution, each of the services tends to resist proposals which, though promising more funds, may lead to a less than proportionate increase in its budget as compared with other parts of the defense establishment. The services individually prefer the certainty of a particular share of the budget to an unknown situation in which budgets may increase but shares may change. For example, in 1957, the Gaither Committee appointed by President Eisenhower recommended substantial increases in the budgets of all three services, arguing the need for secure second-strike retaliatory forces and for larger limited-war capabilities. However, none of the services supported these proposals, in part because none was certain how the expanded budget would be divided.[45]

Organizational Stands

Participants who look to organizational interests to define national security interests seldom feel the need to engage in a full-scale analysis of a particular issue. Rather, their reactions reflect "grooved thinking"— responding to a particular stimulus in a set way. This leads to typical patterns of stands by organizations. We have already referred to the traditional State Department opposition to negotiations by presidential emissaries or the President himself and its opposition to proposals which would appear to require the State Department to involve itself in direct intervention abroad. In negotiations, State typically presses for the talks to be kept going and for concessions to be made to the other side in hopes that counterconcessions will be offered in turn.

Each military service supports foreign policies which will justify the forces it believes are necessary for the essence of the service and favors

45. Morton H. Halperin, "The Gaither Committee and the Policy Process," pp. 360–84.

strategies which presume that precisely those forces will be the ones used in the event of hostilities. Each opposes mixed forces or combined service operations. The military usually also support proposals which will give them new equipment. They tend to emphasize the procurement of forces and of overall force structure even at the cost of combat readiness and real combat capability.[46]

The military view issues involving American bases overseas in terms of the interests of their own organizations. Each service favors the retention of the bases which it uses and which suit a military strategy that accords with its force structure. Senior officers are particularly sensitive to possible actions which might jeopardize their bases. According to Arthur Schlesinger, Jr., Secretary of State Dean Rusk discovered this when he proposed that the Bay of Pigs invasion be transferred to the American naval base at Guantánamo.

He [Rusk] reverted to a suggestion with which he had startled the Joint Chiefs during one of the meetings. This was that the operation fan out from Guantánamo with the prospect of retreating to the base in case of failure. He remarked, "It is interesting to observe the Pentagon people. They are perfectly willing to put the President's head on the block, but they recoil from the idea of doing anything which might risk Guantánamo."[47]

In assessing what forces a friendly country should be encouraged to maintain, the military prefer an organization similar to their own. Thus the Army will be concerned about allied ground forces, the Navy with fleets, and the Air Force with the air arm. They urge the buildup of sister forces and the provision of aid for that purpose.[48]

The "sister service" approach extends to the composition of international forces. In the debates in the United Nations Security Council Committee on the Composition of an International Military Force, the American Air Force representative argued that the contribution of the great powers should be entirely in air forces, while the Army representative, General Ridgway, argued that the United States should contribute ground forces.[49] The same philosophy applies to estimates of enemy forces, each service stressing that the enemy has been building up in its area.

46. Enthoven and Smith, *How Much Is Enough?* pp. 10–11.
47. Schlesinger, *A Thousand Days*, p. 257.
48. For examples of this attitude, see Laurence Martin, "The American Decision To Rearm Germany," p. 649; Arthur J. Dommen, *Conflict in Laos*, p. 101.
49. Ridgway, *Soldier*, pp. 169–70.

In the eyes of American officers, the best way to build up a "sister service" abroad is to supply American training and advisers. Without these, military aid may be useless, they feel.[50] As for the proper size of a military assistance program, in their estimation that depends upon whether military aid will be subtracted from their own service budgets or added on.

The attitude of the military services toward commitments and the use of force is surprising to observers who expect a bellicose outlook. In general, the military oppose new commitments for the United States and have in general been opposed to, or neutral on, postwar American interventions. (On the other hand, when interventions do occur, the services push for authority to employ the full range of available forces.)

The services are often reluctant to take on new commitments, feeling that their forces are already stretched too thin. With regard to allies, they tend to see the defense of Western Europe against a Soviet attack as the main commitment. The military have learned that the allocations given to them do not necessarily correspond to the number of commitments that the United States undertakes, and therefore they see new commitments as adding new obligations on them without yielding additional forces. Dean Acheson relates a typical example from the era when the French wanted help to hold on to Indochina:

As the year wore on without much progress and we ourselves became bogged down in the negotiations at Panmunjom, our sense of frustration grew. A review of the situation in late August, before I left for a series of meetings in the autumn of 1951, brought warning from the Joint Chiefs of Staff against any statement that would commit—or seem to the French under future eventualities to commit—United States armed forces to Indochina. We did not waver from this policy.[51]

On the issue of American military intervention, the armed services have been in general quite cautious. At different times they have resisted proposals for intervention, remained neutral, or asked for authority to use all their existing forces to make the gamble of involvement less risky if taken at all. Professionally they prefer a conservative estimate of the readiness of forces, and they are sensitive to the danger of using forces where they might be defeated or where they would be drawn away from the primary theater of operations. This military attitude first manifested itself

50. Dean Acheson, *Present at the Creation: My Years in the State Department*, pp. 331, 661.

51. Ibid., p. 675.

during the Berlin crisis of 1948. General Lucius Clay, who had direct responsibility for Berlin, favored the sending of an armed convoy down the road from the American zone of Germany to Berlin. President Harry S Truman was prepared to support this proposal if it won the endorsement of the Joint Chiefs. The Chiefs, however, refused to recommend such action. Moreover, the Air Force was itself opposed even to the airlift.[52]

At the time of the outbreak of the Korean War in June 1950, the military made no recommendation for intervention. Indeed, the top commanders were known to believe that though Taiwan was vital to the security of the United States, Korea was not. Consequently Truman was forced to agree to defend Taiwan as the price of gaining military acquiescence in the Korean intervention. The military were not the driving force in planning the Bay of Pigs operation, which was largely a CIA endeavor. In the case of the possibility of intervention in Laos in 1961, the military were opposed unless granted full authority to use all forces. They also pressed for an all-out strike if there were to be any action against Cuba in 1962. The services were not the driving force behind the American involvement in Vietnam.

Paradoxically, however, military reluctance to enter into half-hearted or ill-backed commitments leads to the opposite of caution once intervention begins. As soon as the United States committed itself to the defense of South Korea, the Joint Chiefs pressed for a rapid buildup of American forces. Similarly in the case of Vietnam, the Joint Chiefs pressed for a larger, quicker buildup and for attacks on North Vietnam.

In particular, the services have pressed for the right to use nuclear weapons in any military conflict. The first such effort came during the Berlin blockade when the military, supported by Secretary of Defense James Forrestal, pressed the President to agree that the atomic bomb would be used if necessary.[53] President Eisenhower did make a generalized decision that the armed forces could plan on the use of nuclear weapons in the event of conflict.[54] But he resisted pressure to delegate authority in any particular crisis. The military nonetheless continued to press him—for example, during the Quemoy crisis of 1958.[55] The Joint Chiefs pushed hard

---

52. Murphy, *Diplomat among Warriors*, p. 316; Truman, *Memoirs* (Vol. II: *Years of Trial and Hope*), pp. 124–26. Cited hereafter as *Years of Trial and Hope*.

53. David E. Lilienthal, *The Journals of David E. Lilienthal* (Vol: II: *The Atomic Energy Years, 1945–1950*), p. 406. Cited hereafter as *Journals*.

54. Glenn Snyder, "The 'New Look' of 1953," pp. 427, 433–35.

55. Eisenhower, *Waging Peace*, p. 299.

for advance authority to use nuclear weapons when the Kennedy administration was considering intervention in Laos in 1961.[56]

This chapter is the longest in the book, and the reader may feel somewhat uncertain as to why so much detail has been provided. Recall that our purpose was to explain organizational interests. Career officials, including those who will come to head organizations such as the Joint Chiefs of Staff, often develop their position largely by calculating the national interest in terms of the organizational interests of the career service to which they belong. Even in-and-outers are sometimes "captured" by the organizations which bring them into government. It is necessary to understand the details of these interests if one is to avoid the erroneous notion that organizations simply seek to grow in size. The details of organizational interests, the essence of groups as defined by the members, and the competition of groups over roles and missions are likely to be unfamiliar to readers, and they are important in understanding how a large number of participants come to see issues and what motivates the stands they take. Before discussing specifically which participants come to rely mainly on organizational interests, we need to consider a second major class of interests, those of the President.

56. Hilsman, *To Move a Nation*, pp. 129, 133–34; Schlesinger, *A Thousand Days*, pp. 338–39.

CHAPTER FOUR

Presidential Interests

If some participants, particularly career officials, take their cues to what is in the national interest from their definition of the interests of their organization, others, particularly in-and-outers at high levels, detect clues to the national interest in their conception of presidential interests. Presidents and their close associates frequently come to determine their stands largely in relation to problems of maintaining effective power or getting reelected. Also, Presidents and those concerned with domestic problems and the domestic economy may equate national security with avoiding recession or inflation or promoting specific domestic programs such as welfare reform or highway construction.

It should be noted at the outset that the consideration in this chapter of the domestic political factors entering into presidential stands on foreign policy issues should not be construed as a critical judgment about the legitimacy of such considerations. Foreign policy and national security decisions are multiple-value choices and are rarely reached on the basis of a single, overriding view of any single problem that excludes all other considerations. Domestic political considerations and personal interests are an inescapable part of the decision process, especially at the White House level. However, these are usually dismissed or not considered at all in formal analyses of decision making in the area of national security. This chapter is meant to bring them into focus.

Domestic Politics

There is a very strong and widely held view in the United States that it is immoral to let domestic political considerations influence decisions which may affect war and peace. Supposedly foreign policy should be bipartisan. This belief is so strongly held that senior officials frequently deny in public, and even apparently to themselves, that they take domestic politics into account.

Richard E. Neustadt offers an historical explanation of this phenomenon, contrasting the American situation to that of the British:

I have a strong impression that on his [Prime Minister Harold Macmillan's] side of the water, front-bench politicians of the time could give party-political concerns free play in foreign policy—to say nothing of economic policy—with a straightforward consciousness quite inadmissible, indeed almost unthinkable, for Presidents on our side.

We proceeded then in an inhibiting framework of "bipartisanship" built by FDR and Truman—and maintained by Eisenhower after his own fashion—to afford support for a revolution in our foreign relations, breaching the isolationist tradition. Men who had been bred in that tradition before shifting ground themselves now sought to keep the country with them on the plea that "politics stops at the water's edge." This, for them, could not be a mere slogan. For them it was a virtual imperative of personal conduct. Truman tried to live by it and rarely let his conscious mind admit inevitable lapses. Eisenhower seems to have done the same.[1]

The reluctance to admit that one is taking domestic political interests into account means that they are seldom discussed explicitly within the government. This reluctance is reinforced by recognition that for the public to know that domestic political factors were being openly considered would be extremely damaging because of the belief that such considerations are immoral. Participants are aware that somebody opposed to a certain policy in the area of foreign affairs which is being justified on domestic grounds will almost certainly leak such information. David Lilienthal reports on a discussion within the Atomic Energy Commission about a sensitive issue which the military services sought to raise with the President. He noted in his diary that one member of the commission talked about the "election year political atmosphere in which this issue would be dealt with, saying this was a bad time to raise it." Lilienthal disapproved. "I thought his point was dangerous because there were some who would then assert that a decision against the military would simply be a political decision by the President, which could be quite damaging."[2]

Presidents often instruct officials not to take domestic politics into account in making their recommendations. Thus President Truman is quoted as saying to Secretary of Defense James Forrestal, "Look, Jim,

1. Neustadt, *Alliance Politics*, p. 87.
2. Lilienthal, *Journals*, p. 374.

when you take a thing as serious as this to the American public you should forget about political considerations."[3] Truman also instructed the State Department not to take account of domestic politics in making its recommendations, and here he had an additional reason in mind. He believed, as he once said to State Department officials, "You fellas in the Department of State don't know much about domestic politics."[4]

Beneath the surface, of course, domestic politics do enter into the making of foreign policy. It is incumbent upon political scientists to bring this out even though evidence is relatively hard to come by.

Ted—Have you considered the very real possibility that if we allow Cuba to complete installation and operational readiness of missile bases, the next House of Representatives is likely to have a Republican majority? This would completely paralyze our ability to react sensibly and coherently to further Soviet advances.[5]

This note, passed by Douglas Dillon to Theodore Sorensen at a meeting of the so-called ExCom of the National Security Council during the height of the Cuban missile crisis, is one of the few instances on the public record of a frank consideration of domestic politics. Nevertheless, there is no doubt that domestic interests do affect the stands of participants. In commenting almost a decade later on the Cuban missile crisis, John Kenneth Galbraith laid out the choice of conflicting objectives and the rationale for giving consideration to domestic politics:

In the Cuban missile crisis President Kennedy had to balance the danger of blowing up the planet against the risk of political attack at home for appeasing the Communists. This was not an irresponsible choice: to ignore the domestic opposition was to risk losing initiative or office to men who wanted an even more dangerous policy.[6]

Lyndon Johnson's concern with domestic politics was acute during his consideration of the ABM deployment in 1967. As he considered the recommendations of the military services that an ABM deployment be

---

3. Vannevar Bush, *Pieces of the Action*, p. 295.

4. Quoted in Keith C. Clark and Lawrence J. Legere (eds.), *The President and the Management of National Security*, p. 169.

Glenn Paige, *The Korean Decision*, p. 141, reports that, in response to a request from Under Secretary of State Webb to consider the political aspects of sending the Seventh Fleet into the Straits of Formosa, President Truman "snapped back, 'We're not going to talk about politics. I'll handle the political affairs.' Thus the conference did not consider any questions dealing with domestic politics."

5. Theodore Sorensen, *Kennedy*, p. 688.

6. Galbraith, "Plain Lessons of a Bad Decade," p. 32.

initiated and of his Secretary of Defense that it be postponed, Johnson could not and did not ignore the domestic politics. There could be little doubt in his mind that the Republican nominee, whether it be Richard Nixon or Nelson Rockefeller, could well make weaponry a major issue in the campaign. At the urging of the Secretary of Defense and under intense budget pressures, Johnson had permitted the non-Vietnam portion of the military budget to decline, at least in real terms, and he was regularly rejecting proposals from the Joint Chiefs to develop and deploy a whole array of new weapons systems. Opposition to his defense program was building, particularly among leaders in the Senate and the House. ABM was rapidly becoming a symbol of "preparedness." Johnson had to recognize that, if he did not deploy an ABM, he was open to the political charge of failing to take a step which would save American lives in the event of war. Kennedy had apparently scored effectively against Nixon in 1960 on the missile gap issue, and Johnson was reluctant to run the risk that the "defense gap" issue would be used against him.

A particularly important reason for searching out domestic political considerations in analyzing the foreign policy process is that many career officials routinely (if somewhat surreptitiously) take them into account.[7] Bureaucrats have learned that Presidents will simply not take seriously proposals that are totally out of bounds in domestic politics, and they recognize that Presidents do, in fact, make such calculations. Although domestic considerations are discussed quietly, they are discussed at all levels of decision making on national security issues.

The President and his principal advisers are assumed to weigh the possible effect of foreign policy issues on elections. Secondly, they are assumed to keep the President's overall program in mind in approaching any given decision in the area of foreign affairs.

Presidential Elections

There is much debate among political scientists about the effects of foreign policy issues on presidential elections. Most studies seem to show that foreign policy issues play a relatively minor role although the image of a candidate as being knowledgeable in foreign policy and a man of

---

7. Two former officials who attested this point without qualification are Joseph M. Jones, *The Fifteen Weeks: February 21–June 5, 1947*, p. 149, and Karl Lott Rankin, *China Assignment*, p. ix.

peace is of value.[8] As compared with the analysts, Presidents and potential Presidents themselves see a closer link between stands on foreign policy issues and the outcome of the presidential elections. The range and diversity of issues which Presidents believe can affect their domestic political posture and their chances of reelection are reflected in a study by Philip L. Geyelin of Lyndon Johnson's calculations:

At this point, the Johnson reasoning comes full circle and takes on deep significance in his approach to the major crises of his first two years. For example, the reasoning would begin with his assessment that it would be bad politics at home to cave in quickly to Panamanian rioters (even though he was prepared to be more than generous, by any previous standards, when the appearance of pressure was removed); that it would be unpopular to allow the U.S. position to collapse in Vietnam, even into a "neutralist" solution, because of the "appeasement" stigma this might carry with it; that even slight risk of "another Cuba" in the Dominican Republic would be political suicide; that a full cross-section of Congress was against the MLF; that disarmament proposals or recommendations for easing East-West trade barriers would stir the cold warriors of Congress at a period of maximum tension over Vietnam (but not, let it be noted, at other times); that foreign aid to countries whose citizens burn libraries or whose rulers denounce U.S. policy in Vietnam or elsewhere is political anathema.[9]

Presidential calculations about the impact of foreign policy on elections seem to relate to three kinds of issues: (1) generating a popular image of the President among the electorate; (2) denying a potential opponent a major issue; and (3) appealing to particular interest groups. Each of these is considered in turn.

APPEALING TO THE POPULATION AS A WHOLE

In general, presidential popularity appears to go up—at least in the short run—when the President is seen acting vigorously on almost any issue, even though the consequences of his action are not yet known. Presidential initiatives in foreign policy are frequently seen as desirable because they show a President in command and seeking solutions to problems.

More specifically, Presidents and their domestic political advisers often

8. See, for example, Angus Campbell, Gerald Gurin, and Warren Miller, *The Voter Decides.*

9. Geyelin, *Lyndon B. Johnson and the World*, p. 148.

believe that the President's popularity can be increased, with desirable consequences for the next presidential election, by demonstrating that he is a man of peace willing to take whatever steps short of appeasement are necessary to reduce world tensions. Both James Haggerty, President Eisenhower's press secretary, and Eric Goldman, a sometime speech writer for President Johnson, sought to persuade their respective bosses to undertake a major campaign of speeches and world travel designed to portray them as men of peace, and both advisers expected that such a tour would favorably influence the next election. Haggerty was successful in selling the proposal to Eisenhower, and this resulted in the extended presidential world trip of 1959 which many believe helped Richard Nixon in the 1960 election and was certainly urged on Eisenhower for that purpose.[10] In both cases, the State Department objected because of its concern with maintaining its autonomy and keeping the President out of diplomacy. In Eisenhower's case, with the death of John Foster Dulles and with the new Secretary of State Christian Herter exercising relatively little influence on the President, the State Department objections were overruled. In Johnson's case, LBJ's initial approval of the proposal was changed when Dean Rusk, Secretary of State, strenuously objected.[11] Although no memoirs are yet available, many observers have interpreted various moves by President Nixon, including his visits to Russia and China and the SALT agreement, as aimed in part at creating an image of himself as a man of peace, an image he exploited with great skill in his landslide victory in 1972.

DENYING POTENTIAL OPPONENTS A KEY ISSUE

As has been suggested, President Johnson's ABM decision may have been influenced by the notion that if he failed to deploy an ABM, his opponent in the 1968 election would use the issue against him. Such considerations affect Presidents throughout their first term, for the four-year period between elections looks quite short to them. For example, Theodore Sorensen reports that President Kennedy's decision to proceed with a civil defense program in 1961 stemmed partly from the possibility that a "civil defense gap" would be used against him as he had used the "missile gap" against Richard Nixon.[12]

Postwar Presidents have been particularly concerned about the effects

---

10. Emmet John Hughes, *The Ordeal of Power: A Political Memoir of the Eisenhower Years,* p. 278; Patrick Anderson, *The Presidents' Men,* p. 191.

11. Eric F. Goldman, *The Tragedy of Lyndon Johnson,* pp. 223–24.

12. Theodore Sorensen, *Kennedy,* p. 614.

of permitting a country to "go Communist." All of them have been mindful of the attacks mounted on President Truman because of his refusal to intervene in the Chinese civil war and prevent the Chinese Communists from coming to power. "Do not let a country fall to communism" has been balanced by the second injunction, "Do not commit American troops to ground combat." After President Truman's commitment of American troops to battle in the Korean War, the contradiction between the two injunctions created a dilemma for the Presidents who followed him. Roger Hilsman describes one instance in which contradictory pressures were brought to bear on President Kennedy and his White House advisers in a dramatic and explicit way:

In the midst of the President's nicely balanced political and military moves on Laos, the Republican leadership in Congress chose to make a public statement opposing an agreement in Laos which would lead to a coalition government that included Communists. But when the President consulted the leaders of both parties, he found that they were also united in opposing any commitment of American troops to Laos.[13]

Some interpretations of U.S. policy in Vietnam have argued that Kennedy sought to walk the line between not losing a country to communism and not openly committing ground troops to battle.[14]

Apprehensions about losing a country to communism were always linked with fears of reviving McCarthyism—the search for nonexistent Communists or Communist sympathizers as the source of American defeats. The most explicit suggestion of the importance of these factors in shaping U.S. Vietnam policy is contained in a report by Kenneth O'Donnell, a special assistant to Kennedy, as corroborated by Senate Majority Leader Mike Mansfield. O'Donnell asserts that Kennedy had specifically decided to withdraw from Vietnam but had put it off until after the 1964 presidential elections because of the belief that he could not be reelected if he withdrew from Vietnam and permitted the country to go Communist. This is how O'Donnell has told the story:

In the spring of 1963, Mike Mansfield again criticized our military involvement in Vietnam, this time in front of the congressional leadership at a White House breakfast, much to the President's annoyance and embarrassment. Leaving the breakfast the President seized my arm and said, "Get Mike and have him come into my office." I sat in on part of their discussion. The President told Mansfield that he had been having serious second

13. Hilsman, *To Move A Nation*, p. 134.
14. See, for instance, Leslie H. Gelb, "Vietnam: The System Worked," pp. 140–73.

thoughts about Mansfield's argument and that he now agreed with the senator's thinking on the need for a complete military withdrawal from Vietnam.

"But I can't do it until 1965—after I'm reelected," Kennedy told Mansfield.

President Kennedy felt, and Mansfield agreed with him, that if he announced a total withdrawal of American military personnel from Vietnam before the 1964 election, there would be a wild conservative outcry against returning him to the Presidency for a second term.

After Mansfield left the office, the President told me that he had made up his mind that after his reelection he would take the risk of unpopularity and make a complete withdrawal of American forces from Vietnam. "In 1965, I'll be damned everywhere as a Communist appeaser. But I don't care. If I tried to pull out completely now, we would have another Joe McCarthy red scare on our hands, but I can do it after I'm reelected. So we had better make damned sure that I am reelected."[15]

APPEALS TO PARTICULAR GROUPS

Specific decisions can gain across-the-board support for Presidents or lose them the support of particular groups within the society who have a special interest in foreign policy issues. The appeal to a particular group may be directly by public statements or actions designed to attract them; in other cases, the support may be gained indirectly. An individual who has strong influence with a group may be placated by a particular foreign policy action which in turn leads him to urge support from the group at election time.

The most celebrated case of a President's position on a foreign policy issue being influenced by domestic political considerations involves President Truman and his stand on Palestine. One must note that the evidence here is somewhat ambiguous. Both Richard Neustadt and Dean Acheson concluded that Truman's decisions were not influenced by domestic political calculations. Acheson said flatly: "He [Truman] never took or refused to take a step in our foreign relations to benefit his or his party's fortunes. This he would have regarded as false to the great office that he venerated and held in sacred trust."[16] Other advisers had a different view. Some were constantly urging on him actions which they believed would

15. O'Donnell, "LBJ and the Kennedys," pp. 51–52.
16. Acheson, *Present at the Creation*, p. 176. See also Neustadt, *Alliance Politics*, pp. 83–84.

solidify the Jewish vote and secure funds for his election campaign. On the other side both his Secretary of Defense James Forrestal and his Secretaries of State James Byrnes and George Marshall were convinced that Truman's decisions in this area were largely influenced by the Jewish vote. At a critical meeting to discuss early recognition of the state of Israel, Truman had invited Clark Clifford, one of his principal domestic political advisers but a man who also occasionally involved himself in foreign policy matters. Marshall interpreted Clifford's attendance as a clear indication that Truman would decide the issue on domestic political grounds and was reported to have said, "Mr. President, this is not a matter to be determined on the basis of politics. Unless politics were involved, Mr. Clifford would not even be at this conference. This is a very serious matter of foreign policy determination."[17]

A recent study of the origins of the Cold War further suggests that Truman's concern about the growing disaffection for the Democratic party among ethnic minority groups with Eastern European attachments was one of the motives which led him to take a strong stand against Soviet efforts to establish domination over such countries as Poland, Czechoslovakia, and Hungary.[18]

In some cases, Presidents may appoint particular individuals to public office of one kind or another in the foreign policy field in the hopes of gaining their support in the forthcoming election campaign or gaining the support of ethnic or other minority groups who look to that individual. In his effort to secure Senator Strom Thurmond's support within the Republican party for his presidential election bid, Richard Nixon reportedly promised Thurmond that if he were elected President, he would negotiate a textile agreement which would reduce the importation of Japanese and other foreign synthetic textiles into the United States and that he would support an ABM deployment. Upon election, Nixon apparently felt obligated to seek to meet both of these commitments.[19]

Presidents may also seek to influence elections by awarding defense contracts which gain the support of particular business organizations and perhaps bolster employment in key areas. Herbert York, then a senior Defense Department official, recalls that the contract for a new manned

17. Anderson, *The Presidents' Men*, pp. 118–19. See also *Forrestal Diaries*, pp. 309–10, 347; James F. Byrnes, *All in One Lifetime*, p. 373; and Cabell Phillips, *The Truman Presidency*, p. 198.

18. Wishnatsky, "Symbolic Politics and the Cold War," passim.

19. Lewis Chester, *The American Melodrama: The Presidential Campaign of 1968*, p. 447; Garry Wills, *Nixon Agonistes: The Crisis of the Self-Made Man*, p. 271.

bomber for the Air Force was in serious trouble in the closing days of the Eisenhower administration. But a change came:

Then, during the 1960 campaign for the Presidency, the B-70 was given a brief new lease on life. Even before the new fiscal year started, on July 1, 1960, about $60 million had been tacked onto the originally planned $75 million. This extra money was supposed to be used for development work on some of the most critical weapons subsystems; and in combination with other readjustments in the project, it was to make possible the construction of a single prototype aircraft. However, a program leading to only one prototype never made sense, and going through such a step was nothing more than an exercise in salami tactics. Thus, in August, another $20 million was added for a second plane. Then, just days before the Nixon-Kennedy election contest in November, 1960, the Department of Defense announced that it was bringing the total B-70 budget for the then current fiscal year up to $265 million. As a result of these increased funds, the number of airplanes to be built was increased to four for sure, with eight more possible, and the four were to be prototypes of a "usable weapon system." In California, the announcement of this new lease on life was accompanied by a detailed statement by North American Aviation about the recent sad history of declining employment in southern California and how these funds would change all that.

Although Nixon did carry California in 1960, Kennedy won nationally, and the B-70's new lease on life ran out almost immediately.[20]

Maintaining Presidential Power

In calculating interests in a foreign policy decision, the President and his advisers will be concerned about how the President's stand on a particular issue may affect his ability to accomplish other things. All postwar Presidents have learned, as Richard Neustadt has explained, that the Presidency is simply a license to seek to persuade. Presidential power must be carefully husbanded and used shrewdly if the President's ability to influence events is to go beyond his role as a clerk.[21] One basic aim is to avoid the appearance of failure. To seek to accomplish something and to fail is to signal to others that one can be beaten. Thus Presidents are reluctant to undertake programs in the foreign policy field if they believe that there is only a modest chance of success.

20. York, *Race to Oblivion*, pp. 56–57.
21. Richard E. Neustadt, *Presidential Power.*

The President proceeds warily on those issues that arouse major passions and interests either in the population as a whole or within a significant group whose support he values on other issues, domestic or foreign. We have already mentioned the fear in the 1950s and 1960s of turning loose torrents of domestic opposition by appearing to be "soft on Communism." President Kennedy and his brother Robert, according to the latter's memoirs, discussed impeachment as a possible penalty for failing to get the Russian missiles out of Cuba.[21]

Even when the President is confident of weathering opposition, he dislikes spending his time and energy fighting to regain initiative. Presidents attempt to be careful to choose the issues on which they will fight hard against sustained domestic opposition. They easily convince themselves that an action which is necessary to avoid such a fight is in the national interest because it will leave them free to pursue other programs that are vital to the national security. Lyndon Johnson's decision to involve the United States deeply in Vietnam without making obvious the extent of the commitment was justified by him largely on the ground that this was the posture that would leave him with the time and the political support to pursue the Great Society program.

Sometimes the attitude of small groups or even single individuals is as important to the President as his general popularity.

Presidents are particularly concerned about maintaining the support of their predecessors. Ex-Presidents are likely to give such support or at least to refrain from overt attack on their successors. If they threaten to come out of retirement, however, or if a President feels that his action will bring them out of retirement, he is likely to move slowly. Nothing would more legitimize the opposition than the support of an ex-President. The most dramatic case on record of an ex-President (and ex-Vice President) seeking to influence the policy of a successor is the strong stand on the China question taken by both Eisenhower and Nixon. Eisenhower apparently informed Kennedy that though he hoped and intended to support the new administration on foreign policy issues, he would consider it necessary to return to public life if Communist China threatened to enter the United Nations. In the book he wrote a few years later, Nixon related with satisfaction that he too pressured Kennedy to block China:

I then brought up an issue which I told him [Kennedy] was one on which I had particularly strong views—the recognition of Red China and

---

21. Robert F. Kennedy, *Thirteen Days*, p. 67.

its admission to the UN. I did so because just the day before, Senator George Smathers had told me that Chester Bowles and some of Kennedy's other foreign policy advisers were urging him to reappraise our position on that issue. Kennedy said that he was opposed to recognition of Red China. He indicated, however, that strong arguments had been presented to him in favor of the so-called "two Chinas policy." Under this policy, Nationalist China would retain its seat on the Security Council, and Red China would have only a seat in the Assembly. This would mean that Red China would have only one vote out of about a hundred in the Assembly and would not be able to block UN action by veto. Kennedy said that proponents of this policy were contending that Red China could not do any damage in the UN under such circumstances.

In expressing my strong opposition to this policy, I pointed out that the issue wasn't whether Red China had one vote in the Assembly, or even the veto power. What was really at stake was that admitting Red China to the United Nations would be a mockery of the provision of the Charter which limits its membership to "peace-loving nations." And what was most disturbing was that it would give respectability to the Communist regime which would immensely increase its power and prestige in Asia, and probably irreparably weaken the non-Communist governments in that area.[22]

Under these pressures Kennedy backed off and set the China issue aside.

Another group that Presidents have looked to for support and hence have been reluctant to challenge openly, until Nixon felt forced to do so, is what has become known as the Eastern Liberal Foreign Policy Establishment. Joseph Kraft believes that lack of support from the President's own party as a whole creates a need to turn to this group:

Since they could not count on purely partisan political support, each one of the four Presidents turned, in putting across foreign policy measures, to a grouping of prestigious figures from the worlds of law (John McCloy, Dean Acheson, and Foster Dulles), finance (Averell Harriman, Eugene Black, and Robert Lovett), the press (Henry Luce, Arthur Hays Sulzberger, and Barry Bingham), and the military (Generals George Marshall, Bedell Smith, and Lucius Clay). Time after time, when Administration foreign policy objectives were in hazard before the Congress, members of this group where wheeled up to cow, cajole, or charm the legislators into submission. Because they were all internationalist in outlook, generally connected with the East and its bigger schools and foundations, and usually members of the Council on Foreign Relations in New York, as the years

22. Richard M. Nixon, *Six Crises*, pp. 408–9. On Eisenhower, see Schlesinger, *A Thousand Days*, p. 480.

wore on, the group acquired, from an English counterpart, the name of the Establishment. And to a large extent, it can be said that from 1940 through 1965, the United States followed the Establishment foreign policy.[23]

The desire to have the support of this group probably influenced Kennedy's perception of the Skybolt missile crisis. As his meeting with Macmillan approached, Kennedy received several phone calls from leading members of this Establishment, and he was confronted with a lead editorial in the *Washington Post* warning him not to jeopardize relations with the British. Feeling acutely the need for support from this group of men in any move to reduce tensions with the Soviet Union, Kennedy felt that he had to reach some compromise. He could not challenge them on an issue close to their hearts—good relations with a Conservative leader of Great Britain.

Perhaps the single most important group whose support on a range of issues the President has sought are the leaders of Congress. In cases where congressional action is needed to authorize the expenditure of funds or to ratify a treaty, congressional leaders can virtually exercise a veto. In other cases, the President may have the freedom to act without legislative authorization but hesitate to do so because he recognizes that the move he takes will be exceedingly unpopular with Congress and will generate opposition to other policies, perhaps including policies in the domestic sector.

The concern of congressional leaders, particularly those on the Joint Atomic Energy Committee, to prevent the sharing of American nuclear information and control of American nuclear weapons with any foreign power has played a major role in shaping presidential attitudes toward this question, especially in light of the desire to get the committee's cooperation in promoting the peaceful uses of atomic energy. Acheson in his memoirs relates one critical episode in the continuing effort of the British to get greater cooperation and greater control over the use of nuclear weapons:

> On the last day of the talks we had one of those close calls that lurk in summit meetings. General Collins had given his report from Korea. We were waiting in the Cabinet Room of the White House for a draft from the communiqué writers. The President had taken the Prime Minister to the privacy of his study. When secretaries distributed copies of the draft, our chiefs came back. They had, said the President cheerfully, been discussing the atomic weapon and agreed that neither of us would use these weapons

23. Kraft, *Profiles in Power*, pp. 16–17.

without prior consultation with the other. No one spoke. The President asked the chief drafter to begin reading the communiqué for amendments. As he started, Lovett leaned over my shoulder to say that we were teetering on the edge of great trouble and that I must carry the ball. A whispered conversation with the President and a note passed across the table to Oliver Franks brought the three of us and the Prime Minister together in the President's office, while others continued revision of the draft.

I pointed out that over and over again the President had insisted that no commitment of any sort to anyone limited his duty and power under the law to authorize use of the atomic weapon if he believed it necessary in the defense of the country, and that he had gone far in declaring that he would not change that position. If he should attempt to change it, he would not be successful since Congress would not permit it. The resolution of the twenty-four Republican senators gave fair warning of the temper of Congress. The suggestion he had made in the Cabinet Room would open a most vicious offensive against him and the British, whereas a program of keeping in close touch with the Prime Minister in all world situations that might threaten to move toward violence and hostilities of any kind would be widely approved.

All agreed with this, albeit Mr. Attlee a little sadly, and we began drafting a suitable paragraph, Oliver Franks acting as scribe. The President pulled out the slide at the left of his desk. Oliver left his chair and knelt between mine and Attlee's to write on it. "I think that this is the first time," said the President, "that a British Ambassador has knelt before an American President." Sir Oliver went right on drafting and produced a solution, which was inserted without comment in the communiqué when we returned to the Cabinet Room: "The President stated that it was his hope that world conditions would never call for the use of the atomic bomb. The President told the Prime Minister that it was also his desire to keep the Prime Minister at all times informed of developments which might bring about a change in the situation."[24]

Presidential Stands

The desire to avoid a major domestic row or to keep the good will of a significant domestic group leads Presidents to alter their stands on national security issues in an effort to build a wide consensus or to maintain an ap-

24. Acheson, *Present at the Creation*, p. 484. See also Truman, *Years of Trial and Hope*, pp. 302–4.

pearance of consistency. Presidents will also seek to package their proposals to gain maximum public support and, where necessary, will engage in logrolling. Each of these is discussed in turn.

1. Building a wide consensus.

Presidents are not often content to put together merely the minimum coalition necessary to secure adoption of a policy. In addition to getting particular decisions and actions approved, they have their overall influence and long-run relations to think about and so seek to bring as many groups as possible along with a particular decision. Thus they are often willing to modify and change a proposal even though the advocates of it in the bureaucracy tell them that there is already enough support to have the proposal adopted as its stands. The desire to build a broad consensus is sometimes aimed at bringing a particular group on board which might cause difficulty for the President on some other issue. Moreover, wide support at the outset hampers the remaining opponents who cannot be won over.

2. Maintaining the appearance of consistency.

Presidents guard against any appearance of inconsistency which would give their opponents an opening to attack them in the political arena. For example, after having successfully resisted strong pressure from the Joint Chiefs of Staff and the Republican leaders of Congress to interpose American forces to defend Taiwan following the defeat of the Chinese Nationalists on the mainland, President Truman decided to defend the island when he made the decision to intervene with American forces in Korea. Truman recognized that to fight against Communist expansion in Korea but not in Taiwan would open him to the charge of inconsistency. In order to get the widespread support which he viewed as necessary for his involvement in Korea, Truman felt obliged to reverse the decision and involve the United States in the as yet uncompleted Chinese civil war.[25]

3. Packaging policies for public consumption.

In order to minimize public opposition Presidents will frequently explain and justify their decision in rhetoric which they believe will secure the maximum domestic political support for their proposal even if it does not precisely reflect the reasoning which leads them to the decision. They will seek an explanation that will draw the widest possible support and make it difficult for opposition groups to challenge them.

A fateful example of this was the public rationale given for Truman's

25. Paige, *The Korean Decision*, pp. 62–189; Acheson, *Present at the Creation*, pp. 350, 369, 405–6, 422; Rankin, *China Assignment*, pp. 29, 155; Ronald J. Caridi, *The Korean War and American Politics*, pp. 58–60.

decision to aid Greece and Turkey in 1947. The decision of the British government that it could no longer provide aid to Greece and Turkey was conveyed to the American government in 1947. The reaction of the administration officials was swift and virtually unanimous. Greece and Turkey were seen as states of pivotal importance to checking Soviet military power in the Mediterranean. With the withdrawal of British aid it was clear that the two countries would be under severe pressure unless American aid were given. A task force quickly worked up an aid package; however, the crucial problem was considered to be congressional support. For this purpose, a group of congressional leaders were called to the White House by the President for a critical meeting on February 27, 1947. Secretary of State George Marshall led off the meeting by laying out the administration's case for aid to Greece and Turkey. Marshall evidently presented the argument in the traditional manner in which the issue had been considered within the American government. Greece had been a loyal ally, he asserted, and aid was a matter of humanitarianism. Aid to Turkey could be justified in terms of the importance of maintaining the British position in the Middle East and barring the area to Soviet advances. According to the accounts provided by both Joseph M. Jones and Dean Acheson, this presentation did not go down well with congressional leaders preoccupied with the impact of such aid on the budget. Sensing that the discussion was going rather badly, Dean Acheson moved quickly to try to repair the situation. His report in his memoirs is succinct and vivid:

In desperation I whispered to him a request to speak. This was my crisis. For a week I had nurtured it. These congressmen had no conception of what challenged them; it was my task to bring it home. Both my superiors, equally perturbed, gave me the floor. Never have I spoken under such a pressing sense that the issue was up to me alone. No time was left for measured appraisal. In the past eighteen months, I said, Soviet pressure on the Straits, on Iran, and on northern Greece had brought the Balkans to the point where a highly possible Soviet breakthrough might open three continents to Soviet penetration. Like apples in a barrel infected by one rotten one, the corruption of Greece would infect Iran and all to the east. It would also carry infection to Africa through Asia Minor and Egypt, and to Europe through Italy and France, already threatened by the strongest domestic Communist parties in Western Europe. The Soviet Union was playing one of the greatest gambles in history at minimal cost. It did not need to win all the possibilities. Even one or two offered immense gains. We and we alone were in a postion to break up the play. These were the stakes that British withdrawal from the eastern Mediterranean offered to an eager and ruthless opponent.

According to Acheson, the ploy worked:

A long silence followed. Then Arthur Vandenberg said solemnly, "Mr. President, if you will say that to the Congress and the country, I will support you and I believe that most of its members will do the same." Without much further talk the meeting broke up to convene again, enlarged, in a week to consider a more detailed program of action.[26]

The President's public speech calling for aid to Greece and Turkey thus came to embody the so-called Truman Doctrine which indicated that the United States would supply aid to any free people resisting Communist subversion. As Richard Neustadt has noted, the anti-Russian tone of the case, while somewhat at variance with the internal thinking of the administration, nevertheless helped to crystallize a public and congressional mood which assured a large consensus of support for the policy.[27]

In many cases, a President's choice of men to administer a program will be based on his perception of the need to get wide support for the program. This will often mean appointing an individual who, being less committed to the program than the President, will therefore give skeptics some confidence that it will not run away with itself. For example, Truman appointed Paul Hoffman to run the Marshall Plan as a way of assuring congressional support for the program, and he appointed Bernard Baruch to be the American representative to the UN body seeking to negotiate on nuclear disarmament.[28] In other cases, appointments may be made to assure general support. For example, President Eisenhower apparently felt obliged to consult fully with Senator Robert Taft on his appointment of members to the Joint Chiefs of Staff.[29]

4. Logrolling.

In some cases, the President will see his interest in a particular issue as dominated by his concern to get the desired decision on another issue. President Truman's tenure of office provides two striking examples of presidential interest being defined in such terms and leading to decisions

26. Acheson, *Present at the Creation*, p. 219.

27. Neustadt, *Presidential Power*, pp. 50–51. See also Jones, *The Fifteen Weeks*, pp. 138–43, 154–55; Joseph deRivera, *The Psychological Dimension of Foreign Policy*, pp. 345–48.

28. Dean Acheson, *Sketches from Life of Men I Have Known*, pp. 129–30; Truman, *Years of Trial and Hope*, pp. 7–8; James B. Conant, *My Several Lives*, p. 493.

29. Snyder, "The 'New Look' of 1953," p. 412.

of great significance to relations among the People's Republic of China, the United States, and Japan. The first of these examples, to which reference has already been made, was Truman's decision to defend Taiwan, and the second was his decision to force the Japanese to recognize the government of Taiwan as the government of China.

In recalling the latter episode, it is necessary to remember that, because Britain and the United States could not agree whether the government in Peking or the government in Taipei was the legitimate government of China, neither China was represented at the San Francisco Peace Conference of 1951, where the peace treaty with Japan was signed. The absence of a Chinese signature on the peace treaty raised questions in the United States about which "China" Japan would recognize following her independence. The position taken by John Foster Dulles (who had been appointed especially to negotiate the peace treaty), Secretary of State Dean Acheson, and President Truman was conditioned by their desire to see the Senate ratify the treaty. Any question about what stand on this issue was necessary to secure ratification was removed when fifty-six members of the Senate sent a letter to the President which read as follows:

As Members of the United States Senate, we are opposed to the recognition of Communist China by the Government of the United States or its admission to the United Nations.

Prior to the submission of the Japanese Treaty to the Senate, we desire to make it clear that we would consider the recognition of Communist China by Japan or the negotiating of a bilateral treaty with the Communist Chinese regime to be adverse to the best interests of the people of both Japan and the United States.[30]

In an effort to head off a fight over ratification of the treaty, Dulles made a trip to Tokyo along with Senators Smith and Sparkman. Following their discussions, Japanese Prime Minister Shigeri Yoshida agreed to write a letter to Dulles indicating the intention of Japan to recognize the Nationalist Chinese regime. Whatever Yoshida's own intentions might have been and whatever the views of the American government officials on the desirability of the action, this issue was cast in terms of a trade for Senate support of the peace treaty.

An agreement between President Nixon and Congressman Mendel Rivers, Chairman of the House Armed Services Committee, provides

30. Bernard C. Cohen, *The Political Process and Foreign Policy: The Making of the Japanese Peace Settlement*, p. 151. See also Acheson, *Present at the Creation*, pp. 603–5; William J. Sebald, *With MacArthur in Japan*, pp. 284–87.

another example of trading. In 1970 Nixon agreed to increase spending on naval shipbuilding in order to get the support of Rivers for the Safeguard ABM system. According to reporters, the agreement stipulated that Rivers would go along with the President's request for a Safeguard ABM system provided that the administration would agree to spend additional funds which Congress would appropriate for ship modernization.[31]

In other cases, the trading may occur over a domestic political issue and a foreign policy issue. The President may change his stand on a foreign policy question in order to get support for a domestic issue, or he may alter his stand on a domestic political question in order to get the support of some other actor, perhaps a congressional leader, on a foreign policy question. An example of the former is provided by the decision of the Eisenhower administration in March of 1953 not to cancel development of a nuclear airplane. The President's principal science advisers were united in the belief that such an airplane was, in the words of a National Security Council decision, "not required from the viewpoint of national security." This judgment, however, came up against the view of Representative Carl Hinshaw, who was then Chairman of the Joint Committee on Atomic Energy Subcommittee on Research Development and Radiation. The Eisenhower administration was hoping to get substantial changes in the Atomic Energy Act in order to permit private industry in the atomic power field. Eisenhower thus saw the issue of the nuclear airplane in terms of the needed cooperation of the Joint Atomic Energy Committee on the civilian nuclear power issue, and the nuclear airplane program was reinstated.[32]

The range of presidential interests that affect stands on national security issues clearly goes far beyond the dictates of domestic politics discussed above. Presidents want to do what the national interest demands. Their perspective of the national interest is, as we have seen, often conditioned by an entirely different set of factors from those that condition the bureaucratic perspective. On the one hand, a President inevitably becomes conscious of how his leadership will be assessed in retrospect. On the other, he is constantly faced with a myriad of pressing decisions on both domestic and foreign policy, among which he must make tradeoffs and resolve conflicts. No sector of the national security bureaucracy is faced with either of these situations.

Those who have observed Presidents close at hand have frequently

31. *Washington Post*, April 11, 1970.
32. Lambright, *Shooting Down the Nuclear Plane*, p. 18.

warned of the great difficulty of putting themselves in the shoes of the President and determining where he will look for clues to the national security interest. Theodore C. Sorensen, who was extremely close to President Kennedy, expressed this traditional diffidence:

A President knows that his name will be the label for a whole era. Textbooks yet unwritten and schoolchildren yet unborn will hold him responsible for all that happens. His program, his power, his prestige, his place in history, perhaps his reelection, will all be affected by key decisions. His appointees, however distinguished they may be in their own right, will rise or fall as he rises or falls. Even his White House aides, who see him constantly, cannot fully perceive his personal stakes and isolation. And no amount of tinkering with the presidential machinery, or establishment of new executive offices, can give anyone else his perspective.[33]

As Sorensen suggests, a President often becomes preoccupied, particularly in the later stages of his administration, with how he will come to look in the history books. Presidents often wish to be acclaimed as men of peace who through courage and perseverance reduced the probability of war. A President is also aware of his responsibility for the future of the country and the need to protect it from its enemies. Thus a President must often be a man of peace but a man of strength and courage at the same time. The argument that American strength and determined American action are the ways to secure lasting peace is, in many respects, an effort to avoid this dilemma.

Because many issues come at him at once and from many different directions with many different pressures involved, a President's behavior is characterized, perhaps to a surprising extent, by what we have called uncommitted thinking. He will often respond at any one time to whichever pressures are momentarily strongest, whether they come from particular elements in the bureaucracy, from foreign governments, or from his own domestic political concerns. In the case of the ABM, Johnson's position at any one time may have reflected the strongest pressures being brought to bear on him just then. At some points he seemed to share the arms control interests of his Secretary of Defense, at other times the fears of the military, and on other occasions the concerns of his domestic political advisers.

It would be both impossible and irrelevant to describe here the full range of special presidential interests that affect decision making at the

33. Theodore Sorensen, *Decision-Making in the White House*, pp. 83–84.

White House level. We believe that the types of presidential interests out-lined in this chapter are those that are most likely to be paid attention to within the national security bureaucracy itself. Not only do they shape the President's own perspective and the way he reacts to the bureaucracy, but also many within the bureaucracy can be persuaded sometimes to view the national security in terms of these particular presidential interests. Even many of those who are not necessarily sympathetic to the President's per-spective on national security, particularly with regard to domestic politics, still do take such factors into account in arriving at their own stands on national security issues or in planning strategies for getting the desired decisions. With this in mind we are ready to consider in full how various participants shape their conception of national security.

CHAPTER FIVE

Interests, Faces, and Stands

The previous chapters have suggested a number of interests that officials are predisposed to uphold in developing a position on a matter of national security. Of course efforts are made to determine directly what in the outside world is threatening and how to respond sensibly to those threats; but the interpretation of events inevitably reflects organizational, presidential, and personal interests. For most participants these blur together. Richard Neustadt explains:

For every player, any move toward action brings an element of personal challenge wrapped in a substantive guise. Of these his stakes are made. The substance is important, never doubt it, for that is what the game is all about. But so is the personal element. It makes no difference whether the move is of his own making or arises from sources outside his control. Either way, involvement of his job in some degree involves himself. Attached to his position are assorted expectations in the minds of his associates, evoked by its requirements and his career. Attached to his position also are his expectations of himself. Both sorts of expectations are reflected in his interests. He is man-in-office, with a record to defend and a future to advance, not least in history. The personal is tightly interwoven with the institutional. It is a rare player who can keep the two distinct, much less view both apart from substance.[1]

In general a person's stand derives from his personal experiences, his career pattern, and his position in the bureaucracy. It is not always profitable to look to an individual's personal experiences for clues as to his stand on an issue. The issue may be one that he has not previously been involved in and that does not trigger any highly charged cognitive, emotional, or

1. Neustadt, *Alliance Politics*, pp. 76–78.

psychological reaction. Quite often, however, a particular issue will evoke a deep personal response as the result of earlier encounters. An official may have had professional experience with a related set of issues in the past. Alternatively, the issue may invoke strong feelings because it seems analogous to a historical event or a vivid event in his private life.

The career pattern of a participant also plays a part in predetermining the sources to which he looks for guides to the national security. Career officials are likely to have a different set of guides from in-and-outers with ties in the banking, legal, or academic communities.

The position that an individual occupies in the bureaucracy also helps to determine the clues that he selects to guide him to the national interest. An official with operational responsibilities is likely to be preoccupied with the problems generated by the activities that his bureau or organization must perform. An individual's perceptions will also be affected by whether he receives information from a variety of sources producing conflicting reports about the outside world or whether, on the contrary, his information comes from a single source presenting a unified and sharply defined picture. His perspective is further affected by whether pressures which he receives from subordinates pull him in different directions or press him in a single direction. He will also be affected by how he perceives pressures from above and from colleagues in different agencies and bureaus. In general a person's position in the bureaucracy will determine what face of an issue he sees and what seems important to him.

Career Officials

Within the context of shared images a career official's view is shaped in substantial part by his desire for promotion. Few career officials expect major opportunities for their own personal advancement to emerge outside the government bureaucracy, and they quite naturally attach significant importance to getting ahead within the government. Military officers are concerned about reaching flag or general officer rank, while State Department officials eye ambassadorships. Neither group sees any contradiction between this and national security, believing that the government and the nation will benefit from their services at higher levels.

The desire for promotion will lead a career official to support the interests of the organization of which he is a member, since he recognizes that promotion will, in large measure, depend on the individual being seen as advancing the interest of his organization. He may calculate that if his organization grows, there will be more room for promotion. For immediate purposes, however, he tends to demonstrate loyalty to the particular subgroup that is believed to be the source of promotion. For example, Air Force officers whose primary tour of duty is in the Strategic Air Command look to senior officers of that command to fight for them on promotion boards and hence attach their loyalties to SAC rather than to the Air Force as a whole. Similarly, many Foreign Service officers see their loyalties to a particular subgroup in the service and expect senior officials of that subgroup to protect their promotion.

To be seen fighting for the organization is valued as the way to get promoted. President Nixon's Blue Ribbon Panel on the Defense Department reached this conclusion and stated it in strong terms:

The fact that promotions are within the exclusive authority of an officer's parent Service creates an incentive for an officer, even when serving on assignments with unified organizations, to adhere closely to the official Service position of his parent Service on issues in which he is involved. This circumstance can influence the objectivity of an officer's performance. The extent to which this undesirable incentive motivates officers cannot be precisely measured, but there can be no question that many officers are convinced that any evidence of a deviation by them from their parent Service's official position will seriously jeopardize their chance for further promotion.[2]

In reviewing Foreign Service promotion policies, a Department of State task force found the situation to be similar:

Under the present system, the key factor in determining whether an officer will be promoted is the efficiency report written by his immediate supervisor. The knowledge that the good opinion of his supervisor is crucial in determining whether an officer advances at a normal rate or falls behind and is eventually selected out can act as a powerful deterrent to his forthright expression of views on policy matters which may be at variance with the views of his supervisor.[3]

2. *Report to the President and the Secretary of Defense on the Department of Defense by the Blue Ribbon Defense Panel*, p. 140.

3. William B. Macomber, *Diplomacy for the 1970's: A Program of Management Reform for the Department of State*, pp. 21–22.

Officials learn that it is important to be liked by their superiors, to render them personal services, and to demonstrate their ability to get along not only with superiors but with colleagues. They conclude that one must behave prudently in internecine conflicts and avoid showing any personality traits which could engender disagreements and difficulty.[4]

A former official in the Defense Intelligence Agency (DIA) describes how the taboo against "making waves" affected career military officers assigned to that agency:

Imagine, if you will, what the prospect of a tour with DIA looks like to a military officer. He knows or soon learns that he will be thrust into a position in which, on occasion, his professional judgment will vary markedly from that of his parent service. He will be expected to defend a position that could enrage his Chief of Staff—but officers who do so more than once get known fast and are accorded an appropriate "reward" at a later date in terms of promotion and assignment. Consider also that a tour at DIA— normally two to three years—is very short when compared to a 20-to-30- year military career. And so most officers assigned to DIA go through a predictable pattern. They come on board as "hard-chargers," ready to set the world on fire. They stick to their principles through one or two scrapes. Then they become a little more circumspect, letting individual issues slide by and rationalizing that it wasn't a crunch question anyway. Finally, they resign themselves to "sweating out" their tours and playing every situation by ear. They avoid committing themselves or making decisions. They refuse to tackle the agency's long-term organizational ills because doing so would make too many waves.[5]

The desire to be promoted can also lead an official to undermine the effectiveness of his potential competitors. Such actions must be handled subtly so as not to get the reputation for seeking to hurt others or reducing the effectiveness of the organization. Yet ways are found. One observer of the State Department suggested that briefings of one's superiors and inferiors are carried out largely with this motive in view.

Take the briefing of colleagues prior to their assumption of new assignments. This is of primary importance, yet it is more neglected than performed. Why? Knowledge is power. The mistakes of one's competitors

4. See, for example, Arthur K. Davis, "Bureaucratic Patterns in the Navy Officer Corps," pp. 394–95; Harr, *The Professional Diplomat*, pp. 208–9; Simpson, *Anatomy of the State Department*, p. 33.
5. Patrick J. McGarvey, "The Culture of Bureaucracy," pp. 73–74.

improve one's own chances of advancement. So one is tempted to brief one's colleagues as slightly as possible. This is a subtle means of reducing competition for promotion, and of course it is employed generally against non-members of the fraternity. It obviously can have a disastrous effect on the Department's performance.

The situation is similar for such an elementary technique for coordination and stimulation as the staff meeting. An Assistant Secretary, for instance, will indeed meet with his subordinates as often as three mornings a week. This sounds impressive as an operating device until one finds that too generally the Assistant Secretary tends only to pick his colleagues' brains for information and opinions useful to him in his thrice-weekly meetings with the Secretary, neglecting to make himself useful to *them*— by informing them, stimulating them, pitching their thinking and action to higher, more dynamic levels.

Conversely, most participants in staff meetings are all too often reluctant to bring up matters of real importance. This was pointed out almost twenty years ago as characteristic of the Under Secretary's staff meetings. It is applicable to most meetings today, because few officers wish to appear less than omniscient or wish to invite poaching on their preserves.[6]

The desire to be promoted can likewise lead a participant to hold back information which he believes may create domestic political embarrassment for himself and for his organization. The effect on Foreign Service officers who reported the weakness of the Chinese Nationalists and the strength of the Chinese Communists has apparently had a substantial impact on perceptions of what is safe to report if one wishes to be promoted. James C. Thomson, Jr., discusses the specific impact of this on Vietnam reporting by Foreign Service officers:

In addition, the shadow of the "loss of China" distorted Vietnam reporting. Career officers in the Department, and especially those in the field, had not forgotten the fate of their World War II colleagues who wrote in frankness from China and were later pilloried by Senate Committees for critical comments on the Chinese Nationalists. Candid reporting on the strengths of the Viet Cong and the weakness of the Diem government was inhibited by the memory. It was also inhibited by some higher officials, notably Ambassador Nolting in Saigon, who refused to sign off on such cables.[7]

Few career officials have any qualms about supporting the interest of

6. Simpson, *Anatomy of the State Department*, pp. 40–41.
7. Thomson, "How Could Vietnam Happen?" p. 200.

the organization to which they are attached. It is quite natural for an individual who spends his life within a career service to come to believe that the functions of that organization are vital to the national security. Moreover, as James G. March and Herbert A. Simon have pointed out, the activities of a particular organization are much more concrete than the generalized interest of the government as a whole and hence are felt to be the operational way to promote the national interest.[8] Moreover, an individual comes to know his organization and to believe that it can do a good job. With regard to rival organizations, he is likely to be more aware of shortcomings and hence to believe that tasks assigned to them will not be done well.

Thus for career officials the personal interest in promotion merges with the belief that their organization's welfare is vital to the national security. With a clear conscience they support the interest of their organization and strive for a privileged position for the subgroup to which they are attached.

In-and-Outers

With less time to work for their goals and with other interests to pursue, in-and-outers hope for quick results and look to a variety of sources for guidance. In part their view is shaped by the shared images held by various subgroups within society and by the images prevalent in the professional groups with which they have associated prior to entering the government and to which they may return. These outside reference groups continue to shape their perception of the national interest, and many "temporary" officials have a personal interest in continuing to be respected by their outside professional peer group. Personal experiences are also likely to play a major role separating those who have a deep involvement in an issue beyond official policy from others who come to it fresh with only their experiences in the bureaucracy as a guide. Those with extragovernmental involvement may have a strong attachment to a particular position and exhibit ideological behavior. Some in-and-outers hold general views about international politics which somewhat distance them from the preoccupations of any one organization or administration. Still other in-and-outers contemplate elective office after experience in the bureaucracy.

8. March and Simon, *Organizations*, p. 156.

Involvement and Effectiveness

In-and-outers may be less patient and cautious, but nearly all participants in the policy process desire to be involved in decisions and actions of major importance. They wish to see themselves as being effective and influential in shaping these decisions.

The desire to be involved most acutely affects those participants who are not routinely and inevitably part of the decision-making process. It is difficult for a President not to involve the Secretary of State and the Secretary of Defense in decisions, and in turn it is difficult for these officials to exclude their principal operating offices. Other officials who are on staffs or in advisory or planning positions need to struggle to remain involved. As both Will Sparks and George E. Reedy have observed, this problem is particularly acute on the White House staff. Reedy puts it this way:

> For other White House assistants there is only one fixed goal in life. It is somehow to gain and maintain access to the President. This is a process which resembles nothing else known in the world except possibly the Japanese game of go, a contest in which there are very few fixed rules and the playing consists of laying down alternating counters in patterns that permit flexibility but seek to deny the flexibility to the opponent. The success of the play depends upon the whim of the President. Consequently, the President's psychology is studied minutely, and a working day in the White House is marked by innumerable probes to determine which routes to the Oval Room are open and which end in a blind alley.[9]

Closely related to the desire to be involved is the desire to be effective, to have one's views taken seriously and carry weight with the President. James C. Thomson, Jr., clearly describes the nature of what he calls the "effectiveness" trap, as well as two of its consequences—keeping participants from speaking out or from resigning:

> . . . The "effectiveness" trap [is] the trap that keeps men from speaking out, as clearly or often as they might, within the government. And it is the trap that keeps men from resigning in protest and airing their dissent outside the government. The most important asset that a man brings to bureaucratic life is his "effectiveness," a mysterious combination of training, style, and connections. The most ominous complaint that can be whispered of a bureaucrat is: "I'm afraid Charlie's beginning to lose his

9. Reedy, *The Twilight of the Presidency*, p. 88. See also Sparks, *Who Talked to the President Last?*

effectiveness." To preserve your effectiveness, you must decide where and when to fight the mainstream of policy; the opportunities range from pillow talk with your wife, to private drinks with your friends, to meetings with the Secretary of State or the President. The inclination to remain silent or to acquiesce in the presence of the great men—to live to fight another day, to give on this issue so that you can be "effective" on later issues—is overwhelming. Nor is it the tendency of youth alone; some of our most senior officials, men of wealth and fame, whose place in history is secure, have remained silent lest their connection with power be terminated. As for the disinclination to resign in protest; while not necessarily a Washington or even American specialty, it seems more true of a government in which ministers have no parliamentary backbench to which to retreat. In the absence of such a refuge, it is easy to rationalize the decision to stay aboard. By doing so, one may be able to prevent a few bad things from happening and perhaps even make a few good things happen. To exit is to lose even those marginal chances for "effectiveness."[10]

The striving for power and effectiveness inclines individuals to take stands in favor of those actions which will involve them in implementation and monitoring of what is done; they will favor actions for which they are likely to get the credit. Thus two individuals who agree on objectives may disagree on the means because of their personal stakes in how a decision is carried out.[11] Once an individual is given a mission, he will have a strong desire to "do something" in order to demonstrate his effectiveness and increase the likelihood that he will get future assignments. Henry Kissinger has observed that American negotiators, regardless of their previous positions, often become advocates for the maximum range of concessions in negotiations which they are conducting. They want to claim success.[12] Arthur Schlesinger, Jr., has maintained that Arthur Dean, charged with negotiating arms control arrangements with the Soviet Union by President Kennedy, assumed such a stance, desiring above all to accomplish something.[13]

The desire to remain involved and effective also leads officials whose influence depends largely on the confidence of the President to faithfully execute his decisions and take stands which they believe he would want

---

10. Thomson, "How Could Vietnam Happen?" pp. 201–2. See also Theodore Sorensen, *Decision-Making in the White House*, pp. 62–63.
11. Neustadt, *Presidential Power*, pp. 46–47.
12. Kissinger, *American Foreign Policy*, p. 32.
13. Schlesinger, *A Thousand Days*, p. 505.

them to take. Acheson describes in his memoirs the care which he took to maintain the confidence of the President. Neustadt reports that Dulles was equally motivated by the need to have Eisenhower's confidence if he was to be involved and effective:

Eisenhower first appointed Dulles without knowing much of him except by reputation, and reportedly without much liking him. Dulles took the post intent on gaining presidential confidence. He hungered to be an effective Secretary, and he evidently saw no other way to go. Despite appearances, especially in retrospect, everything I know about their early years suggests that Dulles did not find it easy going. Temperamentally there seem to have been few affinities between them. Operationally, the President had ideas of his own, experience to boot, and an unmatched acquaintance among foreign statesmen, especially in Europe. As Eisenhower took hold of his job he came increasingly to do as other Presidents had done, picking and choosing among numbers of advisers of whom Dulles was but one. Dien Bien Phu affords us an example. There are others. This reached a peak, reportedly, in preparations for the Summit during 1955, where Eisenhower went on Eden's urging to the cheers of aides such as Nelson Rockefeller and Harold Stassen, but not Dulles. There the President assumed the working chairmanship of his own delegation in a burst of personal activity. Six weeks later he was stricken by a heart attack. Only after that attack did Dulles win his way into unrivaled eminence as "Mr. Foreign Policy." He did so by responding scrupulously to his ailing chief's dependence on him.

Thereafter it appears that Dulles kept Eisenhower's confidence in the same way he had won it. During the entire Suez crisis, for example, he apparently cleared every move with Eisenhower in advance, emphatically including cancellation of the Aswan Dam, and also every phase of SCUA [Suez Canal Users Association]. As I read the record, Eisenhower was no "patsy" in this process. Far from it, he was laying down the law: he wanted "peace." Dulles strained to keep it. He had every reason to exert himself. For in his circumstances all the gains of presidential confidence, so recently acquired to his satisfaction, would be risked by warfare with his name on it, with blame, in Eisenhower's eyes, attached to him.[14]

The desire to be involved and influential may also lead participants to hold back from their boss information that they know he would find unpleasant or to avoid issues that they know he would rather leave untouched.

14. Neustadt, *Alliance Politics*, pp. 104–5.

Future Elective Office

One of the things that distinguishes the American system from a parliamentary regime is that most of the President's principal advisers are not themselves competitors for his office or indeed for any elective political office. Whereas congressmen and senators take their prospects for reelection into account in arriving at a stand, most members of the executive branch are not so concerned, since they have no intention of running for public office.

In certain cases, however, such interests do exist and may affect stands on issues. Sorensen points out that presidential advisers with political ambitions of their own may place their own reputation and record ahead of that of the President. He notes that such men are not necessarily suppressing their conscience or forgetting about the national interest; rather, they come sincerely to believe that their own future is important to the national interest.[15] Harold Stassen did not abandon his own presidential ambitions while serving as an aide and disarmament adviser in the Eisenhower White House. Harry Truman's first Secretary of Defense, Louis Johnson, was widely reported to have presidential aspirations, and it was believed that this affected his stands on issues.[16]

Although in recent history very few Cabinet officers have aspired to the Presidency, a larger number have sought election to the Senate, and this may well have influenced their stands on issues. It has been suggested, for example, that in one case Clinton Anderson enhanced his future political prospects while serving as Secretary of Agriculture in the first Truman administration. Anderson was present at a Cabinet meeting in which the focus of discussion was the resignation of Ambassador Patrick J. Hurley as the American representative in China. Hurley had resigned suddenly with a blast at the administration, and the question at hand was what to do and how to replace him. Anderson suggested that the appointment of George C. Marshall, who had been Chief of Staff for the Army during World War II, would take the headlines away from Hurley's resignation. Secretary of Defense Forrestal and Secretary of State Byrnes quickly agreed with this suggestion, and Truman overcame his reluctance to ask Marshall to serve in a difficult post on short notice by asking him to take this on as a temporary assignment rather than serving as ambassador.

Anderson's intention was indeed to drive Hurley out of the headlines,

15. Theodore Sorensen, *Decision-Making in the White House*, p. 75.
16. Paige, *The Korean Decision*, pp. 30–31; Paul Y. Hammond, "NSC-68: Prologue to Rearmament," p. 293.

but a desire to help President Truman was not necessarily his prime motive. Byrnes speculates that Anderson was thinking of his own political future:

Later it occurred to me that there might be a touch of political strategy in Anderson's suggestion of Marshall. Hurley had been in New Mexico for some time since his return from China, and the press had reported that he was considering becoming a Republican candidate for the United States Senate. It was possible that Anderson, a New Mexico Democrat, had in mind that the news of Marshall's appointment would blanket the report of Hurley's resignation. It did. Later, Clinton Anderson and Hurley became candidates for a senatorial seat. Mr. Anderson was elected and has served with distinction.[17]

Official Position

Position within the bureaucracy is also bound to affect an official's stance—whether one has managerial responsibilities, whether one receives information from conflicting sources, whether one is exposed to conflicting pressures from subordinates. Where a participant sits in relation to action channels will strongly bias what kind of issues come to seem important to him and on which he is likely to take a stand and get involved.

A participant's conception of his role (the equivalent for the individual of mission for the organization) further predisposes an official toward a particular view of what constitutes national security. Some in-and-outers guide themselves by explicit theories of the national interest. Others define it in terms of loyalty to the President or to a Cabinet officer or another official who is their immediate boss. Others come to see their loyalties in terms of the organization that they serve. With in-and-outers specifically, the variety of personal experiences they bring to their jobs, the variety of positions they hold in the bureaucracy, and the differences in their conceptions of their role produce a range of answers to the question: what clues do in-and-outers respond to in judging what serves national security? There are several typical patterns which may be identified.

Some senior positions and many junior positions involve primarily the *management of programs*. Individuals in such positions at high levels include the civilian heads of the three military services, the chairman of the

17. Byrnes, *All in One Lifetime*, pp. 328–29. See also *Forrestal Diaries*, p. 113.

Atomic Energy Commission, and the regional directors of AID. Such officials, especially if they have had little previous personal involvement in a
particular issue, are likely to come to reflect the interests of their organization. Much of their time and attention will be taken up dealing with their
subordinates and solving problems put to them by subordinate officials.
Much of their information will come from these subordinates, and they
will soon be keenly aware of the difficulties in operating the program and
believe in its importance to the national security. In several respects these
in-and-outers adopt the outlook of career officials.

Many in-and-outers occupy *staff positions*. That is to say, they are not
in the direct line of responsibility for the management or operation of
programs; rather, they serve either as personal staff assistants to senior
officials or in staff organizations such as the State Department's or the
Defense Department's planning groups. These individuals are frequently
recruited into these positions because they have had a substantial previous
professional involvement with the relevant substantive issues. Often they
will come in with strong views on a particular subject. Such officials, particularly on issues that have previously been of major concern to them, are
likely to exhibit ideological thinking. They will focus on one or two key
variables and see many issues in terms of the pursuit of that variable,
whether it be European integration or disarmament. Here the exchange
of attitudes between careerists and in-and-outers flows the other way.
Some career staff men who have spent most of their service in a planning
or other staff agency with continuing attachment to a single set of issues
may come to reflect the same kind of ideological thinking and often be
indistinguishable from in-and-outers in the same positions. Junior officials
in staff jobs may worry about being "sidelined." Since they have no regularized involvement with issues, they feel they must fight their way in, and
they become conscious of the relationship between the stands which they
take and the degree to which they are involved.

White House staff officials and even Presidents often express the hope
that *Cabinet officers* will take the perspective of the President rather than
reflecting the organizational interest of the department they are heading.
McGeorge Bundy, who was President Kennedy's and President Johnson's
assistant for national security affairs, expressed a typical position when he
asserted that "Cabinet officers are special pleaders" and "should run their
part of the government for the Administration—not run to the Administration for the interest of their part of the government." But as Harold
Seidman observed after quoting McGeorge Bundy, "one might as well

echo Professor Henry Higgins' plaint in *My Fair Lady*, 'Why can't a woman be more like a man?' as ask 'why can't Cabinet members act more like Presidents?' "[18] The pressures on Cabinet officers from their subordinates, as well as from outside pressure groups, is so great that they often come to see themselves as their department's representative to the President. For example, James Forrestal when Secretary of the Navy explicitly saw his job as maintaining the autonomy of the Navy.[19]

Although they are under strong pressure to support the interests of their organization, those pressures are by no means the only ones. Many Cabinet officers feel countervailing pressures from the President and from their Cabinet colleagues. Many of them have not had extensive personal experience with the issues that they are now called upon to confront, and where they have had extensive previous experience, it was not set in the framework of "the national interest." Thus Cabinet officers' behavior is often characterized by what we have called uncommitted thinking. They tend to respond to the immediate pressures on them whether from the President, from their subordinates, or from their colleagues, and their reaction to the push and pull looks to an outside observer like inconsistent behavior.

White House political advisers, particularly those without any regular and routine responsibility for national security matters, often come to see foreign policy issues largely in domestic political terms. They also come to see issues in terms of the possibilities of their own involvement. They are likely to take stands on issues which will increase the probability that they will be involved and are likely to feel the strongest pressures from the President's own concerns.

Thus far we have presented the cast of characters—the participants in the national security policy process—and attempted to explain where they are likely to look for clues to the national security. Shared images limit the extent of disagreement, but within these parameters different experiences and responsibilities, different modes of thinking, and different reference points lead participants to different stands on issues. We are ready now to explore the process by which participants struggle to secure the decisions they want.

18. Seidman, *Politics, Position, and Power*, p. 75.
19. *Forrestal Diaries*, p. 167.

PART TWO

Decisions

CHAPTER SIX

Initiative and Rules

Part II describes the process by which issues get raised and the activities the participants engage in to secure the decisions which their judgment and their interests lead them to want. The main factors that influence the outcome—as far as the bureaucratic system is concerned—are the standing of the participants, the rules (formal and informal) that guide the issue through the system, the information and analysis used by the participants to select from alternative positions and to argue their cases. On many issues, the disposition of the President is a further determinant.

Our presentation concentrates on decisions made at the presidential level. This is not meant to imply, however, that decisions made at lower levels are necessarily less important. Much of the work of the bureaucracy is carried out at lower levels, and many of the decisions made below the presidential level actually determine the outcome of decisions that come to the President for approval.

The bureaucratic system is basically inert; it moves only when pushed hard and persistently. The majority of bureaucrats prefer to maintain the status quo, and only a small group is, at any one time, advocating change. Time and resources of any one person in the bureaucracy are limited, and when a participant does desire change, he must choose carefully the issues on which to do battle.

Most policy issues are not new; they have arisen time and again. Organizations have examined the same or similar issues on a number of occasions in the past and have well-understood positions. Even most senior participants from "outside" are likely to have encountered the issue in the past and to have a view on it. In the majority of cases, moreover, the choice will be between current actions and a single alternative being pushed by those participants desiring a change.

For most participants most of the time the effort to determine their stands on an issue will not involve a canvass of alternatives. Rather, they will examine any particular issue in terms of their own interests and arrive easily at a stand. Even when an issue is new (or new to a particular participant), it is likely to be presented to him in a way that reflects his own interests, and he will be able immediately to identify what his stand should be.

Once an issue has been defined and participants have developed their stands, those desiring change are likely to raise the issue when events, as they perceive them, either provide opportunities for change heretofore absent or increase the cost of continuing to operate without change. Seldom do changes in the environment alone lead to changes in participants' interests or their judgments about the desirability of particular decisions. The Army, for example, had been continuously in favor of an ABM deployment since the mid-1950s when the concept of ABM was developed. However, it pressed hard for deployment only in the late 1950s and again in the mid-1960s when technological innovation, domestic politics, and Soviet action made success seem likely.

In some cases, the degree of determination to seek a decision may be related to a particular event that creates more favorable circumstances for a new decision. Thus, as stated, the stepped-up effort to secure a decision to proceed with ABM followed breakthroughs in technology in the mid-1960s, making an ABM seem significantly more feasible. In other cases, ideological thinking may be the motivating factor for a group to seek a particular decision. They watch constantly for an opportunity to present their desired decision as a solution to a President's or a Secretary's problem. For example, the supporters of a Development Loan Fund in the State Department maneuvered so that Secretary of State Dulles was faced with the need to present some new idea to the Senate Foreign Relations Committee. When they urged the Development Loan Fund proposal on him, they were able to tell him that it would be favorably received by the committee.[1] To cite another example, the Joint Chiefs of Staff found an opportunity in the Vietcong Tet offensive of 1968 to gain their long-sought objective of mobilization of reserve forces in the United States. The fact that Secretary of Defense Robert McNamara was coincidentally being replaced by Clark M. Clifford made the opportunity even more favorable.[2]

---

1. Russell Edgerton, *Sub-Cabinet Politics and Policy Commitment: The Birth of the Development Loan Fund.*

2. Marvin Kalb and Elie Abel, *Roots of Involvement: The U.S. in Asia, 1784–1971,* pp. 214–15.

Pressing for Decisions

We have suggested some of the opportunities that lead participants to seek decisions. These and other circumstances under which issues enter the decision process can be categorized as follows.

1. Dramatic changes in the actions of other nations.

Sometimes the proponents of an issue find in the actions of another nation the rationale for proposing the change they desire. Events abroad may provide opportunities to initiate a general policy review, for instance, and during that review a particular issue can be introduced. The death of Stalin, the French defeat of the European Defense Community, and Castro's takeover in Cuba all allowed officials to argue that the premises for previous decisions had now changed and that a reexamination was in order. Often, in such cases, participants will seek the chance to put forward solutions which they have already developed. When the Soviet Union exploded an atomic bomb, the proponents of a crash H-bomb program in the United States used the occasion to argue that the United States now had to move forward with this program. On the other hand, changes abroad do not guarantee a change of U.S. policy. Participants who fear that a review of an issue will lead to decisions other than those that they desire resist the argument that new decisions are needed.

Some events are so unexpected that they force officials to develop views on an issue which simply did not exist before. For example, when the word reached Washington in June 1950 that the North Koreans had invaded South Korea, senior participants had to make up their minds in a matter of hours whether the United States should use military force to resist an attack on South Korea. Even in these unusual cases, however, established interests influence perceptions. Furthermore, it is quite possible that an issue is foreseen but that no participant has an incentive to seek a decision before the event occurs. High officials, in particular, are usually reluctant to commit themselves on hypothetical situations or to indulge in serious contingency planning. For example, although the possibility of Russian missiles in Cuba had been the subject of much debate before the fall of 1962, only when there was indisputable evidence that Russian missiles were in Cuba did senior participants develop stands on alternative options designed to get the missiles removed.

Conventional analyses of foreign policy usually assume that the actions of other nations are the major stimuli for foreign policy decisions in the United States. We contend that they are only one source of stimulation, and not even the more frequent source. Most decisions are responses to domestic pressures, and the actions of other nations often figure merely as devices for argument.

2. New technology.

Changes in technology may open up new possibilities and force decisions. They may be cited to bolster the plausibility of the argument for a particular decision and hence lead to a more intensified effort to secure the desired result. Thus a major change in the debate about the ABM system occurred in 1965 when breakthroughs in antiballistic missile technology led many scientists and engineers to argue that an ABM was now feasible. Prior to that time, the Army's efforts to press for an ABM could be checked by testimony of most civilian scientists that an ABM system simply could not be designed to intercept a large number of incoming missiles. After 1965, expert testimony went substantially in the other direction, and the Army intensified its efforts to secure a favorable decision.

3. Changes in the shared images of the society or bureaucracy.

Changes in the shared images within the society or within the bureaucracy may be perceived by participants as an opportunity to reopen issues, because they signify a changing domestic mood. For example, efforts to change the China policy of the United States were intensified in the late 1960s and early 1970s to capitalize on the dramatic change in the public attitude toward the "Chinese threat"—a shift that greatly reduced the cost to the President of seeking to move into political and economic contact with the People's Republic of China. Even if a given policy is not shaped mainly by domestic political constraints, changes in the domestic situation may create an opportunity to argue that there are new constraints which require new decisions. For example, many of those arguing against a continuation of the expansion of the American effort in Vietnam in early 1968 did so on the premise that further American aggression would have very serious domestic political costs which would outrun foreign policy gains.

A change in shared images even if it is restricted to the bureaucracy may likewise create an opportunity to put forward a new set of arguments in favor of a decision. Within the Nixon administration, opponents of a large ABM system were able to take advantage of the new acceptance within the bureaucracy of the impossibility of maintaining American strategic nuclear superiority. One could argue that ABM was not necessary for maintaining the American deterrent now conceived as "sufficiency" rather than "superiority" and hence should be ruled out.

4. Routine events.

A number of routine events require the American government, or in some cases the President personally, to state in public or to foreign governments a definite position on a particular issue. Such routine events provide at least an opportunity for participants to get an issue to the President and to press for a new decision. Once again, the case of ABM is illustrative. Since Congress first voted funds for ABM in 1966, the President has been obliged each year to take a stand on ABM deployment in his annual budget message. Because of the public interest in the issue, there has been an annual debate within the bureaucracy about what stand the President should take. International conferences may also force such decisions. If the UN is about to vote on the issue of restrictions on the use of biological weapons, or if the North Atlantic Council is about to take a stand on the desirability of a European Security Conference, the President must make a decision about what positions his ambassador should take.

In other cases, the routine events simply provide an opportunity for raising an issue. Thus if the President of the United States is to make a speech—an annual event such as the State of the Union message or a speech to a convention—"subjects" may be suggested. Visits of foreign leaders to Washington and presidential trips abroad also provide such opportunities.

5. Changes in personnel.

Changes in personnel, particularly shifts among senior participants, are likely to be viewed as providing opportunities for seeking new decisions. Career officers and junior participants may reopen issues on which they have previously lost if they believe that their defeat was related to the position of a departing official. In this spirit, the Joint Chiefs of Staff reopened a number of issues following the departure of Secretary of Defense Robert McNamara, believing that any other Secretary of Defense, and in particular perhaps the new Secretary of Defense Clark Clifford, was more likely to be sympathetic to their position.

New administrations generally feel obliged to review many of the decisions of the previous administration, and in the process career officials may try to push ahead with programs held up in the past. In the case of the Bay of Pigs invasion of Cuba, CIA planners saw an opportunity with the change of administration to press for a firm decision to proceed with an operation which they had been unable to get approved by the Eisenhower administration.

6. Self-generated efforts.

In some cases, participants may decide to seek a decision even in the absence of dramatic changes in the actions of other nations, breakthroughs in new technology, significant changes in shared images, or important changes in personnel. Combinations of minor changes in several of these categories may create the opportunity to seek a new decision. Alternatively, the cost to an organization of the continuation of existing decisions may increase to the point where it is prepared to devote greater efforts to seeking a change than it did in the past. A new approach to a problem may also lead participants to believe that there is opportunity to gain a new decision. For example, the proposal for a multilateral nuclear force was a new approach to nuclear sharing in Europe which led some participants to feel that they could change the U.S. policy of insisting on sole ownership of all nuclear weapons. The cumulative weight of closely spaced events is demonstrated in Herbert York's recollection of developments in the fall of 1952. He mentions "the invention and demonstration of the hydrogen bomb, the election of Eisenhower and the concomitant extensive personnel changes throughout the executive branch (the first complete change in twenty years), and the growing accumulation of intelligence reports which first indicated and then confirmed that the Soviet Union had already launched a major program for the development of large long-range rockets."[3] Out of a reconsideration of the missile question at that time came six crash programs to develop nuclear-tipped missiles.

Rules of the Game

Participation in the decision process does not occur at random. There are numerous written and unwritten rules governing how an issue may enter the system, who can become involved, who must be consulted, etc. The rules of the game are devices for ordering how minds are brought to bear on a problem. Some rules derive from constitutional and legislative delegation of power. Others are spelled out in executive orders and other

3. York, *Race to Oblivion*, p. 83.

executive documents. An unwritten code of ethics determines how a participant must relate to others in the bureaucracy. This code is constantly evolving through changes in the written rules, personnel, and the general environment.

Perhaps the most visible set of rules in the national security bureaucracy involves the use of the National Security Council (NSC). President Truman, under whom the council was created, used it relatively infrequently and in an ad hoc way. President Eisenhower established a very formal National Security Council system, but this was virtually abolished by the Kennedy administration. President Johnson almost never used the council. The Nixon administration reestablished a formal NSC system with a group of subcommittees. However, the attention focused on alternate NSC systems because they are visible tends to obscure the fact that most business is conducted outside of these systems. There always are other procedures for handling routine matters, even those that come before the President, and crises tend to be treated in different ways whether or not there is a formal system. Thus in contrasting administrations it is misleading to focus on the various formal NSC procedures. Rather, one must look at the entire range of established procedures and action channels for moving issues to the President.

Some writers have argued that procedures make no difference—the participants and the setting determine what decisions are made. Procedures are less important than the shared images, the interests of the participants, and their power. Nevertheless procedures can make some difference. After himself playing a part in the abolition of a number of formal requirements, including those in the NSC system, McGeorge Bundy later told an interviewer that he was "less impatient with procedures."[4] President Eisenhower, who received much criticism for his formal NSC system, concluded in his memoirs as follows:

Organization cannot make a genius out of an incompetent; even less can it, of itself, make the decisions which are required to trigger necessary action. On the other hand, disorganization can scarcely fail to result in inefficiency and can easily lead to disaster.[5]

There seems little doubt that procedures do make a substantial difference in determining who is involved, in what order, and with what control over the process.

4. Henry F. Graff, *The Tuesday Cabinet*, p. 96.
5. Dwight D. Eisenhower, *The White House Years* (Vol. I: *Mandate for Change, 1953–1956*), p. 114. Cited hereafter as *Mandate for Change*.

Where Do Rules Come From?

The rules of the game derive from a number of sources, ranging from law to tradition. The Constitution itself establishes the basic framework of presidential and congressional responsibilities as well as limitations on the government's powers. With regard to Congress, the rules of the game require that the views of leaders and committee chairmen (or subcommittee chairmen of appropriation subcommittees) be taken into account before a decision is made. Congress also influences the rules of the game by designing legislation to limit the powers of the executive branch or by demanding information from the executive. Congress has on occasion changed the rules of the game within the executive branch by insisting that certain kinds of determinations be made by particular officials, thereby requiring that they be brought into the game or requiring that the actions be pushed to the level of that official. The President can affect the rules of the game by reorganizing the executive branch of the government through formal orders or through informal directives to the Cabinet officials concerned. The Cabinet officers may, in turn, alter the rules of the game within their own departments by the directives they issue on procedures for making decisions.

Many of the rules of the game, however, develop over time without any changes in the constitutional system, legislation, executive orders, or even orders from department chiefs. They arise from the operational habits and traditions that evolve in bureaucratic organizations. As described by a former State Department official:

Once things have happened [in government], no matter how accidentally, they will be regarded as manifestations of an unchangeable Higher Reason. For every argument inside government that some jerry-built bureaucratic arrangement should be changed, there are usually twenty arguments to show that it rests on God's own Logic, and that tampering with it will bring down the heavens.[6]

How Do Rules Affect the Process?

Rules of the game differ according to what kind of issue is involved. For example, budgets, legislation, cables, and commitments of military force will each move in different channels under different rules. The rules in each case will specify several things:

6. Charles Frankel, *High on Foggy Bottom: An Outsider's Inside View of the Government*, p. 30.

1. *Who has the action?*

"Having the action," a term widely used within the bureaucracy and almost unknown outside, refers to the individual or organization responsible for moving an issue through the government and for taking the initiative in drafting whatever papers are to go to the President. Even if a number of agencies must be consulted, one agency will normally have the action. Within that agency a particular bureau will have the action, and it will be in charge of consulting with and coordinating with other parts of the same agency. Within the other agencies to be consulted one particular bureau will have the action for that agency and will be in charge of consulting with others.

2. *Who must sign off?*

Before a document is addressed by a senior official, either a department head or the President, it must have the concurrence not only of the action bureau but also of a number of other bureaus within the department. In some cases Cabinet officers will not address a memorandum unless it has also been cleared by other agencies involved. An example of how extensive the clearance process can become is offered by Richard Holbrooke:

A new Under Secretary of State discovers that a routine cable—the kind that Under Secretaries are not supposed to see—on the Food for Peace Program has received 27 clearances before being sent out. No one is able to convince him that 27 different people needed to agree to the dispatch of such a message.[7]

When an issue moves to the President for his approval, concurrence will frequently be required from a number of different agencies as well as one or several individuals on the White House staff.

3. *How high up must an issue go?*

The rules generally specify the sorts of issues that have to go to the President, which ones must go to the Cabinet officers, and which ones can be signed off at lower levels. Issues brought up in the form of congressional legislation must receive presidential attention. Executive orders delegate some of the President's authority to specific Cabinet officers. More frequently, however, the operating rules are not written down any place but are understood intuitively by those involved.

4. *Through what channels does an issue move up to the President?*

The rules of the game specify what issues should move via the formal National Security Council procedures, what issues can move by virtue of a memorandum from a particular Secretary to the President, and what

7. Holbrooke, "The Machine That Fails," p. 71.

issues come through budgetary or other special channels. In many cases there will be some flexibility and leeway at certain points in the process, but there will generally be a designated standard procedure for moving a particular issue.

5. *Can informal channels be used?*

In almost all cases there will be alternate ways to secure clearances from particular agencies and departments. Clearances will occur at varying levels in different departments depending upon the informal network of people who know each other and feel solidarity on a particular issue. A President usually has at his disposal information which comes to him informally in what is described in the bureaucracy as "bootleg" copies of memoranda.[8] (Chapter 11 discusses in greater detail the use of informal channels to the President.)

What varies greatly is the willingness of Presidents to act on such information. Truman and Kennedy were more prepared to move on the basis of information obtained in informal ways, whereas Eisenhower and to a lesser extent Johnson insisted on more formal channels. Robert Cutler, who served as Eisenhower's Assistant for National Security Affairs, describes his first and only effort to move informally to the President:

And, when I was new on the job, Pete Carroll and I suggested to the President trying to save the tottering regime of Premier Mayer of France by at once telephoning to Churchill to arrange for the announcement of a U.S.-U.K.-France conference in Bermuda. The President looked at us quizzically: "You boys think you are Assistant Secretaries of State? Go talk to Bedell Smith [General Walter Bedell Smith]." We did.[9]

6. *In what form does an issue come to the President?*

For issues that do move up to the President, the President himself sets the rules that specify either in general or in relation to the issue at hand whether he is to receive an agreed recommendation of his principal advisers, alternative recommendations from each of his principal advisers, or simply a set of stated options from which he may choose a course of action.

On routine matters all Presidents prefer and press for agreed recommendations from their principal advisers. This saves them the trouble of having to get into the issue to make a decision and also avoids putting them into a position of overruling their senior associates. However, Presi-

8. Clark and Legere (eds.), *The President and the Management of National Security*, p. 125.
9. Cutler, *No Time for Rest*, p. 316.

dents differ as to whether on major issues they want an agreed recommendation or the separate views of advisers. President Nixon, in instituting a new National Security Council system at the beginning of his administration, emphasized that he wished to receive from the bureaucracy a series of stated options, regardless of whether they were being recommended by any of his principal advisers. He indicated he would then receive the advice of his principal associates on the various options before making his own decision. President Truman apparently preferred to get alternate recommendations from his principal associates. Both Eisenhower and Johnson, in contrast, emphasized the importance of unanimous recommendations from their advisers. Johnson's memoirs are replete with references to his efforts to get his principal advisers to agree with each other and his reluctance to take action unless they did agree.[10] Eisenhower, even on issues of major concern and personal interest to him, preferred to have agreed recommendation before he acted. Sherman Adams, after reporting President Eisenhower's great interest in disarmament, explains how the issue was handled in the Eisenhower administration:

The President urged Stassen to keep on searching aggressively for a new way to break the disarmament deadlock at the next United Nations Disarmament Subcommittee meeting in London in 1957. Stassen prepared for presentation in London a long list of proposals. When these ideas were ready to be discussed, the President went over them in a meeting attended by Dulles, Stassen, Wilson, Radford, and William Jackson. Stassen wanted to conduct exploratory talks with the British and needed an agreement about the subjects for negotiation. Dulles wanted to try an agreement that would test the intentions of the Soviets. Radford was wary of any agreement to reduce our strength that would be based on the good faith of the Soviets. Strauss talked about the difficulty of detecting underground blasts and of devising a reliable inspection system. Nobody completely agreed with anybody else. His patience exhausted, the President interrupted the game of musical chairs. "Something has got to be done," he declared. "We cannot just drift along or give up. This is a question of survival and we must put our minds at it until we can find some way of making progress. Now that's all there is to it." The discussion began again until it reached the point where the President said to Stassen, "Now take these things we've discussed to Lewis Strauss and the Defense people and get up a paper on which they can agree." As everybody arose to leave the room, Stassen

10. Lyndon Baines Johnson, *The Vantage Point.*

collected his notes and went back to work again. That was how it went with disarmament talks most of the time.[11]

Why Are Rules Obeyed?

Incentives to obey the rules of the game derive from law, habit, and organizational pressures. Some rules must be obeyed on penalty of a jail sentence. The Comptroller General of the United States monitors the actions of the executive branch to be sure that they are in conformity with the Constitution and the laws passed by Congress, particularly with regard to the expenditure of government funds. The Office of Management and Budget performs the same function for the President. Even more important than legality is the strong sense on the part of most participants that the rules of the game ought to be obeyed; an individual who joins an organization implicitly agrees to accept the rules under which that organization operates. This does not mean, of course, that individuals do not ignore some of the rules some of the time or seek to change the rules on occasion to further their own interests and objectives. But in general most participants, especially career officials, simply accept the rules of the game as a matter of course and follow them. Even when habits and legal requirements are not compelling, participants will obey the rules if they feel that the advantages of disobeying or ignoring the rules to achieve a particular objective will in the long run be outweighed by the adverse consequences of having once ignored the rules. For example, participants may calculate that if they redefine the rules of the game so as to exclude a particular individual from the consideration of an issue, he may well exclude them from consideration of another issue when he has the action.

Compliance with the rules of the game is further enforced by monitoring groups within government organizations and by senior officials themselves who may withhold concurrence or refuse to forward a document. Participants find that if they do not follow the rules of the game their proposals simply do not get cleared. Personal relations and anticipated personal reactions also play a role. The probability that an offender or his boss will get an angry phone call as the result of noncompliance with the established rules is, in most cases, a strong incentive to follow the rules of the game.

11. Adams, *Firsthand Report*, p. 326.

Why Do Rules Change?

Changes in rules come about because of personal relationships among participants, because particular participants decide to make an effort to change the rules, or because personnel arrive and depart. The most important of these factors is the personal relationship between Presidents and senior participants and between senior participants and their key subordinates.

PERSONAL RELATIONS

In foreign policy the most important personal relationship is usually that between the President and the Secretary of State. When the President is known to rely heavily on the judgment of his senior Cabinet official and when that official is prepared to assert himself, the rules will be heavily influenced. Truman's relation to Acheson and Eisenhower's to Dulles, for example, meant that, regardless of any formal procedures, the Secretary of State could make decisions affecting other departments and have them obeyed; it also meant that policy issues tended to funnel through the Secretary to the President. When the Secretary of State is unwilling to assert himself or is not seen as being the President's principal adviser, access to the President tends to be more diffused. If several senior participants are equally close to the President, none will yield to the others' judgment.

The determination of who is a senior participant and what rules they observe depends heavily on the inclination of the President. Some participants will be senior, regardless of their formal positions, because of their personal standing in the political or intellectual community. Averell Harriman as Assistant Secretary of State for Far Eastern Affairs under Kennedy was a senior participant, as was Adlai Stevenson when he was Ambassador to the United Nations. In other cases, participants carry weight (or indeed figure in the making of foreign policy at all) because of personal relations with the President. This was true not only of Attorneys General Robert Kennedy and John Mitchell but also of Roger Hilsman, who as Director of Intelligence and Research in the State Department had the ear of President Kennedy.

These same considerations affect the rules of the game within a department. The Secretary's style and personal relations with his subordinates affect the extent to which his Deputy's authority is accepted, who will have access to him, and the extent to which the formal rules are followed. The fact that Secretary of Defense McNamara had confidence in the techniques of systems analysis and in the individuals doing systems analysis in the Pentagon meant that they were consulted and involved in a broad range of issues. Melvin Laird as Secretary of Defense showed less confidence in both the method and the individuals and tended to rely more heavily on military judgments.[12]

ASSERTIVENESS

Another aspect of the influence of personal relations on the rules of the game is the effect of maneuvers by participants who succeed in convincing other participants to involve them in particular actions because it would be costly not to. An individual who will assert his right to be heard on an issue, who is known to complain to the Cabinet officer involved if he is not consulted, is likely to be consulted, because of the perception that not to notify him means unnecessary fuss and disagreement; while an individual who is passive is less likely to be heard. Thus the rules of the game are shaped so that some "country directors" are always consulted on economic or scientific matters pertaining to "their" country, while others are never consulted.

In this way, the role of any particular individual in a particular job can be influenced by the actions of his predecessors. If previous Assistant Secretaries of State for European Affairs have asserted the right to be consulted on trade issues affecting Western Europe, then a new incumbent is likely to be consulted, at least until he indicates a lack of interest in such issues. Alternatively, if his predecessors have not been involved in a question, a new incumbent in a position will have to assert his right to be consulted.

MANEUVERING TO CHANGE RULES

Although most participants obey the established rules most of the time, maneuvers to change rules still occur fairly frequently. Participants often believe that they can change the rules in ways that will increase their influence or get particular decisions or sets of decisions they desire. They think carefully about this if the existing rules have resulted in a bad decision or the failure to focus proper attention on an issue. President Kennedy made a number of changes in the rules of the game as a result of the Bay

12. *New York Times*, September 13, 1969; *Wall Street Journal*, February 10, 1970

of Pigs fiasco. Secretary of Defense McNamara changed a number of internal Defense Department decisionmaking procedures following the TFX controversy in which he attempted to force the Navy and Air Force to buy a single plane for various combat purposes.[13] A new President or a new Cabinet officer may seek to change rules because of a preferred style of behavior or because he believes that things were not done properly under his predecessor. Other changes occur as a result of cumulative frustrations. Thus President Eisenhower devoted a substantial amount of time in the last few years of his administration to changing the decisionmaking procedures within the Department of Defense, and he did so expressly because of his belief that the United States was continuing to spend too much money on defense and getting inefficiently designed forces.[14]

There are a number of ways that participants can alter the rules. Presidents frequently readjust the procedures for making major national security policy decisions, including the form in which they receive suggested options and alternatives. This may drastically affect the degree to which the rules require unanimity among the departments. In some cases, rather than seeking to change the system in general, key participants establish a unique set of rules for a particular activity. General George Marshall, for example, when sent on a mission to China to seek to negotiate a compromise between the Communists and the Nationalists, arranged with Truman for a unique set of decisionmaking arrangements. This involved sending his reports and recommendations to Under Secretary of State Acheson, who in turn carried them directly to the President.[15]

When he feels that a particular approach has not been brought to bear in analyzing a set of issues, the President may create a new office and put into that position an individual whom he expects will bring to bear the kind of expertise and approach to policy issues that he wishes to have.[16] Instead of creating a new position, however, the President may simply direct that certain individuals not previously involved in a particular range of issues now be brought in. Alternatively, a participant can be told that he is no longer to involve himself in a particular range of issues.

Changing the rules may involve the creation of a new channel for mov-

13. Art, *The TFX Decision*, pp. 164–65.

14. Eisenhower, *Waging Peace*, pp. 217, 222, 484.

15. Acheson, *Present at the Creation*, p. 143; Acheson, *Sketches from Life*, pp. 150–51.

16. For a discussion of the different ways in which Presidents have changed or might change the rules in an effort to get better advice from the military, see Morton H. Halperin, "The President and the Military."

ing issues to decision, or it may simply involve moving an issue from one existing channel to another. For example, the ABM question was moved by President Nixon from the channel of direct bilateral relations between the President and the Secretary of Defense into the National Security Council, where a number of other agencies would be consulted. George F. Kennan reports that the role of the Planning Council in the Department of State was substantially changed when he was told he could no longer present papers to the Secretary without the concurrence of the relevant regional Assistant Secretary.[17] Secretary of Defense Louis Johnson substantially changed the system of coordination between the Department of State and the Defense Department by directing that there was to be no coordination below the level of his office and that of the Secretary of State and designating a single individual in his office to carry on all contacts with the State Department.[18]

NEW PARTICIPANTS

Changes in personnel probably account for a substantial part of the changes in the rules of the game, even when this may not be the intention. The replacement of Clark Clifford with Charles Murphy as Special Counsel to the President in the fall of 1949 altered the involvement of the White House staff on national security matters. Clifford had been particularly interested in such matters and had developed a wide range of contacts with officials in various agencies. Murphy, not particularly interested, had not developed comparable contacts and consequently played a negligible role in such matters, reducing the likelihood that the President would receive information informally.[19]

Similarly, changes in personnel bring about changed conceptions of particular roles in the bureaucracy. This can have a major effect on rules, especially where senior participants are concerned. For example, Secretary of Defense McNamara explicitly saw his role as not only arbitrator among the services and manager of the Defense Department but also as innovator in strategy and weapons procurement. Thus the rules of the game on defense budget issues and strategy issues were quite different under McNamara than they had been under his predecessors, particularly Charles Wilson and Neil McElroy.

If the change in personnel consists of promotion of a career official to

17. Kennan, *Memoirs, 1925–1950*, p. 465.
18. Hammond, "NSC-68," pp. 336–37.
19. Ibid., p. 327.

fill the job previously occupied by another career official, the results are likely to be considerably less dramatic. This is especially frustrating when one hopes to find a career official who will challenge the interests of his organization as defined by that organization. President Eisenhower tried to appoint an Army Chief of Staff who would accept his strategy of massive retaliation—a strategy that entailed a severe cut in the size of the Army because of all-out emphasis on nuclear weapons. He was, however, constrained to choose among the senior officers of the Army, and both of the men he appointed to the position, Generals Matthew Ridgway and Maxwell Taylor, ultimately resigned and publicly denounced the policy. Where the issue turns on debate within a service as to its essence, then promotion of particular individuals can make a difference. Thus both sides in the struggle within the Army as to whether heavy emphasis should be given to an Army medium-range missile program sought to put their men into the right positions.[20]

Senior participants, and even some at lower levels, have wide scope within which they can define the nature of their job and their interests. The rules of the game very quickly adjust to the interests of senior participants and the standing of these officials with the President. Each new administration tends to produce its own set of rules.

What we have referred to as the rules of the game are often described as the structure of national security decision making or the organizational arrangements of the foreign affairs bureaucracy. Much attention is given to changes in these structures and in particular to the varying ways in which Presidents use the National Security Council and its surrounding apparatus. The premise of this book is that the rules do not dominate the process, although they do make a difference to the extent that they structure the game. This still leaves considerable flexibility for participants to maneuver. We have seen them maneuvering to change the rules in their favor. We turn now to a consideration of how participants plan their moves within whatever rules exist—plan, that is, to get the decisions they want.

20. Armacost, *The Politics of Weapons Innovation*, pp. 122, 167.

CHAPTER SEVEN

Planning a Decisional Strategy

We use the term "planning" here to describe the process of systematically working out a strategy designed to accomplish the goal that one perceives for oneself in relation to an issue.[1] Usually planning focuses on the President. The decision that one wants is often one that only the President can make. (Sometimes planning in our sense may involve keeping an issue from getting to the President.) Frequently, the central problem in planning is to determine how one can get the issue to the President, put him in a position where he believes he has to make a decision, and then get him to decide in one's favor. This involves structuring the issue and affecting who participates in the process. Of course, the President himself may initiate or engage in planning.

Defining the Issue

Once a participant or coalition of participants reaches the conclusion that the time is right to seek a decision, those parts of the bureaucracy with a direct interest in the issue usually become aware of the movement for change. Initial efforts to head off the reopening of an issue sometimes succeed. If not, however, most officials with an interest at stake will come to accept that an issue is being reviewed and that there is, according to their view, either danger of or opportunity for a new presidential decision. This recognition often occurs sequentially. More and more organizations

1. Confusion is generated by the common use of the word "planning" to mean a number of things. Here it is used in the sense of laying out a scheme designed to secure a desired governmental decision and action. In the title of the State Department's Policy Planning Council, the word meant an organization which would mainly write papers estimating the long-run consequences of possible courses of action if undertaken by the government, although members of the council did from time to time engage in planning in the sense used here.

and participants come to recognize that a presidential decision may in fact be made. In some cases, the recognition moves from the top of the government downward, particularly if it is the President who is initiating policy review; or it may move upward, from lower levels of the government.

Most issues are not new, having already been defined in terms of the interests involved. However, when an issue is revived or when a novel proposal is being made, some participants will analyze the implications for national security as they judge it and for their own interests. Those who do feel the need for such analysis are likely to be those less affected by the outcome than other participants. Often these relatively open-minded participants are the ones whose allegiance is fought over in the struggle to secure the desired presidential decision.

Once he recognizes that an issue is under review, a participant must determine just what kind of decisions he wants and what changes and actions he expects to follow from them. He must also determine what bad decisions he is most anxious to avoid, and finally he must consider what compromises he is prepared to make.

After defining the end goal of his actions, the participant must determine in what order to present the elements to be decided. Often he seeks a decision in principle or a decision that he believes will lead in steps to the ultimate decision he desires. He tries to get the President to make what seems like the easier choice before raising more difficult issues on which the President is less likely to decide his way. In February of 1968 when General Earle Wheeler, Chairman of the Joint Chiefs of Staff, and General William Westmoreland, Chief of American Military Forces in Vietnam, concluded that the United States should invade Laos and Cambodia, they also concluded that, in order to do that, they needed a substantial increase in American forces in Vietnam. General Wheeler decided to take the decisions one step at a time. After a meeting with Westmoreland in Saigon, Wheeler returned to Washington and presented the now famous request for 205,000 additional troops.[2] He did not tell the President or other participants in Washington that the troops were wanted so that the United States could invade Cambodia and Laos. As he later explained:

Back in Washington I emphasized how Westy's forces were very badly stretched, that he had no capability to redress threats except by moving

2. See Lyndon Johnson, *Vantage Point*, pp. 388–415, for the presidential account of this episode.

troops around. I emphasized the threat in the I Corps. More attacks on the cities were, I said, a possibility. I argued that Westy needed flexibility and capability. I talked about going on the offensive and taking offensive operations, but I didn't necessarily spell out the strategic options [i.e., that the troops were to be used to invade Cambodia and Laos].[3]

Dean Acheson in his memoirs explains the same technique in the case of NSC-68. This document, prepared by a group of State and Defense Department planners prior to the Korean War, called for the creation of very substantial forces capable of fighting limited wars. Acheson reports how the proponents sought decisions a step at a time:

While NSC-68 did not contain cost estimates, that did not mean we had not discussed them. To carry through the sort of rearmament and re-habilitation-of-forces program that we recommended, at the rate we thought necessary, for ourselves and with help for our allies, would require, our group estimated, a military budget of the magnitude of about fifty billion dollars per annum. This was a very rough guess, but, as the existing ceiling was thirteen and a half billion, the proposal—or rather the situation out of which it grew—required considerable readjustment of thinking. It seemed better to begin this process by facing the broad facts, trends, and probabilities before getting lost in budgetary intricacies. If that begins before an administration has decided what it wants to do, or made what diplomats used to call a decision "in principle"—in essence—the mice in the Budget Bureau will nibble to death the will to decide.[4]

Having made his calculations about his operational goals and the sequence in which to pursue them, the participant must develop a concrete plan of action. He must determine in what form he should raise the issue, what kinds of policy analyses are likely to be needed, who should be brought in and how, who should be kept out and how, and how high up to go. Will the President come down on the "right" side, or should the issue be kept out of the presidential purview? The participant developing a plan also needs to determine which argument to use with which participants, when and how. He needs in addition to consider the strategy likely to be adopted by his opponents and to develop, at least on a contingency basis, his plans for meeting them. Finally, he needs periodically during the process to reassess where he is going, whether he should change his strategy or abandon his effort to get a favorable decision (or to resist an unfavorable one).

3. John B. Henry II, "February 1968," p. 24.
4. Acheson, *Present at the Creation*, p. 379 (italics added).

Who Is Involved?

A participant seeking a decision or seeking to block one is wise to ask himself who else is likely to be involved in the process. Perhaps the key question is to determine who is likely to be particularly influential with the President on the range of issues involved. Neustadt has said that perhaps the most active game in Washington is seeking to determine who has influence with the President on what issues.

Since officials and advisers often have a choice of whether or not to get involved, the participant planning the strategy will need to consider whom he could perhaps persuade to stay out. He recognizes that some participants are natural allies who, for their own reasons, will be prepared to support the decision he wants. Others are potential converts to his position, who might be brought along by either persuasion or bargaining. Still others he sees as probably neutrals. Finally, there are those participants whose goals are incompatible and whose opposition will have to be overcome. Perhaps the "balance of forces" can be altered by convincing an individual or faction not to participate.

Opting In or Out

Whether to become actively involved will be a critical choice for each potential participant if the rules of the game have not already settled the question. In general, being "in the game" is the more desirable option for most participants, but there are times when some will find it more advantageous to opt out. In some cases the rules of the game make it almost impossible for some officials to remain totally out of a particular struggle, since their views are almost certain to be requested by the President or by a Cabinet officer. Even in such cases, however, they can temporize if they choose. Thus the Joint Chiefs of Staff carried out only the most perfunctory evaluation of the CIA plan for the invasion of Cuba and made it clear that responsibility rested with the CIA. Secretary of State Dean Rusk often managed to avoid involvement in key issues. For example, aware that his presence in Nassau might be interpreted by some State Department officers as a form of support for their desire to eliminate the British nuclear force and convinced that the outcome of the Nassau talks would be the opposite (which he himself desired), Rusk chose to honor a longstanding commitment at a diplomatic dinner rather than accompany

President Kennedy to Nassau to meet Harold Macmillan in 1962.[5] Cabinet officers may find that they must at least appear not to be involved, in order to throw the public off the scent of a crisis issue that has not yet reached decision. Other officials will find that their responsibilities do not routinely involve them but do give them an opportunity to fight to be involved in an issue, and they will have to weigh the advantages of involvement against the cost of fighting their way in.

These calculations and others can be summed up in a hypothetical checklist which a prudent official might draw up for himself in judging whether to involve himself in an impending decision.

1. *Time and energy.*

An analysis of a particular decision frequently misses the fact that no matter how important the issue may appear to an observer in retrospect, it was only one of a large number of issues confronting any senior participant. Participants are concerned about a great many things; the importance of particular issues is impressed upon them by various of their subordinates, and they must pick and choose. They have neither the time nor the energy to fight every issue brought to their attention no matter how important it may seem to their subordinates or to an outside observer. Henry Kissinger offers this explanation of Secretary of Defense McNamara's failure to get involved in a number of early debates about Vietnam strategy:

. . . McNamara's profundity in analysis had to give way to a very practical problem: how many times a month could he go to the mat with the JCS? He had to decide very deliberately which issues he could confront them with. If one wants to explain why it is that McNamara's theories about the war in Vietnam were not always matched by implementation, especially toward the end, the primary reason was that he felt that confronted with issues of ABM, troop deployment, force levels, renewal of the strategic force, and Vietnam strategy, he could only handle so many of these cases simultaneously. He picked those which he thought were crucial at the moment.[6]

2. *Reputation with the President.*

Senior participants value highly their reputation with the President, and they carefully assess how involvement in any particular issue would affect that relation. They want to "win" with the President, they want to

5. Letter to the author from Dean Rusk, January 8, 1973.
6. Kissinger, "Bureaucracy and Policy Making," p. 91. On the general question, see Caraley, *The Politics of Military Unification*, pp. 263–64.

impress colleagues, and they want what they recommend to work if their advice is taken. Secretary of Defense McNamara, for example, was, reluctant to get involved in issues of how to fight the war in Vietnam, for he did not believe that on this issue his competence was greater than that of the Joint Chiefs of Staff.[7] Secretary of State George C. Marshall refused to endorse JCS effort to get a substantial increase in the military budget in 1949, because he did not believe that the Chiefs would spend the money in a sensible way leading to an increase in American security.[8] Senior participants are reluctant to come to the President with what they know is unwelcome advice and risk an argument or quarrel with him. They recognize that any President will tune out senior participants who frequently come to him with counsel that he finds uncongenial, and therefore they will save such attempts for issues on which they feel very strongly. It was this calculation that kept Joseph Califano from involving himself in Vietnam issues when he moved from the Pentagon to the White House to become a principal adviser to the President on domestic policy issues.[9] Desiring to protect their reputation with the President, they are reluctant to challenge him on issues where he does not view them as having expertise or competence. These concerns heavily influenced what issues Secretary of State John Foster Dulles chose to get involved in:

"*Dulles saw himself as Eisenhower's exclusive advisor on foreign policy and went to great lengths to protect this position. But the consequence of this was that the more an issue moved away from the center of foreign policy, the more carefully Dulles would pick his ground before asserting himself with the President. Dulles was very conscious of Ike's military background, and he knew that Ike had a lot of respect for Admiral Radford [Chairman of the Joint Chiefs of Staff]. And on economic matters, he watched what Humphrey would do first. He also thought it was hazardous to guess what Congress wanted. . . .*"[10]

Senior participants are equally concerned with what their colleagues will think if their advice is rejected by the President. They recognize that their ability to operate effectively in the bureaucracy on issues of paramount concern to them depends on being known by other participants for effectiveness with the President. Dean Acheson and John

7. Henry Brandon, *Anatomy of Error*, p. 29.
8. Warner R. Schilling, "The Politics of National Defense: Fiscal 1950," pp. 193–95.
9. Anderson, *The Presidents' Men*, p. 368.
10. Interview with Robert Bowie, October 22, 1964, as quoted in Edgerton, *Sub-Cabinet Politics and Policy Commitment*, p. 8.

Foster Dulles both guarded carefully their reputations, and this is part of the explanation for Dulles' unwillingness to get involved in military budget issues and economic issues. If he lost on these issues, people would begin to wonder whether he would indeed always win on diplomatic issues.

In 1948, Secretary of Defense James Forrestal had to decide whether or not to get involved in what was shaping up as a major confrontation between the Joint Chiefs of Staff and the Chairman of the Atomic Energy Commission, David Lilienthal. At this time, the Atomic Energy Commission had complete custody and control of all nuclear weapons. Contingency plans called for them to be turned over to the military only after the President had authorized their use. The Joint Chiefs, unhappy about this situation because it denied them complete autonomy over the weapons, pressed for a change which would have the weapons turned over to military custody as soon as they were operational. Lilienthal vigorously resisted such a move with the support of members of the White House staff. Forrestal openly succumbed to pressure from the military and weighed in on their side, but only after he had rejected the advice of Lewis L. Strauss. As the latter relates it:

"Don't do it, Jim," I urged. "The President will decide against you."

"Why should he?" he asked.

"For the same reason," I answered, "that the public still fears the 'trigger-happy Colonel.' Don't get yourself into a position where, for the first time in your dealing with him, the President will overrule you. If he does, the fact can't be kept secret. It's bound to leak. An important element in your authority is that the President has always backed you up in everything concerned with national defense."[11]

Despite Forrestal's intervention, Truman sided with Lilienthal, and Forrestal's influence declined as Strauss had warned.

3. *Account with the President.*

Senior participants find that they can get the President to support them from time to time simply by making an issue of personal privilege. Unless there are overriding reasons not to, Presidents tend to give in when their principal advisers feel very strongly about something. However, such influence with the President must be carefully husbanded. If a senior participant too frequently draws upon his personal account with the President, he may discover himself short of influence when a matter of great importance comes along after a series of concessions. In addition, senior

---

11. Lewis L. Strauss, *Men and Decisions*, p. 160.

participants discover that when they ask the President for something, he will ask them for something in return. Are they prepared to pay the price?

4. *Antagonizing others.*

Reluctance to get involved for fear of losing to other senior participants goes one step further in the principle of avoiding conflict with other participants lest they enter battles against "the troublemaker." Secretary of State Dulles was careful to stay out of areas where the powerful Secretary of the Treasury George Humphrey considered his responsibilities to be paramount. In return he expected Humphrey to stay out of foreign policy issues. Dulles drew the line very carefully, and this influenced how far he was prepared to go in fighting for the Development Loan Fund and for aid to the British at the time of the Suez crisis.[12]

5. *Concept of one's role.*

Some participants may stay out of an issue simply because they do not view it as part of their responsibility. Eisenhower's Secretaries of Defense Charles Wilson and Neil McElroy, for example, both viewed their job as being managers of the Pentagon and did not involve themselves in foreign policy or strategic disputes.[13]

Secretary of State Dean Rusk's conception of his role under Presidents Kennedy and Johnson required that he not engage in controversy with his colleagues either in front of the President or elsewhere. He viewed his role as giving private advice to the President and thus did not involve himself when issues were argued out in other forums.[14]

Often several of the motives listed above combine to explain the absence of a major figure from an important controversy. Such was the case for the failure of Henry Kissinger to try to prevent starvation in Biafra following its capture and reincorporation into Nigeria:

A major question is where the President and Henry Kissinger were through all of this. It appears that Kissinger was informed of the controversy in detail, and was deeply concerned, and backed his staff in its efforts to change State Department policy. But Kissinger is one of the busiest men in Washington, and he had other wars, literal and bureaucratic, to fight. Any official must decide his priorities, the issues on which he chooses to spend his capital, and the Nigerian case was not as important to him as

12. Neustadt, *Alliance Politics*, p. 99.

13. Snyder, "The 'New Look' of 1953," pp. 517–18; Halperin, "The Gaither Committee and the Policy Process," p. 373.

14. See the *Life* interview with Dean Rusk, "Mr. Secretary on the Eve of Emeritus," p. 62B.

were some others. Moreover, Kissinger's relationship with Richardson appears to have been an important factor. Because of the power that Kissinger has accrued, and because of Rogers' own relaxed approach to his job, the Secretary of State has become a largely irrelevant figure in the making of foreign policy. The relationship between Kissinger and Rogers is, from several accounts, strained. The axis of power and policy runs from Kissinger to Undersecretary Richardson, a cool, bright, and able man who is Kissinger's close friend. The two men have lunch once a week, and talk on the telephone several times a day. Richardson had charge of Nigerian policy, and Kissinger has confidence in him. Finally, the form in which the issue came up was incompatible with Kissinger's chosen role: he is the foreign policy conceptualizer, the grand strategist; this was an operational issue of a rather mundane sort—malnutrition statistics, trucks, food tonnages.[15]

Drawing the Circle

We have spoken of how officials judge whether it is in their interest to get involved in an issue. We have spoken also of their calculations as to possible allies and possible enemies. Once they become involved and once the calculations are made, a set of maneuvers for including certain participants and excluding opponents comes into play. These efforts will be constrained by the rules of the game, but within those rules there is considerable scope for maneuver, particularly by the President, to reduce the circle, increase the circle, or even change personnel.

REDUCING THE CIRCLE

We have mentioned the technique of persuading an uncommitted official that, given his interests, he should not get involved. If this fails, it may be possible to structure the procedure leading to a decision so that some potential participants are left out.

The usual rationale for excluding particular participants generally makes use of the argument that "security" must be maintained in order that the planned course of action not be revealed prematurely by information being given to allied governments or being leaked to the press. As George Reedy explains, such arguments are likely to be received with sympathy at the White House:

The environment of deference, approaching sycophancy, helps to foster

15. Elizabeth B. Drew, "Washington," p. 24.

another insidious factor. It is a belief that the president and a few of his most trusted advisers are possessed of a special knowledge which must be closely held within a small group lest the plans and the designs of the United States be anticipated and frustrated by enemies. It is a knowledge which is thought to be endangered in geometrical proportion to the number of other men to whom it is passed. Therefore, the most vital national projects can be worked out only within a select coterie, or there will be a "leak" which will disadvantage the country's security.[16]

Such arguments were used effectively in the case of the Bay of Pigs invasion. Kennedy was informed by the CIA that covert operations of this kind needed to be restricted to a very tight circle of those who had "a need to know." On this basis most of those involved in the analysis of foreign events in the CIA and the Department of State were excluded from consideration of the Bay of Pigs operation.

The second set of standard arguments for excluding potential participants relates to the notion that only those with responsibility for a particular issue need to be consulted. To an extent, this can be accomplished in the way an issue is defined. In the case of the ABM, McNamara, in effect, argued that this was a matter which concerned only his department and therefore should be settled bilaterally between the President and the Secretary of Defense with only minimal consultation with other officials.

If the President is firmly committed to moving in a particular direction, the argument can be made to him that individuals who are likely to oppose the action or to raise objections should be excluded. The President may feel that he is thoroughly familiar with the arguments on both sides and does not want to waste time or be bogged down hearing objections or pleas for consultation with allies.

One tactic used on those to be excluded is simply not to inform them that a decision is under consideration. Obviously officials kept in the dark are not in a position even to volunteer advice or information. In planning his invasion of Cambodia in April of 1970, President Nixon apparently did not inform a number of officials of this operation. Even more tightly held was the decision at the same time to engage in limited bombing of North Vietnam. In that case, according to the journalist Hugh Sidey, the Secretary of Defense was not informed of the full extent of the planned bombing operations, and the Secretary of State was not informed at all.[17]

Although it is quite irregular to exclude Cabinet officers from informa-

16. Reedy, *The Twilight of the Presidency*, pp. 10–11.
17. Sidey, "Nixon in a Crisis of Leadership," p. 28.

tion about impending decisions, officials at lower levels are often excluded. The Chief of Intelligence in the Department of State and the CIA's Deputy Director for Intelligence were not informed of the impending invasion of Cuba. Refusal to inform officials can sometimes be carried to the extreme of not telling them "officially" about something which they have already caught wind of. This occurred when the senior officials of the United States Information Agency learned from a reporter that the United States was planning to invade Cuba. Donald M. Wilson, who was then Deputy Director of USIA, describes the bizarre episode:

> I had little to do with the Bay of Pigs operation. USIA was not informed, and I found out about it before it happened in a strange way. I was called on the telephone by Tad Szulc of the *New York Times*. He had been down in Florida and insisted that I join him for breakfast at his father-in-law's house in Georgetown, at which point he revealed all he had found in Florida—only some of which he printed in the *New York Times*— and said that he was convinced that an invasion was about to take place, and I think he talked to me because I was a friend of his and he didn't quite know what to do with it. So I went to Ed Murrow, who was my boss, and Murrow promptly called up Allen Dulles. Murrow and I went over to see Allen Dulles and told him everything Szulc had told me. Allen Dulles didn't give us a thing. He was very bland and he didn't admit that any of it was true and of course we knew it was by then—you could just tell—and Murrow was angry in a way but he was a loyal soldier and he realized, I guess, that he wasn't supposed to know about it. So we went back to USIA and pretty much operated in the dark during the Bay of Pigs thing. It was very unfortunate and poorly handled from all points of view and certainly from the propaganda point of view.[18]

Even when officials are informed or have become aware of a particular issue, they may be denied the right to comment or to prepare a study on the question involved. For example, after Roger Hilsman, who was Director of the State Department's Bureau of Intelligence and Research, inadvertently learned about the planned invasion of Cuba, he confronted Secretary of State Rusk and asked for permission to have his Cuban experts prepare an analysis of the situation. Hilsman was denied permission to do this study.[19]

Preventing the circulation of documents is a tactic to forestall potential

18. Wilson, Kennedy Library Oral History Interview, pp. 14–15. See also Thomas C. Sorensen, *The Word War: The Story of American Propaganda*, p. 139.
19. Hilsman, *To Move a Nation*, p. 31.

participants from drawing in officials on their staff to prepare careful comments on a proposal. Often documents are handed out at a White House meeting but then participants are refused permission to take copies back to their own agencies. This was in fact done during the Bay of Pigs preparations.[20]

Efforts can also be made to restrict the circle by failing to invite a particular participant to a key meeting. The White House staff, which believed that Eisenhower was unduly influenced by the hard-line views of Dulles, tried from time to time to get Eisenhower committed to a particular course of action before the Secretary of State was brought into the picture. Perhaps the most spectacular attempt occurred when Washington was informed that the Russian leader Joseph Stalin was dying. Robert Cutler, the President's Assistant for National Security, called a meeting with the President, a group of White House officials, and Allen Dulles, Director of the CIA. At this meeting it was decided that the President should address a message to the Russian people. John Foster Dulles arrived at the White House after this meeting and expressed serious reservations in an apparent effort to change the President's mind, but to no avail.[21]

WIDENING THE CIRCLE

Presidents, who sometimes themselves try to reduce the circle when they are sure what they wish to do, have methods to check such maneuvers by subordinates. Often they expand the circle precisely to keep certain protagonists from excluding critics. The basic argument used for enlarging the number of participants is the doctrine that the President should hear all points of view. More concretely it can be argued that others whose areas of responsibility are affected by a decision ought to be consulted and that the President should also hear "disinterested" individuals who do not have any bureaucratic responsibilities in the area under consideration. For example, following the Bay of Pigs fiasco, President Kennedy often consulted outside advisers as well as his brother Robert, then serving as Attorney General. President Johnson often consulted Clark Clifford and Abe Fortas, the former a lawyer at the time practicing in Washington and the latter then serving as an Associate Justice of the Supreme Court Sometimes the argument that an individual should be included relates not to the likelihood that he will provide information or options which the

20. Theodore Sorensen, *Kennedy*, pp. 304–5.
21. Cutler, *No Time for Rest*, p. 321.

President will find of value but rather to the fear that his exclusion will entail political costs because of the belief of others, frequently others outside the executive branch, that the individual should be consulted. Presidents often feel pressure, particularly from senior congressmen and senators, to consult military leaders on matters concerning defense budgets or the employment of military force. For this reason General Earle Wheeler, Chairman of the Joint Chiefs, was ultimately included in the Tuesday lunch at which President Johnson made his major Vietnam decisions.[22] Pressure may come from other senators and congressmen to include spokesmen of other viewpoints. Members of the Senate Foreign Relations Committee, for example, often probe the administration as to whether officials of the Arms Control and Disarmament Agency were consulted before decisions were made. Though an individual may be brought in merely so it can be said he was there, that individual once involved may affect the outcome.

There are a number of different ways in which individuals can be brought into the process. This is easier when the individual concerned is anxious or at least willing to be involved, although some techniques can be effective in drawing in a participant who would prefer to remain aloof.

In some cases it is sufficient to inform a participant that a decision is about to be made; for he has no hesitation about being involved, and the rules of the game clearly provide for his involvement should he choose to engage himself. For example, State Department opponents of a proposed sale of American military aircraft to South Africa were able to block the sale by informing the U.S. Ambassador to the United Nations, Arthur Goldberg, of the impending decision. Goldberg phoned Under Secretary of State Thomas Mann and was able to persuade him to cancel the sale.[23]

Another means of expanding the circle is to secure an invitation for a certain individual to participate in an existing forum where an issue is being debated. As indicated above, in 1966 President Johnson invited General Earle Wheeler to participate in the Tuesday lunch discussions at which Vietnam matters were being debated. An alternative technique is to seek to move an issue into a new forum. Often those desiring to have a large number of individuals examine a question seek to move it into a

22. Hugh Sidey, A *Very Personal Presidency*, pp. 204–6. Sidey suggests that the President did not particularly value Wheeler's advice and acceded to this request only to please Congress. President Johnson in his memoirs did not deal with this question, but there is evidence to suggest that he took the military position more seriously following the major escalation of the war in Vietnam.

23. Arnold Beichman, *The "Other" State Department*, pp. 97–98.

formal NSC process which typically involves a number of agencies. In general, the more formal the process the larger the number of participants.

The number of participants can also be expanded by persuading the President to appoint an ad hoc committee, either of executive branch officials or outsiders, to examine an issue which he normally would treat by dealing directly with the principal operating agency concerned. When participants seeking a particular decision find themselves unable to obtain what they want by expanding the circle within the executive branch, they often go beyond it to bring in congressmen or outside individuals. Often the problem is primarily to alert outside parties to an impending decision. This can be done either by providing information privately to a congress-man or senator, by leaking information to the press, or by arranging to have a congressman or senator ask a question which can be answered in a way to provide him with information with which to fight presidential preferences. This latter technique is particularly effective with military officers, since Congress asserts the right to ask military leaders for their "personal" opinions on military issues. This right is jealously guarded by the Congress.[24]

Congressional involvement can be used to bring pressure to bear di-rectly on the President on the substance of the issue, or it can be used to expand the circle. If congressional pressure is not sufficient, people from the private sector who for one reason or another have influence with the President may be pulled in. Harry Truman remembered one episode when his former haberdashery partner was brought into the process in an effort to overturn a presidential decision:

As the pressure mounted, I found it necessary to give instructions that I did not want to be approached by any more spokesmen for the extreme Zionist cause. I was even so disturbed that I put off seeing Dr. Chaim Weizmann, who had returned to the United States and had asked for an interview with me. My old friend, Eddie Jacobson, called on me at the White House and urged me to receive Dr. Weizmann at the earliest pos-sible moment. Eddie, who had been with me through the hard days of World War I, had never been a Zionist. In all my years in Washington he had never asked me for anything for himself. He was of the Jewish faith and was deeply moved by the sufferings of the Jewish people abroad. He had spoken to me on occasion, both before and after I became President, about some specific hardship cases that he happened to know about, but he did this rarely. On March 13 he called at the White House.

I was always glad to see him. Not only had we shared so much in the past, but I have always had the warmest feelings toward him. It would be hard to find a truer friend. Eddie said that he wanted to talk about Palestine. I told him that I would rather he did not and that I wanted to let the matter run its course in the United Nations.

I do not believe that in all our thirty years of friendship a sharp word had ever passed between Eddie and me, and I was sorry that Eddie had brought up the subject.

Eddie was becoming self-conscious, but he kept on talking. He asked me to bear in mind that some of the pro-Zionists who had approached me were only individuals and did not speak for any responsible leadership.

I told him that I respected Dr. Weizmann, but if I saw him, it would only result in more wrong interpretations.

Eddie waved toward a small replica of an Andrew Jackson statue that was in my office.

"He's been your hero all your life, hasn't he?" he said. "You have probably read every book there is on Andrew Jackson. I remember when we had the store that you were always reading books and pamphlets, and a lot of them were about Jackson. You put this statue in front of the Jackson County Courthouse in Kansas City when you built it."

I did not know what he was leading up to, but he went on.

"I have never met the man who has been my hero all my life," he continued. "But I have studied his past as you have studied Jackson's. He is the greatest Jew alive, perhaps the greatest Jew who ever lived. You yourself have told me that he is a great statesman and a fine gentleman. I am talking about Dr. Chaim Weizmann. He is an old man and a very sick man. He has traveled thousands of miles to see you, and now you are putting off seeing him. That isn't like you."

When Eddie left, I gave instructions to have Dr. Weizmann come to the White House as soon as it could be arranged. However, the visit was to be entirely off the record. Dr. Weizmann, by my specific instructions, was to be brought in through the East Gate. There was to be no press coverage of his visit and no public announcement.[25]

When an official is reluctant to get involved in an issue but it is believed that if he does he will support a particular decision, participants favoring

25. Truman, *Years of Trial and Hope*, pp. 160–61.

that decision will seek to force him to become involved. They may do so by urging the President to consult with him, or they may seek to establish on the record that the concerns of his agency are affected. Secretary of Defense Forrestal made a substantial effort to get Secretary of State Marshall involved in a struggle with the President over the size of the military budget in 1948. Forrestal believed that if Marshall were somehow drawn into the process, he would inevitably support a larger budget. He thus sent Marshall a letter in which he raised three questions:

(a) *Has there been an improvement in the international picture which would warrant a substantial reduction in the military forces we had planned to have in being by the end of the current fiscal year?*

(b) *Has the situation worsened since last Spring, and should we, therefore, be considering an augmentation of the forces that we were planning at that time?*

(c) *Is the situation about the same—that is, neither better nor worse?*[26] The ploy failed because Marshall was unwilling to get involved in opposition to the President. Later, in fact, Truman brought him in on his side in the campaign to keep down defense spending.

Who Plans?

The range of options available to any participant, the degree to which he can plan, depends on his position and the kind of issue involved. Every participant will be constrained by the amount of time, energy, and resources available to him to carry out particular objectives.

Some participants seem to plan often, others almost never. In general, staffs without formal operational responsibility have more time and are more likely to be involved in maneuvers to obtain a certain policy. Thus planning of the kind suggested here (to induce a decision) is often done by "planning staffs" in the second sense, such as the State Department's Policy Planning Council. It was a small group of officials connected primarily with the Policy Planning Council of the State Department who favored the multilateral force and engaged extensively in systematic efforts to "sell" it to the administration. Henry Kissinger notes:

... *The MLF was put over by five or six highly motivated, highly in-*

26. Schilling, "The Politics of National Defense," pp. 187–88.

telligent individuals, in a government where a considerable number of people were indifferent and nobody was really opposed. The process by which it was done involved, at least in its early phases, a fairly deliberate manipulation by the bureaucracy of the senior executives.

For example, sentences were put into a Presidential speech which in themselves were perfectly sensible, but the full import of which was perhaps not understood. These were then used to start study groups which were subsequently used to present a new claim for a little more progress, and so on until the point where the prestige of the United States had become heavily committed to something the implications of which, in my judgment, had never been submitted to the adversary procedure.[27]

Organizations as such are most likely to carry out conscious planning in relation to matters affecting their essence. Michael Armacost reports that both the Army and the Air Force engaged in considerable systematic planning in their struggle for medium-range missile deployments.[28]

Although most senior officials are in general too busy to plan, evidence suggests that Presidents and Cabinet officers do plan on a few items of very high priority. McNamara seems to have engaged in some systematic planning to prevent a large-scale ABM deployment. Richard Neustadt's description of the way in which Truman succeeded in getting the Marshall Plan approved by Congress suggests a considerable amount of conscious planning on Truman's part:

The crucial thing to note about this case is that despite compatibility of views on public policy, Truman got no help he did not pay for (except Stalin's). Bevin scarcely could have seized on Marshall's words had Marshall not been plainly backed by Truman. Marshall's interest would not have comported with the exploitation of his prestige by a President who undercut him openly, or subtly, or even inadvertently, at any point. Vandenberg, presumably, could not have backed proposals by a White House which begrudged him deference and access gratifying to his fellow-partisans (and satisfying to himself). Prominent Republicans in private life would not have found it easy to promote a cause identified with Truman's claims on 1948—and neither would the prominent New Dealers then engaged in searching for a substitute.

Truman paid the price required for their services. So far as the record

27. Kissinger, "Bureaucracy and Policy Making," p. 88. See also Steinbruner, *Decisions under Complexity.*

28. Armacost, *The Politics of Weapons Innovation,* esp. pp. 17–18, 92, 97, 169–70.

shows, the White House did not falter once in firm support for Marshall and the Marshall Plan. Truman backed his Secretary's gamble on an invitation to all Europe. He made the plan his own in a well-timed address to the Canadians. He lost no opportunity to widen the involvements of his own official family in the cause. Averell Harriman the Secretary of Commerce, Julius Krug the Secretary of the Interior, Edwin Nourse the Economic Council Chairman, James Webb the Director of the Budget—all were made responsible for studies and reports contributing directly to the legislative presentation. Thus these men were committed in advance. Besides, the President continually emphasized to everyone in reach that he did not have doubts, did not desire complications and would foreclose all he could. Reportedly, his emphasis was felt at the Treasury, with good effect. And Truman was at special pains to smooth the way for Vandenberg. The Senator insisted on "no politics" from the Administration side; there was none. He thought a survey of American resources and capacity essential; he got it in the Krug and Harriman reports. Vandenberg expected advance consultation; he received it, step by step, in frequent meetings with the President and weekly conferences with Marshall. He asked for an effective liaison between Congress and agencies concerned; Lovett and others gave him what he wanted. When the Senator decided on the need to change financing and administrative features of the legislation, Truman disregarded Budget Bureau grumbling and acquiesced with grace. When, finally, Vandenberg desired a Republican to head the new administering agency, his candidate, Paul Hoffman, was appointed despite the President's own preference for another. In all of these ways Truman employed the sparse advantages his "powers" and his status then accorded him to gain the sort of help he had to have.[29]

The Limits of Planning

As Neustadt suggests, even Presidents have to engage in considerable persuasion, bargaining, and coercion if they are to be able to make the kinds of decisions which they wish to make, particularly when they need congressional concurrence. In the next two chapters, we consider the way in which all participants struggle to affect decisions by persuading other

---

29. Neustadt, *Presidential Power*, pp. 52–53.

participants to support them or by maneuvers aimed at bargaining or coercion.[30] Before leaving the subject of planning, however, we wish to reiterate that planning is a variable in bureaucratic behavior. It may or may not be present in any given struggle, and it may or may not be efficacious.

The reader should keep in mind that everything described in the next chapter occurs at the same time. Moreover, it occurs while participants are dealing with a great many other issues. Some of the participants will be spending a considerable amount of time on a particular issue; others will be devoting almost no time to it and simply involving themselves episodically. Some will be carrying out well-formulated plans. Most will be reacting on a day-to-day basis to particular events and to pressures and deadlines. Thus what might be described in retrospect as a maneuver may not actually be consciously thought out by the participants. Moreover, any effort to describe the process involves the great risk of suggesting much greater order, uniformity, and regularity than exists. Indeed, observers who have been involved in government are unanimous in emphasizing the confusion, the great pressure of deadlines, the importance of accident, misunderstandings, and lack of information in determining what occurs. If the reader will keep all this in mind, we may proceed first to consider efforts at persuasion and then to consider maneuvering aimed at bargaining and coercion.

30. This discussion owes much to Caraley's *The Politics of Military Unification*, pp. 272–76. The three categories are drawn from his text. March and Simon in *Organizations* present a similar list. They divide persuasion into two categories, "problem solving" and "persuasion." The first refers to the search for information and analysis of alternatives, and the second refers to efforts to demonstrate that disagreement over subgoals should be merged because of agreement over more relevant, higher criteria. They use the term "politics" rather than "coercion" but seem to mean essentially the same thing, with an emphasis on expanding the number of players in order to get a particular player overruled.

CHAPTER EIGHT

Information and Arguments

Recall from Chapter 2 that participants in the foreign policy process believe the United States should do what is required for national security as they define it. But they become aware that their own view of national interests, shaped as that view is by organizational, presidential, or personal interests, will not necessarily be shared by other participants. They therefore recognize the need to present positive, "impartial" evidence in favor of their position. Often they seek to convince other participants by putting forward information and arguments designed to demonstrate that what they advocate is objectively in the interest of the United States. Generally they relate their arguments to concepts that appeal to the majority and avoid explaining the process of reasoning and the set of particular interests that led to their stand.

Arguments in favor of a decision are the most important form in which information reaches the President and other senior participants. Normally a proposal for a presidential decision will move through the bureaucracy accompanied by a set of arguments initially drafted by advocates and revised to take account of criticisms and to get as many participants as possible on board. Arguments presented formally and in writing must relate to national security in the context of the shared images and rules then operating within the government.

Arguments accompanying a proposal are those that participants believe will lead others to adopt a desired position. This does not mean that they will use arguments they know to be false; rather, they will choose from the wide range of plausible arguments those that seem likely to persuade. For example, in commenting in his journal on his successful effort to persuade President Truman not to turn physical control of nuclear weapons over to the military, AEC Chairman David Lilienthal writes: "I had guessed right on the kind of argument that would appeal to him in his present frame of mind, and his sanguine temperament."[1]

---

1. Lilienthal, *Journals*, p. 595.

Other arguments designed to influence particular participants must be made privately and usually orally. Possibly arguments designed to convince one organization that a proposal is in its organizational interest will turn off other participants, and hence such arguments will be made privately and directly to the organization concerned. There is the fear that arguments which relate to domestic interests will be leaked to the press in an effort to undermine a proposal by showing that it is being put forward only for domestic political purposes.

Those who are exposed to arguments frequently support a recommended decision without accepting the reasoning with which it is put forward. In many cases they see no purpose in explaining their own motivations. Organizational calculations are best kept within the organization. Highly technical considerations are meaningful to some participants, unimportant to others. Senior participants and the President are likely to be concerned with very generalized kinds of national security arguments and (discreetly) with domestic political considerations rather than with the arguments put forward in memoranda. Thus gaps frequently develop between the arguments which the writer and the reader each find persuasive and those which appear in the memorandum proposing a decision.

Despite the fact that arguments put forward may bear very little relation to the motives of either those advocating a policy change or the senior participants who make the decision, such arguments may take on a life of their own. Frequently they are incorporated into presentations made to congressional leaders and into public statements used to justify a policy.

Purposes of Arguments

The arguments accompanying a proposal through the bureaucracy serve a number of different purposes in addition to attempting to persuade other participants that the proposed course of action is indeed in the national interest. To indicate that policy arguments may have one or another of these purposes is not to prejudge the intellectual merits of the arguments or their soundness in terms of policy analysis. Five such purposes may be noted.

1. *To fill in the blank.* The rules of the game require that any proposal to change policy must be accompanied by arguments supporting the change. Participants advocating a change in policy must state *some* argu-

ment in favor of the change even if they do not feel free to state either the reasons that lead them to favor a new policy or those they believe would persuade others in private. Participants wish to avoid arguments that could be used against them in other situations. Consequently they sometimes employ standard arguments, referred to as "boiler-plate" in the bureaucracy. These arguments are simply stated and exploit widely shared values and images. For example, the boiler-plate artist might write, "This action is necessary to stop the spread of Communism."

2. *To demonstrate that there is a national security argument.* Senior players are likely to be more reluctant to support a proposal solely for organizational, personal, or domestic reasons. They must be persuaded that such a stand is also in the interest of the country. Thus one purpose of arguments is to demonstrate to these players that something that they wish to support for other reasons can be supported on national interest grounds. The national interest arguments need not be totally persuasive or irrefutable; they simply must demonstrate that it is possible to support a certain outcome on national interests grounds.

For example, the service secretaries are under tremendous pressure to support the most highly valued proposals of their service. A Secretary of the Air Force who opposed the construction of a new manned strategic bomber would find it very difficult to get the cooperation of his uniformed officers on other issues. Hence he would like to support a manned bomber, but he would be reluctant to do so unless he could be persuaded that a case could be made for its serving the national interest. Air Force officers would thus put forward to him such arguments as could be made with reference to the national interest and could be advanced by him before congressional committees and the Secretary of Defense. Only if he can be persuaded that such arguments are respectable will he be in a position to support the proposal.

3. *To signal policy preferences.* Some arguments simply predict the consequences of changes in policy or patterns of action without making a specific recommendation. Arguments relating only to consequences will be used by participants to signal policy preferences, and those who hear arguments relating to consequences will read policy preferences into them.

This function of arguments is particularly important to the intelligence community, which, under the rules of the game, is limited to predicting consequences of alternate policies and is not permitted to recommend policies. Thus the only way members of the intelligence community can signal what policy they think should be adopted is by shaping the arguments about policy consequences to make clear what they think should be done.

Other participants also find that their policy views are read into their predictions of consequences, and they choose their words accordingly. Karl Rankin, the American ambassador to Nationalist China during the 1950s, explains why he felt it necessary to exaggerate his arguments in order to accomplish his objectives:

Some of these excerpts may sound unwarrantedly alarming or seem to support unduly the side of Nationalist China. This was done deliberately, for my pervading purpose was to assist those in Washington who shared my own sense of urgency about China and the Far East in general and who believed that a positive and active American strategy was indispensable. The milder presentation of so grave a situation could have given comfort in quarters favoring disengagement. With American responsibilities so heavy and widespread, I could not place those with whom I agreed in a position to be told, "What are you worrying about? Our man on the spot doesn't seem alarmed."[2]

4. *To signal the degree of concern.* Participants, including the President, not only weigh the arguments but also take note of who makes them and how strongly the various parties feel. The arguments used are a way of indicating how strongly a participant feels about a proposed outcome. To say, for example, that a proposal is on balance probably not worth the risk signals a certain attitude; to say that the action suggested would gravely threaten the national interest signals quite a different attitude. Participants, recognizing that others will read into arguments the intensity of commitment, will tailor their presentation appropriately.

5. *To report a consensus.* When participants agree on a desired outcome, they wish to appear to agree also on the reasons why the outcome is desirable. Senior participants are more likely to be persuaded to support the change in policy if they believe that there is agreement all down the line. Thus participants seek to draft arguments to which all can subscribe. Because other participants will be gauging concern, such arguments must represent a "highest common denominator"—that is, they must reflect not only consensus but the seriousness with which each of the participants feels that a change in policy is either necessary or dangerous. The pres-

2. Rankin, *China Assignment*, pp. vii–viii.

sures to formulate statements to which all can subscribe frequently lead to the use of broad generalizations as arguments.

Constraints on Information and Arguments

In their efforts to influence others, participants are constrained by: (1) the procedures through which organizations gather and report information, (2) the need to protect numerous long-run interests which may outweigh current issues, (3) the need to defer to experts within the government, and (4) shared images. Each of these constraints is discussed in turn.

Organizational Procedures and Programs

Most of the information and options laid before senior participants is prepared by large organizations such as the Central Intelligence Agency, the Joint Staff and the military services, and the State Department and Foreign Service bureaucracy. Key information may be gathered by a number of different agencies and individuals, some of them located in Washington and some overseas. In order for information to be gathered about many countries and a variety of different issues by a number of different people in several large organizations, it is necessary to adopt standard operating procedures for gathering and transmitting it. Graham Allison has commented on the delay, loss of detail, and filtering out that occur in the process:

Information does not pass from the tentacle to the top of the organization instantaneously. Facts can be "in the system" without being available to the head of the organization. Information must be winnowed at every step up the organizational hierarchy, since the number of minutes in each day limits the number of bits of information each individual can absorb. It is impossible for men at the top to examine every report from sources in 100 nations (25 of which had as high a priority as Cuba). But those who decide which information their boss shall see rarely see their bosses' problem. Finally, facts that with hindsight are clear signals are frequently indistinguishable from surrounding "noise" before the occurrence.[3]

3. Allison, *Essence of Decision*, p. 120.

In his careful study of the Cuban missile crisis, Allison provides a systematic and detailed explanation of how information was gathered about the possible presence of Soviet missiles in Cuba and the way that information was processed within the various organs of the intelligence community. His description, filled with fascinating details, is worth quoting at length:

... *Information about Soviet missiles in Cuba came to the attention of the President on October 14 rather than three weeks earlier, or a week later, as a consequence of the routines and procedures of the organizations that make up the U.S. intelligence community.* ...

The available record permits a fairly reliable reconstruction of the major features of the organizational behavior that resulted in discovery of the Soviet missiles. Intelligence on activities within Cuba came from four primary sources: shipping intelligence, refugees, agents within Cuba, and U-2 overflights. Intelligence on all ships going to Cuba provided a catalogue of information on the number of Soviet shipments to Cuba (eighty-five by October 3), the character of these ships (size, registry, and the fact that several of the large-hatch lumber ships were used), and the character of their cargoes (transport, electronic, and construction equipment, SAMs, MIGs, patrol boats, and Soviet technicians). Refugees from Cuba brought innumerable distorted reports of Soviet missiles, Chinese soldiers, etc. For 1959—before the Soviet Union had begun sending any arms whatever to Cuba—the CIA file of reports devoted solely to missiles in Cuba was five inches thick. The low reliability of these reports made their collection and processing of marginal value. Nevertheless, a staff of CIA professionals at Opa Locka, Florida, collected, collated, and compared the results of interrogations of refugees—though often with a lag, since refugees numbered in the thousands. Reports from agents in Cuba produced information about the evacuation of Cubans from the port of Mariel and the secrecy that surrounded unloading and transport of equipment (trucks were lowered into the holds, loaded, and hoisted out covered with tarpaulins), a sighting and sketch of the rear profile of a missile on a Cuban highway heading west, and a report of missile activity in the Pinar del Rio province. But this information had to be transferred from sub-agent to master-agent and then to the United States, a procedure that usually meant a lag of ten days between a sighting and arrival of the information in Washington. The U-2 camera recorded the highest quality U.S. intelligence. Photographs taken from a height of fourteen miles allowed analysts to distinguish painted lines on a parking lot, or to recognize a new kind of cannon on the wing of an airplane. U-2s flew over Cuba on August 29, September 5, 17, 26, 29, and October 5 and 7 before the October 14 flight that discovered the missiles. These earlier flights gathered information on SAM sites, coastal defense missile sites, MIGs, missile patrol boats, and IL-28 light bombers.

Intelligence experts in Washington processed information received from these four sources and produced estimates of certain contingencies. Hindsight highlights several bits of evidence in the intelligence system that might have suggested the presence of Soviet missiles in Cuba. Yet the notorious "September estimate" concluded that the Soviet Union would not introduce offensive missiles into Cuba. No U-2 flight was directed over the western end of Cuba between September 5 and October 4. No U-2 flew over the western end of Cuba until the flight that discovered the Soviet missiles on October 14. Can these "failures" be accounted for in organizational terms?

On September 19, when the highest assembly of the American intelligence community, the United States Intelligence Board (USIB), met to consider the question of Cuba, the "system" contained the following information: (1) shipping intelligence about the arrival in Cuba of two large-hatch Soviet lumber ships, the *Omsk* and the *Poltava*, which the intelligence report also noted were riding high in the water; (2) refugee reports of countless sightings of missiles, plus a report that Castro's private pilot, after a night of drinking in Havana, had boasted: "We will fight to the death and perhaps we can win because we have everything, including atomic weapons"; (3) a sighting by a CIA agent of the rear profile of a strategic missile; (4) U-2 photos from flights on August 29 and September 5 and 17, showing the construction of a number of SAM sites and other defensive missiles.

Not all of this information, however, was on the desk of the estimators. . . .

Intelligence about large-hatch ships riding high in the water did not go unremarked. Shipping intelligence experts spelled out the implication: the ships must be carrying "space consuming" cargo. These details were carefully included in the catalogue of intelligence on shipping. For experts alert to the Soviet Union's pressing requirement for ships, however, neither the facts nor the implication carried a special signal. The refugee report of Castro's pilot's remark had been received at Opa Locka along with reams of inaccurate and even deliberately false reports spread by the refugee community. That report and a thousand others had to be checked and compared before being sent to Washington. The two weeks required for initial processing could have been shortened by a large increase in resources devoted to this source of information. But the yield of this source was already quite marginal, and there was little reason to expect that a change in procedures, reducing transmission time to one week, would be worth the cost. The CIA agent's sighting of the rear profile of a strategic missile had occurred on September 12; transmission time from agent sighting to arrival of the report in Washington typically took nine to twelve days. That report arrived at CIA headquarters on September 21, two days *after* the USIB meeting. Shortening the transmission time would have imposed severe cost in terms of danger to sub-agents, agents, and communication networks.

U-2 flights had produced no hard indication of the presence of offensive missiles. The flight over western Cuba on September 5 revealed SAM installations approaching completion. Then on September 9, a U-2 on "loan" to the Chinese Nationalists was shot down over mainland China. Recalling the outcry that followed the downing of Francis Gary Powers' U-2 over the Soviet Union on May 1, 1960, the intelligence community feared lest this incident trigger an international stage show that could force the abandonment of U-2 flights, eliminating its most reliable source of information. The Committee on Overhead Reconnaissance (COMOR), which approved each U-2 flight pattern, was quickly convened. The State Department pressed arguments about the political consequences if another U-2 should be shot down, for example, over Cuba. As a result, COMOR decided that rather than flying up one side of the island and down the other, future flights should "dip into" Cuban airspace and peer as much as possible from the periphery. COMOR also decided at this meeting that flights should concentrate on the eastern half of Cuba rather than on the western tip, where SAMs were known to be approaching operational readiness.

Given the information available to them on September 19, then, the chiefs of intelligence made a reasonable judgment in predicting that the Soviets would not introduce offensive missiles into Cuba. And the information available to them included everything that they could reasonably expect.[4]

Organizational standard operating procedures influence the relative weight given to items of information that enter the system. For example, in the early stages of the Vietnam War there was a tendency to take

4. Ibid., pp. 118–21.

seriously reports from South Vietnamese officials. The supposition seemed to be that they were trying as hard as American officials were to get accurate information. Almost no one studied the possibility that the South Vietnamese were supplying information which they hoped would lead the United States to do what the government of South Vietnam wanted.[5]

Standard operating procedures tend also to produce a mass of papers unlikely to hold the attention of senior participants or the President, particularly when routine items must compete with reports of individual visitors and the news media. George Kennan explains:

The regular governmental machinery was designed to serve the President and the Secretary of State in two ways: first, as a source of information, stimulus, and recommendation with relation to the exercise of their responsibility, and, secondly, as a channel for the implementation of their decisions.

So far as the first of these purposes is concerned, it is plain that the contribution the regular apparatus is capable of making bears no proper relation to its size and to the enormity of its effort. This is partly the result of the very limited time the senior officials have in which to absorb information and impulses of all sorts brought to them through the regular channels; but it is also partly a consequence of the inferior form in which this information is produced—inferior, that is, from the standpoint of its effectiveness in engaging and impressing the mind of anyone so busy, so overwhelmed with ulterior preoccupations, and so constituted by education and intellect as most presidents and most secretaries of state are apt to be. On countless occasions subordinates have been surprised and disappointed—sometimes even personally hurt—to find that the Secretary or the President has been more decisively influenced by some chance outside contact or experience than by the information and advice offered to him through the regular channels. Either he has talked with someone from outside whose statements seemed somehow simpler and more striking and appealing than anything he had heard from his own subordinates, or the same effect has been produced upon him by some newspaper or magazine article he read or by something he heard on the radio or saw on the newsreels or on television.

There is, admittedly, a real injustice here in most instances. The statements of the fascinating outsider often prove in retrospect to have been less sound and balanced than the final product of official judgment, and

5. John Mecklin, *Mission in Torment*, pp. 100–102.

the items purveyed by the mass media are found to be dangerously over-simplified and inadequate as a basis for official action.

But the regular subordinates are inclined to forget or ignore the deadening effect of the bureaucracy on all forms of communication, oral and written. Whereas the products of the mass media are designed to strike and to hold briefly the attention of busy people, and whereas the statements of the outside visitor are apt to have at least the charm of the expression of a single human mind, with all its directness and freshness, the products of the official machinery are almost invariably dull and pedestrian, drafted or spoken in the usual abominable governmentese, and even, in many instances, intellectually inferior by virtue of the extensive compromising of language which has preceded their final formulation. In short, the busy senior executive frequently finds more useful and meaningful to him the product of the individual mind than the product of a tortured collective effort; and it is only the latter that he gets from his assistants.[6]

Protecting Other Interests

Participants concerned about organizational and personal interests will see the face of an issue which affects these interests. This, in turn, guides their choice of what information to report or not report, since they will be concerned about the impact of the information on these other interests.

Concern with organizational interests inclines participants to refuse to report or to concede facts which might be damaging in another context. This problem can be particularly acute when it involves competing parts of a particular service. Enthoven and Smith, former senior civilian officials in the Office of Systems Analysis in the Pentagon, report that trying to determine the so-called probability of kill (PK) of existing naval anti-submarine warfare (ASW) forces was quite difficult because of the struggle within the Navy between the submarine and surface faction and the aircraft faction. They explain:

Our effort to come up with a convincing analysis of ASW forces, one that everyone would accept and agree upon, failed. It failed, in part, because the U.S. Navy is made up of three competing branches, each proud of its own capabilities and traditions: a submarine Navy, a surface Navy, and an aircraft Navy. The Navy conducted its ASW studies by committee, with representatives from all three branches present. When it came time

6. Kennan, "America's Administrative Response to Its World Problems," pp. 18–19.

to gather assumptions on which to base the PK's of the various Navy forces, each branch competed with the others in overstating performance claims for its own preferred weapon systems. Each feared that if it did not, future studies would show that all or most of the Soviet submarine force was being destroyed by one of the other branches, which might then get more of the total Navy budget. Also, each branch felt obliged, when stating the PK's of its particular weapons, to use the numbers that it had earlier claimed would be achieved when it justified the R&D programs for these weapons. Thus, if a branch did not claim a high effectiveness for its proposed new weapons, it stood in danger of having its R&D budget cut back.

When all these inflated claims for PK's were put together and run through a total-fleet war game, the results were, predictably, that our side won handsomely with the forces already approved by the Secretary of Defense; in fact, we won not only decisively but within a very few weeks. Indeed, it often appeared that we could have won the war quickly enough with even smaller forces. Given the high PK's, it was apparent that the programmed forces were entirely adequate to do the job.[7]

Intelligence officials in the various services and agencies wish to demonstrate that they are doing a good job and that competing organizations in the intelligence field are less effective. This may lead to a determination to downgrade information provided by other agencies. One observer of the State Department has suggested that the career Foreign Service officers tend to "downgrade or ignore some of CIA's more alarming news, particularly if it did not corroborate their own."[8]

Organizations constantly hedge against unforeseen consequences and the possibility that their private estimates are wrong. This concern leads intelligence organizations continually to predict crises, for when a crisis does occur, they can then point out that they predicted it. General Westmoreland, commander of U.S. forces in Vietnam, was reported to have a favorite story which he recited whenever an intelligence officer told him that he, the officer, had accurately predicted a forthcoming enemy move. Westmoreland, visiting a unit badly hit by the Viet Cong, demanded to know why there had been no warning. The unit's intelligence officer asserted that he had predicted an attack for that day. "Yeah, he's right," interjected the weary unit commander, "but he also predicted an attack for ninety-nine straight days before—and nothing happened."[9]

7. Enthoven and Smith, *How Much Is Enough?* pp. 229–30.
8. Simpson, *Anatomy of the State Department*, p. 100.
9. Don Oberdorfer, *Tet!* p. 134.

Operating agencies tend to hedge by asking for larger forces or more autonomy than they believe they need. This may make an operation look much more expensive or much more difficult than they actually believe it to be. Yet hedging of this kind is held down somewhat by the wariness of officials not in the intelligence community about developing a reputation for false predictions. Joseph deRivera puts the point well:

Within the government, the intelligence service places a high cost on failure to report a signal. Since nobody wants to be blamed for an intelligence failure, far too many false leads swamp the information channels at a high level in the State Department and elsewhere. On the other hand, at the Assistant Secretary level, there is a high cost placed on falsely reporting a signal to be present when actually nothing is there. No one wants to bother a Secretary of State or a President with false information. Unfortunately, the result is a filter which may be at the wrong place in the system. While central decision makers have a broader view of world events, persons nearer the source of intelligence might be better judges of the accuracy and importance of information mainly relevant to one nation.[10]

Personal interest can also affect information which officials are prepared to report. Career officials concerned about promotion will be unwilling to report facts that will undercut the stand taken by the organization controlling their promotion. Men appointed to the White House staff find it extremely difficult to bring "bad news" to the President or to take positions that they know go against the President's own desires. George Reedy, who was Lyndon Johnson's press secretary, reports the great difficulty of saying no to a strong President. "You know that nobody is strongminded around a President; let's get that thing established right now. It just doesn't exist. As far as the President is concerned, it is always: 'yes sir,' 'no sir' (the 'no sir' comes when he asks whether you're dissatisfied)...."[11]

Deference to Expertise

One notion which affects the kind of arguments that can be put forward within the American government is the view that one should defer to expertise. In some respects this notion complements the use of standard operating procedures. No one else need bother with a subject or area routinely "covered" by an expert. When a policy move brings the area to

10. DeRivera, *The Psychological Dimension of Foreign Policy*, p. 56.
11. Quoted in R. Gordon Hoxie (ed.), *The White House*, p. 183.

the fore, the expert is relied upon to suggest the means for reaching whatever goal is decided upon. Robert A. Lovett, who served in the State Department and the Defense Department, believed strongly in bureaucratic specialization. As he expressed it:

Civilian and military executives alike should stick to the fields in which they have special training and aptitudes: if they do, the chance of making the machinery work well is excellent. One of the few humans as exasperating as a civilian businessman who suddenly becomes an expert on military strategy and tactics is the military adviser who magically becomes an expert in some highly sophisticated production problem in which he has no background or experience.[12]

Many in-and-outers defer to expertise in the expectation that they will likewise be deferred to in their own specialty. Senior businessmen brought into the Defense Department as management experts have deferred to the military on what they view as strategic questions and to the State Department on political questions, the assumption being that they in turn deserve the last word on business management issues. In-and-outers without any formally defined expertise have tended to be much more skeptical of expert advice and much more willing to challenge it.

Career officials have a very strong tendency to defer to expertise. Their own involvement and influence depend in large part on other officials deferring to their expertise. To challenge the expertise of another career group is to risk retaliation. Thus Foreign Service officers have been extremely reluctant to challenge the military on strategic questions or to challenge Treasury officials on economic matters.[13]

The great difficulty in challenging what is viewed as expert advice can be seen in the debate in the ExCom of the National Security Council during the first week of the Cuban missile crisis over the option of a "surgical strike" against the missile sites being constructed in Cuba. The idea of a surgical strike was appealing to a number of senior civilian officials. They were unwilling to recommend an all-out invasion, but they doubted that a blockade could be effective when the missiles were already in Cuba and undergoing deployment. The military services were thus pressed very hard to come up with a plan for a surgical strike. Their assertion that such a strike was impossible settled the issue, nevertheless, and moved the option off the feasible list. President Kennedy, not completely satisfied

12. Lovett, "Perspective on the Policy Process," p. 81.
13. See, for example, Robert H. Johnson, "The National Security Council," p. 728.

with this information, himself met with the commander of the Tactical Air Command and was assured that a surgical strike was impossible. Dean Acheson, serving as an ad hoc member of ExCom, strongly favored a surgical strike and experienced great frustration in trying to overcome the military judgment that such a strike was infeasible. He was only one of many.[14]

Deference to expert opinion is based on the belief that the calculation and process of reasoning by which experts reach their conclusion is extremely complicated and impenetrable by outsiders. Frequently, however, this belief is erroneous. Expert judgments may be based on simple rules of thumb, standard operating procedures of the organization, compromises among experts determined to present a unanimous report, and in some cases guesswork.

Debate over the surgical air strike illustrates several of these points. The calculations done by the Tactical Air Command and by the Joint Staff were apparently based on the assumption that the Soviet missiles in Cuba were "mobile"—meaning that they could be moved within a few minutes or a few hours. In fact, the Soviet missiles were "movable" only in the sense that in weeks or days they could be moved to a new location and set up again. Once this mistake was discovered after President Kennedy's speech announcing a quarantine of Cuba, the surgical air strike option was put back on the list of feasible options. The Tactical Air Command's original calculation that a surgical strike was not feasible was based also on the standard military doctrine that if one goes after a military target, one goes all out. TAC calculated that in the event of an attack on missile sites the enemy might send bombers and fighters aloft, and thus it would be necessary to simultaneously hit air bases. Since air bases were going to be attacked, tactical air defense sites would have to be hit as well. Moreover, the military planners felt that an invasion would probably have to follow a large air strike. Thus landing sites and other targets of relevance to a landing should be hit in the first place. In brief, the standard operating procedures by which the military gauged the feasibility of a surgical strike were heavily weighted against the kind of operation supposedly being studied.

The limitations of expert advice can be illustrated by examining the basis upon which a distinguished group of scientists set the performance

14. On this episode, see Schlesinger, *A Thousand Days*, p. 827; Theodore Sorensen, *Kennedy*, p. 684; Kennedy, *Thirteen Days*, pp. 48–49; and Allison, *Essence of Decision*, pp. 202–10.

goals of the first-generation American ICBM. These were stated to be "a one-megaton-warhead explosive yield, 5,500 nautical miles range, and five miles or better accuracy." As Herbert York has reported, military officers and others took these goals seriously, and the goals in fact determined the shape and size of the American program.[15] As is usually the case, the assumption was that these numbers could be "derived from complex mathematical formulae connecting explosive yield, damage radius, target vulnerability and other numerically defined quantities." In fact, the reality was quite different. York, who was a member of the missile science committee and served as the chief scientist in the Pentagon, reveals that the criterion of one megaton and the other numbers were picked arbitrarily through a sort of primitive reflex:

So, why 1.0 megaton? The answer is because and only because one million is a particularly round number in our culture. We picked a one-megaton yield for the Atlas warhead for the same reason that everyone speaks of rich men as being millionaires and never as being tenmillionaires or one-hundred-thousandaires. It really was that mystical, and I was one of the mystics. Thus, the actual physical size of the first Atlas warhead and the number of people it would kill were determined by the fact that human beings have two hands with five fingers each and therefore count by tens.

What if we had had six fingers on each hand and therefore counted by twelves instead of tens? As any school child who takes modern math knows, the number one-million in base twelve is fully three times as big as the number one-million in base ten. Thus, if evolution had given us six fingers on each hand, our first ICBM warhead would have had to be three times as big, the rockets to deliver them would have threatened the lives of up to three times as many human beings, and it would have taken one or two years longer to carry out their development program. Similarly, if we had had only four fingers, like some comic-strip characters, the first warheads and missiles would have been only one-fourth as large, we could have built them somewhat sooner, and the present overkill problem would not be nearly as serious as it is. The only funny thing about this story is that it is true. It really was that arbitrary, and what's more, that same arbitrariness has stayed with us.[16]

The other two numbers were almost equally arbitrary. The 5,500 nautical miles simply made the target area equal to one quarter of the earth's

15. On this episode, see York, *Race to Oblivion*, pp. 88–90.
16. Ibid., pp. 89–90.

surface, and the five miles or better accuracy was a compromise between those who believed that one could do much better and those who thought that five miles would be doing well. It was thus simply "a conservative estimate."

The reluctance of policymakers to go behind the numbers in analyses produced by experts can be found not only in military and scientific affairs but sometimes also in the case of "information" put forth by the intelligence community. David Lilienthal recorded in his journals his amazement at discovering the process by which estimates were made about when the Soviet Union would have atomic weapons:

The thing that rather chills one's blood is to observe what is nothing less than lack of integrity in the way the intelligence agencies deal with the meager stuff they have. It is chiefly a matter of reasoning from our own American experience, guessing from that how much longer it will take Russia using our methods and based upon our own problems of achieving weapons. But when this is put into a report, the reader, e.g., Congressional committee, is given the impression, and deliberately, that behind the estimates lies specific knowledge, knowledge so important and delicate that its nature and sources cannot be disclosed or hinted at.[17]

Expert advice is likely to be challenged only when the policy conclusions which derive from it are strongly inconsistent with the interests of participants in the policy process. Then standard maneuvers come into play. One way to challenge expert advice is to argue that there is an overlapping body of expert opinion which renders invalid the judgment of the particular experts being challenged. Thus military judgments about the proper size of the defense budget are undercut by advice from economists and bankers that the proposed expenditures would bankrupt the government and thus play into the hands of the Kremlin. In other cases, advocates of a certain policy charge that the experts have exceeded the bounds of their expertise. For example, military men often argue that scientific advice has gone beyond the realm of science into military questions. When experts disagree, then one is of course free to choose that advice which most fits with the stand that one has developed.

Shared Images

By definition, most participants share the images dominant within the government at any one time. However, even those who do not will be

---

17. Lilienthal, *Journals*, p. 376.

constrained by their knowledge that the shared images influence others, and this will affect the kind of arguments which are put forward.

Participants will have considerable difficulty getting the ordinary administrator or politician to believe facts that go against the shared images. Officials react as all individuals do to evidence which goes against strongly held beliefs. They either ignore the evidence or reinterpret it so as to change what it seems to mean.

This problem affected American perceptions of what the Soviet Union was up to in Cuba prior to the outbreak of the Cuban missile crisis. There was a widely shared view, held by the Russia experts in the Central Intelligence Agency, the State Department, and elsewhere, that the Soviet Union would never ship nuclear weapons or nuclear delivery systems beyond its borders. To the best of the knowledge of American officials at the time, the Soviet Union had never done so, even to East European countries contiguous with the Soviet Union. The shipment of missiles and nuclear warheads abroad meant running the risk that they would be taken over by unfriendly forces. In view of the Russian government's known caution about dispersing nuclear weapons and the emphasis on maintaining tight command and control over weapons even in the Soviet Union, it seemed wildly implausible to these experts that the Soviet Union would ship missiles and weapons across the seas to Cuba, where they would be particularly vulnerable to an American effort to capture them. Thus evidence that the Soviet Union was installing missiles in Cuba tended to be ignored. John McCone, then the Director of Central Intelligence, did not have an extensive background in studying Soviet behavior and did not himself subscribe to the notion that the Soviet Union was extremely cautious in the dispersal of nuclear weapons. Hence McCone, looking at the evidence, saw a pattern and came to believe that the Soviet Union was in fact in the process of installing missiles in Cuba. However, he was unable to convince anyone else that this was indeed the case.[18]

Participants learn that it is not productive to put forward a proposal or to take a stand in such a way that acceptance depends on rejecting shared images. For example, to reinforce his argument against an invasion or other military action against Cuba in the opening days of the debate within the government about how to react to the Russian missiles on the island, Secretary of Defense McNamara at first suggested that it simply did not matter that the Soviet Union was putting missiles into Cuba. He asserted that "a missile is a missile" and that the Russians could threaten

18. On this point, see Roberta Wohlstetter, *Cuba and Pearl Harbor.*

the United States as effectively from the Soviet Union. This assertion went against the widely shared belief that the establishment of a military base by a hostile outside power in Latin America, especially in the Caribbean, posed a vital threat to the security of the United States, and it met with instant and firm rebuttal. McNamara quickly recognized that the argument he was presenting went against the national security images held by the great majority of the group and thus ran the risk of undercutting his entire credibility as an opponent of the invasion being proposed by Dean Acheson and others. He switched without delay to a different set of arguments.[19]

Participants seem to believe that their influence and even their continuation in office depends on their endorsement or seeming endorsement of shared images. Even men who appear invulnerable to opposition zealously guard their reputations for accepting shared images. Arthur Larson reports, for example, Eisenhower's great concern when he was accused by Averell Harriman of being "soft on communism" during the 1956 presidential campaign. "The President jumped up from his chair, strode across the room, pulled down a copy of *Crusade in Europe*, and read me several strong passages about the threat of international communism and the need to be constantly on guard against the potential aggressiveness of the Russians." Larson reports his surprise that Eisenhower felt the need to do this, "as if he had to defend himself from this unpalatable charge."[20] In such a climate, participants less firmly entrenched positively bend over backwards to show that they support the shared images, particularly those with strong support within the society as well as the government. A number of observers suggest that officials felt the need to go along with the use of military power in Vietnam because of the danger that they would otherwise appear to be rejecting the shared image that the United States had to assume the burden of "world responsibility" and hence be willing to use power to oppose "international communism."[21]

Although fears about nonconformity may be exaggerated and are perhaps self-fulfilling, they are not groundless. John Kenneth Galbraith maintains with good reason that his ability to influence Vietnam policy was substantially reduced by the fact that he was largely recognized as not sharing the belief that the United States had to be willing to use military

19. See Elie Abel, *The Missile Crisis*, p. 51.

20. Larson, *Eisenhower*, p. 81.

21. See, for example, Thomson, "How Could Vietnam Happen?" p. 207; Kalb and Abel, *Roots of Involvement*, pp. 122–33.

force against international communism. He confided to his diary in 1961 that McGeorge Bundy "thinks there is no occasion when I would urge the use of force. I have to admit that my enthusiasm for it is always very low."[22] Similarly, when George W. Ball, the Under Secretary of State, in 1964 warned his close colleagues against an escalation of U.S. involvement in Vietnam, his challenge appears to have been considered more as the interesting view of a skeptic than as a viable option to escalation.[23] President Kennedy himself had been largely responsible for sanctifying the widely held belief that the United States had to use force against local insurgency because behind it lay international communism. Having established the doctrine that native guerrilla movements backed by Russia and China were now the threat which had to be opposed by military force, he created a situation in which other officials felt pressure to indicate their support for this doctrine. As students of this period, Kalb and Abel conclude that "if a high official expressed skepticism about the significance or newness ascribed to this style of warfare, it was said, he risked shortening his tenure in office. McNamara, Taylor, and Rostow became early converts, and their White House standing soared."[24]

As a result of the conditions, lessons, and fears discussed here, a disingenuous style of argument prevails. It can become more complicated and more wearing than the substantive issues themselves.

1. Participants shape arguments in terms of the shared images of the society and the government even if they do not believe that those images are an accurate reflection of the world.

Galbraith, for example, attempting to keep himself involved in the Vietnam debate, argued that his proposals for diplomatic and economic moves would be more effective in preventing the spread of communism than proposals for the use of military force. He presented these arguments despite the fact that he did not really believe that there was much danger of the spread of communism or that increased Communist influence in Indochina would threaten American security interests anyway.

2. Since participants seldom challenge shared images, regardless of their ultimate policy position, the President is rarely exposed to fresh and provocative arguments.

In the ABM debate, for instance, President Johnson was not con-

---

22. Galbraith, *Ambassador's Journal*, p. 243.
23. Ball, "Top Secret: The Prophecy the President Rejected," pp. 36–49. This article is a reproduction of a memorandum written by Ball on October 5, 1964.
24. Kalb and Abel, *Roots of Involvement*, p. 124.

fronted with the argument that simple numerical nuclear superiority was irrelevant, that the United States did not need any sort of an ABM system no matter what the Russians might do. In opposing the ABM, McNamara did not challenge the conventional notion of American superiority. He merely attempted to show that the ABM might increase the probability of nuclear war without saving any American lives.

3. If participants believe that taking a certain stand which they think wise will be interpreted as deviation from shared images, they will take the opposite stand for fear of losing influence or indeed their position in the government.

Arthur Schlesinger, Jr., suggests that this was in fact part of the motivation for the failure of State Department officials to oppose the Bay of Pigs invasion despite their anticipation of its disastrous international consequences. "I could not help feeling," he writes, "that the desire to prove to the CIA and the Joint Chiefs that they were not soft-headed idealists but were really tough guys, too, influenced State's representatives at the cabinet table."[25]

George Ball related a similar episode which occurred during his tenure as Under Secretary of State. In early 1965, Ball found himself Acting Secretary when the decision was being made to begin the bombing of North Vietnam. He recognized that the other participants believed that the United States needed to prevent South Vietnam from being ruled by a Communist government and could do so by using force against North Vietnam. To oppose the decision to begin the bombing, was, Ball believed, to sacrifice all future influence on the Vietnam issue. Thus he supported the initiation of bombing, as he explained it later to a television questioner.[26]

4. In some cases, a devil's advocate is designated, or will emerge, who is known not to accept the shared images which shape a policy or at least agrees to act as if he does not accept it. George Reedy, who served in the Johnson White House, explains this phenomenon of token opposition:

Of course, within these councils there was always at least one "devil's advocate." But an official dissenter always starts with half his battle lost. It is assumed that he is bringing up arguments solely because arguing is his official role. It is well understood that he is not going to press his points harshly or stridently. Therefore, his objections and cautions are discounted

25. Schlesinger, A *Thousand Days*, p. 256.
26. Ball, "Vietnam Hindsight."

before they are delivered. They are actually welcomed because they prove for the record that decision was preceded by controversy.[27]

George Ball, although not pressing his dissent from the set of images guiding Vietnam policy, was soon cast into this role, according to an account written by James Thomson:

Once Mr. Ball began to express doubts, he was warmly institutionalized: he was encouraged to become the inhouse devil's advocate on Vietnam. The upshot was inevitable: the process of escalation allowed for periodic requests to Mr. Ball to speak his piece; Ball felt good, I assume (he had fought for righteousness); the others felt good (they had given a full hearing to the dovish option); and there was minimal unpleasantness. The club remained intact; and it is of course possible that matters would have gotten worse faster if Mr. Ball had kept silent, or left before his final departure in the fall of 1966.[28]

Challenging Shared Images

As we saw in Chapter 2, sometimes changes in personnel or changes in perceptions of reality either at home or abroad lead to changes in shared images without any participant deliberately setting about to create a change. Even without change of that sort, it happens on occasion that a few audacious participants tire of framing every argument in terms of some well-worn orthodoxy. Certain officials conclude that they can get the decisions they want from the government by changing the set of images on which the government operates. If they feel that they have built up a sufficient line of credibility as reputable and reasonable participants in the policy process, they may launch a deliberate effort to change interpretations of reality. One such episode occurred in late 1949 and the first months of 1950. It involved an effort to convince American officials that the serious military threat from the Soviet bloc required a major buildup in American military forces. In order to bring about a substantial increase in military spending, it was necessary also to destroy the conviction that the United States could not afford to spend more than $15 billion a year on defense. President Truman was persuaded to appoint a special committee within the National Security Council system to ex-

27. Reedy, *The Twilight of the Presidency*, p. 11.
28. Thomson, "How Could Vietnam Happen?" p. 201.

amine threats to the United States in light of the changing international environment and to recommend what action needed to be taken. The committee worked slowly to form a consensus within the government. Its members made a deliberate decision to exaggerate possible dangers so that officials who discounted such documents would still feel sufficient concern to accept a change. Economic officials, particularly those on the Council of Economic Advisers, were recruited to counteract the notion that the United States could not afford to increase military spending. As Dean Acheson later explained:

The purpose of NSC-68 was to so bludgeon the mass mind of "top government" that not only could the President make a decision but that the decision could be carried out. Even so, it is doubtful whether anything like what happened in the next few years could have been done had not the Russians been stupid enough to have instigated the attack against South Korea and opened the "hate America" campaign.[29]

A similar effort was made by Robert McNamara in seeking to prevent deployment of an American ballistic missile defense system. McNamara recognized that the prevailing set of images within the American government stressed the importance to the United States of maintaining strategic superiority over the Soviet Union. This superiority was believed to be important politically to the United States, giving it political advantage in diplomatic dealings and in crisis bargainings with the Soviet Union. Superiority was seen as requiring an American countermove to any Soviet military system and the American matching of any Soviet deployment. Thus an ABM system was thought to be necessary because the Soviet Union had such a system and because the Russians were building a large fleet of intercontinental ballistic missiles and the United States needed a defense against such an attack. McNamara, both in his public statements and within the government, sought a fundamental change in the images which guided thoughts about nuclear weapons. Though he had hesitated to challenge the standard images in the Cuban missile crisis, by 1967 he was arguing openly that the concept of nuclear superiority was essentially meaningless. If both sides have the capability to destroy each other, the only benefit that one can get from nuclear weapons is to deter a nuclear attack. He argued that it was useless to try to defend against Russian missiles, for the Russians could easily build additional missiles fully offsetting the value of the defense. Finally, he argued that the United States

29. Acheson, *Present at the Creation*, p. 374. See also Hammond, "NSC-68."

did not need to match every Soviet deployment. If the Russians were wasting money on an ineffective ABM system, it did not mean that the Americans needed to do so as well. However, at the same time he was putting forward these arguments McNamara recognized that the prevailing sentiment in favor of superiority was so comforting to so many people that he would lose his case if it rested solely on the spuriousness of the concept. Thus he compromised by arguing that the United States was maintaining its "superiority" with the multiple, separately controllable warheads known as MIRVs.

Although McNamara ultimately lost the battle and an ABM deployment went forward, his arguments triggered a reassessment of strategic doctrine. The changes in images which he sought came to fruition in the early years of the Nixon administration, leading to President Nixon's espousal of the doctrine of nuclear sufficiency and his specific assertion that the United States would not seek to counter Soviet offensive and defensive moves in a way that might threaten the Soviet deterrent.

With this example, it is time to pass on to another facet of information. Assembling information to prove that what one wants to do is required by the national interest in light of shared images is only one aspect of the problem. The second is getting this information to the right people and keeping "misleading information" away from them. That sort of maneuvering is described in the next chapter.

CHAPTER NINE

Maneuvers To Affect Information

A great deal of the information that reaches the President and other senior participants has been selected because it confirms the position of the officials who report it. Higher-ups in turn may digest the information at their disposal in such a way as to support a given policy line, or they may seek to "recover" facts that have been filtered out. In this chapter we focus on maneuvers commonly used at all levels to affect information in favor of a given decision.

Selective Information

1. *Report only those facts that support the stand you are taking.* For any complicated foreign policy issue there are a very large number of facts that might be relevant to a judgment on what should be done. A participant favoring a particular stand can and frequently does choose among facts, reporting those that back up his position and ignoring those that do not. Harlan Cleveland, who was the U.S. ambassador to NATO, reports how the issue of whether or not the United States could rely on a conventional defense was affected by the selective reporting of information. One example he cites had to do with the aircraft capabilities of the NATO powers versus the Warsaw Pact forces:

Similarly in air power, it is not just how many aircraft each side has on hand, but how good they are, how accurate are their maintenance crews, how well trained are their pilots, how sophisticated are the air defenses they have to penetrate, what stocks of ammunition are within easy reach, what reserves and replacements are quickly available, how vulnerable are the airfields they propose to use, and above all how the commanders and pilots rate themselves and their opposition. If an F-4 Phantom is likely to shoot down three or four MiG-21s before it gets hit—or, what is less likely, vice versa—what does it mean to compare the numbers of strike/attack aircraft?

Yet sober and honest officers will tell you the Warsaw Pact has twice as many first-line planes as NATO and forget to mention that most of the discrepancy is in air defense, not in strike/attack aircraft. They will describe the Warsaw Pact "threat" to the central front as more than a million men, against perhaps three-quarters of a million for NATO, without reminding you of the War College dictum that the attacker needs two or three times as many men as the defender. (This conventional wisdom applies to conventional war; nobody knows about nuclear war.) They will speak of NATO manpower without explaining that the Western allies have committed to NATO varying proportions of their men under arms; some of those armed but uncommitted men, ranging from one-fifth to four-fifths of national totals, would surely be available in a real pinch.[1]

2. *Structure reporting of information so that senior participants will see what you want them to see and not other information.* The quantity of intelligence information produced in the American government each day is overwhelming. Cables arrive from a hundred nations, field reports are sent in by military commands throughout the world, intelligence units in Washington produce long reports. Some of this information, such as the CIA daily report for the President and the State Department summary of major cables, almost inevitably reaches the President. Other information such as pouched reports from embassies about economic and social conditions are unlikely to reach any senior participants at all. Thus a participant can select information which is likely to reach the President by putting it into channels which will assure getting it to the top. Other information can be reported in more routine ways that almost guarantees that it will not surface before senior participants. Thus one can hedge against the charge of being accused of not reporting particular information while structuring that which does reach senior participants.

According to an official then serving in the Defense Intelligence Agency in the Pentagon, this technique was used by the U.S. military commanders in Vietnam to signal either optimism or pessimism:

From 1964–65, when U.S. involvement in Vietnam began to be considerable, until late 1966 or early 1967, the generals in Saigon worked to build up U.S. troop strength. Therefore, they wanted every bit of evidence brought to the fore that could show that infiltration was increasing. DIA

1. Cleveland, *NATO*, p. 85.

obliged and also emphasized in all reports the enemy's capability to recruit forces from the South Vietnamese population. In 1967 a second period began. The high priests of Saigon decided that we were "winning." Then the paramount interest became to show the enemy's reduced capability to recruit and a slowdown in infiltration due to our bombing. The tune and emphasis of reports from the field changed radically, and so did those put out by DIA.

It should not be concluded that anyone suppressed evidence. No one did. The military in Saigon sent all the facts back to Washington eventually. During the buildup period, infiltration data and recruitment data came in via General Westmoreland's daily cablegram. Data from field contact with enemy units came amid the more mundane cables or by courier up to five weeks later. Cables from Westmoreland, of course, were given higher priority in Washington. When we started "winning," detailed reports highlighting "body counts" and statistics on how many villages were pacified were cabled with Westmoreland's signature; recruitment studies were pouched or cabled with the reports on the fluctuating price of rice. It was all a matter of emphasis.[2]

3. *Do not report facts which show danger.* The experts in charge of a program or an operation are frequently the only ones knowledgeable enough to report the dangers and difficulties inherent in an operation. If they are pressing for an approval of a weapons system or an operation, they may well be reluctant to gratuitously inform top leaders of dangers which those leaders would otherwise not be aware of. President Eisenhower's discussion of the U-2 flights over the Soviet Union, for example, suggests that he was not informed of the increasing concern that Soviet missiles would be able to bring down a high-flying intruder in the relatively near future.[3]

In the case of the Bay of Pigs, President Kennedy was informed that if the landing failed to establish a beachhead, the invading forces would move to the nearby mountains. No mention was made of the fact that there was a virtually impassable swamp between the landing site and the mountain sanctuary.[4]

4. *Prepare a careful and detailed study to present facts in what appears*

2. McGarvey, "The Culture of Bureaucracy," pp. 71–72.

3. Compare the account in Eisenhower's *Waging Peace*, pp. 544–59, with the discussion in Francis Gary Powers' *Operation Overflight*, p. 353.

4. Schlesinger, *A Thousand Days*, p. 293; Haynes Johnson, *The Bay of Pigs*, pp. 68–69, 224; Theodore Sorensen, *Kennedy*, p. 302.

to be an authoritative manner and to discover new facts which may bolster your position. Participants conduct within their own organization a detailed study of a proposed decision. In most cases they do so knowing in advance which position they support and seeking to enhance the credibility of that position by presenting in a formal and detailed manner the results of a study based on extensive expertise and careful analysis.

General Matthew Ridgway reports, for example, that in his efforts to prevent a decision by the Eisenhower administration to intervene in Indochina in 1954 he had the Army Staff prepare a detailed study based on the trips to the field and an analysis of requirements for intervention. Ridgway indicates that this study enabled him to be somewhat more persuasive with the President in arguing against allied intervention to save the French in Indochina.[5]

5. *Request a study from those who will give you the desired conclusions.* In many cases it is much more effective to ask for a study from an ostensibly impartial or external body, knowing in advance that it will produce facts to support your stand. The United States intelligence community has a procedure to produce what is known as a National Intelligence Estimate (NIE) or a Special National Intelligence Estimate (SNIE). The estimates are produced in crisis situations or in case of unexpected developments to evaluate possible American courses of action. In some cases officials impartially request such studies. Often, however, there is a debate within the government about whether an SNIE should be requested, whether it is appropriate in the given circumstances. Frequently those arguing in favor of an SNIE have reason to believe that the Intelligence Board which approves such estimates will take a position favorable to the stand they are advocating, whereas those arguing against have reason to doubt that they will be supported by the intelligence community. For example, those who believed that the United States was not doing well in Vietnam and who favored a retrenchment argued in 1968 that the intelligence community should be asked to prepare an SNIE on the pacification program. They knew that those who would be responsible for drafting the estimate believed that the pacification program was not going well. Officials who felt on the contrary that such pessimistic information would hurt *their* position argued that pacification was an allied program and hence should be evaluated by the operators in the field and not by the intelligence community. In the closing days of the Johnson ad-

---

5. Ridgway, *Soldier*, pp. 276–78.

ministration an SNIE was finally produced, and it took the pessimistic position that those seeking such an estimate believed that it would.

Authoritative advice can also be sought from an ad hoc group of presidential advisers or from a formal presidential commission. In some cases the President himself will use this device to build support within his administration and within Congress for a desired program. For example, President Eisenhower, desiring a new trade policy for the United States, appointed a carefully selected commission under Clarence Randall, who had recently retired as chairman of Inland Steel Company. Sherman Adams, Eisenhower's principal assistant, explains that Randall was selected not because anyone wished to know whether free trade was a good idea but because Randall was likely to be effective in advocating free trade. "Randall's position as a capitalist was unassailable," Adams writes. "He was also a brilliantly intelligent man who had traveled widely around the world and shared Eisenhower's convictions about the need for free trade as a peace weapon. He had remarkable ability in an argument to explain a complex proposition with clear simplicity and to stick to a position with calm control."[6]

When the President's mind is not made up, one or more of his advisers may recommend a convening of a presidential panel in hopes that its recommendation will persuade him in the desired direction. Thus during March of 1968 in an effort to get President Johnson to cut back on the U.S. involvement in Vietnam, Secretary of Defense Clark Clifford proposed that a panel of the "Wise Men" be convened. This was a group Johnson had consulted from time to time on Vietnam, and Clifford had reason to believe that the group had moved substantially from the hawkish position that it had reported to the President some months before. After convening and listening to government briefings, the group did urge the President to "de-escalate." (In this case, LBJ said later, he discounted their views because they were based on the mood of pessimism in the United States rather than the detailed reports the President was receiving from the field.)[7]

In other situations advisory committees may be appointed at lower levels within the departments in the hopes that their prestigious conclusions will serve to influence the President and his principal counselors. For example, in an effort to get the strategic missile program moving over the opposition of the Air Force (which was more concerned with bombers),

6. Adams, *Firsthand Report*, p. 383.
7. Lyndon Johnson, *The Vantage Point*, pp. 409, 416–18, 422.

the civilian director of the program in the Pentagon, Trevor Gardner, created a Strategic Missiles Evaluation Group whose members were appointed on the basis of their commitment to ICBMs and their influence with senior officials.[8]

6. *Keep away from senior participants those who might report facts one wishes to have suppressed.* White House officials are sometimes able to control a briefing presented to the President, and they use this power to keep out undesirable information. In other cases participants maneuver to keep out of the process individuals who are likely to report information contrary to what they wish to have presented to the President. Thus in the case of the Bay of Pigs both the State Department Bureau of Intelligence and Research and the CIA's Intelligence Branch were not informed of the impending invasion and were thus unable to report to the President their own view that an invasion was unlikely to spark the uprising in Cuba which the operations branch of the CIA was promising.

7. *Expose participants informally to those who hold correct views.* Maneuvers may also be planned to see to it that senior participants are exposed to the views of those who speak authoritatively for the favored position from a different frame of reference. President Eisenhower, for example, was reported to be anxious to have all the Joint Chiefs attend National Security Council meetings because he had also invited his Secretary of the Treasury George Humphrey. Eisenhower believed that Humphrey might be effective in convincing the Joint Chiefs that the fiscal requirements of the nation meant that the military spending had to be reduced.[9]

George Kennan reports an elaborate plot on the part of Kennedy to have him in attendance at the White House when some senior congressmen were present so that the President could casually introduce Kennan to them and have him explain his position on aid to Yugoslavia.[10]

8. *Get other governments to report facts which you believe will be valuable.* Officials seeking to convince the President that the facts which they have reported are correct may seek to get a foreign government to convey the same information to the United States. Proponents of the MLF, for example, used this technique to counter doubts about the intensity with which governments in Europe favored the American plan for a multilateral nuclear force. They persuaded a number of foreign officials

8. Armacost, *The Politics of Weapons Innovation,* p. 57.
9. Snyder, "The 'New Look' of 1953."
10. Kennan, Kennedy Library Oral History Interview, p. 79.

to express support for the proposal.[11] In other cases an effort may be made to get foreign governments to share in evaluation of a situation in a third country.

9. *Advise other participants on what to say.* When they recognize that other senior participants are looking to a particular official or organization for authoritative judgment on a question, participants will attempt to get that official or organization to say the right thing. If one is not certain that the other participant shares one's stand, the effort may be subtle. For example, in the case of the 1965 U.S. intervention in the Dominican Republic, the acting U.S. ambassador, W. Tapley Bennett, received strong hints from Washington that it would like him to report that "a rebel victory would probably lead to a pro-Communist government." The hints were conveyed to Bennett by Secretary of State Rusk and Secretary of Defense McNamara, who both asked him by telephone if he did not agree with this judgment which had been reached in Washington. Bennett, who favored intervention to put a pro-American government in power, was quick to pick up the clue and report that there was danger of Communists coming to power.[12]

In some cases, career officials may have to be bludgeoned into presenting the desired information by reminding them that their parent organization controls their promotion. A former DIA official recalls how General Westmoreland and other officers were able to influence the estimates prepared by the Defense Intelligence Agency, their leverage being the control the armed services wielded over their representatives in the agency. According to this official:

In one instance the Air Force Chief of Intelligence called my boss at DIA about a nearly completed estimate on U.S. bombing in Laos. He told him that he was sending a team down to change the wording of the estimate and that my boss had better remember what color his uniform was. Of course it was the same as the General's blue. The team arrived, and, over the protests of the DIA analysts, a compromise was reached.

The classic example of command influence on intelligence matters occurred just after the Tet Offensive in January, 1968. In the early weeks of February the JCS insisted that the offensive was total military defeat for the enemy—General Westmoreland told them so in his daily cables. DIA didn't agree with this interpretation, but it watered down every paper it

11. Steinbruner, *Decisions under Complexity.*

12. John B. Martin, *Overtaken by Events: The Dominican Crises from the Fall of Trujillo to the Civil War*, p. 659.

wrote on this subject so that its position was impossible to determine. Then General Wheeler went to Saigon and came back with Westmoreland's request for 206,000 troops to "clean up" the "defeated" enemy. Suddenly it was legitimate to say that the Tet Offensive had really "set us back." Everybody on the service staffs, with DIA leading the pack, started writing gloomy estimates with unaccustomed forthrightness and clarity.[13]

10. *Circumvent formal channels.* So-called "back channel" messages are an effective way to tell an already committed participant what line to take. Military and Foreign Service officials in Washington often send private messages to the field so that officials there will know the best way to answer questions put to them from Washington. Roger Hilsman reports one such episode. At an NSC meeting it was decided to pose a series of questions to General Paul D. Harkins, then the U.S. commander in Vietnam. A back channel Pentagon message advised Harkins as to the most effective answers to the questions. In this case President Kennedy and State Department officials discovered the maneuver, but often it goes undetected.[14]

In some cases the problem is not to get recognized officials to say what one desires but rather to get information to the President and other senior participants which one cannot move through formal channels. If members of the intelligence community refuse to accept information developed at lower levels within their organizations or if Cabinet officers are reluctant to bring information to the attention of the President, it may still come to him informally, often through members of the White House staff. Arthur Larson, who served on Eisenhower's staff, reports that Foreign Service officers unable to get information past their ambassadors into Washington would often send him frantic appeals, such as one from an American official in a Southeast Asian country which said, "For God sakes, tell John Foster Dulles that Ambassador X is backing the wrong horse here and that the situation is about to blow up!"[15]

The armed services frequently use military assistants in the White House to get information informally to the President. Dean Acheson described an episode when he was Secretary of State in which information from the President's naval attaché went directly to President Truman, who in turn raised the matter with British Foreign Secretary Anthony Eden:

After dinner the President and Prime Minister withdrew to the aft

13. McGarvey, "The Culture of Bureaucracy," p. 73.
14. Hilsman, *To Move a Nation*, pp. 492–93.
15. Larson, *Eisenhower*, p. 19.

saloon while the table was being cleared, in a few minutes sending for Mr. Eden and me. The President opened by a complaint that I instantly recognized as coming from a persistent and infuriating practice of the Navy. Through his naval aide the President would be given what was known in the trade as "raw intelligence," reports not analyzed and appraised in accordance with required procedure—in this case a list of British ships, with the gross (not cargo) tonnages, said to have called at Chinese ports over the past year. The practice, as in this case, resulted in extreme and unsupportable conclusions being drawn and caused considerable trouble until the ounce or two of truth had been extracted from the blubber. Our guests were understandably disturbed by possible conclusions. I pointed out that the matter had not been brought to my attention, as it should have been, and asked that it be left to Mr. Eden and me to investigate. When fully analyzed and put together with other data, including known trade between Hong Kong and the mainland, this Navy bombshell amounted to very little.[16]

11. *Distort the facts if necessary (and if you can get away with it).* Participants seem to strain very hard not to say anything which they know to be false either in internal argument or publicly. Nevertheless, when it appears necessary to secure approval of a project, they are sometimes prepared not only to use each of the maneuvers described above but also to distort the facts. Gary Powers, the pilot of the ill-fated U-2, believes that Eisenhower was deceived about the ability of the aircraft which he flew over the Soviet Union to destroy itself. Eisenhower wrote in his memoirs:

There was, to be sure, reason for deep concern and sadness over the probable loss of the pilot, but not for immediate alarm about the equipment. I had been assured that if a plane were to go down it would be destroyed either in the air or on impact, so that proof of espionage would be lacking. Self-destroying mechanisms were built in.[17]

Powers, after quoting this paragraph, asserts:

If Eisenhower was told this, he was deceived. Had we been carrying ten times the two-and-a-half-pound explosive charge, there would have been no guarantee that the entire plane and all its contents would have been destroyed. Nor was the single mechanism "self-destroying." It would have to be activated by the pilot.[18]

A combination of the maneuvers enumerated above can lead to a sub-

16. Acheson, *Present at the Creation*, p. 598.
17. Eisenhower, *Waging Peace*, p. 547.
18. Powers, *Operation Overflight*, p. 353.

stantial distortion of the information available to the President. When there are advocates of different positions within the administration and when participants on all sides have their own access to sources of information, the President tends to be informed of the problems and difficulties of various alternative positions. When, however, the advocates of a certain policy are able to keep out of the process those with alternate sources of information and expertise, the distortions can be very great. The Bay of Pigs invasion provides an example of obvious distortion of the information available to the President when making a critical decision. Sorensen, in writing about the episode, sums up the number of ways in which the President was either misled or deceived about the facts:

1. *The President thought he was approving a quiet, even though large-scale, reinfiltration of fourteen hundred Cuban exiles back into their homeland. . . . Their landing was, in fact, highly publicized in advance and deliberately and grossly overstated. . . .*

2. *The President thought he was approving a plan whereby the exiles, should they fail to hold and expand a beachhead, could take up guerrilla warfare with other rebels in the mountains. . . . The immediate area was not suitable for guerrilla warfare, as the President had been assured; the vast majority of brigade members had not been given guerrilla training, as he had been assured. . . . [A move to the mountains] was never even planned by the CIA officers in charge of the operation, and they neither told the President they thought this option was out nor told the exiles that this was the President's plan.*

3. *The President thought he was permitting the Cuban exiles, as represented by their Revolutionary Council and brigade leaders, to decide whether they wished to risk their own lives and liberty for the liberty of their country without any overt American support.* Most members of the brigade were in fact under the mistaken impression, apparently from their CIA contacts, that American armed forces would openly and directly assist them, if necessary, to neutralize the air (presumably with jets), make certain of their ammunition, and prevent their defeat. . . .

4. *President Kennedy thought he was approving a plan calculated to succeed with the help of the Cuban underground, military desertions, and in time an uprising of a rebellious population. In fact, both Castro's popularity and his police state measures, aided by the mass arrests which promptly followed the bombing and landing, proved far stronger than the operation's planners had claimed. The planners, moreover, had no way to alert the underground without alerting Castro's forces. . . . As a result . . .*

no coordinated uprising or underground effort was really planned or possible.

5. *The President thought he was approving a plan rushed into execution on the grounds that Castro would later acquire the military capability to defeat it. Castro, in fact, already possessed that capability.*[19]

Presidential Efforts To Expand Information

For getting information to certain participants in order to persuade them, the President has available to him some of the same devices listed above. He, too, can arrange to expose other participants informally to views of persuasive individuals, and he can seek to influence what field commanders, ambassadors, or even other countries report to Washington. He can seek to suppress facts or to keep certain participants out of a particular dispute.

Presidents find, however, that the real test of their ability is to expand their own information, because they learn that the information being provided to them by subordinates is designed not so much to enlighten them as to convince them to adopt certain positions. Sometimes it may take a President a year or more to discover that he cannot rely on the information he is being given. Only by 1965 did Lyndon Johnson begin to understand that the optimistic statistics being reported to him from Vietnam were meaningless.[20] It was not until the spring of 1962 that Kennedy, addressing a group of Foreign Service officers in the State Department auditorium, remarked: "Winston Churchill once said that the secret of the survival of the British Empire was that they never trusted the judgment of the man on the spot. I never understood that until recently."[21]

When he is dissatisfied with the information reaching him, the President can do a number of things:

1. *Instruct the White House staff to seek alternate sources of information on critical issues.* Every postwar American President has come to see the White House staff as a means of getting information that the departments would not wish him to have. This function was drastically expanded after the Bay of Pigs operation when Kennedy, believing that the White

19. Theodore Sorensen, *Kennedy*, pp. 302–3 (italics added).
20. Sidey, *A Very Personal Presidency*, p. 220.
21. John P. Leacacos, *Fires in the In-Basket: The ABC's of the State Department*, p. 301.

House staff was not in a position to keep him fully informed, instructed McGeorge Bundy, his Assistant for National Security Affairs, to increase staff capacity substantially and to see that the President was fully briefed. As a result, Bundy arranged to have much of the raw material coming in from the field, including State Department, CIA, and military cables, sent directly to the White House situation room. Prior to that time only those cables the departments chose to send over reached the White House. Since 1962, the White House staff has been in a much more effective position to monitor information coming into Washington and report it to the President. It is more difficult for the White House to get access to information that does not come into Washington or reaches Washington through informal channels and back channel messages.

2. *Create new channels of reliable information.* When the President feels that he has fully tapped existing sources of information and is still receiving biased reports, he may find it convenient to create an entirely new vehicle for the gathering and processing of information on national security issues. President Truman proposed the creation of a centralized intelligence system to eliminate conflicting and self-serving intelligence reports from each agency.[22] President Nixon, twenty-five years later, believing that the national estimates now being produced by a centralized apparatus had become sterile bureaucratic compromises, created special panels to evaluate weapons problems and events in Vietnam.[23]

3. *Surround himself with divergent views.* To guard against biased information, a President may surround himself with individuals who have divergent views on particular issues and who are likely to call attention to facts supporting different positions.

4. *Ask for the separate views of each adviser.* The President frequently presses his advisers for a unanimous judgment as to what should be done. However, where he has doubts about the information being presented, he may ask each adviser to give a separate view (in an effort to uncover hidden differences). Kennedy resorted to this technique when confronted with the question of whether or not to intervene in Laos. "Thank God the Bay of Pigs happened when it did," he told Sorensen on the eve of a UN address. "Otherwise we would be in Laos by now—and that would be a hundred times worse."[24] Anxious in this case to discover whether his

22. Truman, *Memoirs* (Vol. I: *Year of Decisions*), pp. 98–99. Cited hereafter as *Year of Decisions.*
23. Richard M. Nixon, *U.S. Foreign Policy for the 1970's.*
24. Theodore Sorensen, *Kennedy*, p. 644.

advisers did in fact all agree, he had pressed for the separate views of each of the Joint Chiefs and in hearing them discovered that they in fact had very divergent notions as to what was going on in Laos, what American forces would be needed, and what the danger of Chinese intervention was.

5. *Encourage adversary proceedings.* A refinement of the new-channels and divergent-views technique is for the President, when he feels he needs to hear all sides of an issue, to have a group of participants with different interests and direct stakes in the issue sit down and fight it out in front of him. Presidents Truman and Kennedy frequently resorted to this technique.[25]

6. *Call middle-level officials and permit them to call.* In an effort to go beyond the information provided formally by the senior participants who have direct access to him, the President can seek to establish informal channels of communication with middle-level officials. In most cases, this is done through the White House staff. A substantial part of its job in ferreting out additional information for the President is to maintain informal contact with middle-level officials in various departments whose views are unlikely to get through the filter of each agency. In some cases, however, the President himself will seek to establish such contact. Kennedy appears to have done more of this than any other postwar President. He frequently would telephone middle-level officials or bring them into White House meetings. Often Kennedy would call the man that he thought had written the memo that came to him with the signature of the Secretary of State.[26]

7. *Contact ambassadors directly.* Presidents sometimes encourage their ambassadors to communicate directly with them or through the White House staff in addition to using the formal channels of communication which flow through the State Department. Again Kennedy seems to have favored this technique more often than any other postwar President, making it a point to see ambassadors when they were in Washington and encouraging them to write directly to him.[27] Ambassadors, of course, will be

25. Alexander George, "The Case for Multiple Advocacy in Making Foreign Policy," pp. 751–85, expands this point into a scheme which he believes might overcome the liabilities of bureaucratic politics in the foreign policy process. In essence, he prescribes a system in which all the arguments bearing on an issue are brought into focus and fought out under the direction of a disinterested "custodian" at the special assistant level.

26. See the numerous references to this technique in the Oral History Interviews in the John F. Kennedy Library.

27. Ibid.

interested in establishing this kind of direct communication, because they often feel that their side of a story does not get beyond the country desk in the State Department.[28]

8. *Send representatives to the field.* Presidents come to distrust the information being sent back to them through formal channels. They may send their personal emissary to the field for a direct assessment of the situation. Cabinet officials are sometimes chosen for this role but, because their views are likely to be affected by the stands and interests of their organization, are more often passed over in favor of White House officials or ad hoc personal advisers. Thus during the long history of the Vietnam War a number of different presidential emissaries were sent to assess the situation. President Nixon, for example, once sent the British counter-insurgency expert Sir Robert Thompson, and Maxwell Taylor was sent on such a mission by President Johnson. In one of the earliest such episodes President Kennedy sent a Foreign Service officer and a general to Vietnam together on an inspection trip for him. The civil official came back with a deeply pessimistic report, and the military officer came back greatly encouraged by what he had seen. This led to the famous presidential response, "Were you two gentlemen in the same country?"[29]

Kennedy's dilemma in this case reflects a frequent presidential problem. If an individual with a lack of prior experience or involvement in the issue goes out, it is difficult for him to penetrate beyond the formal briefings. If, on the other hand, a career official intimately involved is sent to the field, he is likely to report back whatever serves the interests of the organization in whose career pattern he moves. In the days prior to his authorization of the Bay of Pigs invasion President Kennedy asked a Marine colonel who was an old friend to evaluate the situation. His enthusiastic concurrence in the optimism of the CIA was apparently important in overcoming Kennedy's doubts.[30]

9. *Go outside the government.* Finally, a President has the option of expanding his base of information by seeking opinions outside the executive branch and outside the government. One of the most common methods of getting information from beyond the confines of the bureaucracy is the presidential commission. Presidents often consult with congressmen and senators from relevant committees, with former government officials,

28. For a discussion of this issue, see William Attwood, *The Reds and the Blacks*, pp. 157–58.

29. Schlesinger, *A Thousand Days*, pp. 992–93.

30. Haynes Johnson, *The Bay of Pigs*, p. 73.

and with academic experts, and they confer with foreign ambassadors stationed in Washington.

One of the most important ways in which both the President and the other participants maneuver to affect information is by seeking to influence what is reported in the press (and other news media) about any particular subject. This maneuver has not been included in the foregoing discussion because its aspects are varied and deserve more detailed treatment in a separate chapter. Thus the following chapter provides that treatment and in so doing extends our discussion of maneuvers to affect information.

CHAPTER TEN

Uses of the Press

Information that appears in the American press (and over television) plays a major role in shaping presidential decisions. Much of the information available to senior participants on any issue consists of what they encounter in the media. Some of the information reaches the press routinely or through the persistence of reporters, but some is put there by participants in an effort to influence presidential decisions. This chapter explores the techniques that bureaucrats employ in using the press. We do not suggest that "leaking" is the only, or even most important, way that information gets into print, but we wish to discuss the use of leaks as a standard bureaucratic maneuver.

Releasing Information

Most of the news about national security issues that reaches the press concerns formal governmental decisions. A decision is made, and then as a matter of routine it is announced to the press either because this is part of the process of implementation (to be discussed in the following section) or because it is simply assumed that the public should be informed about major presidential or cabinet-level decisions and not have to learn about them by observing implementation. However, a substantial fraction of what appears in the press is there for other reasons, some of which are related to efforts to affect presidential decisions.[1]

Most of the information about national security issues that reaches the press is released by participants in the executive branch, either in official handouts or in press conferences. Often such press conferences are on the record: that is, journalists are free to report that the conference was held

---

1. See Leon V. Sigal, *Reporters and Officials*, pp. 131–50.

and to identify and quote directly the officials who spoke to them. In other cases, the press conference is on a "background" basis. That is, reporters may use the information but instead of quoting directly must attribute it to some vague source, such as "high administration officials" or "State Department officials." Only senior participants are in a position to call press conferences, whether "on the record" or "for background," though occasionally they sponsor one conducted by a relatively junior official. During the Kennedy and Johnson administrations, Secretary of State Dean Rusk and Secretary of Defense Robert McNamara held background briefings weekly.[2] Presidential adviser Henry Kissinger frequently held background briefings following a major presidential speech or in the midst of a foreign policy crisis. Usually a conference is open to all reporters, but in some cases a specific group of journalists hold a luncheon or breakfast to which they invite an official and ask for a background briefing. Though the material given in a background press conference normally can be attributed to "high officials," in some cases a conference is designated "deep background," and the reporter must write the information on his own initiative without attributing it to any official source. President Kennedy, for example, held such deep backgrounders at the end of each year, leading to a series of stories saying, "The President is known to believe that...."[3]

Apart from these official forms of release, an important fraction of the material supplied to the press by participants in the executive branch is in the form of "leaks." Leaking is accomplished in many ways, such as private and off-the-record interviews, vague tips to reporters to look into a particular subject, or actually handing official papers to a reporter surreptitiously.

Most White House leaks occur at the President's initiative. However, some reporters seek to establish a general relationship with the White

2. Stewart Alsop, *The Center: People and Power in Political Washington*, pp. 186–89; Edward Weintal and Charles Bartlett, *Facing the Brink: An Intimate Study in Crisis Diplomacy*, p. 163.

3. Public knowledge of what is said at background briefings is generally limited to news stories. For two complete texts of background briefings, see Deputy Under Secretary of State Alex Johnson's remarks on the return of Okinawa to Japan, *United States Security Agreements and Commitments Abroad*, Hearings before the Subcommittee on United States Security Agreements and Commitments Abroad of the Senate Committee on Foreign Relations, 91 Cong. 2 sess. (1970), Pt. 5, pp. 1439–46; and presidential assistant Henry Kissinger's remarks on the Indo-Pakistani war of 1971, *Congressional Record*, Vol. 117, Pt. 35, 92 Cong. 1 sess. (1971), pp. 45734–38.

House such that they may be provided with leaks in return for a promise to report the information in a way that will accomplish the objectives of the President in leaking the material. Joseph Alsop, a Washington syndicated columnist, has frequently been successful in establishing such relations and apparently takes the initiative in seeking to do so. Robert Cutler, President Eisenhower's Special Assistant for National Security Affairs, reported being approached by Alsop early in the Eisenhower administration in an attempt to set up such an arrangement.[4]

Another ploy reporters use on their own initiative is to call officials, act as if they know that something has occurred, and get implied confirmation from them, often in the form of a refusal to discuss the subject. Thus on one occasion, alerted almost inadvertently by McGeorge Bundy to the fact that there was a major news story waiting to be discovered, Chalmers Roberts and Murray Marder of the *Washington Post* began calling administration officials and asking them, "What was in the message from Khrushchev to Kennedy about the Il-28's?" On one call Roberts finally got the response, "For Crissakes, how did you know about that? I can't tell you what was in the message."[5] On this basis, the *Post* was able to print a story indicating that Khrushchev had sent a message to Kennedy on the Il-28's in the closing days of the Cuban missile crisis.

Less often, officials will describe a document in detail to favored journalists or actually let them see the document or take a copy away—with or without their superior's knowledge. Presidential assistant Walt Rostow, for example, would frequently, on Johnson's orders, call in a group of reporters and permit them to read intelligence reports on the Vietnam situation.[6] Following the Indo-Pakistani war of late 1971, some officials gave to Jack Anderson, a syndicated columnist, the full text of a number of documents, including three reports of meetings of the Washington Special Actions Group, a senior-level group chaired by Henry Kissinger.[7]

Leaks come from many different sources, but it is the judgment of most reporters that the greatest single source of leaks is the White House.[8] Reporters themselves have told of receiving highly sensitive information

4. Cutler, *No Time for Rest*, pp. 317–19.
5. Alsop, *The Center*, pp. 165–67. See also Chalmers Roberts, *First Rough Draft*, p. 207.
6. *Newsweek*, July 5, 1971, p. 21.
7. The three documents were reprinted in the *Washington Post*, January 5, 1972.
8. See, for example, James Reston, *The Artillery of the Press: Its Influence on American Foreign Policy*, p. 66.

directly from the President. Both Max Frankel and Benjamin Bradlee were briefed by President Kennedy on his meeting with Nikita Khrushchev in Vienna in 1961.[9] In other cases the source of a story may be Congress or a foreign embassy.[10] For example, one of the most famous leaks of the Johnson administration, that of the fact that General Westmoreland had requested an additional 206,000 troops to be sent to Vietnam following the Tet offensive, was apparently leaked to the press from Capitol Hill.[11]

Senior officials have a choice among leaks, background press conferences, and statements on the record. They may choose to use a background press conference or a leak because the material that they have given out is unauthorized. That is, they do not have authority from the President to give it out, and they fear being fired or more likely cut out from the circle of participants involved in a particular issue. Junior participants because of the same fears take elaborate precautions to protect themselves when they leak material. Another reason for resorting to leaks or background press conferences is to conceal the source of information so as to make it appear to be some more authoritative or expert source. In other cases, a participant is concerned about "multiple audiences." He may desire to make clear to a domestic American audience or to the bureaucracy what the position is without conveying a formal statement to a foreign government, or he may wish to launch a trial balloon, or to give guidance to the bureaucracy without making a formal commitment for the President. For all these reasons officials will resort to leaking, background press conferences, and other techniques of putting information into the press without first securing a presidential decision that such material should be released. What specifically do participants hope to accomplish in providing material to the press?

Why Information Is Leaked

In general information is provided to the press either to directly affect bureaucratic maneuvers or to alert and bring into the process participants from outside the bureaucracy.

---

9. *Washington Post*, June 22, 1971; *Washington Post*, July 9, 1971. See also Arthur Krock, *Memoirs*, p. 27.
10. Douglass Cater, *The Fourth Branch of Government*, p. 125.
11. Kalb and Abel, *Roots of Involvement*, p. 238.

To Get the Message Through

Providing material to the press is often designed to expose senior participants to a certain view of what is happening and the likelihood of certain developments. Much of the information about the world which reaches senior participants comes through the press. The feeling is that "everyone" in Washington reads the *New York Times* and the *Washington Post*. The reality reflected in those newspapers, in other newspapers, and on radio and TV helps shape the way senior participants see the world. For this reason participants may talk to reporters in a manner designed to get them to present their stories in a particular light, hoping that the daily reading of the press will gradually lead senior participants to interpret an issue in a given way. For example, during the early 1960s different officials in Saigon leaked conflicting reports about the Vietnam War to American reporters in hope of convincing senior participants in Washington either that the war was a civil war or that it was essentially an invasion from the north. These two conflicting notions of what was going on in South Vietnam implied quite different policy stands.[12]

To Undermine Rivals

Leaks are often used in an effort to drive a participant entirely from the executive branch or to reduce his influence substantially. This is done by trying in a variety of ways to bring his behavior into question.

One technique is to try to show that a participant was in favor of a policy which lacks any support in the country. Following the Cuban missile crisis, opponents of UN Ambassador Adlai Stevenson hinted to newsmen that Stevenson had favored appeasement of the Soviet Union by advocating a trade of missiles in Cuba for missiles in Turkey. The intent was to show that Stevenson was so "soft" that his views could not be taken seriously. If this could be shown, Stevenson's enemies believed, then President Kennedy would feel pressed to remove him from office or to ignore him.[13]

A closely related technique is to try to have the press portray a particular participant as not a loyal supporter of the President. As with other aspects of leaking to the press, the machinations can become quite involved. Following the Bay of Pigs invasion, news stories appeared indicating that Chester Bowles, the Under Secretary of State, was one of the few

12. Hilsman, *To Move a Nation*, p. 499.
13. Beichman, *The "Other" State Department*, pp. 146–47; Schlesinger, *A Thousand Days*, p. 835.

officials who had opposed the operation. Opponents of Bowles charged that he had deliberately leaked this story in order to ingratiate himself with the left wing of the Democratic party but in doing so had undercut the President's effort to maintain a united front. It is not impossible that the initial stories were leaked by opponents of Bowles in order to put them in a position to make the charge.

Leaks may also be designed to show that a particular participant is incompetent or doing a poor job. Such leaks frequently occur when two senior participants are in a feud with each other and each is prepared to use any available means to undercut the other's position. Thus when Harold Stassen and John Foster Dulles competed for the ear of the President on disarmament matters and when Secretary of State Dean Acheson and Secretary of Defense Louis Johnson feuded, the press was full of stories about the positions of each of these officials.[14] Participants may also seek to undercut the position of an opponent by showing that he does not have the support of the President. Often the President himself will engage in such leaking as a way of advising other participants that they need not take the views of this particular individual or organization as seriously as they had in the past. James F. Byrnes, Truman's first Secretary of State, believed that he was subjected to such a move on the part of the President.[15] President Kennedy sought to undercut the position of the Joint Chiefs of Staff following the Bay of Pigs operation by telling Arthur Krock, the Washington correspondent of the *New York Times*, that he had "lost confidence" in the Joint Chiefs and permitting Krock to publish this information on his own authority.[16]

Leaks may be utilized to indicate that a participant has lied to the public, thereby making it an embarrassment to the President to keep him in office. This was one explanation offered for the leak of documents relating to American policy during the Indo-Pakistani war of 1971. The leaks seemed to show that presidential assistant Henry Kissinger had lied to the press in describing American policy, and some observers believed that the purpose of the leak was to discredit Kissinger.[17]

Accusing an official of leaking something is itself a way of discrediting his reputation within the bureaucracy. John Mecklin, the U.S. Public Affairs Adviser in Vietnam in the early 1960s, reports that because he was

14. Bernard C. Cohen, *The Press and Foreign Policy*, p. 197.

15. Byrnes, *Speaking Frankly*, p. 238.

16. Krock, *Memoirs*, p. 371.

17. See, for example, Joseph Kraft, "Undermining Kissinger," *Washington Post*, January 11, 1972.

friendly with two reporters, Neil Sheehan of UPI and David Halberstam of the *New York Times,* he was accused of leaking stories to them. Such complaints were conveyed by Secretary of State Dean Rusk and CIA Director John McCone to the head of the USIA. Mecklin concludes that "the damage done to my reputation at such a level also severely compromised my future with the government."[18]

Machiavellian use of the press to discredit one's opponents attains its highest levels within the White House staff itself. George Reedy describes the atmosphere:

The only aspect of "palace-guard" politics which requires subtlety is the use of the press. The inexperienced courtier may make the mistake of using his press contacts (which it takes a positive effort of will not to acquire) to secure favorable mention of his name in public. But the wilier practitioners of the art of palace knife-fighting take a different tack. They seek to feature their competitors' names in a context which will displease the man who holds the real power. This reverse-thrust technique is somewhat more complex than it appears on first glance. It is not inconceivable, for example, that a newspaper story speculating on the promotion of an assistant to higher office may be the death knell of that assistant's governmental career. It all depends upon the psychology of the president, but whatever that psychology, there will always be people around him who are willing to play it for whatever it is worth.[19]

Leaks to the press can be designed to affect relations between organizations as well as individuals when this is believed necessary in order to attain a desired outcome. The Army, attempting to get permission for development of a medium-range missile, at one point sought to cement an alliance with the Navy by inflaming relations between the Navy and the Air Force. Army colonels leaked to the Pentagon reporter of the *New York Times* an Air Force staff paper which deprecated the contribution of Forrestal-class carriers to the overall strategic mission. The aim was to deceive the Navy into thinking that the Air Force was leaking papers prejudicial to the Navy's interest.[20]

To Attract the Attention of the President

Getting a story into the news media is sometimes a way of bringing issues to the attention of the President. As one former high official ob-

18. Mecklin, *Mission in Torment,* pp. 184–86.
19. Reedy, *The Twilight of the Presidency,* pp. 90–91.
20. *New York Times,* May 20, 1956; cited and explained in Armacost, *The Politics of Weapons Innovation,* p. 93.

served: "The amount of high-level interest in an issue varies with potential press interest."[21] Particularly when preparing for press conferences, the President will be informed by his aides as to what questions are likely to be raised by reporters. In this process he may learn of issues which would otherwise remain buried in the bureaucracy. One clue that the aides use in determining what questions reporters are likely to raise are leaked stories which have appeared in the press in recent days. Thus an official anxious to bring an issue to the attention of the President may plant a story with the expectation that the subject will then come up in the preparation for the press conference.

To Build Support

Presidents may use press leaks to give what bureaucrats call a "hunting license"—meaning that they let their inclination in favor of a particular proposal be known as it is winding its way through the bureaucracy. By having reporters write stories saying that the President favors moving in a particular direction, the White House strengthens the hand of those advocating that move. The advocates will point to the story as an indication of presidential concern justifying movement.

To Ensure Implementation

Many times a leak follows a presidential decision and is designed to enforce implementation. This aspect of leaking is discussed in Part III.

To Alert Foreign Governments

In some instances, press leaks are used to bring the influence of foreign governments to bear on a policy question. NATO countries are likely targets for such operations. Officials in those countries read the American press carefully and are sensitive to American actions which they think may undercut the NATO alliance. George Kennan explains in his memoirs how a leak was used to kill a plan for a partial withdrawal of American forces from Europe in the early postwar period.[22] Maxwell Taylor states that a leak undercut a plan by Admiral Arthur Radford during the latter's

21. Quoted from an anonymous former official by Holbrooke, "The Machine That Fails," p. 72.
22. Kennan, *Memoirs, 1925–1950,* pp. 444–45.

term as Chairman of the Joint Chiefs of Staff to withdraw a substantial number of American forces from Europe. The report in the press that such a plan was afoot led German Chancellor Konrad Adenauer to send the chief of the German armed forces to Washington to express great concern.[23] This brought forth from the European allies intense complaints which forced the U.S. government to suspend consideration of a reduction of forces. One of the first notorious leaks of the Kennedy administration involved such a maneuver. Secretary of State Rusk had on February 15, 1961, sent a memorandum to Secretary of Defense McNamara outlining the American military forces which he believed were required to support the proper foreign policy objectives. In the course of the memorandum Rusk emphasized the need for general-purpose forces, and this could be construed as supporting the Army budget against that of the Air Force. The memorandum was leaked to the press within two weeks in a badly distorted form suggesting that Rusk favored abandonment of the nuclear deterrent in Europe. The episode was typical in that what finally reached the press was a distorted version designed to create the maximum sense of fear in the intended audience.[24]

Going Outside the Executive Branch

Most leaks are designed to put information into the public domain which would not otherwise be available, and the purpose of putting it there is to influence Congress or the public as a whole and thereby to influence presidential decisions. The decision to leak information to the press is taken by those who are dissatisfied with decisions being taken within the executive branch and who have reason to believe that public attitudes are likely to be more favorable to their position. A participant who recognizes that public and congressional views are likely to be even more opposed to his position has no incentive to alert newsmen despite the expectation of an adverse presidential decision. Thus the sort of information disclosed changes from time to time in light of executive branch views of public and congressional attitudes. Leaks may be designed simply to alert participants outside the executive branch in order to enable them to bring influence to bear, or they may be designed to affect the informa-

23. Taylor, *The Uncertain Trumpet*, pp. 41–42.
24. Kraft, *Profiles in Power*, pp. 115–18; Douglass Cater, *Power in Washington*, p. 48.

tion which the public and the Congress has and which will lead them to make up their mind in a particular way on a particular issue. Frequently the stand which a particular group or individual has taken on an issue is made known through leaks when it is believed that knowledge of this stand will affect the attitudes of leading congressmen and important groups. Finally, leaks related to domestic politics may be designed to create the expectation that something which is favored by important segments of the public will in fact occur. Each of these uses of the press is discussed in turn.

Alerting Outside Supporters

In some situations participants recognize that there are a number of supporters of their position in key congressional positions and in interest groups. The problem is simply that these potential allies are not aware of the fact that a presidential decision is about to be made. The purpose of leaks is to inform these individuals that an issue is up for decision, so that they can make their views known. Officials will find it more difficult to act to the contrary after they have been informed in advance about the strong views of individuals whose support they need on a wide range of issues. Roger Hilsman, who was then the Director of the Bureau of Intelligence and Research (INR) at the State Department, describes an episode in which he had the agreement of State Department officials to transfer to the Central Intelligence Agency what he viewed as certain peripheral functions then being performed by INR with funds transferred from the CIA:

But I had not reckoned on Congress. I had Rusk's approval, but before the decision was final I had to touch base with the Bureau of the Budget, the CIA, and others. Before I could complete the rounds, there was—inevitably—a leak, and a leak designed to block the move. A national news magazine reported that I was about to sell half the personnel of the bureau "up the river"—literally up the Potomac River to the CIA headquarters at Langley, Virginia. Wayne Hayes, Chairman of the Subcommittee on State Department Organization, and the entire membership of the House Foreign Affairs Committee were furious at what they thought was a further enhancement of the power of CIA. For the Foreign Affairs Committee shared many of the State Department's resentments of the CIA, and for many of the same reasons. Knowledgeable and sensitive to the political considerations in our dealings abroad because of their work on the committee, the members decried the growth of the CIA, its ubiquitous

ness, and the political handicaps which the United States' seemingly excessive reliance on secret agents and cloak-and-dagger techniques brought
in their wake. They also resented the fact that the CIA had a special relationship with a secret subcommittee consisting of members from the
Appropriations Committee and the Armed Services Committee—bypass-
ing the Foreign Affairs Committee on a number of matters they considered
their proper responsibility. I was ordered to appear before the subcommittee the next day.[25]

If outside opponents of a favored line of action are known to exist, strenu-
ous efforts will be made to keep a matter from leaking before a presidential
decision can be announced. For example, in planning his trip to Peking,
President Nixon went to great lengths to keep the matter from leaking to
supporters of the Chinese Nationalist regime in the United States until he
could announce that he had accepted an invitation from Chairman Mao.
Similarly, great efforts were made to prevent any leaks of the proposed
American plans to support an invasion of Cuba in 1961.[26]

Affecting Public Information

In other cases the problem is more complicated. Participants believe
that there is potential support for their position among the public but
that they need to focus this support by providing information which will
make clear why their position is important to the national security. In
such cases the leaks, besides alerting the public to the fact that an issue
is up for debate, must also present information which will galvanize outsiders into action. The information leaked to the press may be designed to
warn the public of the great dangers which would flow from a decision
that participants fear the President will make. Their aim will be to increase the domestic political cost to the President by generating public
fears. Admiral Arthur Radford may have resorted to this technique as
part of the campaign to get Eisenhower to approve military intervention
in Vietnam in 1954. According to one study:

An important section of the military led by Admiral Arthur Radford,
the Chairman of the Joint Chiefs of Staff, increasingly identified the Indochina War with centralized Communist planning in Moscow and Peking.
The French, in this view, were fighting to defend the free world, to hold
back the yellow hordes of Communist-indoctrinated peasant guerrillas
bent on conquering all of Asia—first China, then Vietnam, and which

25. Hilsman, *To Move a Nation*, p. 71.
26. Schlesinger, *A Thousand Days*, p. 261.

country next? The analogy of a line of falling dominoes was used to illustrate the danger confronting the American defense system based on a chain of islands from Japan to Formosa and the Philippines. It was argued that intervention to meet the threat, either alone or in concert, was preferable to a negotiated surrender. As the *New York Times* put it in a dispatch printed on May 2, the Radford school argued that there should be "no agreement to cease firing or to an armistice or to any settlement that will permit the Communist Viet Minh to build up their strength and resume fighting more effectively later." The article concluded that "In essence, any solution in Indochina short of outright military defeat of the Viet Minh rebels is opposed by the men responsible for the military security of the United States."[27]

Many leaks relate to supposed "enemy" capabilities. The military services seek to generate support for their proposed weapons systems by leaking information to the press about enemy capabilities. In some cases the estimates which are leaked may be wildly exaggerated or even totally false. One example of the latter was the story put out surreptitiously by the military that the Soviet Union had tested a nuclear-powered bomber. In fact no such test had taken place, and no information existed which suggested that it would.[28] Many leaks relating to Russia's capabilities occurred during the SALT negotiations.

Other leaks are aimed at extolling the virtue of one military capability as compared with another. These show up especially when the services are developing two closely related systems such as the Polaris and Minuteman missiles.[29] Leaks are also devised to emphasize "gaps" in U.S. capabilities if it is thought the gaps may then be "overcome" to the advantage of the armed forces. Thus when the military were denied operational control over nuclear weapons by President Truman, they leaked the fact to the press along with hints that this interfered with the operational readiness of the Air Force.[30]

Informing a Constituency

Matters of allegiance and personality sometimes lie behind leaks. The position taken by a key individual or organization on a particular issue may be made known through a leak if important groups outside the executive

---

27. Dommen, *Conflict in Laos*, p. 47.
28. Lambright, *Shooting Down the Nuclear Plane*, p. 17.
29. James Baar and William Howard, *Polaris*, pp. 215–16.
30. Nuel Pharr Davis, *Lawrence and Oppenheimer*, p. 287.

branch take their cues from the stands of specific participants within the executive branch. If participants have no following, their position is rarely leaked. Thus one seldom learns what the career officials in the various State Department regional bureaus think about an issue. When, however, groups with prestige outside the executive branch fear that their positions will not be accepted by the President, they are likely to see to it that their supporters know what is happening. In some cases the leak originates with other officials anxious to get the support which will come from letting it be known that a prestigious group supported their position.

Because of the prestigious position which the military services have had in most of the postwar period, their views on a number of issues are leaked to the press in an effort to increase the domestic cost to the President of overruling the military. For example, in the early postwar period the fact that the Joint Chiefs of Staff favored German rearmament was made known to Congress in an effort to pressure the State Department into support of that position.[31] The objections of the services to limitations imposed by a President on defense budgets are also frequently reported in the press. The views of particularly prestigious military leaders also may be made known. General Douglas MacArthur frequently resorted to this technique in an effort to pressure President Truman. MacArthur, rather than resorting to leaks, simply made public statements, on one occasion announcing plans to withdraw a substantial number of American military forces from the occupation of Japan and in another announcing that he thought a Japanese peace treaty could come fairly soon.[32] During the Korean conflict MacArthur revealed in a letter to Representative Joseph Martin, which the latter made public, that he favored an expansion of the war.[33]

Leaking the views of one prestigious group or individual can be countered by leaking the position of another. This form of counter-leaking was a key part of the effort to use the press to influence a decision by President Nixon in the spring of 1971 on the number of troops that he would then withdraw from Vietnam. The maneuvering began on March 16, 1971, with Secretary of Defense Melvin Laird asserting that the Nixon administration was committed to continuing its current rate of withdrawal from Vietnam through late 1972. Laird was quoted in next day's news-

31. Laurence Martin, "The American Decision To Rearm Germany," p. 651.

32. Truman, *Year of Decisions*, p. 520; Frederick S. Dunn, *Peace-Making and the Settlement with Japan*, p. 63.

33. The episode was described by Truman in *Years of Trial and Hope*, pp. 445–46.

papers as saying that the President would withdraw at least 12,500 men a month from Vietnam "from now on."[34] Two days later, the *New York Times* published a story out of Saigon reporting the concern felt by the United States military command in Vietnam that budget restraints and manpower ceilings were forcing withdrawals from Vietnam faster than would be dictated by the President's "Vietnamization" program. The reports seemed to challenge the idea of a fixed rate of withdrawal by referring to the President's remark that forces would be withdrawn from Vietnam only as Vietnamization, the level of enemy activity, and progress in Paris permitted.[35] At the end of the month Joseph Alsop filed a dispatch from South Vietnam in which he said that General Creighton W. Abrams, the U.S. commander in Vietnam, had proposed a "pause" in the American withdrawal from Indochina. Alsop reported that Abrams would be gravely concerned if the withdrawal continued at the current rate.[36] The day after Alsop's column, the *Washington Post* had another story reporting that General William C. Westmoreland, Abrams' predecessor in Vietnam and now the Chief of Staff of the United States Army, favored a six-month halt in any withdrawals from Vietnam. It was reported that Westmoreland had ordered a full study of the risks of various withdrawal schedules, and the story confirmed the view that Abrams was concerned about withdrawals at the current rate.[37]

The White House the next day refused to comment on these various reports, claiming that the President had not made up his mind; however, a Pentagon spokesman asserted that "I have seen nothing that would indicate a delay in the Vietnamization program."[38]

On April 9, President Nixon announced that he would make a troop withdrawal announcement after April 15. This precipitated a rash of stories underlining where various administration officials stood. The *New York Times* reported on April 10 that the Chiefs of Staff had formally recommended a delay of up to sixty days before further troop withdrawals were decided upon or announced. Whoever provided this information to the *Times* also informed the newspaper that Secretary Laird would reject this recommendation and urge the President to announce additional cuts. The *Times* reported that the Joint Chiefs were particularly concerned about events in Laos and Cambodia. The same story confirmed that

34. *Washington Post*, March 17, 1971.
35. *New York Times*, March 18, 1971.
36. *Washington Post*, March 30, 1971.
37. *Washington Post*, March 31, 1971.
38. *Washington Post*, April 1, 1971.

General Abrams had expressed a hope for a delay and for a reduction in the rate of withdrawal.[39] On April 19, on the eve of the President's address to the nation on Vietnam, William Beecher, the *New York Times* military correspondent, published a story which made clear where everyone stood. He indicated that Secretary Laird was known to favor an increase in the withdrawal, while military leaders were pressing for a delay. He suggested that the President was searching for a compromise because, as someone had stated to Beecher, "if a real crisis should develop over the next few months, Mr. Nixon would not want to be in a position of having grossly ignored the military advice and endangered American troops in Vietnam."[40]

The President faced a dilemma. If he acceded to the Joint Chiefs' request to delay any troop withdrawals, he would do so with the public knowing that his own Secretary of Defense believed that troop withdrawals could go forward on schedule. Thus the doves would be aroused. On the other hand, if he announced that he was withdrawing troops on the current schedule, it would be known that he was doing so over the strong recommendations of the Joint Chiefs of Staff and of the American commander in Vietnam. Thus the hawks would be aroused. The President pulled a rabbit out of the hat by announcing the withdrawal of 150,000 men from Vietnam over the next twelve months (thus maintaining the current rate of withdrawal) but then apparently agreeing privately with the military that they could postpone any withdrawals during the first sixty days of the twelve-month period.[41]

Announcing a Policy

The press can be used to create the impression that a decision has been made. If the news is well received by the public, the President must go along or else appear in the unwelcome role of an executive reversing a popular policy. The announcement of a policy in hopes of pressuring the President to accept it may be done in a backgrounder or in a press leak, but it is much more effective when done on the record.

The technique is limited to senior participants such as Cabinet officers who are in a position to call a press conference. When maneuvering in this way, a senior participant announces to the press on the record that

39. *New York Times*, April 10, 1971. The *Washington Post* reported the same information on the following day.
40. *New York Times*, April 19, 1971.
41. *New York Times*, April 22, 1971.

the government has made a particular decision. He does so only if he has tried and failed to get the President to make that decision, only if he feels very strongly that the proposed decision is in the national interest, and only if he thinks that by publicly announcing the policy he can change the consequences for the President sufficiently so that the President will not publicly challenge him or otherwise revert to the previous decisions. Naturally, also, the man who tries this ploy must choose a time when there is strong and widespread public support for the decision which he announces.

Secretary of Defense Clark Clifford used this maneuver in the spring of 1968 after he had sought and failed to get President Lyndon Johnson to change his Vietnam policy in several respects. Clifford had recommended to the President that the United States declare that it would send no additional troops to Vietnam. During March of 1968 the President decided not to meet General Westmoreland's specific request for 206,000 men, but he was unwilling to announce categorically that no additional troops would be sent.

Nevertheless, in the weeks following President Johnson's March 31 speech, Clifford announced to the press (largely in response to questions so that there was no text that needed to be cleared in advance) that the United States had decided to put a ceiling on its effort in Vietnam, that America would no longer pour troops into a bottomless pit, and that as a matter of fact the United States did not intend to send any additional troops to Vietnam.

Obviously, in rejecting Clifford's advice that he announce such a decision, the President sensed the great domestic popularity the announcement would have, but he apparently felt that the adverse consequences for national security outweighed the possible domestic gains. However, once Clifford announced the policy, the President's choice was either to go along or to publicly engage in a hassle with his Secretary of Defense over the question of whether or not he would send additional troops to Vietnam. Having, he said, renounced another term as President to work for peace in Vietnam, Johnson was not in a very strong position to argue in public that additional troops might have to be sent to Indochina. This maneuver changed the domestic political consequences for President Johnson to the point where they outweighed his estimate of foreign policy consequences, and he went along with the change in policy.[42]

42. Philip Goulding, *Confirm or Deny*, pp. 323–33.

Trial Balloons

In some situations the press is used in an attempt to learn more about the likely domestic consequences of a proposed course of action. Thus what is known as a trial balloon may be issued on the record by a Cabinet officer or in a background briefing or through a leak. The effort is to see what sort of public debate is generated by the news that a proposed decision is under consideration, thus providing the President with additional information as to the likely domestic consequences. Often after a decision is made, the press is used to test various ways of softening these feared adverse domestic consequences.

Presidential Speeches

The President can himself use each of the techniques listed above. He can command much more press attention than anyone else whether he is speaking on the record or offering background information or carefully leaking something. Presidents often obtain press coverage by delivering a major foreign policy speech.

The great advantage of this device for a President is that he can in effect implement decisions himself soon after making them. Presidents often find that the most effective way to settle an ongoing bureaucratic squabble is with a public statement. "Faced with an administrative machine which is both elaborate and fragmented," Henry Kissinger has written, "the executive is forced into essentially lateral means of control."[43] Thus many public speeches, though ostensibly directed to outsiders, may perform a more important role in laying down guidelines for the bureaucracy. The chief significance of a foreign policy speech by the President may be that it settles an internal debate in Washington. A public statement is more useful for this purpose than an administrative memorandum because it is harder to reverse.

In some cases the President may be unwilling to settle a bureaucratic conflict definitively but may wish to give a hunting license to a particular group. To do this he may in a speech indicate his general support for a particular policy approach. He thereby avoids putting himself in a position of having definitively overruled a major part of the bureaucracy, but at the

---

43. Kissinger, *American Foreign Policy*, p. 22.

same time he increases the probability of getting the outcome which he desires. The hunting license will serve the purpose only if important elements in the bureaucracy attach high priority to the proposal to which the President has given impetus and are prepared to pick up his hunting license and move with him.

In some cases the President seeks in a speech not to settle an ongoing bureaucratic dispute or to give a specific hunting license but to set an entire new direction for the foreign policy of his administration. He realizes that he is going to be moving against the strongly held views of a number of factions in his bureaucracy. Each postwar President has made such speeches, and they have followed a strikingly similar pattern. Avoiding the usual procedure of informing the bureaucracy that the President plans to give a major speech and requesting inputs to it, the White House in the cases we are talking about here keeps to itself the fact that any speech is contemplated. A draft is put on paper in secret after consultation among a few key White House advisers. Only after this draft is discussed with the President and he has given it his approval is any effort made to notify the bureaucracy. At that time, the coordination usually takes place at very high levels. A senior White House official conveys the speech to the Secretary of State and the Secretary of Defense, informing them that the President has already approved the text and that he plans to give the speech in a very few days. Under an obligation not to show the text to their subordinates, key officials almost always go along with the President's proposed text, because any suggestion for change would mean challenging a presidential decision that had already been made. Thus speeches clear quickly at high levels.[44]

Senior participants and representatives of organizations quickly come to recognize the importance of major presidential speeches. Those who are frustrated in other ways in getting the bureaucracy to adopt a policy will frequently recommend that the President give a "new directions" speech. Others will seek to slip a key idea into a paragraph of a speech being drafted. They hope to affect future decisions within the bureaucracy by being able to cite a presidential source for endorsement. The aim, for example, may be to set the tone which will affect an issue up for decision,

44. For examples of this approach, see Hughes, *The Ordeal of Power*, p. 107, relating to a major peace speech by President Eisenhower delivered in April 1953. See Schlesinger, *A Thousand Days*, p. 900; Theodore Sorensen, *Kennedy*, pp. 730–31; Henry Brandon, "Schlesinger at the White House," on President Kennedy's American University peace speech. President Nixon has resorted to this technique more often than any of his predecessors. He appears to have employed it first in delivering his initial major Vietnam speech in May of 1969.

such as the American stand in an ongoing negotiation. George Kennan relates just such an episode which came after he was appointed to chair an interdepartmental committee to try to settle differences between Treasury Secretary John Snyder and the State Department about how to deal with a British request for a substantial loan shortly after the end of World War II. He writes:

Three days later, while my interdepartmental committee was still at work, the department received the draft of a speech the President proposed shortly to give which included a paragraph addressed to the forthcoming arrival of the British statesmen. It seemed to me cold and wholly devoid of sympathy of understanding for the British position. I therefore dictated a paragraph for inclusion in it; the Secretary read this over the phone to Clark Clifford in the White House; and to my own surprise it found its way into the speech. It was to the effect that the British statesmen would find the usual warm welcome in our country; that we would not forget our wartime associations with Britain or the strains and stresses to which the British people had been subject in the postwar years; that we would regard the matters under discussion as a common problem and would sit down to the discussions in a spirit of friendliness and helpfulness. When this speech appeared in the papers, on August 30, the general reception was highly favorable, but I later heard that it was the occasion of much anguish, and even phone calls of protest to the President, on the part of Secretary Snyder, to whom a friendly word of this sort appeared to harbor sinister dangers.[45]

Because officials are always on the lookout for opportunities to insert in the President's speeches statements that they can later cite to serve their special purposes, he must be wary. "The executive thus finds himself confronted by proposals for public declarations," Henry Kissinger has written, "which may be innocuous in themselves—and whose bureaucratic significance may be anything but obvious—but which can be used by some agency or department to launch a study or program which will restrict his freedom of decision later on."[46]

George Ball, Under Secretary of State in the Kennedy administration and one of the men in favor of creating a multilateral nuclear force, relates one episode which demonstrates the high value placed on even the most tenuous presidential hunting license inserted into a speech. In May of 1961, when a speech by Kennedy was scheduled, there was much opposition within the government to the American proposals for creating an

45. Kennan, *Memoirs, 1925–1950*, pp. 460–61.
46. Kissinger, *American Foreign Policy*, p. 23.

interallied nuclear force. Thus the best that Ball and his colleagues were able to get was a presidential statement that "beyond this we look to the possibility of eventually establishing a NATO seaborne force, which would be truly multilateral in ownership and control, if this should be desired and found feasible by other allies, *once NATO's nonnuclear goals have been achieved.*"[47] Opponents of the MLF viewed this statement as entirely innocuous, since everyone understood that NATO's nonnuclear goals would in fact never be achieved. Nevertheless, as Ball himself explains, the statement was exploited as a presidential "mandate" and formed the basis for an effort by Ball and his colleagues within the State Department to convince the Europeans to support the MLF proposal.[48]

Astute bureaucrats thus view major presidential speeches both as a danger and as an opportunity. Dean Acheson, writing from the vantage point of his experience as Secretary of State, sums up the perspective of the senior participants on this aspect of maneuvering within the government:

The Secretary, if he is wise, will join the fray himself, with his own draft, and try to guide and direct it. He can carry more weight than any of his associates, particularly in the final stages when the President himself, as I knew the procedure, joins the group and makes the final decisions.

It may seem absurd—and doubtless is—for a Secretary of State to be spending his time as a member of a Presidential speech-writing group. But this is often where policy is made, regardless of where it is supposed to be made. The despised speech, often agreed to be made months beforehand without thought of subject, a nuisance to prepare and annoyance to deliver, has often proved the vehicle for statements of farreaching effect for good or ill. As both a junior and a senior official, I have fought this guerrilla warfare; sometimes to get things done which would otherwise be stopped, and sometimes to prevent others from doing the same thing.[49]

Implications for Decisions

At the top levels of the American government the belief is held that anything of importance, especially if it touches on domestic political in-

47. Presidential address at Ottawa on May 17, 1961, quoted in George Ball, *The Discipline of Power*, p. 207 (italics added).
48. Ibid., pp. 206–9.
49. Acheson, "The President and the Secretary of State," p. 44.

terests, will be leaked to the press by some participant unhappy with the drift of presidential decisions. Because this belief is so widely held, it tends to influence significantly the way issues are handled in the executive branch. Often an option under consideration will be rejected on the grounds that it could not be implemented before it was leaked and not successfully implemented unless put into effect before it leaked.

The extremes to which a President may conclude he has to go to keep things from leaking is illustrated by the preparations for the trip by presidential assistant Henry Kissinger to Peking to arrange a visit by Nixon. Apparently no more than four or five Americans, inside or outside government, at any level, were aware of these preparations. All the great departments of the government, including the State Department (with the possible exception of the Secretary of State himself), were kept in the dark. Although the secret was kept, it entailed a substantial cost. The President was denied the expertise of the bureaucracy in designing the probe toward China, and allied governments could not be informed, an omission which caused a crisis in American relations with Japan. It was only because the President had great confidence in his national security adviser and therefore was prepared to move without the advice of the State Department and the intelligence agencies, and only because the action to be carried out was one that could be performed by a very small number of people, that this secret probe toward China was possible. In some situations the calculation that a leak will occur and would be disastrous leads a President and other senior participants to reject proposed courses of action.

Knowing of the fear of leaks, participants opposed to a particular course of action sometimes seek to prevent it by warning participants higher up that, if the action is taken, it will quickly be leaked with detrimental effects. For example, during the Indo-Pakistani war of 1971 the White House was pressing for an anti-Indian position which was being resisted by the bureaucracy. When Henry Kissinger informed the senior AID official that the President desired to tightly restrict aid to India, the following exchange took place:

Kissinger: The President wants no more irrevocable letters of credit issued under the ninety-nine million credit. He wants the seventy-two million PL 480 credit also held.

Williams: Word will soon get around when we do this. Does the President understand that?

Kissinger: That is his order, but I will check with the President again....[50]

The threat is always made in the passive voice. Not "I will leak it" but "It will leak." When they feared that President Kennedy might cancel the Bay of Pigs invasion, CIA officials pressed him very hard with the argument that, if the invasion were called off, the fact would certainly leak from the Cuban refugees, who would provide a highly distorted view of the probability of success of the operation and the American reasons for cancellation. Arthur Schlesinger reports the arguments as they were put to the President:

As [Allen] Dulles said at the March 11 meeting, "Don't forget that we have a disposal problem. If we have to take these men out of Guatemala, we will have to transfer them to the United States, and we can't have them wandering around the country telling everyone what they have been doing."[51]

Since a President believes that anything of importance may leak, he will be concerned about the possibility of a leak even if no explicit threat is made or the possibility is not pointed out by other participants. Apparently one of President Johnson's concerns in considering whether to continue with the Vietnam policy which he inherited from President Kennedy was the fear that if he changed course, the advisers whom he also inherited and who had framed the policy in the first place would contrive leaks to imply that the new President was jeopardizing the security of the United States.[52]

When a revealing story does appear in the press, a President sees it as a confirmation of his view that participants with different objectives will leak things through the press. Presidents tend to ignore the possibility that the leak resulted from some source outside the executive branch or that the story appears as a result of a reporter's initiative. At one point, in a desperate effort to convince President Johnson that many of the stories appearing in the press did not get there as a result of deliberate leaks from his staff, presidential assistant McGeorge Bundy asked Philip Potter, who had just written an accurate account of President Johnson's policy on aid to India, to explain how he had got the story. "Would you mind giving me a memorandum on how you came to write that story?" he

---

50. *Washington Post*, January 5, 1972.
51. Schlesinger, A *Thousand Days*, p. 242.
52. Tom Wicker, *JFK and LBJ*, pp. 203–4; David Halberstam, "The Very Expensive Education of McGeorge Bundy," p. 31.

asked. "I'd like to show it to the President. I know you got the story legitimately, but this President never believes a reporter can get a story like that unless the secret paper is filched or a Cabinet member suborned."[53]

Because of the importance of the press in the policymaking process as a whole and because of the analytical value of considering the press's role in a single place, we have been somewhat deflected from our effort to trace a particular issue through the government to a presidential decision. Recall then where we are. Participants with varying interests and constrained by the rules plan strategies to get the decisions they want. Part of the strategy relates to information content and dissemination of information. It is this aspect we have been concerned with thus far and which led us to a discussion of the role of the press. The second strand of the process relates to how the issue moves through the system toward the President and toward a decision. It is to that aspect that we now turn.

53. Quoted in Alsop, *The Center*, pp. 203–4.

CHAPTER ELEVEN

Involving the President

As we saw in Chapter 7, ascertaining whether the President is to be involved in a decision is one of the crucial steps in planning to gain the decision one wants. The rules of the game, particularly those set by the President, may necessitate the President's involvement, or they may specify that the issue be decided at another level of the bureaucracy. Often, however, the rules of the game are sufficiently flexible that they do not prescribe the exact progress of a decision through the bureaucracy. The first part of the present chapter discusses the reasons why participants prefer consensus below the President. The second part deals with the options open to participants to affect the way issues reach the President in those cases where his involvement cannot be avoided (or, less frequently, when a participant decides that presidential involvement is more desirable). Finally, we consider two key elements in securing a presidential decision: securing a consensus and creating a deadline.

Agreeing without the President

When there is a choice, participants prefer to reach consensus and decision below the President. This is true for a number of reasons.

Participants recognize that they are likely to have much more *control over what is decided* if it is the result of a compromise among the organizations and individuals directly involved in an issue. If an unresolved issue were taken to the President for a decision, the White House might shape its own compromise, taking into account the President's domestic political concerns, and this compromise might substantially reduce the autonomy of an organization with operating responsibilities. Moreover, bucking an issue up to the President for a decision, calling upon him to overrule one or another organization, runs the risk that the locus of decision making in general will move upward toward the White House, thereby reducing the autonomy of all organizations in the bureaucracy.[1]

In some cases, participants have a strong *need or desire to get a decision quickly* which will permit them to go forward with various actions. They recognize that it may be difficult to persuade the President to involve himself in an issue or that in any case it may take a substantial period of time before he will make a decision. Thus there is strong pressure to compromise in order to get a unanimous decision below the President which will permit actions to go forward. In such cases a participant who is less eager for action can frequently have his way by threatening to take the matter to the President. John Kenneth Galbraith, for example, reports that while he was ambassador to India, he quarreled with the State Department and the White House about the text of a letter to go in the President's name to Indian Prime Minister Nehru. Galbraith, receiving a draft unacceptable to him, sent it back with his recommended changes and "asking that my recommended changes, or my reasons for them, be sent to the President himself." He notes he got his way by relying on the fact that, "since getting his [the President's] attention was difficult, the alternative would be to accept them. So it happened."[2]

Fear of losing, and thus of hurting their reputation, is another reason why participants are reluctant to take issues to the President. Also they recognize that when they ask the President to overrule another official, they are using up one of the limited number of occasions on which the President will go to such lengths for them. For example, when Secretary of State John Foster Dulles clashed with Secretary of the Treasury George Humphrey about a proposal for a development loan fund (under which the United States would provide loans on lenient terms to developing countries), both felt under strong pressure to reach an agreement so that neither of them need go to the President and ask him to overrule the other. Dulles by invoking foreign policy considerations of high importance was able to get Humphrey to retreat from the position that the fund would have to be financed by annual appropriations. At the same time Dulles ac-

1. As Alexander George observes in "The Case for Multiple Advocacy in Making Foreign Policy," p. 753: "Left to their own devices, those subunits which share responsibility for a particular policy area often adapt by restricting competition with each other. As a result, policy issues may not rise to the presidential level, or when they do, they often take the form of concealed compromises that reflect the special interest of actors at lower levels of the hierarchical system."

2. Galbraith, *Ambassador's Journal,* p. 516 (n. 28).

cepted Humphrey's position that appropriations would have to be requested for the first year. As Russell Edgerton has observed in his careful
study of the loan fund, despite the fact that the agreement was not fully
satisfactory to either official, *"Neither man went to the President."*[3]

The considerations involved here are the same as those that lead participants to stay out of an issue. When they cannot, these pressures lead them
in the direction of a compromise below the President.

Getting to the President

It may happen that participants have no choice but to go to the President. Perhaps he asks that an issue be referred to him for a decision, or a
matter arises that requires a presidential decision according to the rules of
the game. The importance of an issue will be a factor, as when someone
wishes to send troops into combat in a conflict just developing or when
successful implementation of a policy would require a presidential commitment which can be revealed to other governments. In other cases, a
participant may elect to take an issue to the President because he is dissatisfied with the compromise which can be negotiated below the President and prefers to take his chances on a decision from above. If an issue
is to be taken to the President, participants have a number of choices
about how to do so.

Through Channels

The most straightforward way of bringing an issue to the President is
to do so through the formal channels prescribed by the rules of the game.
In some cases this will call for introducing the question into a formal
National Security Council system such as that used by Presidents Eisenhower and Nixon. If there is no formal NSC system or the issue does not
warrant introduction into that system, the procedure calls for a memorandum from the relevant heads of departments, generally the Secretary of
State and the Secretary of Defense and/or the Secretary of the Treasury,
with a recommendation for a particular course of action.

The rules of the game will prescribe whether in the formal procedures

3. Edgerton, *Sub-Cabinet Politics and Policy Commitment*, pp. 140–41.

the President is to be presented with a single recommended option or a variety of options from which he can choose. Where a single option is called for, an effort will be made to negotiate a compromise option with which all the relevant departments and participants are satisfied. Where the rules of the game call for several options, participants will seek to arrange the options so that in the package is only one viable option acceptable to all of them. If this cannot be done, then the President may be confronted with real options each advocated by different parts of the bureaucracy.

Often this path will appear to be extremely risky. Participants, uncertain of how the President will react to various options, do not know how to shape their proposal and take their stance so as to get the desired decision from him. For this reason, a participant who has control of the action often tries to get to the President by a different route in order to maximize his chances of getting the desired decision. Senior participants have a number of routes open to them, some of which are also open to junior participants intent on circumventing their nominal superiors.

Going Alone

The ideal situation for a senior participant is to be able to take a controversial issue to the President and get him to decide it without further recourse to other participants. An official whose relationship permits him to bring issues forward in this way will nevertheless use the privilege sparingly, recognizing the price that the President will pay with other participants. Officials with direct access to the President are most likely to take issues to him in hopes of a quick decision when there is substantial disagreement or when others plan to act without informing the President.

Dean Acheson has recounted a number of occasions when he acted this way in the face of intense squabbling within the government, particularly when the Pentagon refused to accept his judgment on political matters. Acheson reports that he saw the President alone each Monday and Thursday and had an opportunity to bring up such matters.[4]

Few officials, however, have the confidence of the President to such an extent that he is prepared to decide a controversial issue simply upon hearing one side of the story and without at least pretending to have a formal

---

4. Acheson, "The President and the Secretary of State," p. 45.

review of the matter in regular channels. More often an issue will be taken privately to the President for his tentative judgment subject to review and confirmation when the issue comes through formal channels.

Acheson frequently used this technique when he was Secretary of State. He would discuss an issue with Truman to assure himself of the President's support and then orchestrate with the President how to handle the more formal meeting with other officials. He reports that he tried this again under President Kennedy when assigned by him to try to work out a solution to the American balance-of-payments problem. In this case, as Acheson relates, it did not work as well, apparently because there was no commanding figure under the President to whom others were prepared to defer. According to Acheson:

After I got this down, I had another talk with the Treasury, and I got the impression that Roosa would go along with this perfectly well, and I talked with Doug Dillon about it, talked with people in State. Then I had another session with the President, and I said, "You know, I think that if you study this, then call everybody together and say, let every man now speak if he wants to but later hold his peace—then decide what should be done." He thought that was a good idea, and we had such a meeting. It just didn't turn out the way I thought it was going to.[5]

Nevertheless, members of the White House staff often work with sympathetic Cabinet officers and with the President to determine in advance how he wishes to decide an issue and to help to conduct a meeting so as to minimize tensions.

In other cases, a senior participant goes to the President separately in the hope that by explaining the issue in his own way he can get the President firmly on board before others present their side of the issue. In some cases, it is important to a participant to learn what the President's position is likely to be, so that he can know whether he is better off compromising or standing firm with the confidence that the President will then support his position.

David Lilienthal, when he was head of the Atomic Energy Commission, frequently used this technique. He relates one episode when he was fighting with the military about the degree of control that the AEC would have over weapons laboratories. He was relieved to find that Truman appeared to be fully in support of his position:

Well, of course, we were "charmed" by this clear-headed and simple

5. Acheson, Kennedy Library Oral History Interview, p. 33.

talk. *I went on to explain how we planned the transfer, that he would be asked to sign certain orders. "Send them along; I'll sign whatever you recommend." I said that we might as well mention the fact that, though we hoped for agreement with the War Department, there might be some differences we couldn't adjust that would have to come to him. "I expect that. The Army will never give up without a fight, and they will fight you on this from here on out, and be working at it in all sorts of places. But you can count on it, I am your advocate."*

"No, you're not an advocate, Mr. President," I said, "you are the judge—and it's a lot better to have the judge on your side than the most persuasive advocate." This seemed to amuse him a lot, and he said, "Well, I know how they are, they are trained never to give up. I know because I am one of them." "Well," I said, "if you are, you are a lay brother." This was all lighthearted, but very, very important. It meant that in our negotiations with the Army about transferring Sandia and so on we could draw the line where we thought it wise, rather than where we thought we must as a compromise.[6]

Knowledge of such private meetings is often kept from other participants, who might complain of unfair treatment if they heard that the President had already talked to one of the parties and reached at least a tentative decision. For this reason, there are very few reports of such meetings on the public record, although one suspects that they occur frequently.

In a few instances a participant will seek to inform others of his private meeting with the President in an effort to get them to go along without needing to bring the issue back to the President. William Attwood, U.S. Ambassador to Guinea at the time, succeeded in getting President Kennedy on board with a proposed program and then went out of his way to contrive circumstances in which others would learn of the President's support:

After talking to McGeorge Bundy—at the President's suggestion—I returned to the State Department to find the task force already arguing over the draft of my instructions. With things about to get unraveled, I picked up the phone, called Rostow at the White House, and, with the task force silently attentive, told him about my talk with the President and said we nevertheless seemed to be running into problems. It didn't take too long after that to get the instructions approved, and I left Washington that night.[7]

6. Lilienthal, *Journals*, p. 118.
7. Attwood, *The Reds and the Blacks*, p. 40.

Going through the White House Staff

Often participants bring issues to the President through the White House staff rather than going themselves or going through formal channels. In some instances senior participants use the White House staff simply as a quicker and less conspicuous route to the President than if they themselves asked for an appointment. Lilienthal, as head of the AEC, frequently went through the White House staff to get a presidential reading on an issue before taking the matter to the President through regular channels. He used this technique, for example, in dealing with the requests from the military and Defense Secretary Louis Johnson that custody of nuclear weapons be turned over to the military. After assuring himself of the President's support through Clark Clifford, the President's counselor, and Jim Webb, the Director of the Bureau of the Budget, Lilienthal recommended that the President receive the issue in a formal way and send back a formal response.[8]

Senior participants recognize that they pay a price in going alone to the President without informing their colleagues. Rather than do this, they may seek to interest a member of the White House staff in a proposal and have him carry the ball in bringing the issue to the President. For example, when Secretary of Defense Robert McNamara reached the conclusion that the United States government was not giving sufficiently serious attention to seeking to get a treaty banning the spread of nuclear weapons, he was reluctant to carry the issue to the President. Since this was primarily a foreign policy matter, the major responsibility for recommendations to the President in this area lay with Secretary of State Dean Rusk. For McNamara to bring the issue to President Johnson would appear to be undercutting Rusk and would complicate his relations with the Secretary of State. Thus McNamara avoided this route by having his Assistant Secretary for International Affairs, John T. McNaughton, speak privately to presidential aide Bill Moyers. McNaughton explained to Moyers the importance of preventing proliferation and quietly pointed out the ways in which the State Department was failing to give this top priority. Moyers, convinced, went to the President, who upon being convinced himself called in Dean Rusk and gave the orders which led to a change in American policy and eventually to a non-proliferation treaty.[9]

In other cases, recourse will be had to the President through the White

8. Lilienthal, *Journals*, pp. 376–77, 384.
9. Anderson, *The Presidents' Men*, p. 344.

House staff when one urgently needs a means of preventing another part of the government from acting and one doesn't feel that one has the personal standing to take the issue to the President. Lilienthal resorted to a call to Clark Clifford to prevent the Joint Chiefs of Staff from releasing a report on an American nuclear test which the Chiefs apparently planned to make public without getting presidential approval. Clifford brought the report to the President, who then insisted upon clearance.[10]

In some cases, senior participants find it difficult to get through to the President on a particular issue and resort to friends on the White House staff who they believe are likely to be sympathetic to their position. On several occasions, Averell Harriman, while serving in the State Department, used this technique to get presidential attention, often going through Arthur Schlesinger, Jr., who, though he had no formal role, was able to reach the President. While negotiating on Laos, Harriman received instructions from the State Department that he was not to talk to the Chinese. He informed John Kenneth Galbraith, the U.S. Ambassador to India, who in turn communicated with Schlesinger, who informed the President. As a result Harriman was given instructions to talk to anyone he wished. Harriman used the same technique during the Cuban missile crisis, going through Schlesinger to get across his interpretation that Khrushchev was desperately seeking for a way out.[11]

The Joint Chiefs of Staff are likely to pass the word quietly through a White House staff member when they are unhappy about being overruled by the Secretary of Defense and are prepared to take their case to the Congress. For example, in the preparation for the fiscal year 1972 defense budget several staff members in the Bureau of the Budget persuaded the Budget Director that a cut of almost two billion dollars in the defense budget could be made. The Budget Director, George Shultz, in turn convinced the Secretary of Defense, Melvin Laird, to go along with these cuts. When informed of this, the Joint Chiefs went to the President's Assistant for National Security Affairs, Henry Kissinger, and persuaded him to take the issue to the President, at which point the funds were restored to the budget.[12]

Junior staff members frequently take issues to White House staff members when they cannot get their superiors to make a formal recommenda-

10. Lilienthal, *Journals*, pp. 233–34.
11. Schlesinger, *A Thousand Days*, pp. 821–22; Brandon, "Schlesinger at the White House."
12. *New York Times*, April 9, 1971.

tion to the President. They hope that the President will act or instruct departments to act on a matter which might not otherwise gain presidential attention. This technique shaped the Point Four Program under which President Truman, in his inaugural address, proposed technical assistance to developing countries. State Department officials who had long favored such a program found it impossible up to that point to gain any support within the department. In preparation for his inaugural address, Truman had instructed the White House staff to seek fresh ideas which he could talk about. In searching for ideas, White House staff assistant George Elsey came upon the proposal for a technical assistance program. Working with State Department staffers in favor of this proposal, Elsey developed a paragraph for the President's speech. When the draft was sent to the State Department for comment, the paragraph was removed; however, Elsey put it back, and the President delivered the address with Point Four intact.[13]

Senior participants sometimes calculate that, by choosing which White House staff member handles the issue and what face of the issue the President sees, they can influence the outcome of a presidential deliberation. For example, Harold Stassen as head of the Mutual Security Agency recognized that the White House staff member most friendly to his cause was Eisenhower speech writer Emmet John Hughes. Thus instead of seeking to gain approval through normal budgetary procedures for a proposed level of spending, Stassen simply put the figure he desired into a draft of a presidential text on mutual security and sent it off to Hughes' office. Hughes reports that he edited the message in the morning and then quotes from his diary as to what happened after that. His description is worth quoting in full, not only to illustrate this use of the White House staff, but also to guard against the tendency of the reader to assume that the processes being described are orderly ones:

On returning to my office from lunch, I find a huge hassle on. The issue, boiled down: does the Administration really want $5.8 billion—or would, say, a billion dollars less do just as nicely? Incredible—but no one has made a decision. And I quickly gathered a few other incredible facts. One: The State Department had neither seen the message nor knew its contents till this noontime. Two: Joe Dodge at the Budget Bureau likewise had not seen it. Three: State thinks the message is too weak, asks for not enough. Four: Budget thinks the message is too strong, asks for too much. Five:

13. Jonathan Bingham, *Shirt-Sleeve Diplomacy*, p. 10; Louis J. Halle, *The Society of Man*, pp. 21–23, 29–30.

Neither Dulles nor Adams can be reached till the end of the day, for they are locked in a conference of state governors in the old State Department building. *Six:* Committee hearings on the request—whatever it turns out to be—start on the Hill at 10 A.M. tomorrow morning.

It took a while—and maybe a dozen phone calls—to piece together a coherent picture of all this incoherence. On one side, Douglas MacArthur at State lamented to me: "I'm terribly worried about this. There's no water in the $5.8 billion figure, and if we don't get all of it, we're in *real* trouble." (And Dulles somehow sent me a note, perhaps by carrier pigeon, from his closed conference with the governors—to the same effect.) From the other side, came the voice of Joe Dodge: "Nonsense! State's going to have to have a lot of unspent funds at the end of this year. I just don't want to see the President getting out on a limb asking for so much money as a *must* when he may damn well take a licking on the request." To compound confusion, Herb Brownell somehow learns of the clash. Shows up in the White House, and corners me in the corridor to back Dodge vehemently, adding: "What the hell, if we do need more money later, we can always ask for it then." A remarkable theory: call it "Planning for Yesterday?" Finally, to cap all, Jerry Persons emerges from the President's office, vaguely reporting this and other business, to advise that the President wants Dodge to be the deciding voice. At best, this seems odd, for I'm sure no one had briefed the President on the substance of the disagreements.

After some hours of this nonsense, and running between the White House and State, carrying the crumpled message-draft—by now it is beginning to have the feel of a battered and half-unfeathered shuttlecock—I decided to get Adams out of his conference. As he glowers kindly at the interruption, I tell him: "This is all too damn serious to be decided in a series of side-of-the-mouth corridor conversations. We just have to hold it till the morning when we can get to the President directly and quietly." Garrulously, he grunts: "Okay."

The circus continues after sundown. I finally locate Stassen, Stassen heads for Dodge's office, and after some three-way phone-negotiating we all reach agreement of a sort on the message language—roughly close to original, with the dollar figure intact. No sooner is this compact contrived than Dulles' office phones to suggest to me still stronger language in the request. Arbitrarily I decide to put it in and leave it to State to so advise Dodge and Stassen.

We come full circle next morning, when Adams and I see the President. He buys "strong" message as I've written it, even though we report both Brownell's (political) and Dodge's (fiscal) aversion to it. With marvelous disregard of his nomination of Dodge yesterday to be deciding voice, he shrugs off such reservations. Message swiftly typed in final form and rushed to the Hill.

How reassuring it would be to all governments of our allies around the world—if they could see the disciplined and dedicated way we plan and provide our economic assistance![14]

Other Paths to the President

The most frequently used paths to the President are described above. Other things being equal, participants prefer to take a consensus position to the President; or when he demands options, they prefer to structure a series of options such that only one is the viable alternative that the President can choose. When it is not possible to put together a consensus, or when certain senior participants are unwilling to take an issue to the President, other participants will resort to either going alone to the President and attempting to arrange things with him or working through members of the White House staff believed to be friendly to a given position. When none of these methods succeeds, alternative routes to the President will be tried.

One such method is to work through individuals from Washington known to have direct access to the President. Most Presidents have a few Washington advisers from outside the government. If these individuals can be persuaded to interest themselves in a problem, they provide a route to the President. In addition, senior leaders of the Congress have access to the President and are often asked to bring up with him items which are known to interest them.

As we saw in Chapter 10, the press can also be used as a way of getting issues to the President.

Foreign governments, too, can be used for this purpose. If a foreign government can be persuaded to raise a question or make a proposal which it requests be considered at the highest levels of the American government, then this can be a route for forcing an issue to White House attention. Often an American ambassador in the field can stimulate such a request.

Negotiating teams sent out by the United States are often in a position

14. Hughes, *The Ordeal of Power*, pp. 82–83.

to raise issues which they could not get to presidential attention in any other way. While W. Averell Harriman worked in Washington as the President's special representative for Vietnam negotiations, he had to channel his proposals through the Secretary of State. When he went to Paris as the head of the Vietnam negotiating team, however, his cables from Paris automatically went to the President and other senior officials. Thus from the vantage point of Paris, Harriman was able to get through to the President with proposals that otherwise would not have reached him.

Another technique used is to propose the creation of a commission on a general subject with the hope that the commission members will make the proposal that one is advocating.

Securing a Presidential Decision

Even when an issue reaches the President, participants continue to maneuver to get him to make a decision and the right decision. This may involve promoting as broad a consensus as possible for the desired decision and establishing a deadline so that the President feels a need to decide.

Building a Consensus

Because of his concern about maintaining the support of his principal subordinates and because of his recognition of the need for widespread support in order to gain congressional and public acceptance of a proposal and its implementation by the bureaucracy, a President is reluctant to overrule key individual supporters or major institutions such as the Joint Chiefs of Staff. Participants, discovering this over time, feel the need to forge a consensus in order to increase the probability that the President will act and act in the way they desire. Therefore at the crucial time proponents intensify their efforts to get all the key participants on board, hopefully with their active support or at least with their agreement not to report to the President their dissent from a proposed decision. This is primarily a bargaining process.[15] A number of techniques are used by participants in pursuit of a broad consensus.

15. See Schilling, "The Politics of National Defense," p. 22.

PERSUASION

Persuasion involves an effort, without changing a proposal, to convince a participant that it is in his interest to support it. This can be done, as we suggested earlier, either by relating arguments to the national interest (conceived in terms of the shared images of the participants) or by appealing to particular organizational, personal, or domestic political interests of the participants.

Where the appeal is to interests other than the national security interests, care must be taken to see that the arguments are presented only to those who will be influenced by them. This must be done because certain forms of argument—for example, those relating to domestic politics or personal interests—are considered questionable, and there is a danger that they will be leaked to the press. Moreover, arguments relating to one set of organizational interests may underline the danger to other organizations of a particular proposal.

The need to keep arguments related to other interests from getting broad dissemination means that they are almost always put forward orally. This is because of the recognition that almost anything put in writing will be duplicated and widely distributed within the government and is likely to be leaked if leaking would help those who oppose the arguments put forward. In some cases the arguments are stated orally and privately to a single individual in an effort to persuade him to support a particular position. Thus there appears to be no written record of any discussion about the impact of an ABM deployment on domestic politics and in particular on the presidential election of 1968. Certainly none of the papers coming from the Pentagon to the President discussed this matter. It appears that all such discussions, assuming they took place, were confined to very private conversations between President Johnson and the Secretary of Defense McNamara, in which the President sought to convince McNamara or at least explain to him why he felt that some sort of ABM was necessary if the President was to be reelected and to avoid the charge of a ballistic missile defense gap.

Participants who do not have an opportunity for private conversation with the President may have to bring up in wider meetings their arguments relating to other interests. In that case they are likely to speak in a veiled and elliptical manner. For example, one of the strongest arguments which the CIA had for going forward with the Bay of Pigs invasion was that cancellation would weaken the political position of President Kennedy, since he had promised during the election campagin to assist Cuban refugees in seeking to "liberate" their homeland. The CIA leaders simply pointed out that if the invasion were cancelled, the Cuban brigade would disperse, and many of its leaders would return to the United States. They did not have to spell out the fact that these people would talk to their friends and ultimately to the press, making it known in Washington that the President had prevented what these leaders would of course describe as a sure-to-succeed invasion. Kennedy no doubt got the point without needing explicit reference to domestic politics.

The appeal to organizational interests frequently takes the form of suggesting a delayed benefit. For example, in trying to make the case for Army control of a medium-range missile the Army explicitly adopted Navy doctrine. The admirals had long argued that they needed to have offensive missiles in order to destroy targets of particular concern to the Navy, such as Russian submarines. The generals now argued that they needed to have offensive missiles to destroy targets such as enemy staging areas and enemy launching sites for missiles aimed at troops. The Army appealed to the Navy for support on the grounds that the proposal would reinforce the principle that each service should have the offensive forces to deal with threats to its own particular mission.[16]

COMPROMISE

In bargaining, one offers to alter the proposal on which one seeks to have a decision in order to make it more palatable to a participant or to change the consequences for him of accepting or rejecting the proposal. One way in which a proposal is frequently changed in order to seek consensus for it is to omit items which are known to be controversial even though they seem to go to the heart of what is being recommended. For example, in the preparation of NSC 68 in 1950, a study which advocated substantial American rearmament in order to deal with what was seen as a growing Russian military threat, a conscious decision was made to omit costs and to omit the details of what increases in military capability there should be. This was done explicitly to avoid interservice conflict and to provide a document to which all the services would give their support. This was felt to be necessary if there was to be any hope (as explained below) of securing the support of the Secretary of Defense which was in turn needed if there was to be any chance of getting presidential support.[17]

16. Armacost, *The Politics of Weapons Innovation*, p. 94.
17. Hammond, "NSC-68," pp. 319–20.

An alternative way to create a consensus is to add items to the package so that there is something in it for everyone. This is what is typically done in creating what is known somewhat humorously in the bureaucracy as Option B. If the President has asked for a statement of alternative options, he may receive a list with two extreme options, A and C, both of which are clearly unacceptable and impossible to carry out, and a consensus "Option B," the item around which the bureaucracy is coalesced and which they are urging the President to implement. Often a consensus has been attained for this option by including in it many of the things that each organization wishes to do and stating the principle or "policy" so generally that each organization is free to continue behaving as it has in the past. This maneuver seemingly was much used in Washington during the Vietnam War. For example, in the debates in late 1964 and early 1965 over what to do about the rapidly "deteriorating" situation in South Vietnam some argued for a substantial bombing campaign against North Vietnam, and others argued that the only way to save the situation was to send large numbers of ground troops into South Vietnam. In the end the President was confronted with a compromise "Option B" which called for both a bombing campaign against North Vietnam and the introduction of substantial ground combat troops into the south.[18]

A similar process occurred in an attempt to develop a unified proposal for President Truman regarding the beefing up of the defense of Europe after the outbreak of the Korean War. The State Department, believing that some symbolic gestures were necessary quickly, urged the appointment of an American Supreme Commander and the creation of an integrated military force. The Joint Chiefs, more concerned with actual military capability than with symbols, were pressing for early rearmament of Germany. Even though Secretary of State Dean Acheson recognized that a proposal to rearm Germany would meet stiff opposition not only in France but in Germany itself, he agreed to go forward with this recommendation to President Truman, who ultimately approved what Acheson has referred to as the "one package" decision.[19]

Generally speaking, changes in the wording of proposals to secure the support of a particular participant or organization have more to do with getting them accepted than with altering what is proposed. In some cases the change will be perceptible only to those involved in the bureaucratic

18. Thomson, "How Could Vietnam Happen?" p. 208.
19. Acheson, *Present at the Creation*, pp. 437–38, 440, 459; Laurence Martin, "The American Decision To Rearm Germany," pp. 656–67.

infighting. Acheson tells of a typical incident which occurred among the members of the U.S. delegation to a NATO meeting in which the principal protagonists were Averell Harriman, then an Assistant to President Truman for National Security Affairs, and General Omar Bradley, Chairman of the Joint Chiefs of Staff. Acheson explains:

Almost at the beginning of the Lisbon week a heated disagreement in our own delegation between Harriman and General Bradley showed me how thin was the ice we had to cross. Harriman pressed the General to endorse the view that the military forces which the Temporary Committee report recommended as being within the economic capability of the European countries would provide an adequate defense for Europe. Bradley refused to do so. I listened to the discussion until it seemed to be getting out of hand and then adjourned the delegation meeting, asking the disputants to meet alone with me. Pointing out that General Bradley was being asked to lend his great reputation to the support of a proposition that one could see was, at least, open to doubt, I asked whether he thought the forces recommended were better than what we had, were the best we could get, and, taken together with our nuclear capacity, would have a strong deterrent effect upon any desire to test their adequacy. The General said that he most certainly did think so. Harriman, I urged, ought to be able to find language that Bradley could accept and would carry the desired meaning. This was done.[20]

ABM deployment and the Bay of Pigs invasion stand as more complicated illustrations of the same tendency. In the case of the ABM, Johnson was seeking to get McNamara to agree to some sort of deployment. For Johnson's purpose of heading off a domestic political struggle he needed only a token ABM deployment which the Joint Chiefs and ABM's leading supporters in the Congress could describe for their own satisfaction as the first step toward the large anti-Russian system which they desired. His problem was that McNamara was strongly opposed to any actual large anti-Russian system and would not agree to deployment which was the beginning of such a system. The compromise that Johnson offered McNamara was to permit the Secretary of Defense to describe the proposal any way that he chose and to accompany it with as strong a warning as he wished to make against a large system, provided only that the actual deployment which he authorized was one which the generals and senators such as Richard Russell could urge be made the first step toward

20. Acheson, *Present at the Creation*, p. 623.

a major system. In turn Johnson appears to have authorized the Joint Chiefs to condition their acceptance of the proposed deployment with a statement to congressional committees that they were going along with it only because they viewed it as the first step toward the large anti-Russian system that the Secretary of Defense was simultaneously resisting. Thus without altering in any significant way the actual physical first-stage deployment of the ABM system, Johnson by letting McNamara and the Joint Chiefs describe it as they chose was able to secure the consensus which kept his Secretary of Defense from resigning and kept the Joint Chiefs from coming out against him.

In the case of the Bay of Pigs the problem for the CIA was to convince President Kennedy that the invasion should be authorized. In order to do so, they agreed in principle to cut back the size of the invasion and to eliminate any overt U.S. involvement. There appears to have been very little change in what they actually planned to do, but a substantial change occurred in the President's perception of what he was authorizing.[21]

CHANGING THE CONSEQUENCES

If the proposal itself cannot be sufficiently altered to secure the support of key participants, it may be possible to gain their support by altering the consequences for them of the proposal. The change of consequences may relate either to their perception of national security interests or to other interests. One device frequently used to change consequences is to give a friendly foreign government some crucial information. For example, in the case of an argument within the American government about whether to respond to an increase in Russian military power, the consequences will be seen as very different if the increase in Russian power is known to allies of the United States. If American allies are informed, then failure to respond to the Russian move could (it will be argued) increase their concern about whether the United States intends to meet its commitments.

A second frequently used technique is to arrange for an issue to come up in an international forum. It is one thing for the United States to avoid taking a position publicly on an international issue; it may be quite another to vote against a stand which has wide support. For example, the

21. How far this change went is not entirely clear, but it is worth noting that Secretary of State Dean Rusk assured his Under Secretary, Chester Bowles, who had reported to him great qualms about the proposed invasion, that the planned operation had been reduced to the point where it would not be reported on page one of the *New York Times.* See Bowles, *Promises To Keep: My Years in Public Life, 1941–1969,* p. 239 (n. 2).

position of a number of participants in the American government on the question of trade with Rhodesia and relations with South Africa has probably been affected by the fact that this issue comes up in the United Nations General Assembly. So also has the American position on seabed mining been affected by the need to take positions in General Assembly debates.

The chief obstacle to changing national security consequences is the difficulty of getting other governments to take actions. For this reason participants may have to seek to manipulate consequences in relation to other interests. In some cases the other interest may be an extremely narrow one of convenience. For example, the military services have been known to persuade an ambassador to permit a military attaché section to be added to an embassy by indicating that an airplane goes with an attaché's office and hence would be at the disposal of the ambassador.[22] In other cases the consequences are more substantial. Typically an effort will be made to convince a participant that to hold out on support for a proposal moving toward the President will be to isolate himself from everybody else in the government and create a situation in which he is in effect asking the President to overrule everybody else and support him. Participants are reluctant to do that, recognizing that there are only a few occasions on which they can ask the President to support them against everybody else. If a participant can demonstrate the likelihood of presidential support, he can change the consequences for other participants by putting them in a position of seeking to oppose what the President will want to do. In an effort to affect consequences in this way, participants will seek to get a presidential speech which suggests support for the principle involved in a particular proposal, hence creating in people's minds the increased likelihood that the President will support the participants who influenced the speech. Or bureaucratic strategists may seek to gain the support of all other relevant officials before approaching an official known to be likely to oppose a particular proposal.

This was done with some skill in the case of NSC 68. Secretary of Defense Louis Johnson was known to be strongly opposed to any substantial increase in defense spending. Thus it was clear from the start that Johnson would be the principal opponent of the report advocating a major buildup of military forces. The Defense Department officials working on the study kept Johnson less than fully informed about what they were doing. After the study was completed, a meeting was arranged between

22. See, for example, Attwood, *The Reds and the Blacks*, p. 152.

Johnson and Secretary of State Acheson to discuss the report. When Johnson refused to be stampeded by this meeting and left the room in anger, the supporters of the proposal resorted to a different technique. After the paper was approved by Acheson, it was sent to the Defense Department to receive the endorsement of the Joint Chiefs of Staff and various departmental committees as well as the secretaries of the three services. Finding the document so authoritatively "certified" by the time it came to him, Johnson decided to sign it, thus making it a unanimous report of the President's advisers.[23]

Another technique to change consequences for a participant is to link a particular issue to other issues and to promise support to him on these in return for his support on the issue then under discussion. In some cases this type of logrolling can be done by actually joining two issues together and bringing them up to the President simultaneously. In other cases, the problem is not of support on another issue but the implicit threat that one will fight a participant on issues of concern to him if he fights on this issue.

Still another stratagem is to set up pessimistic beliefs about what may be done if a particular proposal, though not really welcome itself, is rejected. If participants come to believe that the alternative will be even worse in terms of their perception of national security interests, they may be prepared to go along with a proposal which they would otherwise vigorously oppose. Participants feel that they cannot fight every suggestion, and they tell themselves that they have to support the lesser of two evils. President Johnson recalled using this technique on the U.S. Ambassador to Vietnam, Ellsworth Bunker. During March of 1968 when he was considering a partial bombing halt, Johnson sent Bunker a cable outlining what he described as two pending suggestions. One proposed that all bombing be stopped, and the other proposed that there be a partial halt. As Johnson predicted, Bunker came back reluctantly accepting the partial halt while strongly opposing a complete halt.[24]

Deadlines and Delays

Getting an issue onto the President's desk with a consensus in support of a position is only a part of the battle. The problem then is to get him

23. Acheson, *Present at the Creation*, pp. 373–74; Hammond, "NSC-68," pp. 325–26.
24. Lyndon Johnson, *The Vantage Point*, pp. 408, 411.

to make a decision. Presidents and senior participants have time to do only what they think they must do. Richard Neustadt has well described the world of executive pressure:

A President's own use of time, his allocation of his personal attention, is governed by the things he has to do from day to day: the speech he has agreed to make, the fixed appointment he cannot put off, the paper no one else can sign, the rest and exercise his doctors order. These doings may be far removed from academic images of White House concentration on high policy, grand strategy. There is no help for that. A President's priorities are set not by the relative importance of a task, but by the relative necessity for him to do it. He deals first with the things that are required of him next. Deadlines rule his personal agenda. In most days of his working week, most seasons of his year, he meets deadlines enough to drain his energy and crowd his time regardless of all else. The net result may be a far cry from the order of priorities that would appeal to scholars or to columnists—or to the President himself.

What makes a deadline? The answer, very simply, is a date or an event or both combined. The date set by MacArthur for a landing at Inchon, or the date set by statute for submission of the budget, or the date set by the White House for a press conference, these and others like them force decisions on a President, pre-empt his time. And statements by MacArthur, or a Humphrey press explosion, or a House appropriations cut, or sputniks overhead, may generate such pressure inside government or out as to affect him in precisely the same way. Dates make deadlines in proportion to their certainty; events make deadlines in proportion to their heat. Singly or combined, approaching dates and rising heat start fires burning underneath the White House. Trying to stop fires is what Presidents do first. It takes most of their time.[25]

Thus a participant who wants a presidential decision must find a way to attach a deadline to his issue or attach his issue to a pre-existing deadline. In the first case he must find a way to convince the President of the necessity of deciding on this issue now. In the second, his effort is to convince the President that an already recognized problem can be solved by this proposal. As we mentioned before, those in the State Department who favored a major American technical assistance program were able to get the President to announce such a program because it was an answer to his problem of finding something new and dramatic to say in an in-

25. Neustadt, *Presidential Power*, pp. 155–56.

augural address. Such opportunities crop up from time to time—the President or a Cabinet officer has a speech to give or testimony to present before Congress, or he is going to an international meeting, or he feels under pressure to demonstrate that he is resolute. At such times, participants with a favorite proposal put it forward in the hopes that the President (or a department chief) will find it a solution to his problem.

Some issues carry with them a deadline which forces a presidential decision. The President's budget message is the most inexorable deadline. Each year in late January the President must present a budget to the Congress. In doing so, he must take at least an implied stand for or against those items in the budget which are of public or congressional concern. This means that any part of the bureaucracy vitally concerned about an issue can stimulate public or congressional interest in the issue and thereby force it into the open at budget time. Since there was great congressional and public interest in the ABM, Lyndon Johnson could not duck the issue in his annual budget messages. Instead, he had to discuss the subject and state clearly why he was for or against the ABM. Because this was an annual budget issue, proponents of the deployment of an ABM system had no difficulty in reaching the President and getting him to make a decision. For the same reason, opponents could present their case each year, so long as they suggested a plausible public anti-ABM stand which could be elaborated by the Secretary of Defense under congressional questioning. Thus at each budget cycle the proponents of ABM had a natural deadline, and opponents, because of the same deadline, had to devote considerable effort and energy to finding a rationale that the President would be prepared to use in explaining why he was not going forward with an ABM deployment.

In some cases a deadline arises out of a scheduled international meeting. For example, the debate within the United States government about whether or not to seek permission of European governments to deploy Thor and Jupiter intermediate-range ballistic missiles (IRBMs) in Europe came to a head in the preparations for a summit meeting of the North Atlantic Treaty Organization in mid-December 1957. The United States could not go to that meeting without raising the IRBM issue, because of its importance in the wake of the Sputnik launching. Thus a decision had to be made.[26]

Congressional hearings can also impose a deadline on decisions. If a

---

26. Armacost, *The Politics of Weapons Innovation*, p. 187.

committee is known to be strongly interested in a question and if the Cabinet officer can therefore expect to be intensely drilled, there is strong pressure to establish an administration position before he testifies. For example, Secretary of State Dulles found himself about to face the Senate Foreign Relations Committee on the subject of foreign aid. He was informed that the committee was particularly interested in a proposal for long-term financing and would press him on the creation of the proposed development loan fund. Knowing that the committee would demand something new from him and informed of its support for this particular proposal, Dulles decided to go forward and announce administration support for the fund.[27]

An event abroad may also create a deadline. Thus the death of Stalin, clearly necessitating some sort of presidential statement, posed the question of what kind of initial appeal Eisenhower would make to the new Russian leaders. The decision could not be delayed.

In some situations a scheduled presidential speech is inevitably related to a particular subject. If the President is to address the United Nations General Assembly, it is difficult for him not to comment on major issues of concern to the Assembly. Thus a deadline is imposed for taking a position on such an issue.

To keep such examples in perspective, it may be well to close our discussion of deadlines with a reminder that nearly every bureaucratic maneuver is subject to counter-maneuvers. Participants who favor delay, for instance, find ways to evade deadlines. Frequently, they do nothing, counting on the fact that their opponents will not be able to establish a deadline or attach their proposal to a deadline. If those favoring a decision seem to be succeeding, those who favor delay can and will propose a number of procedural devices to put off a decision. They will, for example, suggest that a document has not been fully cleared with all of those who are concerned and that a decision should be postponed until additional agencies and individuals are consulted. Alternatively, they can argue that the proposal really belongs in a different channel and should be delayed until it comes up through that channel. For example, the existence of a formal National Security Council system permits participants to argue that a proposal cannot come simply from one Cabinet officer to the President but must go through formal consideration not only by the National Security Council but also by its subordinate organs. Proponents of delay

27. Edgerton, *Sub-Cabinet Politics and Policy Commitment*, pp. 129–31.

can also call for further study, indicating that additional information is needed before a sensible decision can be made. They can themselves promise to provide additional information, insist that the proponents must provide it, or propose the creation of a special study group. If all else fails, they will put forward arguments against acting now. They may suggest that the process is moving too quickly and that there is danger in haste, or they may argue that the international situation does not at present permit the proposed actions.

Through examples of these and many other maneuvers and counter-maneuvers, we have now traced the policy process through to presidential decisions, but in doing so we have assumed, more or less, that all of the maneuvers described were available equally to all of the participants. Clearly this is not the case. Sources of influence are unequally distributed, and this affects what issues get to the President and how he decides them. This is the subject of the last chapter of Part II.

CHAPTER TWELVE

Influence and Decisions

We have discussed shared images, interests, the rules of the game, and stratagems both for advancing proposals and for blocking them. A great number of officials operate within this framework, subject to the same constraints. What personal characteristics enable some of them consistently to have more influence over decisions than the rest?

In brief the list reads as follows: (1) ability to gain the confidence of the President; (2) willingness to assume responsibility; (3) finesse in threatening to leak information or to resign; (4) staff skill in performing the functions of the bureaucracy; and (5) aptitude for mobilizing support outside the bureaucracy. To fully understand politics inside government, it is useful to examine each of these characteristics in action.

Relations with the President

The single most important determinant of the influence of any senior official is his relationship with the President. Indeed, a main topic of conversation in Washington is who is "in" with the President now.[1]

"Confidence" is the key concept in establishing a good relationship. As Dean Rusk explains:

The real organization of government at higher echelons is not what you find in textbooks or organizational charts. It is how confidence flows down from the President. That is never put on paper—people don't like it. Besides, it fluctuates. People go up—and people go down.[2]

Generally to win the President's confidence, an official must demonstrate both that he has mastered his area of responsibility and that he has the

1. See, for example, Attwood, *The Reds and the Blacks*, p. 108.
2. Rusk, "Mr. Secretary on the Eve of Emeritus," p. 62B.

President's interest at heart. By following his own precept, Rusk himself gained more power in Washington than most observers realized. This is borne out in the recollections of Lyndon Johnson's Press Secretary George Christian, who commented:

... Johnson's faith in Rusk never wavered. He listened to Clifford, Mc-Namara, George Ball, and others who sometimes differed with Rusk on specifics, and he might blend these views into a decision; but mainly it was Rusk's judgment he wanted in the end, and Rusk's judgment he followed.[3]

Confidence leads to the feeling on the part of the President that he should defer to a particular individual. The feeling is reinforced when an issue falls into that individual's area of responsibility. Presidents come to feel that, having made a man Secretary of State or Secretary of Defense, they owe him their support and ought not to undercut him. Several of President Eisenhower's closest advisers, including Sherman Adams, reported that Eisenhower frequently felt obliged to yield to Secretary of State John Foster Dulles on what he viewed as a diplomatic question even though Eisenhower was more eager for détente and arms control agreements with the Soviet Union than was his Secretary of State. Eisenhower speech writer Arthur Larson tells of one key episode, which revolved around a proposed speech to the American Society of Newspaper Editors:

... President Eisenhower had practically decided to call off the Editors' speech. The main reason was that he was in disagreement with John Foster Dulles on the content and tone of the speech. Dulles wanted to stress our accomplishments in the past in working toward peace. President Eisenhower wanted to stress how dark things were at that very moment and why all-out efforts were needed to get at the cause of tension. He showed me his exchange with Dulles and said, "I don't like to make a speech on foreign policy that my Secretary of State disagrees with." Moreover, Dulles had pooh-poohed his idea of inviting several thousand Soviet students and had raised many objections. The letter to Bulganin, as far as I know, was never actually sent, and the idea of bringing in three thousand Russian students was never followed up.[4]

The power of individuals close to the President, either personally or by position, is increased by virtue of the fact that they are better able to predict what arguments will be most persuasive with him. Other participants rely on these key officials for a judgment as to whether it is worth taking an issue to the President and, if so, in what form it should go. Success in

3. Christian, *The President Steps Down*, p. 115.
4. Larson, *Eisenhower*, pp. 72–73. See also Adams, *Firsthand Report*, p. 87.

gauging likely presidential responses increases the probability that one will be consulted on other issues and have one's views taken into account in shaping options for the President.

A participant who has the President's ear quickly acquires a reputation for being able to win. Not only will his support be sought, but proposals will be dropped rather than brought forward against his opposition. The great strength of Secretaries of State Dean Acheson and John Foster Dulles was the widely held perception in Washington that they would win if others carried a diplomatic or foreign policy issue to the President over their objections. Similar considerations affect the influence of junior participants in relation to their principals. Thus, if a Cabinet officer feels confidence in a particular individual or feels that he should defer to him because of his position, or if that participant has an ability to predict what the Secretary is likely to do and what will persuade him, he will come to have substantial influence within the bureaucracy.

It was suggested at the beginning of this section that there is nothing that Washington officials watch more closely than the relationship of particular individuals to the President. When a participant's standing is going up, the sense that one should defer to that individual rather than taking issues to the President will increase. When the reverse occurs, when an individual or an organization is seen to go down in presidential standing, then the sinking party will begin to find it necessary to compromise and yield to other groups whose status has, at least by comparison, risen. Roger Hilsman, who was then Director of Intelligence and Research in the Department of State, describes this rather subtle process at work as a result of the decline in presidential respect for the Central Intelligence Agency after the Bay of Pigs fiasco:

> ... What no one in Washington had failed to notice was that the Bay of Pigs debacle, the public display of the CIA's feet of clay, and, within the administration, the President's obvious disenchantment were all having an effect. On May 15, 1961, Allen Dulles called me to say that although he still had a few qualms, he was withdrawing his objections to the State Department's plan to consolidate its staffs and procedures for "co-ordinating" intelligence and political action proposals. More importantly, the letter to the ambassadors from the President giving them clear authority over all United States agencies abroad was cleared and shortly thereafter, on May 29, 1961, dispatched. Over the next few weeks, the ambassadors at all our missions overseas received briefings on the operations of all the agencies represented at their posts. Another, more subtle change also became ap-

parent—everyone had been burned so badly by the Bay of Pigs that fewer of the "political action" kind of operations were now being proposed for interdepartmental approval, and fewer still were approved. Not all of this became known immediately, but it was not long before even those of our allies who were most dependent on CIA saw the way the Washington wind was blowing. Finally, our ambassadors in those countries began to feel the change reflected in the officials with whom they dealt. When notables from these countries visited Washington, for example, they paid far fewer calls on the Director of Central Intelligence than had once been customary. CIA's power had been at least slightly reduced, in other words, even though no formal organizational changes had actually been made.[5]

Willingness To Assume Responsibility

When asked by a former colleague in the State Department to name the quality which he thought most necessary in a Secretary of State, Dean Acheson reportedly without hesitation replied, "The killer instinct."[6] Acheson was not thinking of foreign adversaries in making this remark. Rather, he was referring to the Secretary's relation with officials from other departments and members of the White House staff. One key component of a killer instinct is a drive for power. Because many do not have this instinct, those who do can wield substantial influence. In addressing the senior officials of the State Department at the beginning of the Kennedy administration, Secretary of State Rusk noted, "The processes of government have sometimes been described as a struggle for power among those holding public office." But, Rusk continued, this is true only in the sense that people struggle for formal bureaucratic trappings such as "water bottles." He argued that in fact most officials shy away from power and that the struggle is far more "the effort to diffuse or avoid responsibility." Therefore, he said, "Power gravitates to those who are willing to make decisions and live with the results."[7] Coupled with the drive for power must be an understanding of what makes for influence in Washington. Acheson and Dulles, for example, both understood the critical importance of maintaining the President's confidence and the perception in Washington that

5. Hilsman, *To Move a Nation*, pp. 80–81.
6. Kraft, *Profiles in Power*, p. 178.
7. Rusk speaking to the policymaking officers of the Department of State, February 20, 1961, as quoted in Hilsman, *To Move A Nation*, p. 15.

they had that confidence. They thus avoided fights that they knew they would lose and were careful to check with the President before undertaking a major battle.

Another element affecting personal power is one's ability to get mad, to display a temper. Referring to his experience as an ambassador to India, John Kenneth Galbraith observed that "a bad temper, real or contrived, serves as a 'No Trespassing sign.' "[8] One must be willing to confront those who seek to usurp one's power and to deal with them in an ungentlemanly way. One can thereby head off attempts by power seekers to move into one's domain and have them move on to others who are less assertive. For example, after the appointment of former Texas Congressman George Bush as President Nixon's representative to the United Nations, a number of officers in the State Department feared that Bush might move into their territory. After Bush made a comment about Middle Eastern policy at his first press conference, Joseph Sisco, the Assistant Secretary of State for Near Eastern Affairs and a man with a large reputation for power instinct, reportedly called Bush and told him "politely but firmly that he would give out the news about this area including any leaks."[9] No doubt Bush got the message. If he sought to move in on Sisco, he would have a brawl on his hands.

A reputation for chutzpah also helps. Acheson relates an incident in which he dealt with an attempt by the Department of the Interior to discredit the State Department's adviser on petroleum problems:

So when Mr. Hull, during the oil-to-Spain controversy, received a letter from his Cabinet colleague bitterly attacking our Petroleum Adviser, Max Thornburg, I intervened. The letter, copies of which had been sent to the President, Vice President, and others, charged that Thornburg, one of the officers principally concerned with the Spanish oil problem, was improperly influenced by connections in the oil industry. It was true that Thornburg, like Churchill, was in favor of a more liberal oil allowance to Spain than were most of the rest of us, but he was no more moved to judgment by improper influences than Churchill was. While Harold Ickes' charges were quite unfounded, the source of the argument ad hominem was not obscure. The Petroleum Adviser to Ickes had been a rival officer in the same company with Thornburg. Their opinions of one another were not laudatory, and this was not the first spat they had had. Since the oil controversy provided enough inflammable material without added charges of this

8. Galbraith, *Ambassador's Journal*, p. 106.
9. *Washington Post*, March 18, 1971.

nature, I asked Mr. Hull to allow me to handle the matter, and he, glad to be rid of the whole disagreeable business, assented.

Max Thornburg agreed to my plan. I telephoned Harold Ickes, told him that Mr. Hull had demanded an investigation of his charges, and said that one would be held that afternoon, with witnesses to be sworn and their testimony reported.

"Investigation!" he roared. "Before whom?"

"Before you," I said.

"What in hell is going on?" he demanded. "Are you crazy?" I explained that I was not; that, although it was well known that he was a curmudgeon, I was betting that he was an honest curmudgeon and would be willing to hear and decide upon the evidence my contention that he was mistaken about Thornburg. As the enormity and, at the same time, the humor of my effrontery sank in, he murmured, "Well, I'll be damned," and set an hour to receive us.

We went through with the judicial farce: witnesses sworn by a court reporter, testimony taken stenographically, and cross-examination offered to the Solicitor of Interior—now an eminent justice. The substance of the charges was disproved. No improper interest in conflict with Thornburg's duty had influenced his advice. Ickes agreed to this and was about to dismiss us when I pointed out that the retraction, like the charges, should be in writing and go to the same people. He agreed to this, also, and called a secretary and dictated an ungrudging letter saying that on further investigation he found that he had been mistaken and withdrew what he had said. A copy was given to the reporter.

We had risen to leave when in an audible sotto voce Harold added, as a postscript, "Anyway, I still think he's a so-and-so."

"Mr. Thornburg," I said, "resume the stand. Do you know the ordinary and usual meaning of the term Secretary Ickes has just used?"

"Oh my lord," Harold shouted, "skip it. I withdraw that, too. Now get out of here and let me do some work."

"Good-bye," I said, as we filed out. "I'll see you at six o'clock." And I did.[10]

Though Acheson has written more clearly than almost any other former bureaucrat about the need to assert oneself in the bureaucracy, President Truman evidently feared that Acheson was no match in this regard for Secretary of Defense Louis Johnson. Truman took aside his

---

10. Acheson, *Present at the Creation*, pp. 62–63.

newly appointed Budget Director, James Webb, and told him: "Acheson is a gentleman. He won't descend to a row. Johnson is a rough customer, gets his way by rowing. When he takes out after you, you give it right back to him."[11]

A special case of willingness to take responsibility—sometimes the source of it and sometimes a manifestation of it—is passion and devotion to an issue. If power in general depends on relations with the President, power on a particular issue may depend much more on the amount of time, energy, and interest one is prepared to devote. A senior official who is prepared to devote substantial energy to a problem can exert influence far beyond his ordinary performance. The same is often true of a junior official who has the confidence of his principal and devotes himself passionately to any one issue.

The Threat of Resignation

Even if a President does not warm up to particular senior participants or does not feel that their standing entitles them to great deference, he may feel obliged to take their views into account because of the fear that they otherwise may resign and politically embarrass him. Presidential sensitivity on this score is well known inside the government. Theodore Sorensen, speaking while still a White House senior adviser, commented:

Whenever any President overrules any Secretary, he runs the risk of that Secretary grumbling, privately, if not publicly, to the Congress or to the press (or to his diary), or dragging his feet on implementation, or, at the very worst, resigning with a blast at the President. It is rare, of course, for any appointee leaving office to have more public appeal than a President in office. The whirlpools he expects to stir up with his dramatic resignation and published exposés are soon lost in a tide of other events over which the President continues to ride.

Nevertheless, the violent resignation of almost any Secretary of State, Secretary of Defense, or Secretary of the Treasury could cause his chief considerable trouble; and other appointees could cause trouble in their own circles.[12]

Even when the President *asks* for the resignation of a senior partici-

---

11. Lilienthal, *Journals*, p. 565. In recording this episode, Lilienthal writes: "mystified Webb; doesn't me."

12. Theodore Sorensen, *Decision-Making in the White House*, p. 80.

pant, he does so in a way that avoids a public break. This will be particularly the case if the senior participant is seen to have his own following outside the executive branch. Thus when President Kennedy decided that he needed to replace Chester Bowles as the Under Secretary of State, he went to great lengths to persuade Bowles to take a different job in the government and ultimately to leave quietly without expressing his great misgivings about the current direction of Kennedy foreign policy.[13]

Knowing of presidential sensitivity on this score, senior officials on occasion explicitly threaten to resign if their views are not somehow accommodated. Secretary of Defense James Forrestal recorded in his diary a conversation with President Truman in which he stated what he would have to do if his views on defense reorganization were not taken into account:

I said I also wanted to make it clear that while I recognized that the genius of our government made it necessary for the President to have the support of his Cabinet members, I could not get myself into the position of agreeing to support by testimony before committees of Congress a bill which did violence to the principles which I outlined above. I said I recognized clearly that a member of the President's Cabinet should support his policies and that therefore I did not wish to set myself up as any source of embarrassment to him in the carrying out of his policies, and that, if I could not support with conviction and sincerity a bill introduced by the administration, I would have to ask him to accept my resignation. The President said in response to this that he expected no such necessity need arise.[14]

Warner Schilling later expressed the conventional opinion on why Truman chose to compromise in such a case. "The President," Schilling wrote, "was far better suited to cope with the arguments of an acting Secretary in private than he was to risk hearing them from an ex-Secretary in public, especially in an election year."[15]

An interesting question remains, however, so far as civilian officials are concerned. The fact is that not once in the postwar period has a senior civilian official involved in the making of foreign policy attacked the President's position after resigning. Not even the Vietnam War, which provoked substantial disagreement within the Kennedy and Johnson administrations, produced a civilian resignation followed by a blast at the

13. Bowles, *Promises To Keep*, pp. 352–64.
14. *Forrestal Diaries*, p. 205.
15. Schilling, "The Politics of National Defense," p. 158.

President's policies. Does this mean that the risk of embarrassment exists mostly in the President's mind and is simply exploited from time to time by adroit bureaucrats? Or does it mean that the risk assumes such importance that every President brings all his powers to bear to prevent an open break?

The one group that has clearly been prepared to follow up on threats to resign in protest is the military. American military officers feel strongly about the organizational interests of their service. They have often had broad support among the public and in the Congress and have demonstrated a willingness to resign "noisily" if overruled on key issues. This combination has made the threat of resignation of prominent military officers a very real one to every President.

The calculation of whether to resign depends in part on the perception of what sort of public reaction one will get. Thus in the late 1940s General Omar Bradley considered resigning but held off because of his belief that his plea for increased spending on the Army would fall on deaf ears in a period when Congress and the public favored a drive for economy.[16] A number of admirals outraged by Truman's refusal to build large carriers did resign in the so-called "revolt of the admirals" because of their strong feeling on the issue. Although they recognized that they could probably not win with the public, they perhaps expected some shift of attitudes in their direction. During the Eisenhower administration both Matthew Ridgway and Maxwell Taylor resigned from the post of Army Chief of Staff because of their opposition to the doctrine of massive retaliation. They took their case to the public, though without any great expectations of winning in the short run.

The most potent threat the military can make is the threat of the resignation en masse of all of the Joint Chiefs of Staff. President Johnson was apparently confronted with such a threat in 1966. The Chiefs, sensing that Secretary McNamara's standing with the public and the President had begun to fall, pressed the White House for higher budgets and threatened to resign en masse unless programs of each service, the ABM system, the new manned bomber, and ship construction were carried forward.[17] Johnson, deciding he could not tolerate a mass resignation of the Chiefs in the middle of the controversy about the Vietnam War, ap-

16. Ibid., pp. 160–61.
17. Hoopes, *The Limits of Intervention,* p. 90; Lawrence J. Korb, "Budget Strategies of the Joint Chiefs of Staff," pp. 14, 17. Korb cites as his source an interview with the Chief of Naval Operations, Admiral McDonald.

parently took steps to mollify them, including the decision to go forward with the Sentinel ABM system.

Staff Skill

A bureaucrat can make use of the skills of his trade in increasing his influence. Staff skill is in part a matter of knowledge, of "understanding" in detail how the system works, how various components such as the Joint Chiefs or the United States intelligence bureaus make their decisions, what is likely to influence them, and with what timing new information should be introduced. Staff skill also involves knowing the position of different individuals, knowing whom one should go to for a particular stand on a particular issue or to get a particular fact which others may be seeking to bury. It means knowing whom to call in a particular agency, because that individual is likely to favor what one wants done and can exert the necessary influence. It means knowing when to question the expertise of others and how to do so.[18] A key component of bureaucratic skill is the knowledge of how to make planning effective. Adam Yarmolinsky explains how this was done in the Office of the Secretary of Defense in which he served:

In the area of direct relations with State, the planning function was similarly integrated with operations. Within the Office of the Assistant Secretary of Defense for International Security Affairs, the Assistant Secretary set up a policy planning staff as a kind of free-wheeling adjunct to the regional and subject-matter specialized units within the office to work on whatever problems might be assigned to it from time to time. This staff examined the long-range planning implications of immediate decisions facing the department, but it did so always in the context of a matter that was very much at the top of the Assistant Secretary's immediate priority list. It did not produce policy papers in vacuo, but rather made recommendations for action in areas where the Assistant Secretary and the Secretary were prepared to act.

By contrast the policy planning function in the State Department has been lodged in a policy planning council, a group of senior foreign service

---

18. On these points see, for example, McGarvey, "The Culture of Bureaucracy," p. 75; Anderson, *The Presidents' Men*, p. 330; Robert Johnson, "The National Security Council," p. 727; Adam Yarmolinsky, "Bureaucratic Structures and Political Outcomes"; Hilsman, *To Move a Nation*.

officers assigned for this purpose, who have largely generated their own agenda, but whose work product has had very little visible impact on the decision-making that goes on at the other end of the building.

The Defense Department approach to policy planning in the foreign area has the obvious defect of limiting the opportunities for the planning staff to raise questions that are wholly outside the current concerns of decision-makers. But this function is one that, realistically, must be performed outside government if it is to be performed effectively and if the result is to draw the attention of busy men at the top of any government structure. On the other hand, the Defense Department approach to the planning process reinforces the effectiveness of the department in generating immediate policy proposals, and particularly in taking a more active and less reactive position on matters that are on the joint State-Defense agenda.[19]

One key skill is the ability to write short and concise memos which explain an issue in a way likely to seem persuasive to the President and other senior officials. McGeorge Bundy, Special Assistant for National Security to Kennedy and Johnson, had a reputation for writing excellent memoranda.[20] The State Department, on the other hand, has always had a reputation for writing memos much too long and lacking in persuasiveness. Under Secretary of State George Ball, for example, is reported to have wondered aloud on one occasion "why State Department officials never seemed to be able to write anything under ten pages."[21] A former White House official has noted the following episode in which State lost the battle of the briefings:

When he called for briefing papers on short notice from State for a Presidential overseas trip, his first deadline passed without any response. He then turned to the office of International Security Affairs at Defense, which responded with a complete, concise, and thoroughly indexed briefing book. State finally crashed through with several cardboard cartons of unsorted cables on the countries listed in the President's itinerary.[22]

The effective bureaucrat will take considerable time on an important memo in an effort to make it both short and persuasive to the President.

19. Yarmolinsky, "Bureaucratic Structures and Political Outcomes," p. 232.
20. Halberstam, "The Very Expensive Education of McGeorge Bundy," pp. 28–29.
21. Attwood, *The Reds and the Blacks*, p. 106.
22. Adam Yarmolinsky, *The Military Establishment*, p. 34. Though this example may be extreme, it is not atypical. See, for example, the first memorandum presented to President Truman by the Department of State and reprinted by him in *Year of Decisions*, pp. 14–17.

David Lilienthal, then Director of the TVA, describes one working session:

Owen had been working several days on such a memo. It was very long and quite preachy, and full of a tone of preoccupation with ourselves that doesn't seem to me very persuasive. But it had the essential points. I suggested a different approach: one that I thought built upon the President's own experience and interests. This was to assert that TVA was still in danger from its enemies, but that this time the danger came from efforts to break down the autonomy and freedom from red tape that provides our chief armor against attacks; namely, our ability to do a good job and one that evokes the approval and support of the people. So I drafted a rough statement along that line. By the time Owen and Clapp rewrote it, it was again obscure and much too long, I thought. By this time it was 10:30 P.M. This went on and on. At 12:40 A.M. we had another draft, briefer, but still not too good. I was so whipped down that I would have accepted it, but Owen saw its weaknesses and insisted on doing something with it. At two o'clock we quit, still without a memorandum. I didn't get to bed until 3 A.M.

I got off by myself at 9:15 and wrote the introductory part on a new basis, in longhand, and revised the balance; Clapp made some suggestions, and at 2:45 I was with the President's special counsel, Captain Clifford, with a copy of a 5½ page, double-spaced draft.

This tale of a memo is almost incredible—that's why I have taken the trouble to tell its story in such fullness. No one seeing the memo would believe that it represented so much work.

But it appears that the care was worth it. For the President did read it, and he began our meeting this morning by pointing to it on his desk and saying, "I've read your statement and I agree completely. But where are we going to get someone to take your place so TVA can go on that way, the way I want it?"[23]

Ability To Mobilize Outside Support

A major form of influence within the bureaucracy is the ability to mobilize the support of influential groups outside the executive branch.

23. Lilienthal, *Journals*, p. 93.

These are groups that matter to the President, either because they affect his ability to pursue the particular policy under discussion or his more general ability to function effectively and to be reelected. The most potent such groups are leading congressmen and senators, as well as major groups within the President's political party and interest groups whose support the President needs to have. The ability to mobilize outside groups comes in part from their perception that particular participants within the bureaucracy should be deferred to in defining the national interest. It may also come from a belief that the particular participants inside represent the interests of the outside group.

The substantial influence of senior military officers has rested in part on the prestige and influence that military leaders have enjoyed in the past with leading figures in the Congress. Many congressmen have defined the national interest in terms of what the military believe is necessary for national security. Other groups in the society, including some newspaper editors, American Legion officials and to some extent American labor unions, have also defined the national interest largely in terms of deference to military perceptions. The influence of the military services has been enhanced by their willingness and ability to make their views known outside the executive branch. In testifying before congressional committees, senior military officers will make clear where their judgment differs from that of the President, particularly as reflected in budgetary decisions. Military officers are also quite willing to talk to members of the press about their views on security matters. Presidents are aware that, if the military is unhappy, Pentagon press reporters will report the existence of military disaffection. For many years Hanson Baldwin, for example, the military editor of the *New York Times,* reported accurately on the views of the Joint Chiefs and particularly of the Navy. On some issues the influence of the military has virtually amounted to a veto. On matters of reorganization of the Defense Department, for example, both President Truman and President Eisenhower carried on extensive negotiations with the military in the recognition that they were unlikely to be able to get any reorganization plan through the Congress which did not have military support.

The military services offer perhaps the leading example of achieving influence within the American government in the postwar period through ability to call on outside groups of importance to the President. But such influence has not been limited to the military. Bernard Baruch, for instance, despite Truman's impatience with him, had considerable influence within the Truman administration, without holding any official position, because it was recognized that he had important influence with congressional leaders and with the business community.[24]

The Elusiveness of Decisions

The effort to describe the process by which decisions on national security issues are made within the American government is at an end. What is contained in these past six chapters may be misleading, inasmuch as it gives the reader too great a sense of orderliness. In reality, as we have hinted from time to time, there is much confusion, much that occurs by accident and without the intent of any particular participant. There is much also that remains inscrutable. All close observers of presidential decisions have warned of the difficulty of analyzing decision making in the White House. In John F. Kennedy's words: "The essence of ultimate decision remains impenetrable to the observer—often, indeed to the decider himself. . . . There will always be the dark entangled stretches in the decision-making process—mysterious even to those who may be most intimately involved."[25] And George Reedy, a close observer of President Johnson, has warned us:

The fact is that a president makes his decisions as he wishes to make them, under conditions which he himself has established, and at times of his own determination. He decides what he wants to decide, and any student of the White House who believes that he is making a contribution to political thought when he analyzes the process is sadly mistaken. At best— at the very best—he can only contribute to human knowledge some insights into the decision-making process of one man.[26]

On major issues the President does decide. But, as we suggest in Part III, the process is then by no means over.

24. See, for example, ibid., p. 163.
25. Theodore Sorensen, *Decision-Making in the White House*, pp. xi–xiii.
26. Reedy, *The Twilight of the Presidency*, p. 31.

PART THREE

Actions

CHAPTER THIRTEEN

Decisions and Implementation

The reader has every right to expect to be at the end of the book. For one thing it is already quite long. For another, we have reached the end of the topic as it is normally discussed. We have traced the foreign policy process inside the government to the point of presidential decisions. But the process is by no means over. If our question is not "How do Presidents decide?" but "How does the United States act?" then we need to explore the relationship between presidential decisions and the subsequent actions of government officials.

Presidential Decisions

Presidental decisions vary in specificity. They are often conveyed only in policy statements expressing a sentiment or intention. The statements may indicate in general that certain kinds of actions should be taken but not say who should take them. Even if they do specify the actor, they seldom indicate when the action should be taken or the details of how it should be done. In fact the instructions are often so vague as to leave all the actors free to continue behaving as they have in the past.[1]

Even if a decision results from a long struggle among his advisers—indeed, especially when it results from such a struggle—the President tends to delay decisions and then decide as little as possible.[2] Furthermore, the President seldom makes a single comprehensive decision covering a wide range of interrelated issues. More often he decides a series of questions

1. On this general point, see Taylor, *The Uncertain Trumpet*, pp. 82–83; and W. W. Rostow, "The American Agenda," p. 17.
2. On this point, see Warner Schilling, "The H-Bomb Decision: How To Decide without Actually Choosing." Our description here draws heavily on this article as well as Schilling's "The Politics of National Defense."

discretely, each one on its own merits, adding up to a series of diffuse and, on some occasions, contradictory guidelines to the bureaucracy about what should be done.

There are a number of reasons why a President may not want to state definitely what should be done to implement his decision. In many cases, the consensus which has been built for the decision may in fact depend on the vagueness of what the President decides. In the case of the ABM, Secretary of Defense McNamara was prepared to go along with a limited deployment provided he could announce it as anti-Chinese and express strong opposition to erecting any large system supposedly designed to counter a Russian missile attack. At the same time, the Joint Chiefs of Staff and Senate leaders, such as Chairman of the Senate Armed Services Committee Richard Russell, were prepared to go along with limited initial deployment provided they could describe it as the first step toward a large anti-Russian system. In order to keep this "coalition" together the President's decision had to be vague enough so that participants on each side could believe that he had decided in their favor (and in any case so that participants on each side were free to describe the decision as they chose). President Truman was confronted with a similar problem of differing views about whether or not the United States should begin the development of a hydrogen bomb. With Atomic Energy Commission Chairman David Lilienthal against any deployment, with the military in favor of proceeding with a deployment, and with the State Department in favor of exploring the options, Truman settled on a tentative and minimal decision which kept everybody on board by giving Lilienthal no target to shoot at but the military enough of a move in their direction that they were prepared to acquiesce.[3]

Often reinforcing the desire to maintain a semblance of harmony by expressing his decision in vague terms is a presidential desire not to be committed to the details of a decision. Presidents typically confront an issue on a very general and theoretical level without much discussion of the details of the best way to implement a decision. When he has not spent time on details and has not looked into the possible problems buried in one kind of decision or another, the President prefers to express only a general desire to move in a particular direction and leave it to a battle among his subordinates to fill out the details. He is likely to assume that important issues will be brought back to him for further decision.

3. Schilling, *The H-Bomb Decision*, pp. 38–42.

In many cases, a President, after making a decision, wishes it to be kept secret for a while in order to head off attacks on the decision before actions are under way. He recognizes that the further down in the bureaucracy a piece of paper gets which specifies that the President has decided something, the more likely the piece of paper will be leaked. In Washington what the President decides is news, and low-level officials are eager either to show that they know what the President wants or to undercut a policy which they oppose.

In addition, the President may feel that his time must not be squandered in providing specific instructions. Robert Cutler, at one time Assistant to the President for National Security Affairs, reports that this was Eisenhower's view:

Eisenhower believed that policy decisions at the apex of Government should afford general direction, principle, and guidance, but should not be spelled out in detail. The Council dealt with strategy, not tactics. A Supreme Commander's orders are directed to Army groups and armies; they do not deal with battalions and companies. The last throw of Ludendorff in 1944 [sic] failed, in part, because his orders meddled with the battle movement of small elements. President Eisenhower was as impatient with too much detail as he was with lack of clarity in stating general policy.[4]

Whether or not he considers attention to "details" appropriate, a President when he is new in office tends to assume that faithful subordinates all down the line will labor to put into practice the policies he outlines. One of President Eisenhower's speech writers commented on Eisenhower's initial faith of this kind: "Nowhere did the lack of civilian experience so betray itself as in this system's cheerful assumption that, once the Chief Executive had pointed in a certain political direction, the full force of government would move in that direction, in concert as precise and as massive as battalions and divisions wheeling through field maneuvers."[5]

Even when he comes to understand that specification of detail is necessary if one wishes to have faithful implementation, a President will not have on tap at the White House experts to draft decisions in specific terms in all areas. Nor does the White House staff, whatever its own expertise, have time to prepare detailed instructions on many issues.

Because presidential decisions are seldom formulated in a way that

4. Cutler, *No Time For Rest*, p. 300.
5. Hughes, *The Ordeal of Power*, p. 153.

conveys in detail what should be done and because the President himself is seldom the actor to carry out the decision, it is true only in very special cases that presidential decisions are self-executing. Usually, in fact, they begin a process. The President often announces a policy decision in conversation with senior officials who head the organizations which will be responsible for implementing his decisions. On their understanding or recollection of what was said depend the first steps toward concrete action. In other cases, the President decides alone or in the company of White House officials, and the decision is then conveyed (sometimes orally) to the heads of the departments concerned or to a subordinate official who is believed responsible for supervising the required actions. They in turn issue instructions to those who, according to the rules of procedure, are responsible for actually carrying out the decision. Frequently this involves not only distributing directives to subordinates in Washington but also sending out cables to American ambassadors and military commanders in the field. This is not a trivial matter. Turning the sketchy language of a presidential decision into precise terms which can be understood and acted on in the field is extraordinarily difficult and may have to be done at high speed. During the opening days of the Korean War, for example, the senior civilian and military officials, after meeting with the President and getting his oral instructions, would move to the Pentagon or the State Department and improvise written instructions to the field.[6]

Once orders are written and sent to the individuals who should act, one might at last expect faithful implementation of the presidential decision, but this does not occur either. Why it does not is our next subject.

Limits on Faithful Implementation

There are three basic causes for failure to comply with presidential or other directives: (1) officials at the operations level may not know what it is that senior officials want them to do; (2) they may be unable to do what they believe they have been ordered to do; (3) they may resist doing what they have been ordered to do. Each of these is discussed in turn.

6. This process and the difficulty of translating orders into operational form in the opening days of the Korean War are described by Glenn Paige in *The Korean Decision*, pp. 138–39, 142, 161, 163, 245–47, 250–51, 321–23. See also Beverly Smith, "Why We Went to War in Korea," p. 80.

Uncertainty about Orders

In approaching the question of why presidential orders may not be obeyed, it is important to keep in mind the vast size and diversity of the federal government. Few officials see the President at all. Even fewer see him often enough to have a good feel for his approach to problems. Many of those who have to implement decisions are not privy to conversations between the President and his principal advisers or between those advisers and their subordinates. The orders which they receive in writing or orally are not only very general but are often the only clues they have. Thus the ambassador or first secretary in the field, the commander of a bomber squadron, an assistant secretary in Washington, a Treasury official visiting a foreign government—all may have little information on which to determine what it is the President wants them to do.

In some cases, officials at the operations level may not even know that the President has issued orders in a particular area. After an American U-2 was shot down over the Soviet Union, a public affairs officer in the National Aeronautics and Space Agency held a press conference at which he asserted that the plane had accidentally drifted over Russian territory. This happened long after President Eisenhower and his senior advisers had decided that only the State Department would make any comment.[7] Senior officials, too, may sometimes be unaware of the President's plans. For example, Secretary of Defense Melvin Laird, while visiting Japan, made a number of statements which led to press reports that the United States favored a Japanese nuclear capability. Unknown to Laird, these statements were made at precisely the time that presidential assistant Henry Kissinger was in Peking negotiating with Chou En-lai about the possibility of a trip by Nixon to China. It is believed these comments by Laird greatly complicated Kissinger's mission. Laird was not disobeying orders. He was simply uninformed about Nixon's approach to China and therefore unaware of the fact that what he was saying might halt or at least complicate implementation.

Misunderstanding about what a subordinate is ordered to do crops up. The most dramatic case on record of a pure misunderstanding resulted in President Eisenhower's invitation to Soviet Premier Nikita Khrushchev to visit the United States. Eisenhower had decided that he would be pre-

7. David Wise and Thomas B. Ross, *The U-2 Affair*, pp. 78–84.

pared to invite Khrushchev to the United States *only if* there was progress at the ongoing foreign ministers' meeting which would justify the convening of a four-power summit conference. The invitation to the Russians was to be conveyed by Under Secretary of State Robert Murphy, who was to meet Soviet Deputy Prime Minister Koslav during the latter's visit to the United States. Murphy's instructions were given him directly by the President but were oral. Evidently, even this direct communication could not prevent misunderstanding. Murphy conveyed through Koslav an unconditional invitation to Premier Khrushchev, rather than the one that the President wished transmitted (contingent upon progress in the four-power talks). Confronted by this misunderstanding, Eisenhower felt obliged to honor the invitation.[8]

More often, it is not that the official is totally uninformed or that he completely misunderstands his orders. Rather, he has no way of grasping the nuances behind decisions, no guidance as to exactly why he is told to do what he has been told to do. This makes it very difficult for him to implement the policy, to make the day-to-day implementing decisions in conformity with the President's desires. George Kennan explains:

In the execution of policy, we see the same phenomenon. Anyone who has ever had anything to do with the conduct of foreign relations knows that policies can be correctly and effectively implemented only by people who understand the entire philosophy and world of thought of the person or persons who took the original decision. But senior officials are constantly forced to realize that in a governmental apparatus so vast, so impersonal, and lacking in any sort of ideological indoctrination and discipline, they cannot count on any great portion of the apparatus to understand entirely what they mean. The people in question here are in large part people they do not know personally and cannot hope to know in this way. Considerations of security alone would make it difficult, in many instances, to initiate into the reasons of action all those who might be involved if one were to use the regular channels. The expansion of the governmental apparatus has led to a steady inflation of titles roughly matching that of the growth of the apparatus itself.[9]

The problem has gotten even more acute since Kennan wrote. An examination of the State Department prepared by a group of Foreign Service officers in 1970 related this problem to the Nixon National Security Council system:

8. Eisenhower, *Waging Peace*, pp. 405–8.
9. Kennan, "America's Administrative Response to Its World Problems," p. 19.

Specific decisions are generally communicated promptly and clearly to the implementing units. On occasion, however, the implementing unit is not specified precisely, and the system suffers. More often, the specific decision is transmitted without reference to the broader objectives which should guide the action office in carrying it out. Action offices thus must rely on rather rough and ready guidance of their own making, extrapolating from the specific decision and the very broad-brush generalizations contained in public pronouncements by the President and the Secretary. The result can be either inconsistency in implementation or excessive caution. One reason for this lack of guidance is that Departmental inputs to NSSM's [National Security Study Memoranda] are often not framed in such a way as to produce it. Also the Department usually does not participate in drafting NSDM's [National Security Decision Memoranda] it is required to implement.[10]

The problem of determining what one is supposed to do is further complicated by the fact that no official receives just one order. The directive comes as an item in a flow of paper across an official's desk. He is receiving instructions to do things because other officials have made decisions. He is receiving requests from his subordinates for authority to take actions within existing directives. He is receiving reports of ongoing activities. Whatever effort he makes to implement a particular directive must be within the context of his attempt to implement other directives which have come to him before. He may see a conflict between two very specific directives—a conflict of which senior officials may not be aware. He may perceive a contradiction between a specific directive and a more general policy statement which is received in writing or which he gleans from public presidential and departmental statements. Such a conflict accounts in part for the failure of the State Department to remove missiles from Turkey in 1961. President Kennedy had ordered American missiles removed from Turkey. But he had also ordered the State Department to invigorate the NATO alliance, and, indeed, one of his campaign pledges had been that he would bolster NATO. At the same time, his Secretary of Defense, Robert McNamara, was engaged in an effort to persuade the NATO countries to take conventional military options more seriously. The State Department officials concerned were well aware of the fact that this effort was causing great difficulties within the alliance. The officials who received the directive to remove the missiles from Turkey also felt themselves to be

10. Macomber, *Diplomacy for the 1970's,* pp. 556–57.

operating under a more general presidential directive to strengthen the troubled alliance. They did not believe that the order to remove the missiles from Turkey was meant to contradict the order to strengthen NATO. They raised the issue in a tentative way with the Turkish government. When that government registered strong objections, they held off obeying the order to remove the missiles.

Whereas missiles remained in Turkey because of conflicting directives from the President, in other cases uncertainty arises from the fact that an official receives conflicting orders from two or more of his superiors. The President may in effect tell him to do one thing. The Secretary of the Navy or the Chief of Naval Operations seemingly tell him to do another. In such cases, the official often makes his own judgment about which orders have higher priority.

The Difficulty of Implementation

Some orders direct an official to gain a certain outcome but do not specify any particular action. For example, an official may be told to secure ratification of a nonproliferation-of-weapons treaty by a particular government, or he may be told to persuade a certain country to increase its military forces. In such cases, the implementation of the order depends on the cooperation or at least the yielding of a foreign government. In other cases, implementation may depend on the cooperation of Congress or other groups outside the executive branch and beyond the control of the official being given the order. Under those circumstances he may find it impossible to comply.

In still other cases, limits of compliance come from the fact that most presidential orders need to be carried out by large complex organizations. Some presidential decisions can be carried out by a relatively small number of presidential advisers without regard to the capability of large organizations. When President Nixon decided he wished to establish contact with the People's Republic of China, he was able to dispatch Henry Kissinger, his Assistant for National Security Affairs, to Peking. Kissinger could carry on discussions in China without reference to the standard operating procedures of the Department of State. However, when the action to be carried out requires the cooperation of large numbers of people in the major organizations of the American government, what the President can order done is much more limited. For example, when North Korean forces attacked South Korea in June of 1950, President Truman could only order into the fight those forces which already existed and which could reach the battlefield; these were the occupation forces in Japan under General Douglas MacArthur. When President Kennedy in 1961 wished to step up the number of American "advisers" in Vietnam, he could only send those "counterinsurgency" specialists who had already been trained by the government, either in the CIA or in the armed services.

The organization designated to carry out an action will use its standard operating procedures (SOPs) to do so. These procedures are routine methods which permit coordinated and concerted actions by large numbers of individuals. The rules for this purpose need to be simple in order to facilitate easy learning and unambiguous application. Clusters of standard procedures comprise a program for dealing with a particular situation. A set of programs related to a particular type of activity constitute an organization's repertoire. The number of programs in a repertoire is always quite limited. Thus activity according to standard operating procedures and programs does not constitute a farsighted, flexible adaptation to the decision made by the President. Rather, detailed implementation of actions by organizations is determined predominantly by organizational routines. Since the programs cannot be tailored to the specific situation, the organization, when striving to obey presidential decisions, will use whatever program in the existing repertoire seems most appropriate, given its limited understanding of the purposes of the decision.[11]

Again we can cite Kennedy's experience with Vietnam. When he increased the number of American military personnel in Vietnam from 685 in 1961 to 10,000 in 1962, one observer noted that "there was no change in the advice provided by the advisor; there were just more advisors."[12] In general, the American troops later sent to Vietnam performed very much as they would if sent to fight a large-scale military battle on the plains of central Europe—toward which most of their training had been directed. The State Department, AID, and USIA missions likewise performed in accordance with their standard procedures.[13]

Large organizations find it extremely difficult to develop new plans quickly or to implement plans developed for a different purpose. When the Soviet Union constructed the Berlin Wall in 1961, Kennedy found

11. Allison, *Essence of Decision*, pp. 67–100.
12. Corson, *The Betrayal*, pp. 45–46.
13. Charles Cooke, "Organizational Constraints in U.S. Performance in Vietnam."

that he was offered no suggested choices of action by his advisers. All the contingency planning had been directed to other possible provocations such as a closing of the access routes between West Berlin and West Germany.[14] Routine behavior will be followed even when it appears foolish to an outsider. During the Cuban missile crisis, for example, intelligence officers reported that Russian and Cuban planes were inexplicably lined up wingtip to wingtip on Cuban air fields, making perfect targets. Kennedy, recognizing this as a standard military practice, had a U-2 fly over the American air fields in Florida and discovered that American planes were similarly lined up.[15]

When a senior official gives an order to an organization to carry out an action, he is likely to have an idealized picture of what will then occur. He assumes that the organization will quickly grasp what he is trying to accomplish and adapt its behavior creatively to the particular purpose. The truth is, however, that action, when it involves large numbers, may turn into something quite different from what the official had in mind. One such episode occurred during the summit meeting of 1960. Secretary of Defense Thomas Gates, who had accompanied Eisenhower to Paris, learned that Khrushchev was making rather strong demands and became convinced that the summit conference was about to end in disagreement. He therefore decided on Sunday night to order a worldwide alert of American military forces, feeling that it would be prudent to have local commanders alerted at battle stations all over the globe. He sent a message to the Pentagon calling for a "quiet" alert on a "minimum need to know basis." The Secretary, however, was not familiar with the set of alert patterns that had been developed and did not specify which alert, among alternatives numbered one to five, he wished to have implemented. The Joint Chiefs, feeling the pressure of time and having to guess what Gates wished to accomplish, concluded that alert number three was in order but adhered to Gates's injunction about restricting information. Gates evidently had not visualized that there would be any movement of weapons or troops, but the Pentagon announced that both the continental air defense command and SAC had conducted "limited routine air alert activities." The alert quickly became visible throughout the country and undoubtedly was visible as well to the Soviet Union, sending a signal far different from Gates's simple desire to have the military ready in case the situation should deteriorate.[16]

14. Theodore Sorensen, *Kennedy*, p. 594.
15. Kennedy, *Thirteen Days*, pp. 59–60.
16. Wise and Ross, *The U-2 Affair*, pp. 146–47.

Resistance

Thus far we have explored why presidential decisions may not be obeyed even though implementers seek faithfully to do what the President or his principal associates have ordered them to do. For that reason, the discussion has been somewhat artificial, for in fact those who are assigned to implement presidential decisions often do not feel obliged to execute their orders. Neither career officials nor political appointees necessarily feel that a presidential decision settles the matter. Participants still have different interests and still see different faces of an issue and have different stakes. They may believe that their conception of what is in the national interest is still correct, and they will resist efforts to do things which they feel are contrary to the national interest or to their own organizational or personal interest even if they have been directed by the President. Henry Kissinger explained the problem to a journalist after serving for several years as President Nixon's Assistant for National Security Affairs:

The outsider believes a Presidential order is consistently followed out. Nonsense. I have to spend considerable time seeing that it is carried out and in the spirit the President intended. Inevitably, in the nature of bureaucracy, departments become pressure groups for a point of view. If the President decides against them, they are convinced some evil influence worked on the President: if only he knew all the facts, he would have decided their way.

The nightmare of the modern state is the hugeness of the bureaucracy, and the problem is how to get coherence and design in it.[17]

This problem is not a new one. It has confronted every American President in the modern period, and they have reacted either by seeking to concentrate power in the White House or by trying to get the departments under control. Truman in his memoirs revealed his strong feelings on the subject:

The difficulty with many career officials in the government is that they regard themselves as the men who really make policy and run the government. They look upon the elected officials as just temporary occupants. Every President in our history has been faced with this problem: how to prevent career men from circumventing presidential policy. Too often career men seek to impose their own views instead of carrying out the established policy of the administration. Sometimes they achieve this by

17. Saul Pett, "Henry A. Kissinger: Loyal Retainer or Nixon's Svengali," p. B-3.

influencing the key men appointed by the President to put his policies into operation. It has often happened in the War and Navy Departments that the generals and the admirals, instead of working for and under the Secretaries, succeeded in having the Secretaries act for and under them. And it has happened in the Department of State.

Some Presidents have handled this situation by setting up what amounted to a little State Department of their own. President Roosevelt did this and carried on direct communications with Churchill and Stalin. I did not feel that I wanted to follow this method, because the State Department is set up for the purpose of handling foreign policy operations, and the State Department ought to take care of them. But I wanted to make it plain that the President of the United States, and not the second or third echelon in the State Department, is responsible for making foreign policy, and, furthermore, that no one in any department can sabotage the President's policy. The civil servant, the general or admiral, the foreign service officer has no authority to make policy. They act only as servants of the government, and therefore they must remain in line with the government policy that is established by those who have been chosen by the people to set that policy.

In the Palestine situation, as Secretary Lovett said to me after the announcement of the recognition of Israel, "They almost put it over on you."[18]

This view that one knows what is best for national security affects not only career officials but also political appointees even when they clearly understand the President's own perspective. When at the first meeting of the Eisenhower Cabinet, even before inauguration, General Eisenhower expressed his strong support for increased trade with the Soviet Union, Secretary of Defense Charles Wilson said, "I am a little old fashioned. I don't like to sell firearms to the Indians." Eisenhower then explained in detail why he thought that such trade was good. Obviously, however, he failed to convince Wilson to go along, for the discussion concluded with Wilson saying, "I am going to be on the tough side of this one."[19]

One of the reasons the President is overwhelmingly busy is that so many officials maneuver to line him up on their side of an issue. Then, precisely because of the heavy demands made on his time, in part by them, Cabinet members and staff officers get away with ignoring his orders. One

18. Truman, *Years of Trial and Hope*, p. 165.
19. Adams, *Firsthand Report*, p. 68. See also Hughes, *The Ordeal of Power*, p. 76.

observer has commented succinctly on the game of outwaiting the President:

Half of a President's suggestions, which theoretically carry the weight of
orders, can be safely forgotten by a Cabinet member. And if the President
asks about a suggestion a second time, he can be told that it is being in
vestigated. If he asks a third time, a wise Cabinet officer will give him at
least part of what he suggests. But only occasionally, except about the
most important matters, do Presidents ever get around to asking three
times.[20]

As a President discovers that his decisions are being resisted, he tends
more and more to keep the bureaucracy in the dark and work through
outside channels. This further reduces loyalty as well as contributing
to inadvertent disobedience, which in turn reinforces presidential inclinations toward secrecy. Henry Kissinger, writing before he became an assistant to President Nixon, described the vicious circle that
results:

Because management of the bureaucracy takes so much energy and
precisely because changing course is so difficult, many of the most im
portant decisions are taken by extra-bureaucratic means. Some of the key
decisions are kept to a very small circle while the bureaucracy happily con
tinues working away in ignorance of the fact that decisions are being made,
or the fact that a decision is being made in a particular area. One reason
for keeping the decisions to small groups is that when bureaucracies are so
unwieldy and when their internal morale becomes a serious problem, an
unpopular decision may be fought by brutal means, such as leaks to the
press or to congressional committees. Thus, the only way secrecy can be
kept is to exclude from the making of the decision all those who are
theoretically charged with carrying it out. There is, thus, small wonder for
the many allegations of deliberate sabotage of certain American efforts, or
of great cynicism of American efforts because of inconsistent actions. In
the majority of cases this was due to the ignorance of certain parts of the
bureaucracy, rather than to malevolent intent. Another result is that the
relevant part of the bureaucracy, because it is being excluded from the mak
ing of a particular decision, continues with great intensity sending out
cables, thereby distorting the effort with the best intentions in the world.
You cannot stop them from doing this because you do not tell them what
is going on.[21]

20. Jonathan Daniels, *Frontier on the Potomac*, pp. 31–32.
21. Kissinger, "Bureaucracy and Policy Making," p. 89.

The Struggle over Implementation

What we have said thus far should explain why a presidential decision simply opens a new round of maneuvers rather than settling the question of what is to be done. The process which occurs after a presidential decision goes along in much the same way as the efforts to get a presidential decision. Indeed, in many areas the two processes overlap, since there may be some presidential decisions and a simultaneous struggle over the implementation of them and of the drafting of new decisions. The participants are often the same as those who were involved in framing the decision, although many more lower-level officials may be involved among those responsible for actual implementation, and senior officials are likely to devote less attention. The participants involved will bring to the process the same range of conceptions of what is in the national interest; they will tend to see different faces of the issue, have different stakes, and fight for different kinds of action. Participants have to decide again whether or not to get involved in the process, and some will develop strategies designed to secure the implementation of the President's decision if they favor it or to resist implementation if that is their position. They are constrained by rules of the game which determine who has the responsibility for implementing the decision, whose concurrence will be needed in any orders given, and who will have the right or responsibility to monitor compliance with the decision. If they favor the action, officials charged with implementation are likely to be able to proceed despite the opposition of other groups. If they resist, then the problem of securing implementation is much more difficult. However, the President's problem is difficult even if officials at the operations level favor his policy.

Overzealous Implementation

When the President approves a decision urged on him by those who will be responsible for its implementation, they often feel that he has not gone far enough, or they may choose to interpret the President's decision as giving them more license than he intended. They are then likely to act in a way which looks from the President's point of view to be overzealous implementation. Truman recalled how this happened to him in connection with his agreement to terminate lend-lease to America's European allies following the surrender of Germany:

Leo Crowley, Foreign Economic Administrator, and Joseph C. Grew, Acting Secretary of State, came into my office after the Cabinet meeting on May 8 and said that they had an important order in connection with Lend-Lease which President Roosevelt had approved but not signed. It was an order authorizing the FEA and the State Department to take joint action to cut back the volume of Lend-Lease supplies when Germany surrendered. What they told me made good sense to me; with Germany out of the war, Lend-Lease should be reduced. They asked me to sign it. I reached for my pen and, without reading the document, I signed it.

The storm broke almost at once. The manner in which the order was executed was unfortunate. Crowley interpreted the order literally and placed an embargo on all shipments to Russia and to other European nations, even to the extent of having some of the ships turned around and brought back to American ports for unloading. The British were hardest hit, but the Russians interpreted the move as especially aimed at them. Because we were furnishing Russia with immense quantities of food, clothing, arms, and ammunition, this sudden and abrupt interruption of Lend-Lease aid naturally stirred up a hornets' nest in that country. The Russians complained about our unfriendly attitude. We had unwittingly given Stalin a point of contention which he would undoubtedly bring up every chance he had. Other European governments complained about being cut off too abruptly. The result was that I rescinded the order.[22]

President Kennedy was confronted with an example of overzealous implementation in the case of a proposed multilateral force. A group of officials in the State Department favored the creation of a jointly manned and jointly owned nuclear force of surface ships to be operated by the NATO alliance. Upon securing from Kennedy a decision to ask the European allies of the United States whether they favored such a force, the advocates took this as an indication that the President wished them to seek to persuade others to join the force. Their own reasoning was that the President knew that "nothing happened" in Europe unless the United States forcefully advocated it. Therefore, from their perspective, simply asking the Europeans whether they were interested guaranteed that nothing would happen. Kennedy, on the other hand, apparently assumed that he had authorized only quiet exploration and was surprised to discover the Europeans believed that he was pressing hard for the multilateral force.[23]

22. Truman, *Year of Decisions*, pp. 227–28.
23. Theodore Sorensen, *Kennedy*, p. 569; Schlesinger, A *Thousand Days*, p. 875.

Disregarding Orders

As noted above, officials find ways to overlook, twist, or resist orders. Franklin Roosevelt once gave a classic description of how this is done in general:

The Treasury is so large and far-flung and ingrained in its practices that I find it is almost impossible to get the action and results I want—even with Henry [Morgenthau] there. But the Treasury is not to be compared with the State Department. You should go through the experience of trying to get any changes in the thinking, policy, and action of the career diplomats, and then you'd know what a real problem was. But the Treasury and the State Department put together are nothing compared with the Na-a-vy. The admirals are really something to cope with—and I should know. To change anything in the Na-a-vy is like punching a feather bed. You punch it with your right and you punch it with your left until you are finally exhausted, and then you find the damn bed just as it was before you started punching.[24]

Orders are often disregarded more or less openly. Participants make no effort to disguise the fact that they do not favor the presidential decision and will do what they can to thwart it. For this purpose they set in motion one or more of the following maneuvers.

1. *Do not pass on orders.* One technique available to senior participants is not to pass on to those who actually have to carry out the directive the order received from the President. "Forgetting" and "overriding circumstances" serve as excuses. During the preparations for the Bay of Pigs invasion, for example, President Kennedy directed that if the invading forces were failing to establish a beachhead, they should move quickly to the mountains and become a guerrilla force. However, the CIA did not pass this instruction on to the leader of the brigade. CIA officials later explained that they felt that to do so might weaken the brigade's resolve to fight and that the brigade might choose the alternative plan when the going got rough, even though the invasion still had a chance of success.[25] More than once a Secretary of Defense has kept a presidential directive to himself in the belief that to pass it on would greatly complicate the problem of dealing with the Joint Chiefs of Staff. Both Secretary of Defense Charles Wilson under Eisenhower and Secretary of Defense James For-

24. Marriner S. Eccles, *Beckoning Frontiers*, p. 336.
25. Haynes Johnson, *The Bay of Pigs*, p. 86.

restal under Truman failed to deliver presidential directives establishing ceilings on force levels.[26]

2. *Change "cosmetics" but not reality.* A second technique is to change the formal procedures regarding what is to be done but make it clear to subordinates that the reality is to remain the same. Eisenhower during the course of his presidency became increasingly aware of the limited authority of "unified" military commanders who were supposed to be in charge of all of the American forces in overseas areas such as Europe or the Far East. He therefore devoted considerable energy to persuading the services to accept and Congress to enact a change in procedure which would strengthen the area commander's authority. In presenting the 1958 defense reorganization act to the Congress, Eisenhower stated that "each Unified Commander must have unquestioned authority over all units of his command. . . . The commander's authority over these component commands is short of the full command required for maximum efficiency."[27] At the time that Eisenhower sent his message to Congress, the authority of area commanders was known as "Operational Control." The 1958 act invested in the area commander "full operational command," indicating an intent on the part of the Congress to overcome the deficiency pointed out by Eisenhower. However, as a Blue Ribbon Defense Panel subsequently concluded, "[With respect to] Unified Action Armed Forces (JCS Pub. 2) which sets forth principles, doctrines, and functions governing the activities and performance of Forces assigned to Unified Commands, the JCS now define 'Operational Command' as being synonymous with 'Operational Control.'" According to the panel, the command arrangements remained "substantially unchanged," and "the net result is an organizational structure in which 'unification' of either command or of the forces is more cosmetic than substantive."[28] Thus there was a change in wording but no change in the reality, despite a clear presidential and congressional directive.

3. *Do something else.* A more blatant form of disobedience is to simply ignore a directive and do something else which either runs contrary to what the President ordered or simply does not take into account what the President sought. On August 15, 1945, for example, Truman sent a for-

26. Lilienthal, *Journals*, p. 355; Larson, *Eisenhower*, p. 23; Hammond, "Super Carriers and B-36 Bombers," p. 478.

27. Cited in Blue Ribbon Defense Panel, *Report to the President and the Secretary of Defense*, p. 50.

28. Ibid., p. 50.

mal memorandum to the Secretaries of State, War, and Navy, to the Joint Chiefs of Staff, and to the Director of the Office of Scientific Research and Development. In that memorandum he directed that they "take such steps as are necessary to prevent the release of any information in regard to the development, design, or production of the atomic bomb."[29] Soon thereafter, these agencies released the so-called Smyth Report which contained considerable information about the design and production of the atomic bomb!

Truman was confronted with similar disobedience from the State Department during his efforts to take charge of American policy toward Israel. Truman had directed that the United States should support partition of Palestine. The American delegate to the UN, Warren Austin, despite the fact that he was aware of this presidential directive, declared in public at the United Nations that the United States was no longer for partition. This step was taken with the concurrence of the State Department but without Truman being informed.[30] Nor was Truman the only President treated in this way by his subordinates. Eisenhower relates one episode when Secretary of State John Foster Dulles, who on the whole bent over backward to follow specific presidential directives, probably ignored one:

In the period between the Summit Conference and the Foreign Ministers' meeting, I became ill. Before Foster left to attend the meeting he came to Denver so that we could confer in my hospital room. He had prepared a draft of a reply to Mr. Bulganin, who had asked us for a further explanation of my July proposal for exchanging "blueprints" of military establishments. Inadvertently, Foster had omitted my statement to the Soviet delegation at Geneva that if they would accept an aerial inspection system, I was quite ready to accept their proposition for ground teams. With this correction made, I signed the letter to Bulganin.[31]

It is difficult to believe that the omission was in fact inadvertent.

4. *Delay.* Another technique to avoid the implementation of a presidential decision is simply to delay, either not taking the action that the President has directed or moving very slowly toward implementing it. A view of this technique at work in a specific setting is offered by a former high official of the CIA who reports on CIA resistance to a presidential directive:

29. Truman, *Year of Decisions*, p. 524.
30. Alfred Steinberg, *The Man from Missouri*, p. 307.
31. Eisenhower, *Mandate for Change*, p. 527 (italics added).

Despite that, shortly thereafter a National Security Council directive ordered the Agency to implement certain of the recommendations. I remember having lunch with Najeeb Halaby and discussing the report and directive. Jeeb Halaby, who later became nationally known as the administrator of the Federal Aviation Administration, was then serving in the office of the Secretary of Defense on matters that later were organized under the assistant secretary for International Security Affairs. He had considerable dealings with the CIA and was anxious to see it develop into a strong agency. I recall the conversation vividly because we both agreed that the report and directive were an important step forward, but I predicted that they would not be implemented at that time. Halaby expressed incredulity, noting that it was a Presidential Directive, but I maintained that bureaucracy grinds exceeding slow and if a directive was unpopular with the bosses it could grind even slower.

Such proved to be the case. When General Smith arrived in Washington in October 1950, nearly a year later, to take over from Hillenkoetter, who had gone on to another naval assignment, little had been done to implement the report.[32]

5. *Obey the letter but not the spirit of the orders.* Because orders are expressed in generalities and the implementing instructions themselves tend not to be very precise, officials at the operations level frequently have leeway to implement the decisions as they choose. They often do this in ways which follow the letter of what they are told to do but not the spirit of what the President had in mind, even insofar as they understand that spirit.

This sort of behavior occurred on March 31, 1968, when the American military officers, in planning the first bombing of North Vietnam after President Johnson's speech announcing a cutback of the bombing, chose to obey the letter of their instructions rather than the spirit of the President's address. Johnson had publicly declared:

I am taking the first step to de-escalate the conflict. We are reducing—substantially reducing—the present level of hostilities . . . unilaterally and at once. Tonight, I have ordered our aircraft and our naval vessels to make no attacks on North Vietnam, except in the area north of the Demilitarized Zone where the continuing enemy buildup directly threatens allied forward positions. . . .[33]

The unmistakable implication of what he said was that the remaining

32. Lyman B. Kirkpatrick, Jr., *The Real CIA*, p. 89.
33. *New York Times*, April 1, 1968.

bombing would be related to tactical targets in order to provide protection for U.S. ground forces immediately below the Demilitarized Zone. Later press reports made it clear that the orders to the field directed the military simply to cease all bombing north of 20 degrees, but presumably the text of the President's speech was also available, at least informally, to those planning bombing raids. Nevertheless, much of the weight of the first bombing raids on April 1, 1968, was directed at the only large city below 20 degrees in North Vietnam. The ultimate "message" conveyed not only to the North Vietnamese but also to the American people was one of selected devastation rather than de-escalation. Thus the credibility gap widened even though the commander-in-chief of U.S. forces in the Pacific, who directed the bombing raids against North Vietnam, was acting fully within his orders in carrying out the strikes on North Vietnam.[34]

Whereas the military can generally stretch orders involving combat operations, the State Department often has this flexibility in drafting cables. Elizabeth Drew describes one episode in a fight by the State Department to resist White House orders to step up American economic aid to the secessionist province of Biafra in Nigeria:

When Biafra fell, the White House announced that the President had placed on alert, for relief purposes, transport planes and helicopters, and was donating $10 million. This was done on White House initiative. . . .

This difference was fought out, as such issues usually are, in seemingly minor bureaucratic skirmishes over such things as the wording of cables, and the tone of statements to the press. State, for example, drafted a cable instructing our representatives in Lagos to emphasize that the helicopters and planes were only on standby, and that the $10 million had only been made available because British Prime Minister Harold Wilson had told President Nixon that there was concern over the relief effort. The White House rewrote the cable, deleting the apologetic tone and emphasizing the President's concern that the Nigerians speed relief. It is in such ways that the United States government's posture in a crisis can be determined.[35]

Changing Decisions

The maneuvers that we have discussed so far involve finding ways not to do what one is ordered to do. Different maneuvers exist for resisting a decision by seeking to get it changed by the President or (in spite of the President) by Congress.

34. Kalb and Abel, *Roots of Involvement*, p. 255.
35. Drew, "Washington," pp. 6, 10.

1. *Insist on a personal hearing before obeying.* Most often presidential orders have passed on to other officials either in writing or through a member of the White House staff. When they do not like such orders, senior officials can demand a hearing from the President, insist that, before they will accept his orders, they must be sure that he has heard their side of the argument and that the orders are being transmitted accurately to them. As part of this ploy they are likely to claim that the President may well have been misunderstood, and they may enlist the support of a friendly member of the White House staff.[36]

2. *Suggest reasons for reconsidering.* A related technique which can be used even when one has gotten an order from the President is to insist upon going back to him to "report unforeseen implications." This technique is easiest to use when the President has turned down a request for permission to do something, but it also can be used when the President very specifically directs that a certain action be carried out. Dean Acheson describes in his memoirs in vivid detail the aftermath of a presidential decision to send a cable to General MacArthur ordering withdrawal of a message that MacArthur planned to make public regarding the terms for peace in Korea:

For some time the President had had a meeting scheduled with the Secretaries of State, Treasury, and Defense, Harriman, and the Joint Chiefs of Staff for nine-thirty on that morning. When we filed into the oval office, the President, with lips white and compressed, dispensed with the usual greetings. He read the message and then asked each person around the room whether he had had any prior intimation or knowledge of it. No one had. Louis Johnson was directed to order MacArthur from the President to withdraw the message and report that he (MacArthur) had done so. The President himself would send directly to MacArthur a copy of Ambassador Austin's letter to Trygve Lie, from which he would understand why the withdrawal order was necessary. The business for which the meeting was called was hastily dispatched.

When we left the White House, nothing could have been clearer to me than that the President had issued an order to General MacArthur to withdraw the message, but Secretary Johnson soon telephoned to say that this could cause embarrassment and that he (Johnson) thought it better to inform MacArthur that if he issued the statement "we" would reply that it was "only one man's opinion and not the official policy of the Government." I said that the issue seemed to be who was President of the United

36. One such episode, involving the fiscal 1958 foreign aid bill, is described in Edgerton, *Sub-Cabinet Politics and Policy Commitment,* pp. 121–22.

States. Johnson then asked me an amazing question—whether "we dare send [MacArthur] a message that the President directs him to withdraw his statement?" I saw nothing else to do in view of the President's order.

At Johnson's request, I asked Averell Harriman whether he was clear that the President had issued an order. This shortly resulted in another call from Johnson saying that the President had dictated to him this message to go to MacArthur: "The President of the United States directs that you withdraw your message for National Encampment of Veterans of Foreign Wars, because various features with regard to Formosa are in conflict with the policy of the United States and its position in the United Nations."

Still Johnson doubted the wisdom of sending the order and put forward his prior alternative. Stephen Early, his deputy, came on the telephone to support him, raised the question of General MacArthur's right of free speech, and proposed that the President talk to General MacArthur. At this point I excused myself and ended the conversation, duly reporting it to Harriman, saying that if Johnson wished to reopen the President's decision, he should apply to the President to do so. The President instructed Harriman that he had dictated what he wanted to go and he wanted it to go. It went. MacArthur's message was both withdrawn and unofficially published.[37]

3. *Go to the Hill.* Another way to fight a presidential decision is to bring the matter to Congress, either in open testimony or privately. This maneuver is of course most effective when the presidential decision requires congressional concurrence such as appropriation of funds, approval of a treaty, or the enactment of legislation permitting government reorganization. The channel of communication usually runs between career officials of an organization in the executive branch and staff members of congressional subcommittees. Congressmen often see it as their duty to protect the permanent bureaucracy against encroachments of the President and the Cabinet officers.[38]

The undercutting of the President can be done quite subtly, simply, for example, by not showing the necessary enthusiasm for a proposal to get it through. Sherman Adams, President Eisenhower's principal White House assistant, describes one such episode during Eisenhower's long campaign to get a reorganization of the Defense Department approved by the Congress:

37. Acheson, *Present at the Creation*, pp. 423–24.
38. For an account of a "protective" episode involving the State Department and USIA, see Larson, *Eisenhower*, p. 24.

Unfortunately for the President, his Secretary of Defense, Neil McElroy, did not appear to share Eisenhower's spirited dedication to the reorganization plan when he appeared to testify on it before the House committee. In sending his recommendations to Congress, the President had drafted most of the wording of the bill himself. This was a rare procedure. Usually the President left the drafting of a bill to the ranking member of his party on the appropriate committee to work out with the department head concerned. This time, because Eisenhower had drafted himself, almost word for word, the legislation that he wanted enacted it was assumed in the House that he was taking an unshakable no-compromise stand on it. But McElroy gave the committee the impression that the administration would be willing to make concessions. He was unable to give the inquiring Congressmen any specific examples of the "outmoded concepts" that Eisenhower had cited as the main reason for the need of unification. He indicated that the terms of the bill were in some respects broader than was necessary, but the President was in some degree responsible for McElroy's comment since he had said that he did not regard the exact language of the bill as necessarily sacrosanct. This weakened the President's case somewhat and gave Uncle Carl Vinson the opening to drive in objections to some of the key provisions.

After McElroy left the door open, the President jumped up fast to close it, but the room was already filled with snow. McElroy admitted to Uncle Carl's committee that the Secretary of Defense did not actually need the sweeping powers to assign and transfer that the bill conferred upon him. The President reversed the Secretary and came back strongly to assert that any retreat from this position of demand for supervisory control would make unified strategy impossible. Eisenhower sent word to Congress that no concessions would be made because they had already been made before the bill was submitted. What they were considering were the bare essentials, he declared.[39]

Military officers more often than others have resorted to Congress—in part because of the automatic support they have found there for their views. Many legislators insist that Congress has a duty to hear the views of career military officers who disagree with the President. The White House naturally opposes this outlook, and over the years efforts have been made to reduce the freedom of the military to testify independently before Congress. Under Truman, military officers had the freedom to volunteer the information that they disagreed with an administration proposal and,

---

39. Adams, *Firsthand Report*, pp. 418–19.

after making clear that the administration favored the proposal, to express their personal views against it. Secretary of Defense McNamara in the 1960s sought to impose a much more restrictive rule: that the military reveal differences only if pressed and then in admitting the disagreement to give the administration's side of the case as well.[40]

4. *Go public.* One way to alert Congress as well as the public is to provide information to the press. Here the hope is that news of disagreement over a decision will stir up public or congressional opposition forcing the President to back down. In 1961, for example, the Army, concerned about the fact that President Kennedy was forcing on the military a counter-guerrilla strategy in Vietnam which would impair the ability of the South Vietnamese forces to resist a conventional invasion from North Vietnam, leaked news of Kennedy's action and the Army's objections to the press.[41]

5. *Go to another government.* If all else fails, those seeking to oppose implementation of a decision can go to another government and try to get them to intervene. Where the action directed was to try to persuade a second government to do something, this can be resisted by quietly urging that government not to go along with the U.S. demands. Averell Harriman believes that this was done during his efforts to negotiate an agreement concerning Laos. He maintains that the head of the right-wing forces, General Phoumi, was advised by some U.S. officials to hold out against U.S. pressures for a compromise settlement.[42]

Resisting Requests for Proposals

Thus far we have considered mainly those cases in which the President gives an order to do something, often something that may affect the behavior of another government. Occasionally, however, the President orders his staff to work up a proposal *for* doing something in a certain area. In such cases, the bureaucracy's ability to ignore presidential demands is probably greater. Among the techniques commonly used are the following.

1. *Do not respond.* Presidents often make requests for imaginative or new proposals in a particular area. Such requests are often ignored, and then, when the President inquires, he is told the problem is so difficult

40. *Forrestal Diaries,* p. 119; Korb, "Budget Strategies of the Joint Chiefs of Staff," n. 15.

41. Hilsman, *To Move a Nation,* pp. 415–16.

42. Harriman, *America and Russia in a Changing World,* p. 112.

that a proposal is not yet ready. This technique is particularly convenient when the President insists that he receive a proposal unanimously agreed to by all his advisers. President Eisenhower, for example, apparently believed strongly that the United States should put forward more imaginative proposals in the arms control field, and he continuously pressed his advisers to come up with proposals which could be put to him for his approval. But he also expected his advisers to agree with each other, and such proposals were seldom forthcoming.[43] The no-response technique can be used even when the President's request is a relatively simple and straightforward one and he asks not for opinions but simply for a procedural plan to implement a proposal already decided upon. One example is the way the State Department delayed action upon President Kennedy's wish to create the post of Under Secretary of State for Latin American Affairs. As Arthur Schlesinger, Jr., relates the incident:

The President was more troubled than ever by the organization of Latin American affairs within our own government. Late in October he discussed with Richard Goodwin and me the old problem which Berle had raised in 1961 of an Under Secretaryship of State for Inter-American Affairs, embracing both the Alliance and the political responsibilities of the Assistant Secretary. Kennedy, remarking sharply that he could not get anyone on the seventh floor of the State Department to pay sustained attention to Latin America, dictated a plain-spoken memorandum to Rusk saying that he wanted to create the new Under Secretaryship. "I am familiar," he said, "with the argument that, if we do this for Latin America, other geographical areas must receive equal treatment. But I have come increasingly to feel that this argument, however plausible in the abstract, overlooks the practicalities of the situation." Historically Latin America was an area of primary and distinctive United States interest; currently it was the area of greatest danger to us; and operationally it simply was not receiving the day-to-day, high level attention which our national interest demanded. "Since I am familiar with the arguments against the establishment of this Under Secretaryship," his memorandum to the Secretary concluded somewhat wearily, "I would like this time to have a positive exploration of its possibilities."

He had in mind for the job Sargent Shriver or perhaps Averell Harriman, whom he had just designated to lead the United States delegation to the São Paulo meeting. We later learned that Rusk sent the presidential memorandum to the Assistant Secretary for Administration, who passed

43. See, for example, Hughes, *The Ordeal of Power*, pp. 203–4.

it along to some subordinate, and it took Ralph Dungan's intervention to convince the Secretary that this was a serious matter requiring senior attention. Receiving no response, the President after a fortnight renewed the request.[44]

2. *Not now.* An alternative to no response at all is a plea for postponement. State Department officials often caution the White House that the timing is wrong for a particular initiative because of the delicate political situation. John Foster Dulles was able to use this technique with great effectiveness because of President Eisenhower's feeling that he should defer to Dulles on diplomatic issues. As Eisenhower implied in an interview shortly after leaving office, it was this maneuver that kept the United States from withdrawing any troops from Europe despite the President's strong feelings that they should come out and despite his expertise as a former commander of those forces.

Though for eight years in the White House I believed and announced to my associates that a reduction of American strength in Europe should be initiated as soon as European economies were restored, the matter was then considered too delicate a political question to raise. I believe the time has now come when we should start withdrawing some of those troops.[45]

3. *Come back with a different proposal.* A further technique for stalling is to come back and present to the President a proposal significantly different from the directive that he has put forward. Often the proposal will take account of the organizational interests of the bureau or department involved. When President Kennedy was preparing to ask General Lucius Clay to go to Berlin as the President's principal adviser, reporting directly to Kennedy and taking overall charge of the situation, the State Department and the Defense Department combined to change the draft so that Clay became simply an adviser with no operational control over the military or diplomatic mission in Berlin.[46]

Thus far we have emphasized the ability of participants in Washington to resist presidential orders. The President is not without resources to combat resistance. Before looking into that aspect of foreign policy, however, we want to devote a chapter to how decisions from Washington are treated in the field.

44. Schlesinger, *A Thousand Days*, pp. 1001–2.
45. Interview with Eisenhower, *Saturday Evening Post*, October 26, 1963, as quoted in Charles H. Percy, "Paying for NATO," p. 36.
46. Clay, Kennedy Library Oral History Interview, pp. 5–6.

CHAPTER FOURTEEN

Actions in the Field

Foreign policy decisions made by the President must of course many times be implemented in the field by ambassadors and their subordinates or by military commanders. The relationship between officials in the field and the President are similar to those between Washington agencies and the White House, but there are enough differences to merit discussion in this separate chapter.

We begin with a discussion of the structure of field operations and why and how the perspective of those in the field differs from that of officials in Washington. Then we consider the range of specific maneuvers open to those in the field to resist Washington decisions or to act in the absence of them.

Field Perspectives

The core of an embassy, as most ambassadors conceive it, is the group of Foreign Service officers in the political and economic negotiating and reporting sections. An embassy of any size also has a number of officials from the Department of Defense (military attachés and advisers), the Central Intelligence Agency, and the United States Information Agency. In developing countries there will be an AID mission, and in developed countries officials will be present from Treasury, Agriculture, Commerce, and other government agencies. A military command in the field consists of a commander-in-chief and his staff plus subordinate commanders for each of the services whose personnel are involved in the area. All of these officials see the national interest partly in terms of the interest of their organization and their own interest in promotion. The key to promotion lies in their home agency in Washington, and they will be responsive to its commands and its interests.

The different interests and perspectives of the various groups in an embassy or military command thus produce a replica of the situation in Washington. The military commander or ambassador is only nominally in full control of those beneath him. Although ambassadors and field commanders often strive to maintain control over all channels of communications between their post and Washington, in fact many different agencies have direct private channels of communication with their officials in the field.[1]

Subordinate officials use all the techniques in dealing with orders from their ambassador that are used by officials in Washington and discussed in the previous chapter. For example, they often say things to their counterparts in the host government which violate the ambassador's instructions.[2] Even outright disobedience is not uncommon. A Marine colonel who served in Vietnam describes one such episode:

Before we begin our discussion on Phong Bac, it should be noted that the course of action selected was and is contrary to the spirit and intent of every directive, regulation, or order issued by COMUSMACV (Commander U.S. Military Assistance Command Vietnam) and the U.S. Embassy in Saigon, all of which require U.S. forces to serve as a forerunner of GVN control. For this breach of discipline the responsibility is mine. The men who participated in Phong Bac's pacification carried out my orders and plans because they were good Marines and because they believed in and understood what they were doing. My primary purpose was to protect American lives and property—pacification was the means. The secondary goal was to enable the people of Phong Bac to become strong enough to resist the predatory incursions of both the GVN and the Vietcong.[3]

In many cases the ambassador does not wish to know what is going on. Ambassadors are often uninterested in AID programs and are quite prepared to give wide latitude to their AID mission in dealing on economic matters with the local governments. In the case of the CIA, they often prefer not to know about certain of its activities so as not to be embarrassed in case of disclosure (should CIA communication with anti-government leaders in the country be exposed, for example). The CIA often operates simply without informing the local ambassador. Earl Smith re-

---

1. On communications between an agency and its officials in the field, see, for example, Galbraith, *Ambassador's Journal*, pp. 465–66, and Sebald, *With MacArthur in Japan*, pp. 120–21.

2. See, for example, John Martin, *Overtaken By Events*, p. 389.

3. Corson, *The Betrayal*, pp. 155–56.

ports that while he was Ambassador to Cuba, the CIA established relations with Castro's rebel forces and that he did not learn of this until much later when there was a court-martial of some Cuban naval officers who participated in an early Castro revolt.[4]

At the same time, the members of the diplomatic team or military command tend to share a common bias against "interference" from Washington. They are likely to be strongly motivated to improve relations with the country to which they are assigned and to take actions that accomplish this goal even at the cost of hurting relations with neighboring countries. Officials in the field are often persuaded that improving relations with their host country is vital to the security of the United States, whereas priorities decided upon in Washington seem out of touch. In the journal he wrote while serving as Ambassador to India, John Kenneth Galbraith provides a typical perspective:

Yesterday an incredible telegram came from the Department washing out the C-130 offer I was to come back to India and try to sell as a substitute for MIG's. And likewise any suggestion of military aid. All in craven reaction to the Congress and, I fear, to the President's displeasure with India. The Department was so obviously off base that I decided on a soft answer and spent most of the day on it. For the rest, I am beginning to contemplate a quiet withdrawal.[5]

Believing that they are much more adept at dealing with the local government and understand its complexities, officials in the field feel that they should make policy decisions and that Washington should simply support them. They assume that Washington simply does not understand "the problem" in substantive terms or the difficulty of running an embassy and dealing with the local government. John Harr in his study of the American career foreign affairs official concludes as follows:

A familiar theme in the literature in public administration is the set of problems often found in relationships between a home office and its field posts—lack of understanding, faulty communication, distrust, poor coordination. A normally bad situation is compounded in foreign affairs by remoteness and some of the other problems already discussed—the intangibility of goals, the multi-agency mix, and the lack of systematic tools. The feelings run worse from the field to Washington than vice versa. Operators

4. Earl E. T. Smith, *The Fourth Floor: An Account of the Castro Communist Revolution*, pp. 31–34. For a description of a similar incident in an unnamed country, see Holbrooke, "The Machine That Fails," p. 66.

5. Galbraith, *Ambassador's Journal*, p. 399.

in the field are prone to see Washington as a great bureaucratic sludge which is either unresponsive when something is wanted or bristling with bright ideas that no one needs. The lack of a systematic, meaningful dialogue between Washington and the field is a severe handicap to effective coordination. Repeated so often that it has become a cliché is the view that Washington should have a Country Team set-up like the field does.[6]

Indeed, the behavior of Washington begins to seem quite irrational to field officials preoccupied with their own perspectives and their own problems. Jonathan Bingham, entrusted to head an aid mission (then called TCA), records his early introduction to the insanity of Washington as seen from the field:

I felt better until I got back to the embassy, and found Brown, white-faced, holding a long telegram. It was from Washington, apparently a circular which had been sent to other T.C.A. missions as well. It began something like this:

"For Congressional hearings on MSP starting March 15, need (a) detailed discription TA program your area this fiscal year, including description of going activities, summary of project agreements signed, sums obligated and sums expended, and (b) outline program for FY 53, including amounts needed under each activity classification and justification for same. Telegraphic summary of material must reach TCA/W not later than March 1, detailed documentation by March 7."

The telegram then went on with a careful outline for the "documentation," specifying all the factors that should be taken into account, and ending with a bland request for a "rough projection of amounts expected to be needed in each of next five years."

Livid with rage, I stormed into the ambassador's office. To my surprise he was quite calm, although he had a copy of the telegram in his hand. "But this is absurd," I shouted. "They can't expect me to do this. They know I've only just arrived. They must have sent it here by mistake, or else they've gone nuts."

The ambassador let me blow on for a while, and then he cut in. "Take it easy," he said. "This kind of thing happens all the time. It can't be helped. The point is that the Congressional Committees will want this information. If we don't do it here, as best we can, the boys in Washington will have to dream something up themselves. Would that be any

6. Harr, *The Professional Diplomat*, pp. 301–2.

better? You know more than you did a week ago. I'll put my two economic people on it with you."

I calmed down, and we set to work, pretty much night and day. We got some sort of a telegram off by March 3, two days late, and put the whole job in the air pouch on March 6. It looked pretty good to me. If we could carry out a program such as we had projected, we would have accomplished something.

The next day, the 7th, a telegram arrived from Washington, changing the outline all around but not changing the deadline. It had been delayed in transit, but even so it had left Washington only on the 4th. The Foreign Service people accepted this much more philosophically than I did. "Probably had trouble getting it cleared," they suggested. Again we buckled down, hoping that what we sent in would suit their royal highnesses.

At this point I began to appreciate the difficulty of doing business over a long cable wire. It was reminiscent of communicating with Sears Roebuck about a mail order. You know, like the man who ordered a case of red raspberries c.o.d.; after he had refused a case of black raspberries three separate times, he wrote and gave them hell; they sent him an apology and a refund check for three cases of red raspberries. The State Department isn't quite that bad, but almost, and of course they think the same of us. Answers to urgent questions come in late and garbled, or they give irrelevant information, or they don't come at all, week after week. It isn't anybody's fault. Everybody has too much to do. It's just that the world isn't as small as we sometimes say it is.[7]

This general perspective on Washington—that the home office has the wrong priorities, that it does not understand the local situation—is applied in reaction to specific Washington decisions communicated to the field. Officials in the field, whether military commanders or ambassadors, are remote from the Washington decision-making process. They may from time to time be called back for consultation or receive cables indicating that Washington is contemplating a particular decision and asking for their comments on it. But they do not have the benefit of sitting in the meetings where the new policy has been worked out. They are not informed as to the context in which a decision was made, of the national security considerations that influenced the President, and of the bureaucratic factors that also affected his decision. When the problem of arriv-

7. Bingham, *Shirt-Sleeve Diplomacy*, pp. 32–34.

ing at a decision is tortuous, officials are reluctant to bear the further burden of attempting to clear a cable explaining to the field just why the decision was made. With such an incomplete idea of how a decision was reached, those in the field may feel little commitment to implementing it.

In an effort to learn what is going on in Washington, ambassadors and field commanders try to come back to Washington repeatedly to learn what is going on. In the interim, top officials in the field carry on correspondence, known in the bureaucracy as "official-informal," with the country director in Washington. In such letters, the country director often tries to give an ambassador a sense of the context in which policy decisions have been made and an explanation of the cables he is receiving. Ambassadors look to American newspapers and news magazines to supply a context.[8] They sometimes speak with officials of the country to which they are accredited who have been to Washington. Galbraith comments on one such episode: "B. K. Nehru is back for consultation. By querying him on a recent conversation with the President and Secretary, I got an improved view of American policy. One must use the available channels."[9]

When he receives a message, an ambassador seldom knows how high up the cable went before it was cleared. Since all cables are signed officially with the name of the Secretary of State, he cannot tell whether this is a directive from the President, Secretary of State, Assistant Secretary, or simply the country director under pressure from other agencies. Occasionally, there will be clues in the cable indicating that it actually comes from the Secretary, but in the absence of such clues the ambassador is left guessing whose wrath he risks incurring if he ignores the instruction.[10]

The factors discussed above combine to create a situation in which ambassadors and military commanders in the field can easily come to feel that it is their responsibility in certain situations to effectively *shape* policy toward the country to which they are accredited or the zone of conflict where their forces are engaged. They may view "Washington" as an irrelevant meddler rather than the source of instruction and guidance. Career ambassadors in particular tend to trust only the country director in the State Department (except for a few major countries), feeling that

---

8. See, for example, Hughes, *The Ordeal of Power*, p. 157.
9. Galbraith, *Ambassador's Journal*, p. 315.
10. Eleanor Lansing Dulles, *American Foreign Policy in the Making*, p. 59.

senior departmental officials and White House counselors are ignorant and constitute an obstacle to be overcome. Political appointees to ambassadorships, on the other hand, often disregard the departmental desk officers in the belief that they do not know what the President wants.

One way or another, most officials in the field come to believe that Washington has to be handled with care but circumvented to maintain flexibility for independent action in the field. Bedell Smith, a retired military officer who served as American ambassador in Moscow in the early postwar period, expressed this attitude:

We knew, of course, that there would be difficulties. The time difference between Moscow and our several capitals was one source. I think we also were conscious of the fact that back in the Foreign Offices at home there were a lot of very able young experts who would feel quite sure (possibly with some reason) that they could conduct the negotiations far better than we could. For this reason we agreed that we would have to be tactful but firm with our own Foreign Offices in order to maintain some freedom of maneuver. Most important of all was the necessity to safeguard carefully the position of our military commanders in Germany, who did not operate directly under Foreign Office or State Department instructions. I had, from the time I arrived in Moscow, been in close touch both officially and personally with General Clay and Ambassador Murphy in Berlin.[12]

Note the comments of a career ambassador on the incompetence of Washington and the need for ambassadors to save Washington from ineptness as well as folly:

Consider the widely-believed statement that "an ambassador is merely a Washington messenger boy." That was clearly invented by someone who never served in an embassy. The person who is content to carry messages is in fact a messenger boy, but he has no business being an ambassador. How an envoy delivers a message can be as important as the communication itself. What the ambassador says when he delivers the views of his government can cause the representations to prosper or to fail, regardless of the eloquence of the prose confected in Washington. . . .

There are many awkward or infelicitous Washington messages that are rescued from failure by experienced ambassadorial handling. It is the responsibility of the ambassador, as his government's senior agent abroad, to protect his principal from the effects of his folly as well as his wisdom—

12. Walter Bedell Smith, *My Three Years in Moscow*, pp. 241–42.

and always to have Washington think it has cornered the market on clairvoyance.[13]

Perceptive officials in Washington, catching glimpses of this attitude, come to understand how little control they have. Dean Acheson wrote that "authority fades with distance and with the speed of light."[14] George Kennan offers a warning on the military commands established abroad: *Whoever in Washington takes responsibility for placing a major American armed establishment anywhere beyond our borders, particularly when it is given extensive powers with relation to civil affairs in the area where it is stationed, should remember that he is not thereby creating just an instrument of American policy—he is committing himself seriously to the insights, interests, and decisions of a new bureaucratic power structure situated far from our shores and endowed with its own specific perspective on all problems of world policy; and to this extent he is resigning his own power of control over the use to be made of America's resources in the process of international life.*[15]

Evading Instructions

In addition to inadequate information and conflict over control versus autonomy, field operations bear the burden of conforming to standard operating procedures. When given an order from Washington, organizations in the field typically begin to function according to the standard operating procedure closest to what they are ordered to do. The simple application of existing routines, once Washington accepts or condones a general policy, often leads to a situation in which Washington finds that the constraints that it wished to impose are ineffective. McGeorge Bundy explains how this process led from authorization for a very narrow use of tear gas and herbicides in Vietnam to almost complete freedom on the part of the military in the field to use these weapons as they chose:

There is, however, one specific lesson from the past which seems to me worth holding in mind. Both in the case of herbicides and in that of tear gas, the initial authorizations for military use in the early 1960's were narrowly framed, at least as understood by civilians in Washington.

The first authorized use of herbicides, as I recall it, was for defoliation

13. Briggs, *Farewell to Foggy Bottom*, pp. 5–6.
14. Acheson, *Sketches from Life*, p. 48.
15. Kennan, *Memoirs, 1925–1950*, p. 372.

along narrow jungle trails. I remember no talk of crop destruction at the beginning. The initial use of tear gas was for situations involving the need to protect civilian lives, in conditions closely analogous to those of a civil riot at home, and indeed in his first public statement on the subject Secretary Rusk made it clear that it was the policy of the administration to authorize the use of such agents only in such riot control situations. But as time passed, increasingly warlike uses were found for both kinds of agents, and in testimony before Congress senior military officials have made it clear that in their view both herbicides and tear gas are now legitimate weapons for use wherever they may do some military good. For example, in authoritative testimony in 1969 before a subcommittee of the House Committee on Foreign Affairs, a senior Pentagon official identified six varied battlefield uses of tear gas, and five separate classes of military use of herbicides. Thus under the pressure of availability and battlefield urgency, the initial authorizations from Washington have been steadily widened. This is not a matter of bad faith or deception. Nor is it primarily a failure of command and control, although tighter and more explicit guidelines could have been useful in limiting the use of these agents. What happened here is what tends to happen quite remorselessly in war: unless there are very sharp and clear defining lines against the use of a given weapon, it tends to be used. Our experience in Vietnam with herbicides and tear gas is a compelling specific demonstration of the weakness of partial and ambiguous limitations. The only reliable way to keep chemical warfare off any future battlefield is to keep it off in all its forms. And the best way to do that, I repeat, is for the United States to accept the prevailing international view of the meaning of the Geneva Protocol.[16]

Thus Washington lost control over a major issue without a conscious effort by those in the field to usurp presidential prerogatives. In many cases, however, there is conscious maneuvering by officials in the field because of their belief that they know better than Washington what should be done. These maneuvers are similar to those carried on in Washington, but the field officials have the enormous advantage that their actions are much more difficult to monitor. Moreover, there is a strong feeling in Washington that field commanders should be given wide latitude in carrying out combat operations. Foreign Service officers also tend to feel that ambassadors should be given latitude (although this view is not generally shared at the top levels of the government). In describing imple-

16. Bundy, "The Consideration of the Geneva Protocol of 1925," p. 186.

mentation in general and the perspective from the field, we have already mentioned the techniques employed, but it is worthwhile to emphasize further the effects of great distance and Washington's unfamiliarity with the local situation.

1. *Do something else.* Specific instructions to officials in the field are often ignored, and sometimes the actions taken are actually contrary to these specific instructions. For example, despite President Kennedy's explicit instructions that no Americans were to be included in the task force invading Cuba at the Bay of Pigs, an American, in fact, was the first to land.[17]

In many cases, the action taken in violation of instructions will come after an official in the field has pleaded for new instructions and has been refused. For example, many attempts were made in Washington to change the famous JCS 1067 directive which excluded a number of former Nazis from key job categories in Germany following World War II. According to Robert Murphy, when these had failed, General Lucius Clay, the American commander in Germany, simply "went out on a limb and announced that thereafter we would employ ex-Nazis in skilled jobs. The American government never did cancel this JCS 1067 prohibition; it merely refrained from repudiating Clay's action."[18]

John Kenneth Galbraith, Ambassador to India, persisted in telling the Indians that the United States was no longer seeking military alliances in that part of the world, and he did so despite clear instructions from Washington, including a personal cable from the Secretary of State, instructing him not to say any such thing.[19]

Action in the face of repeated refusal by Washington to change policy may not come until frustration has built up in the field over an extended time. But it can happen that in a crisis officials in the field act as they think best because they believe that Washington simply does not understand the situation. John Bartlow Martin, Ambassador to the Dominican Republic during a coup designed to overthrow the popularly elected Juan Bosch, reports that he sent a cable to Washington urging that he be authorized to take strong action to support the Bosch government. He relates what happened next:

And then the cable we had been waiting for came in. It said that the Department could do little more to save Bosch in view of his past per-

17. Haynes Johnson, *The Bay of Pigs*, p. 101.
18. Murphy, *Diplomat among Warriors*, p. 284.
19. Galbraith, *Ambassador's Journal*, p. 150.

formance despite all my efforts to persuade him to govern effectively. The forces arrayed against him were largely of his own creation. Now he must save himself. The Department did not oppose the moves I had already recommended to him but warned me not to tie such moves to any commitment by the United States. It suggested that perhaps he also should take some "positive" steps. (I wondered how.) As for the aircraft carrier, the Department refused to intervene militarily unless a Communist takeover were threatened. A show of force that we were not prepared to back up would only be a meaningless gesture, ineffective in a situation which had gone so far.

I presumed the cable had been cleared with the White House. I showed it to King and Shlaudeman and told them that *nevertheless we would do everything we could to save Bosch tonight.* I went up to the Residence, telling the Marine to put any calls through to me there.[20]

Ambassadors engaged in negotiations likewise often feel that the situation is breaking too quickly to permit them to accept Washington's instructions. This is often the case at the United Nations when votes have to be cast on resolutions. Moreover, many American delegates to the UN, including Henry Cabot Lodge and Adlai Stevenson, have not felt bound to accept State Department instructions.[21] The temptation is especially keen if ambassadors engaged in negotiations judge that by stretching their instructions they can attain an agreement. They believe that if they do get an agreement, Washington will then overlook the fact that they ignored their instructions. If the effort fails, the consequences can be serious for the negotiator. In one famous case, Harold Stassen, U.S. representative at an international disarmament conference, had instructions not to make any proposals to the Russians without clearing them first with Britain and France. Stassen, believing that he was close to a dramatic agreement with the Russians, advanced a proposal without consulting either of the two allies. However, before the Russians could react to the proposal, the British and French learned of the maneuver and complained to Washington. Stassen was quickly recalled to Washington and removed from his post because of this incident.[22]

This technique of stretching instructions in a gamble to get an agreement is evidently common at the meetings of the permanent delegates of

---

20. John Martin, *Overtaken by Events*, p. 570 (italics added).

21. Murphy, *Diplomat among Warriors*, p. 367; Attwood, *The Reds and the Blacks*, pp. 140–41; Beichman, *The "Other" State Department*, passim.

22. Larson, *Eisenhower*, pp. 77–78.

the North Atlantic Council. Harlan Cleveland, who was U.S. Ambassador to the Council during most of the 1960s, gives the following account:
The advantages of consultation are bound to be more obvious to the full-time consulters, such as an Ambassador at NATO headquarters, than to officials preoccupied with executive decision-making and congressional salesmanship in Washington. Indeed, the best reason for conducting consultations multilaterally in the North Atlantic Council and its subordinate bodies is that the full-time practitioners of multilateral diplomacy develop a "habit of consultation"—that is, they get in the habit of moving slightly beyond their formal instructions.

In a typical case the discussion starts with known governmental positions that are clearly inconsistent with each other and will, if maintained, create a stalemate. But the study of these positions, when they are all laid on the same conference (or luncheon) table, enables each representative to make a judgment about how much his own instructions would have to be bent in order to meet his colleagues'—if they succeed in bending their instructions too. Each representative then reports to his government that a new proposition, not contained in anybody's instructions, might just make it possible to secure agreement. Each representative, in the elementary exercise of bureaucratic caution, attributes this composite formula to one or more other governments, and most of our allies are likely to attribute it to the United States. Without representatives who are willing to operate in that diplomatic no-man's-land beyond their formal instructions, the efficiency of collective diplomacy would be greatly reduced, and governments might just as well send messages directly from capital to capital even on issues that involve many nations.[23]

The official who stretches or distorts his instructions may or may not report this fact to Washington. He may go so far as to suggest that he took the action instructed. Washington will often have difficulty learning the truth. Even if he reports that he disobeyed instructions, Washington may have to accept a fait accompli. Or perhaps it will turn out that nobody in Washington is prepared to use the energy necessary to get out the second cable instructing the ambassador to correct his actions. Indeed, the extreme opposition demonstrated by the ambassador may weaken the coalition that was strong enough to get out a cable, to the point where they cannot clear a second one.

2. *Delay.* Often the most effective technique for an embassy when it

23. Cleveland, *NATO*, pp. 28–29.

receives a specific instruction it does not wish to carry out is simply to delay taking the action. If pressed, the embassy can report that it plans to
move but at the appropriate time and in the appropriate way. Washington
is often not in a position to specify when an action should be taken. It is
frequently at the mercy of the ambassador or the field commander to
determine at what speed and in what form the action should be carried
out. George Kennan, at the end of a long description of the process by
which the National Security Council reached some fundamental decisions on occupation policy in Japan, writes with skepticism about how
much difference these decisions made with regard to what was done in
Japan:

These recommendations were passed on by the Secretary of State to the
Far Eastern Division for its critical comment and clearance. The division
accepted them with only one or two minor modifications. But because
they involved so heavily our military interests and because their implementation had to proceed primarily through our military authorities, they
had also to be submitted to the National Security Council, on which the
armed services were powerfully represented, and thus to receive presidential sanction. This took time. Not all of the recommendations were agree-
able to all echelons of the armed services whose responsibilities were
engaged. Some of the recommendations would interfere, not only with
existing armed service policies, but with cherished personal privileges,
amenities, and advantages. Nevertheless, the recommendations met after
some delay with practically complete acceptance in the National Security
Council, and thus became, with presidential approval, the basis for orders
issued—mostly at the end of 1948 or the beginning of 1949—by the service
departments to the occupational headquarters in Tokyo.

How, at what stages, and in what degree these decisions finally found
realization in the actions and practices of SCAP, I cannot tell. I think it
likely that General MacArthur, being largely in agreement with them and
well informed of the deliberations in Washington that led to their final
adoption, anticipated them at many points by the exercise of his own great
executive powers. Part of them were no doubt well on the way to implementation before Washington had even finished its deliberations. If, on
the other hand, there were certain features that did not meet with General
MacArthur's full approval, he had ample means of delaying, if not frustrating, their execution. For these reasons the effect of the decisions in Japan
was probably a gradual and to many an almost imperceptible one. Mr.
Sebald says nothing in his memoirs to indicate that he ever heard of these

decisions, though he does refer to a number of the changes pursuant to them that took place in 1949. The memoirs of General Willoughly, too, reveal no awareness on his part of any of the above. One has at times the feeling that Washington did not loom very large on the horizons of this highly self-centered occupational command.[24]

3. *Do nothing.* Rather than taking a different action or implementing a decision slowly, officials in the field may simply do nothing when they receive a cable. On occasion they count on the fact that Washington will find it difficult to enforce action or indeed even to monitor noncompliance. For example, in the midst of one of the many Laotian crises, the U.S. Ambassador to Vientiane, Winthrop Brown, received a cable advising him to take such action as would remove Kong Le, who had then seized power, from the scene as expeditiously as possible. Since the message gave no specific orders as to how Brown should accomplish this objective, and since in his view it was impossible to do so, he simply ignored the cable and made no move against Kong Le.[25]

4. *Obey the letter but not the spirit.* Following the letter of instructions but ignoring their spirit can take a number of different forms in the field. A diplomat who is under orders to press a foreign government to carry out some action may go through the motions but slant his conversation in a way that makes it clear to the foreign official that he does not agree.

Alternatively, one can convey information to a foreign government through a channel which makes it almost certain that the message will be ignored. Elizabeth Drew describes one such episode during the period following the collapse of Biafra:

Another interagency meeting was convened on January 21, and it adopted most of the proposals that had been deferred almost a week earlier. Ten days had passed since the collapse of Biafra. The embassy in Lagos was instructed to bring the Western report to the attention of the Nigerian government. Two days later, the embassy sent word back that the report was given to the Ministry of Health by an AID doctor who, it added, could not be expected to support its findings. The embassy said that it believed another survey was necessary. This transmittal of the report—routine, at low levels, with no sense of urgency—was not what Washington had in mind. The Ambassador, William Trueheart, reported that despite

24. Kennan, *Memoirs, 1925–1950*, pp. 392–93. See also Dunn, *Peace-Making and the Settlement with Japan*, pp. 74–78, where Kennan's analysis of the very gradual pace of the implementation of this policy change and the ability of General Mac-Arthur to resist change is corroborated in detail.

25. Dommen, *Conflict in Laos*, pp. 157–58.

Washington's instructions he did not believe that 10,000 tons a week was necessary, and that he could not be expected to convince the Nigerians of the revised, higher need. He argued that the problem needed more study, and that there was a better chance of getting the Nigerians to act if they were not "nudged."[26]

One can also report that the official to whom one is told to speak is not available and therefore one has taken up the matter with a lesser official who will report the information to the senior official.

A more subtle way of obeying the spirit but not the letter is to "over-achieve." Galbraith describes one incident when as Ambassador to India he thwarted the will of the State Department by pressing even harder than the department wanted him to on making concessions that would ease the Kashmir dispute.

Actually, one thing was accomplished. Until last week, the Department had felt I was dragging my feet. In the course of the week, there was increasing alarm that I was pressing Nehru too hard. A telegram questioned my "all or nothing" approach. They felt I left inadequate room for retreat. This is one of many cases where the element of personal strategy enters diplomacy. My instinct was against pressing Nehru too hard. We stood to lose some of the character we gained last fall, make cooperation on other matters more difficult and probably accomplish nothing. But if I did not press hard, the failure would be blamed on me. "Galbraith was reluctant to come to grips with the great man; another ambassador protecting his client." Apart from being bad for me personally, this would have meant pressure for a new effort later on. So I made the best of a bad situation and tried too hard. I won't be blamed for failure, and won't be asked for more effort.

I have the feeling these may be the last of the talks.[27]

5. *Ask them to reconsider.* If an ambassador in the field is reluctant simply to disobey or ignore an order, he can send back to Washington a cable explaining why the action proposed would not be sensible and asking for a new decision. For reasons indicated above, this often works. The narrow coalition put together in Washington to get a proposal through may be shattered by a strong cable from the ambassador asking for reconsideration. Often tired by the first battle, those who press for a particular decision will not have the energy to renew it. They sense that even if they get out a reaffirming cable, the ambassador may then resort to one of the other techniques to avoid putting the decision into effect. They must also

26. Drew, "Washington," p. 21.
27. Galbraith, *Ambassador's Journal*, p. 564.

allow for the possibility that the ambassador may be correct in saying that the action he opposes will not accomplish the purpose intended.[28]

Actions in the Absence of Decision

Field missions, like agencies in Washington, prefer if possible to act without presidential decisions. Karl Rankin, a career official who was Ambassador to Taiwan, reflects the prevalent view:

An unwritten law in the Foreign Service is: Never ask for instructions from Washington if you can help it. It is presumed that the officer in the field is familiar with official policy; in most cases he is in a better position than anyone else to decide how a given problem should be handled in the light of that policy, and whether circumstances demand that he ask for instructions.[29]

Emissaries may feel that they have no choice but to respond to a question put to them by a foreign leader. Failure to respond, they fear, will demonstrate either their own lack of knowledge of policy (and hence reduce their effectiveness as an envoy) or will reveal that Washington is without a policy. Alternatively, they may fear that Washington's answer, although it would authorize them to respond as they would like, would come too late to be effective. Dean Acheson relates one such incident when he was briefing French President Charles de Gaulle on the Cuban missile crisis:

"Suppose they don't do anything—suppose they don't try to break the blockade—suppose they don't take the missiles out—what will your President do then?" When I left Washington nobody had told me the answer to that question. I don't know whether a plan existed, but if it did, I didn't know it. But I thought it would be most unwise to indicate to General de Gaulle that we were not absolutely clear as to what we were going to do in each stage of this—and I said, "We will immediately tighten this blockade and the next thing we would do is to stop tankers—and this will bring Cuba to a standstill in no time at all." He said, "That's very good" again. I said, "If we have to go further why, of course, we'll go further." He said, "I understand."[30]

---

28. For examples of reclaimers, see Attwood, *The Reds and the Blacks*, pp. 92–93; Hilsman, *To Move a Nation*, pp. 488–89; Beichman, *The "Other" State Department*, pp. 80–81.

29. Rankin, *China Assignment*, p. ix.

30. Acheson, Kennedy Library Oral History Interview, p. 28.

In a similar episode, when he was without instructions but would not admit it, William Attwood, then Ambassador to Guinea, reports that he responded affirmatively to a request for help. "I made this offer on my own, knowing that Washington would have approved, but also would have been bureaucratically unable to get the approval to me in time had I requested it."[31]

One reason for taking action without requesting approval is of course to avoid the refusal that might have ensued. Adlai Stevenson made such a move while Ambassador to the United Nations in an effort to break a deadlock over Article 19, which provided that countries in arrears in their payments to the UN could not vote. Stevenson on his own arranged a meeting with the Soviet Union's Ambassador to the United Nations. During the course of this meeting Stevenson and Ambassador Fedorenko worked out an arrangement under which the General Assembly would meet but postpone any votes about the status of the Soviet Union. Stevenson reported this to the State Department, which felt under pressure to go along.[32]

If they are not prepared to act without instructions, ambassadors can take steps which maximize the probability of getting the decision they want. The mildest form of this maneuver is simply to propose to Washington the instructions that one would like to have, recognizing that this cable is likely to become the basis for the drafting of instructions in Washington and that one has gained a substantial advantage by having others work from one's draft.

A stronger version is to indicate the course of action that one plans to take and to state that one proposes to act by a certain date unless the department advises to the contrary. This puts the supporters of the proposed action in Washington in a strong position, since they only have to find ways to delay sending out a cable.[33]

Even ambassadors who ask for instructions sometimes find that they must act before instructions arrive. Henry S. Villard, a career Foreign Service officer who was then Ambassador to Libya, tells of a typical episode in which he was involved:

> ... The [Libyan] Prime Minister had resigned and flown off to Rome, his nerves frayed by the thankless task of guiding a newborn state. The King was ill, in seclusion; there was a rumor in the bazaars that he might abdicate. The whole government structure seemed about to collapse. I had

31. Attwood, *The Reds and the Blacks*, p. 63.
32. Beichman, *The "Other" State Department*, pp. 149–58.
33. Galbraith describes one such episode in *Ambassador's Journal*, p. 391.

just reached a vital point in negotiations for an air-base agreement. So when the Libyan cabinet asked me to fly to Italy and persuade the Prime Minister to return, I cabled the Department urgently for permission to make the try.

Time was of the essence, yet the hours ticked by without response. In Washington, the wheels ground methodically. Committee met with committee, weighing the pros and cons of my recommendation. The Pentagon had to be consulted. Policy factors had to be considered; so did tactics, in the light of progress to date on the air-base negotiations. Suggestions at a lower level had to be referred to a higher level for further discussion. I sent a second cable. No reply.

Finally, I decided to act on my own. I boarded the plane of my Air Attaché, flew to Rome, and called on the Prime Minister at his hotel. With all the eloquence I could muster, I urged him to come back and steer the ship of state through the storm, pointing out that the fate of his country—and our delicate negotiations—rested in his hands alone. He heard me in silence, still smarting from the political wounds which had caused him to resign. He would think it over; he would give me his answer that evening.

At eight o'clock I was again at the Prime Minister's door. His face was wreathed in smiles. He would do as I asked, and to mark the occasion he invited me to dine with him downstairs. With a load like lead off my mind, I was enjoying the repast when I spied an officer of our Rome Embassy discreetly waving a piece of paper from behind the potted palms. I made my excuses, rose, and went over to receive the message—a priority cable to Tripoli, repeated to Rome for information. At long last, Washington had moved. There were my orders. Under no circumstances was I to follow the Prime Minister to Rome, for that, the Department feared, might be interpreted as interference in the domestic affairs of a sovereign country.[34]

Having explored some of the reasons why participants neglect to implement policy and having outlined techniques available to them, both in Washington and in the field, to resist presidential or departmental directives, we are ready to consider the options left to the President for gaining compliance.

34. Villard, "How To Save Money: An Open Letter to Congressman John J. Rooney," pp. 20–22. For a similar episode, see Attwood, *The Reds and the Blacks,* pp. 200–202.

CHAPTER FIFTEEN

Presidential Control

According to some standard accounts of the U.S. govern-
ment, the only time the bureaucracy can ignore presidential orders is when
the President is uninterested or unconcerned in a matter. If the President
devotes his personal attention to a matter, it is said, the bureaucracy and
his principal subordinates have no choice but to obey. Yet the evidence
indicates the contrary. Even when the President does devote his time and
effort and the issue is critical, disobedience can occur.

The Cuban missile crisis is often taken as the extreme example of presidential involvement. President Kennedy did almost nothing during the
period of the Cuban missile crisis but work on this question, devoting his
attention to even the most minute detail. In Robert Kennedy's words:

*Despite the heavy pressure on the big decisions, President Kennedy fol-
lowed every detail. He requested, for instance, the names of all the Cuban
doctors in the Miami area, should their services be required in Cuba. Learning that a U.S. military ship with extremely sensitive equipment (similar to
the Liberty, which was struck by Israel during the Israeli-Arab war) was
very close to the coast of Cuba, he ordered it farther out to sea, where it
would be less vulnerable to attack. He supervised everything, from the
contents of leaflets to be dropped over Cuba to the assembling of ships
for the invasion.*[1]

Yet during that crisis, on a number of critical issues, the orders of the
President were not obeyed in the manner that he had intended. At one
point a tentative presidential decision that he would authorize bombing
of Cuba if an American U-2 was shot down was taken by the Air Force as
sufficient authority to proceed with bombing when an American U-2 was
attacked. It was only at the last minute that this was discovered and the
attack called back. Although the President had given no orders which
would permit American vessels to attack Soviet submarines and believed

---

1. Kennedy, *Thirteen Days*, p. 86.

that there had been no contact between Soviet and American forces, in fact the American Navy was throughout the period of the crisis forcing Soviet submarines in the Caribbean to surface. Despite the President's order to put forces on the alert in case of military confrontation, American aircraft remained lined up wingtip to wingtip on air fields in the southern part of the United States. Despite an explicit presidential order, issued over intense Navy opposition, to move the blockade line closer to Cuba, the line remained where the Navy wanted it. Despite a presidential order to avoid provocative intelligence operations, an American U-2 strayed over Soviet territory at the very height of the crisis.[2]

President Truman fared little better during the opening days of the Korean War, despite his personal attention to the matters at hand. American pilots failed to attack invading tanks in the Seoul area, despite Truman's explicit decision that they should be permitted to do so. Without authorization from Washington, General MacArthur ordered an attack on an air field in North Korea.[3]

Such resistance can even extend to the most trivial items. For example, President Kennedy was unsuccessful in his desire to choose the names for American ships. As Theodore Sorensen explains:

On the other hand, a President's personal interests may draw to him decisions normally left for others. Roosevelt, for example, took a hand in deciding postage stamp designs. I have seen President Kennedy engrossed in a list of famous Indian chiefs, deciding on an appropriate name for a nuclear submarine. (Inasmuch as most of the chiefs had earned their fame by defying the armed might of the United States, it was not an easy decision. In fact, when he finally decided on Chief Red Cloud, the Navy protested that this name had undesirable foreign-policy implications.)[4]

As Truman summed up in his often quoted remark about Eisenhower: "He'll sit here and he'll say, 'Do this! Do that!' *And nothing will happen.* Poor Ike—it won't be a bit like the Army. He'll find it very frustrating."[5]

Presidential Strategies To Gain Compliance

If the thrust of Truman's observations is correct, nevertheless it is not true that nothing ever happens. The resistance of the bureaucracy to im-

2. See Allison, *Essence of Decision*, pp. 137–42; Abel, *The Missile Crisis*, pp. 193–94; Schlesinger, *A Thousand Days*, p. 828; Hilsman, *To Move a Nation*, p. 221.
3. Paige, *The Korean Decision*, pp. 181, 364–65.
4. Theodore Sorensen, *Decision-Making in the White House*, p. 17.
5. Quoted in Neustadt, *Presidential Power*, p. 9.

plementation has a vital effect on the way that decisions are made in the first place, and Presidents, as they become accustomed to resistance, tend to develop ways to deal with it.

By the authority of his office and the position from which he plays the game, the President enjoys certain privileges of power that make it possible for him to break down some of this bureaucratic resistance. Richard Neustadt's study of presidential power provides a cogent summary of what these assets are:

Governmental power, in reality not form, is influence of an effective sort on the behavior of men actually involved in making public policy and carrying it out. Effective influence for the man in the White House stems from three related sources: first are the bargaining advantages inherent in his job with which to persuade other men that what he wants of them is what their own responsibilities require them to do. Second are the expectations of those other men regarding his ability and will to use the various advantages they think he has. Third are those men's estimates of how his public views him and of how their publics may view them if they do what he wants. In short, his power is the product of his vantage points in government, together with his reputation in the Washington community and his prestige outside.[6]

By virtue of these assets peculiar to his position, the President may maneuver in a number of ways to increase the probability that his orders will be obeyed.[7] His demonstrated willingness to use these maneuvers increases the likelihood that in the future his orders will be obeyed without his implementing some of the more drastic measures. The maneuvers available to the President include the following:

Persuasion

One of the President's most important assets is his ability to persuade his principal associates that something he wishes to do is in the national interest. Most participants believe that they should do anything which is required for the security of the United States. They recognize that the President is the only official elected by the whole people and that he there-

---

6. Ibid., p. 179.

7. Most of these maneuvers will be familiar to the reader because they are similar to those discussed in the section on the decision process. The distinction being made here is the effect of resistance to implementation on the way a President maneuvers to gain compliance. It is obvious that the processes of decision making and implementation are so interrelated that it is impossible to separate one from the other completely.

fore has a much stronger mandate than they do to define what is in the national interest. Moreover, the President is seen as having a wider area of responsibility. Thus participants will take very seriously arguments from the President, particularly when delivered by him personally and when he invokes national security considerations. In fact, every President spends a good deal of time capitalizing on these beliefs to convince principal associates that they should do what he has decided should be done. As President Truman once put it, "I sit here all day trying to persuade people to do the things they ought to have sense enough to do without my persuading them. . . . That's all the powers of the President amount to."[8]

A President is most persuasive when he makes his pitch personally in direct conversation with those involved. This may mean the President's meeting with officials with whom he does not normally confer or holding a meeting in order to be sure that those who must implement a decision already made have a chance to argue with him personally and hear directly from him what he wants them to do. President Truman, for example, determined to reassert civilian control over atomic energy, called in the officer he was about to appoint as the Army's director of the nuclear weapons program to replace the legendary General Groves who had run the program during World War II. Although there was no question but what he would approve the appointment, Truman recognized the importance of laying down his own position in person. David Lilienthal, then Chairman of the Atomic Energy Commission, describes the scene:

Talked to Secretary Royall and Col. Nichols outside the President's office; they said they didn't know what the meeting was about, that Royall hadn't asked for it.

The President said he had before him the recommendation of the promotion of Col. Nichols as head of the Armed Forces Special Weapons Project, that he wanted to have a talk with us before acting on it. "I don't want another General Groves incident." Royall injected to say that he saw after his trip West that that situation was as I had said it was, quite impossible.

The President said, "I want it clearly understood before I act on this appointment that this is a civilian-run agency, and I thought I ought to say this to you directly. It requires cooperation between the civilian and the military, of course." Nichols said, "You can count on 100 percent cooperation." I said, "You have a team, Mr. President."[9]

8. Quoted in Neustadt, *Presidential Power*, pp. 9–10.
9. Lilienthal, *Journals*, p. 303.

Unless the President can succeed in persuading his principal associates, he is likely to find that his decisions do not turn into effective actions.

Negotiation

When the President cannot persuade, he must seek to negotiate. His principal associates and the career organizations of the government constantly need things from the President and wish to avoid an all-out confrontation with him. Thus on an issue about which the President feels very strongly, if they are not willing simply to obey his directives, they are likely to be willing to compromise. A President who is prepared to negotiate and to throw other issues into the pot can often persuade others to go along with what he wants. However, in the absence of such negotiations, he is unlikely to get cooperation in seeking to override strong organizational interests.

President Eisenhower in his conversation with President-elect Kennedy during the transition period was amazed to discover that Kennedy seemed unaware of these limitations on presidential power to enforce decisions. Kennedy had raised with Eisenhower questions about the desirability of a rather sweeping reorganization of the Department of Defense which had been proposed to him by a task force. Eisenhower, who had spent the better part of his second term using all the prestige of a war hero and former five-star general to get enacted a much more limited reorganization, was appalled at Kennedy's assumption that the only issue was whether or not the reorganization made sense. He was conscious that any such reorganization would require endless negotiations and compromise. In a memorandum to himself describing the conversation, he put the point well:

I did urge him to avoid any reorganization until he himself could become well acquainted with the problem. (Incidentally, I made this same suggestion with respect to the White House staff, the National Security Council, and the Pentagon.) I told him that improvements could undoubtedly be made in the Pentagon and the command organization, but I also made it clear that the present organization and the improved functioning of the establishment had, during the past eight years, been brought about by patient study and long and drawn out negotiations with the Congress and the Armed Services.[10]

10. Eisenhower, *Waging Peace*, p. 713.

Personal Abuse

A switch from persuasion to bullying and hectoring is a way adopted by some chief executives to keep subordinates in line. The President in ceremonial terms stands above his colleagues in a way that no Prime Minister in a parliamentary system does. He is "Mr. President" even to those who have known him long and intimately prior to his election, and he is treated with the deference of a head of state while functioning as a head of government. If he is prepared to use the leverage that this accords him and exploit the extreme reluctance of others to engage in a rough and tumble argument with him, he can gain some control over his senior associates. Presidents Truman, Kennedy, and Nixon are in general identified with considerate treatment of subordinates, though exceptional incidents might be cited. On the other hand, the famous Eisenhower temper exploded occasionally, and Lyndon Johnson was well known for his abuse of his subordinates. Philip Geyelin describes one of the first such occasions, when Johnson and his principal advisers were preparing for a visit of British Prime Minister Harold Wilson to Washington to seek agreement to move forward on the MLF:

> In the course of the protracted conferences in preparation for the Wilson visit, Johnson assailed the men around him, questioning their competence as well as their counsel. It was at one of these sessions that Johnson ticked off each man in turn. Ball was upbraided for the "disgraceful" caliber of ambassadorial candidates served up by the State Department. Dean Acheson, sitting in as private consultant, was needled "as the man who got us into war in Korea" and had to "get Eisenhower to get us out of it." McNamara was derided for his easy assurances that the MLF could be sold to Congress; commended, sarcastically, for his command of Senate politics, and reminded that if MLF was to be sold to Congress, the job would have to be done by the President himself. Acheson, according to reports, finally broke the mounting tension by declaring: "Mr. President, you don't pay these men enough to talk to them that way—even with the federal pay raise."

Rough as some of the sessions apparently were, they were also instructive. Few who were there or heard about it would thereafter make any quick assumptions about what would be palatable and what would not, when presented to Lyndon Johnson. Few would come unprepared to present their case in minute and, if possible, irrefutable detail. And few would presume to speak for the President without being quite certain where he stood. It was a memorable object lesson in Johnson decision-making, a major development in the President's move towards mastery of the "processes," a significant turn in the U.S. approach to Alliance policy.[11]

Taking Over as Desk Officer

Another source of power that the President has is the ability to personally take charge of as much execution of a policy as possible. When the President makes the decision to communicate certain information to another government or to the American public and then does so himself in a speech, he is combining the roles of decision maker and practitioner in a way that gives him maximum control over the implementing process. This is also the case when the President calls in a foreign ambassador resident in Washington and conveys his views on a particular subject. As Theodore Sorensen explains, this is what Kennedy did in dealing with the Berlin crisis:

His second basic decision was to take complete charge of the operation. For months he saturated himself in the problem. He reviewed and revised the military contingency plans, the conventional force build-up, the diplomatic and propaganda initiatives, the Budget changes, and the plans for economic welfare. He considered the effect each move would have on Berlin morale, Allied unity, Soviet intransigence, and his own legislative and foreign aid program. He talked to Allied leaders, to Gromyko, and to the Germans; he kept track of all the cables; he read transcripts of all the conferences; and he complained (with limited success) about the pace at the Department of State, about leaks from Allied clearances, and about the lack of new diplomatic suggestions.[12]

The President of course pays a price for taking direct charge of operations. He and his staff may lack all of the relevant facts. More important, the President uses up time which could be employed to involve him more intensively in several issues. Consequently he may limit his involvement somewhat, especially when negotiations need to be conducted overseas, by appointing a trusted agent but in effect playing the role of desk officer with respect to that agent. This is what Kennedy did in the test ban negotiations, sending Averell Harriman and taking personal charge of the communications with him.[13]

11. Geyelin, *LBJ and the World*, pp. 162–63.
12. Theodore Sorensen, *Kennedy*, pp. 586–87.
13. Ibid., p. 735.

An active President not only makes speeches and issues press statements. On occasion he becomes a "working member of the bureaucracy" by giving out announcements in the name of his press secretary or a Cabinet officer or arranging leaks to the press in order to communicate to his own government as well as foreign governments. Thus, determined to put an end to excessive American pressure for a multilateral force, Lyndon Johnson first had his advisers prepare a precise memorandum laying out what could and could not be done. Then he not only sent this to senior participants but leaked the entire memorandum to the *New York Times,* thereby communicating it to lower-level officials who supported his position as well as to foreign governments. The implied message was that any American official who applied pressure on behalf of the MLF was acting without the President's support.[14]

Changing Personnel

The President has almost unlimited legal power to appoint and replace his principal advisers. In the case of posts occupied by military officers he is constrained to appoint career people from the established services, but even then he has latitude as to whom he appoints and whether people are kept in positions. A President determined to enforce a particular policy can do so in part by systematically removing from office anyone who opposes that policy. President Truman, battling against the pressures for preventive war in the early postwar period, removed Secretary of the Navy Francis P. Matthews from the Cabinet and named him Ambassador to Ireland after Matthews made a speech calling for preventive war, and Truman retired the Commandant of the Air War College who also made such a proposal.[15] Admiral George W. Anderson, after he resisted Kennedy's orders during the Cuban missile crisis, was appointed Ambassador to Portugal.[16]

As these examples suggest, an official who has influence with an important group either in the bureaucracy or beyond, usually receives another post rather than outright dismissal. When President Kennedy decided that he had to replace Chester Bowles, a leader of the Democratic Party's left wing, as Under Secretary of State, long negotiations ensued to be sure

14. Geyelin, *LBJ and the World,* pp. 175–76.
15. Acheson, *Present at the Creation,* p. 478. See also Truman, *Years of Trial and Hope,* pp. 383–84, on the decision to relieve General MacArthur.
16. Korb, "Budget Strategies of the Joint Chiefs of Staff," p. 6.

that Bowles would not resign with a blast at the President's policy. Bowles was ultimately persuaded to accept the position of special presidential adviser on developing nations.[17]

Appointing an Agent

Rather than seeking to fill an existing position with a new official, a President often resorts to the technique of appointing a special agent who does not have commitments to a particular bureaucratic organization and is free to cut across the concerns of various departments. Henry Kissinger, writing before he joined the Nixon administration, explains the maneuver:

... *The executive [is driven] in the direction of extrabureaucratic means of decision. The practice of relying on special emissaries or personal envoys is an example; their status outside the bureaucracy frees them from some of its restraints. International agreements are sometimes possible only by ignoring safeguards against capricious action. It is a paradoxical aspect of modern bureaucracies that their quest for objectivity and calculability often leads to impasses which can be overcome only by essentially arbitrary decisions.*[18]

President Nixon has often relied on Henry Kissinger in precisely this way, as John F. Kennedy relied on Averell Harriman to negotiate both the Laos agreement and the test ban treaty. Harriman was given wide discretionary powers and authority to deal directly with the President, and his appointment signaled to the Russians a serious intention to negotiate.[19] President Truman resorted to a special agent to break a log jam on the question of a Japanese peace treaty. With the State Department pressing for an early treaty and the Joint Chiefs of Staff and the Secretary of Defense resisting, Truman decided that he wanted to move forward and recognized that the only way to do so was to find a man with influence and energy and give him the mission of getting a peace treaty. As Dean Rusk recalls the episode:

One of the most effective task-force exercises was the practically one-man task force that John Foster Dulles constituted in getting the Japanese Peace Treaty. I think that had we tried to handle that problem on an interdepartmental committee basis, we could never have gotten that peace treaty negotiated and ratified. He simply took it on with a two-page

17. Bowles, *Promises To Keep*, pp. 360–67.
18. Kissinger, *American Foreign Policy*, p. 511.
19. Brandon, *Anatomy of Error*, p. 16; Schlesinger, *A Thousand Days*, pp. 902–3.

letter from the President, saying, "Dear Mr. Dulles: I want you to get a peace treaty of this sort with Japan." On the basis of that, he could cut away the stacks of materials that had developed over the years in the departments. He concentrated on a simple treaty of reconciliation. My job then, as Assistant Secretary of Far Eastern Affairs, was not only to support him, but to block off interference from all the other agencies. They knew that if they wanted to interfere they had to go to the President, and this was difficult to do.[20]

Creating a New Institution

When the President wishes to negotiate with a foreign government, he may be able to do so himself or to pick an individual from outside of channels in order to accomplish his purpose. However, when he wishes to use military force or otherwise have carried out a large complicated project, it is necessary to rely on a major formal organization. If the President realizes that the existing organizations are not carrying out his decisions, he may seek to alter the organization or to create a new one. This is a difficult and time-consuming task which a President will undertake, if at all, only after much hesitation. Tired of receiving conflicting intelligence reports from different agencies, Truman insisted upon the creation of a central intelligence agency following World War II. President Eisenhower agreed to the creation of the National Aeronautics and Space Agency after the military services showed they would not be willing to concentrate on the scientific aspects of space exploration. President Kennedy sought, in effect, to create a new institution in the form of the Army Special Forces, converting them from a guerrilla force for a large war in Europe to an organization which would have a strong counterinsurgency mission. Arthur Schlesinger describes the great difficulties and resistance that Kennedy encountered:

Guerrillas were also an old preoccupation of Walt Rostow's [sic]. When Kennedy read Lansdale's report about guerrilla success in Vietnam, he asked Rostow to check into what the Army was, in fact, doing about counterguerrilla training. He was soon informed that the Special Forces at Fort Bragg consisted of fewer than a thousand men. Looking at the field manuals and training literature, he tossed them aside as "meager" and inadequate. Reading Mao Tse-tung and Che Guevara himself on the sub-

20. Rusk, "The Secretary of State," p. 269. See also Acheson, *Present at the Creation*, p. 432; Cohen, *The Political Process and Foreign Policy*, p. 127.

ject, he told the Army to do likewise. (He used to entertain his wife on country weekends by inventing aphorisms in the manner of Mao's "Guerrillas must move among the people as fish swim in the sea.") He asked General Clifton, his military aide, to bring in the Army's standard antiguerrilla equipment, examined it with sorrow and ordered Army research and development to do better. Most important of all, he instructed the Special Warfare Center at Fort Bragg to expand its mission, which had hitherto been largely the training of cadres for action behind the lines in case of a third world war, in order to confront the existing challenge of guerrilla warfare in the jungles and hills of underdeveloped countries. Over the opposition of the Army bureaucracy, which abhorred separate elite commands on principle, he reinstated the SF green beret as the symbol of the new force.[21]

Degrees of Control

In previous chapters we surveyed the array of maneuvers available to the bureaucracy and its representatives in the field to resist presidential orders or to carry on in their absence. In the present chapter we have covered countervailing maneuvers open to the President. What determines the outcome of the struggle? And how does this reflect back on the decision process?

Where the line is drawn between presidential influence, the interests of subordinates, and the standard procedures of their organization depends on several factors. One is the degree of presidential involvement, which can vary enormously. Obviously the deeper the President involves himself in operations, the more influence he will have over what is being done. In part, this is simply because he is able to do more of it himself, but also the President, by devoting a substantial amount of time to an issue, makes it clear to his subordinates that it is something he cares a great deal about. Officials recognize that to fight the President on such an issue is likely to cost them dearly in terms of their relation with the President. They also recognize that the President is much more likely to learn of a failure to implement a decision on an issue that he is closely monitoring than one, such as missiles in Turkey, where he made a single decision and then assumed that it was being followed. When the President is actively involved in an issue, he is also likely to speak out publicly on it,

21. Schlesinger, A *Thousand Days*, p. 341.

thereby committing his prestige in Washington, the country, and the world.

The second major factor affecting the line between presidential influence and the influence of other participants is the nature of what the President wants to have done. At one extreme, if an action is a simple one capable of being carried out by a single individual in Washington without detailed technical expertise or training, presidential influence is likely to be overwhelming. To the degree that an action is a complicated one, requiring the cooperation of large numbers of people, many of them stationed outside of Washington, presidential influence on implementation fades. Two of President Nixon's decisions in regard to U.S.–China policy illustrate the point. The first involved the President's determination to arrange for a trip to Peking, and the other involved his decision to make an effort to keep the Chinese Nationalists in the United Nations. In the first case, while effective action depended on the cooperation of the People's Republic of China, it required very little cooperation from the American bureaucracy. The President was enabled to entrust the task to one man, Henry Kissinger, who could operate almost independently of the existing bureaucratic organizations. In the other case of seeking to persuade a hundred and six governments in the United Nations that they should permit Taiwan to remain in the UN, implementation depended on a large number of officials in the State Department and a substantial number of American ambassadors. The President was dependent on them to convey the message in a way that he wished to have it conveyed to persuade other governments to support the American decision. The State Department, in turn, could proceed only according to its standard operating procedures in carrying out such a complicated operation.

Finally, the degree of presidential control is determined by whether or not the action can be carried out by different organizations, whether the President has the flexibility to choose among implementers and can find one in sympathy with what he wishes to have done. Presidential control over military operations tends to be more limited than his control over diplomacy precisely because in the military field he has few options. Furthermore, as we saw in the last chapter, the President's influence is greater if the officials carrying out an action are in Washington. Those in the capital can be summoned easily into his presence and have a better feeling for what he wants done.

Thus far we have been considering instances in which the President wishes to have something done and is resisted by subordinates. There are, however, times when the President rejects a proposal for action but certain officials are still eager to take it. If the prospective implementers agree with the President's decision, then it is almost impossible for others to get the action which the President has rejected. On the other hand, if the implementers were turned down, they may be able to find a way to take the action even without presidential concurrence. In particular, the military services have often found ways to keep projects alive after they have been cut out of the budget by the President and the Secretary of Defense. The most spectacular such instance occurred with the Army space program. The Army, ordered not to engage in the development of a missile which could place objects in orbit around the earth, nevertheless proceeded with its program and ultimately put the first satellite in orbit after the authorized Navy program failed on several occasions. General John P. Medaris, who was in charge of this Army program, describes in his memoirs just what was done:

Gen. H. N. Toftoy, who was in charge of Redstone Arsenal at that time, came up with what for those days was an outrageously ambitious project to build such a complex on the top of a hill at the Arsenal. The Army had no mission beyond the Redstone missile itself, which was well along in development, and there was no possible way that the research people could finance such a test complex because they could find no real excuse for it. Yet if anything significant were to be done in the future, the construction of such a complex would have to start right away. Construction time would be a couple of years at least, and in the meantime nothing bigger, or more advanced, could be undertaken. It was the old story that still haunts the programs of the Army, where you can't get what you need for future work until the work itself is approved, and when that happens it is too late to build what you needed in the first place.

If anything was to be done, it seemed to us that it would have to be accomplished with production money. Now the rules say that production money cannot be used for research and development projects. Yet there was a fair amount of money available in the production budget for building or acquiring facilities, and there was none in the Research and Development budget. Finally we cooked up a plausible story of needing the test tower and other test facilities in order to carry on the required quality control and inspection testing that would be needed when the Redstone missile went into production. On the basis that the facilities were to be used for the testing of items in production, rather than for development tests, we could legally use production money.

I do not think anyone in the Army knew what we were up to, but I watched the campaign carefully and finally wangled it through with approximately 13 million dollars as an initial increment. I very carefully avoided even mentioning any R&D work that might be done on these facilities, because I knew this would prejudice our chances. The people who were responsible for approving these projects were, I am afraid, not too well informed with respect to the guided missile area, and they swallowed our story. It is interesting to note that had not this project been rammed through and approved when it was not really justified by either the ground rules or the needs of the moment, there would have been nothing available to make possible the rapid development of the Jupiter missile or the test work that made the satellites possible.

I was convinced by this time that the future of the Ordnance Corps was in large part in guided missiles. Few were interested in old-fashioned munitions, and getting money to build modern tanks or new rifles or develop new vehicles was very difficult indeed. On the other hand, missiles were beginning to capture the public imagination, and support could be had for additional work and new projects.[22]

Many of the actions taken by officials of the American government do not result from explicit presidential decisions. As was suggested above, many of them are the result simply of individuals continuing to do what they have done before. When asked about the impact of the transition from Johnson to Nixon, outgoing Secretary of State Dean Rusk suggested the importance of continuity and consistency in government behavior.

A transition is not so earth-shaking. Of the thousand or so cables that go out of here every day, I see only five or six and the President only one or two. Those who send out the other 994 cables will still be here. It is a little bit like changing engineers on a train going steadily down the track. The new engineer has some switches he can make choices about—but 4,500 intergovernmental agreements don't change.[23]

Sometimes actions result from more generalized presidential decisions which no one foresaw would promote a particular action in a particular area. Presidential budget cuts, for example, often lead to unpredictable changes in military behavior. It was a reduction in the Navy budget which led the Navy to cease patrolling the Taiwan straits, an event that may have been read as an important signal by the People's Republic of China.

22. Medaris, *Countdown for Decision*, pp. 63–64. See also Armacost, *The Politics of Weapons Innovation*, pp. 54, 114; York, *Race to Oblivion*, pp. 105, 135.
23. Rusk, "Mr. Secretary on the Eve of Emeritus," p. 62-B.

In other cases, an organization may initiate a change in its own behavior because of its perception of organizational interests and be in a position to do so on its own without needing to secure presidential approval. Often changes in personnel brought about through routine rotation and retirement lead to substantial changes in the behavior of the United States. These most often occur in the field with the change of ambassadors or military commanders who have substantial freedom.

Thus we can see that most governmental actions, which look to the casual outside observer as if they resulted from specific presidential decisions, are more often an amalgam of a number of coincidental occurrences: actions brought about by presidential decisions (not always those intended), actions that are really maneuvers to influence presidential decisions, actions resulting from decisions in unrelated areas, and actions taken at lower levels by junior participants without informing their superiors or the President. If one is to explain a series of actions, one must consider not only the relevant presidential decisions but also these other sources.

At last we are done, and the framework for explaining national security decisions and actions is in place. What we have described here should not, however, be considered a causal theory by which one may determine which variant of this complex process will be operative under what conditions. The highly politicized policymaking process for national security (and probably most other areas of national interest) can take any one of a rather large number of variations. For any one case in national security decision making, such as the ABM case we are about to revisit in the next chapter, the framework developed here really only provides a starting point and research orientation that serves to sensitize the analyst in examining the available evidence. We do not claim that this broad framework is a substitute for rigorous historical explanation. Nevertheless, we do feel that it will aid the analyst to interpret more realistically the reasons for foreign policy decisions and actions.

PART FOUR

Conclusions

CHAPTER SIXTEEN

Back to ABM: Some Tentative Answers

We are now ready to return to the puzzles posed in Chapter 1 about the decision to deploy the ABM. Some tentative answers emerge when the framework presented in the intervening chapters is employed in the search for explanation.

Bureaucratic Tug-of-War

Our first question is why in January 1967 did President Johnson ask Congress to appropriate the funds to deploy an ABM but state that he would defer the deployment pending an effort to get the Soviet Union to engage in talks on limiting the arms race?

Technological improvement is part of the answer. The technology of ballistic missile defense had in certain respects improved remarkably in the preceding few years. Those responsible for the program in the scientific community, in the Defense Research and Engineering (DDR&E) office and its operating arm, the Advanced Research Projects Agency (ARPA), as well as in the Army, were now arguing that an effective ABM system could be built and could ultimately be improved to handle even a large Russian attack. In past years the contrary testimony of these scientists had offset the pressure from the Joint Chiefs of Staff and enabled McNamara to persuade the President and the Congress that ABM deployment was not technologically feasible. The scientists now thought otherwise.[1]

Soviet ABM deployment became an accepted fact. There was growing evidence that the Soviet Union was beginning to deploy an ABM system around Moscow. In the past the intelligence community had been split as to whether another system, the so-called Tallin system deployed across

1. Edward Randolph Jayne II, "The ABM Debate," pp. 308–9.

the northern part of the Soviet Union, was in fact an ABM system. Though some military intelligence agencies had pressed the view that Tallin was an ABM system, a majority in the intelligence community concluded that it was an air defense system. However, there was no dispute at all that the new system being deployed around Moscow consisted of ABMs. This added to pressures to begin an American deployment in order to avoid an ABM gap.

JCS pressure increased. In part because of the changes in technology and the Russian ABM deployment, the Joint Chiefs of Staff were no longer willing to acquiesce in delaying ABM deployment. They were determined to go firmly on record before Congress in favor of a deployment *now* and, in particular, for a deployment that would develop eventually into a large anti-Russian system.

Senate pressure also increased. Pressure was mounting from Senate leaders for initial ABM deployment. Among others, Russell, Jackson, and Thurmond had all spoken out in favor of an early ABM deployment. The general expectation in the executive branch was that Congress would put great pressure on the President to agree to a deployment if he did not include one in his budget message.[2]

Republican pressure was feared. It was becoming evident that the Republican Party planned to make a campaign issue out of an alleged ABM gap. Michigan Governor George Romney, then believed to be leading Republican candidate for the presidential nomination in 1968, had, on a "Meet the Press" broadcast in November, talked of an ABM gap and made it clear that this would be an issue in the campaign. Moreover, the GOP Congressional Policy Committee led by Melvin Laird had decided to make the ABM issue a vehicle to challenge Lyndon Johnson's strategic policies. Senator Thurmond spoke as a leading Republican expert on defense matters as well as a Senate leader in attacking the failure to deploy an ABM.[3]

There was no doubt that JCS demands for an immediate ABM deployment would be made known to leaders on the Hill, as would the growing evidence of a Soviet ABM deployment around Moscow. Congress had in the previous year included funds for ABM deployment even though the President had not requested any, and the stage was set for a

2. See, for example, *Baltimore Sun*, November 21, 1966, and December 3, 1966; *Washington Post*, November 24, 1966.
3. Jayne, "The ABM Debate," p. 346.

confrontation should Johnson again accept the advice of his Secretary of Defense and delay an ABM deployment.

The President's choices toward the end of 1966 seemed to be rather narrow. He could reject ballistic missile defense, embracing McNamara's arguments against deployment, and prepare to take his case to congressional leaders and the public. Alternatively, he could proceed with a ballistic missile defense deployment at the cost of overruling his Secretary of Defense. The odds were high that the President would proceed with the ballistic missile defense deployment being pressed on him by the Joint Chiefs and the Senate leaders. Only if he could find another option did McNamara stand any chance of again delaying a presidential commitment to ballistic missile defense.

It appears that McNamara first discussed the subject with the President at meetings held on his Texas ranch on November 3 and November 10. These discussions were reported to focus on two matters: ABM and the question of bombing additional targets in North Vietnam.[4]

Following the November 10 meeting, McNamara reported at a press conference that the Russians were now believed to be deploying an ABM system around Moscow. McNamara's initiative in releasing this information made it possible for him to pre-empt an inevitable news leak and, at the same time, to air his view that the Russian ABM deployment required improvements in U.S. offensive capability rather than a matching deployment. McNamara noted that the United States was moving ahead with Minuteman III and Poseidon and therefore was fully confident of its ability to offset the Russian ABM. He declared that it was too early to begin deployment of an anti-Chinese system and that no decision had been made on other possible reasons for a deployment.[5]

The decisive meeting with the President appears to have been held on December 6. At this meeting—attended by the President, Secretary McNamara, Deputy Secretary of Defense Cyrus Vance, the Joint Chiefs of Staff, and presidential assistant Walt Rostow—the Joint Chiefs were given the opportunity to put forward their argument for what was then called Posture A, a full coverage of the United States with a system designed for defense against more than a Chinese attack. The Joint Chiefs made it clear that they saw Posture A going into Posture B, a larger anti-Russian system designed to reduce casualties in the United States in the

4. This and the subsequent meetings are described in ibid.
5. *New York Times*, November 13, 1966.

event of a large attack, and that they would accept nothing less. Mc-Namara countered by presenting the arguments against an anti-Russian system, emphasizing that the Soviet Union could be expected to increase offensive capability to the extent necessary to fully offset the value of a U.S. ABM. At this point he appears to have suggested to the President two possible compromises. The first, which he was ultimately able to persuade the President to accept, called for (1) procurement orders for those ABM components which it would take a long time to produce, (2) postponement of a decision as to what system, if any, would be deployed, and (3) an effort to begin arms limitation talks with the Soviet Union. The second option was to begin deployment of a small anti-Chinese system. The meeting ended with Johnson agreeing that the State Department should begin to probe the Russians on the possibility of talks, but apparently withholding any decision on ABM deployment.

The State Department thus proceeded to explore the possibilities of arms limitation talks with the Soviet Union. Meanwhile McNamara wrote up and presented to the President a memorandum summarizing his arguments against an anti-Russian system but suggesting that an ABM defense against China might prove useful.

To demonstrate that he was not the only opponent of a large Soviet-oriented ABM system, McNamara arranged for the President and the Joint Chiefs of Staff to meet in early January 1967 with past and current Special Assistants to the President for Science and Technology and Directors of Defense Research and Engineering. None of the scientists present dissented from the view that an ABM to defend the American people against a Russian missile attack was not feasible and should not be built. There was some discussion of an anti-Chinese system and some divergence of views, but with a majority opposed to deployment.[6]

Following this meeting, McNamara was apparently able to persuade Johnson to delay any deployment, whether anti-Russian or anti-Chinese, and to pursue the option of initial procurement combined with a concentrated effort to open arms limitation talks with the Soviet Union.

The proposal for such talks seemed to be a vehicle for the pursuit of a number of presidential objectives. Johnson was haunted, as all of his post-

6. The scientists present were science advisers James R. Killian, Jr., George B. Kistiakowsky, Jerome B. Wiesner, and Donald F. Hornig and defense research directors Herbert York, Harold Brown, and John S. Foster, Jr. This meeting is described in York, *Race to Oblivion*, pp. 194–95; Jayne, "The ABM Debate," pp. 347–48; and Anne Hessing Cahn, "Eggheads and Warheads," pp. 37–38.

war predecessors had been, by the specter of nuclear war. He was anxious to try to do something to bring nuclear weapons under control. Moreover, it was an issue on which the President could appeal to the general public desire for peace and specifically to the left wing of the Democratic Party, which was becoming increasingly disaffected on Vietnam. It was also an issue that could make history for Johnson, as the man who had made the decisive move to end the nuclear arms race which threatened mankind's doom. Johnson was quick to sense these possibilities.

McNamara was able to argue that an American decision to proceed with ballistic missile defense would hamper arms limitation talks with the Russians, since one of the main purposes of such talks would be to seek an agreement by both sides to avoid ABM deployment. McNamara could also argue that a dramatic act of restraint by the United States would increase the probability that the Soviet Union would respond favorably and that the talks would begin. In any case a bold gesture by the President for peace would undercut much of the opposition to his decision not to proceed right away with a ballistic missile defense.

At the same time, by asking for funds for ABMs and implying that he would be prepared to spend them if talks did not get underway, the President was able to avoid making the argument that the United States should unilaterally forego deployment of a ballistic missile defense. Johnson would be able to tell the military commanders and the congressional leaders that he had certainly not ruled out a ballistic missile defense, in fact had taken a major step toward such a deployment, but that he was postponing the actual deployment pending an effort to get an arms control agreement with the Soviet Union. Although the military and congressional leaders might be somewhat uneasy about the further delay, they could not effectively mount a campaign against an effort to seek agreement with the Soviet Union, given the widespread popularity of such efforts.

Thus the proposal to link the two issues enabled McNamara to gain a further delay, hoping it might last indefinitely as the talks continued. The President could avoid paying any major price in his relations with McNamara, the Joint Chiefs, or Congress. He put off a hard choice and opened up the possibility of an arms control negotiation which would substantially enhance his domestic position and insure a favorable spot in the history books.[7]

7. On the tendency of chief executives to make the minimum commitment necessary, see Schilling, "The H-Bomb Decision," pp. 24–46.

Something for Everyone

We wish to ask further why the decision to deploy an ABM was announced at the tail end of a speech whose whole structure and purpose
was to explain that an ABM defense against the Soviet Union was impossible. Why did the Secretary of Defense describe the system as one
directed against China, while the Joint Chiefs of Staff and their allies in
Congress described it as a first step toward a full-scale defense against the
Soviet Union?

What has been said thus far should make it clear that the answers lie
in the bargaining between McNamara and Johnson as affected by the
positions of the Joint Chiefs and certain leaders in Congress.

The effort to get the Soviets to agree to set a date for arms limitation
talks was unsuccessful. When President Johnson met with Premier Kosygin at Glassboro, New Jersey, on June 23 and 25 at a hastily arranged
summit conference, there was still no Soviet agreement to talk. Johnson
brought McNamara along, and while the two leaders ate lunch the Secretary of Defense gave them a lecture on nuclear strategy, previewing his
San Francisco speech and emphasizing the value of an agreement to both
sides. The Russian leader was unyielding; he described ABMs as defensive
and unobjectionable and was not prepared to agree to talks.[8]

Following this conference at Glassboro in June of 1967, there could be
little doubt that talks would not be under way before the President's next
budget message in January 1968. Almost immediately Johnson informed
McNamara that some kind of ABM deployment would have to be announced by January at the latest. The President would then have to account for the disposition of ABM contingency funds he had requested
and state whether he was seeking additional sums for deployment of an
ABM system. Given his stakes and given the implicit commitment that
he had made in January of 1967 to go forward in the absence of arms
limitation talks, the President's decision was not difficult to predict. January 1968 would be Johnson's last chance to announce the deployment in a
budget message before the November presidential elections. To hedge
again, stating that he was still seeking talks, would have seemed uncon-
vincing. The intermediate options had run out. The President was determined to go ahead, even if it meant paying a price in his relations with the
Secretary of Defense. Apparently, Johnson also felt that by beginning to

8. Jayne, "The ABM Debate," pp. 366–69.

deploy an ABM he might convince the Russians to enter into arms limitation talks.[9]

Having decided to proceed with an ABM deployment, Johnson was obviously concerned about minimizing the cost in terms of his relations with McNamara. He was willing to let the Secretary announce the deployment in any way that he chose. For the sake of military and congressional acceptance, the President may have insisted that the deployment be such that others could describe it as the first step toward an anti-Russian system.[10]

From McNamara's point of view the primary goal remained that of preventing a large system directed at the Soviet Union. If the United States were to go forward with any ABM deployment, it was important to him to do what was possible to create in the public mind a clear difference between the system being deployed and a large system. Thus it was in McNamara's interest to be able to explain his view of the arms race, explain his opposition to a large anti-Russian system, and only then announce an ABM deployment. The apparent contradiction in the speech was deliberate. McNamara may have hoped that his speech would generate substantial public opposition to an ABM deployment.

McNamara had recognized several years before that he might lose the battle against deploying any kind of ABM system, and he had begun laying the groundwork for a fall-back position in the form of a small ABM system directed against China. In February 1965 McNamara publicly raised the possibility of ABM protection against a small nuclear attack from China but argued that even on those grounds the decision was not then needed because "the lead-time for additional nations to develop and deploy an effective ballistic missile system capable of reaching the United States is greater than we require to deploy the defense."[11]

Thus in September 1967 McNamara could announce that the lead time required for American deployment of ABM was now about the same as the lead time for a Chinese deployment of ICBMs in significant numbers. Therefore it was now prudent to proceed with the sort of ABM installation which he had been discussing for several years. And McNamara appears to have been convinced that in its own terms ABM defense against

9. Ibid., pp. 372–73.

10. Johnson had apparently been told explicitly by General Earle Wheeler that the Army would support a limited deployment only if it could describe it as the first step toward a large system. See Cahn, "Eggheads and Warheads," p. 37.

11. Jayne, "The ABM Debate," p. 273.

China was, as he described it in his speech, "marginal" but nevertheless "prudent." Thus in announcing the decision to deploy an ABM system against China McNamara could put forward arguments which he believed.

Even more important was McNamara's desire to prevent a large deployment directed at the Soviet Union. Such a system, he felt, would force the Russians to respond and thereby set off another round of the arms race. An anti-Chinese system could be more easily limited than a small system directed against the Soviet Union. One alternative was to describe the system as one designed to protect the U.S. Minuteman missiles, although it would be difficult to justify on cost-effectiveness grounds. Moreover, a system deployed only around missile sites would have been resisted by the Joint Chiefs and the Senate leaders, since it would not pave the way for a larger system against the Soviet Union and could not be described as the beginning of a larger system. Whether McNamara himself or the President ruled out this alternative is not clear.[12]

Pressures for Expansion

There is a final question we want to answer. Why was the system authorized for deployment designed as if its purpose was to protect American cities against a large Soviet attack?

Once a presidential decision is made on a policy issue, the details of implementation must be turned over to an individual or organization. In the case of ABM there was no choice but to assign responsibility to the Army. Although McNamara could and did attempt to monitor how the Army would deploy the system, he was unable or unwilling to direct that

12. In his San Francisco speech McNamara stated, with regard to Minuteman defense, that "the Chinese-oriented ABM deployment would enable us to add—as a concurrent benefit—a further defense of our Minuteman sites against Soviet attack, which means that at modest cost we would in fact be adding even greater effectiveness to our offensive missile force and avoiding a much more costly expansion of that force." A short time later, in an interview, "Defense Fantasy Now Come True," pp. 28A–28C, elaborating on the speech, he stated unequivocally that ABMs would be emplaced to defend Minuteman missiles. However, following a trip to Europe for a meeting of the NATO Nuclear Planning Group, McNamara stated that no decision had been made as to whether the option to defend Minuteman would be exercised.

the system be designed so as to minimize the possibility of growth. The Army's freedom may have been enhanced by the fact that McNamara's scientific and technical advisers themselves tended to favor keeping open the option for the system to grow into a large ABM system. Deputy Secretary of Defense Paul Nitze, to whom general responsibility for much of the day-to-day administration of the Pentagon fell as McNamara devoted more and more of his time to Vietnam, tended also to favor keeping open the option for a large system.

But there was a more fundamental problem. Once a decision was made to proceed with a ballistic missile defense directed against China, there was strong pressure to move forward quickly. The President could not then admit that the government had no hardware for such a system and that three or four years of research and development would be necessary before this deployment would begin. Thus deployment began with the components that were already developed, even though they were far from the optimal ones for a missile network that would serve against China but not grow into a large ABM system turned toward the Soviet Union.

Geography also worked against a limited system. Both Russian and Chinese ICBMs are set up to approach the United States through the same corridor over the pole. Radars for an anti-Chinese system would be the same as those for an anti-Russian system, and long-range missile launchers would be useful against both threats.

DDR&E, which favored a large Soviet-oriented system, had no motive to use its ingenuity to develop components that could be effective against China but with little potential for a large anti-Russian system. And in making precise decisions about where to locate radar and missile launching sites the Army in fact chose sites close to cities, to permit the deployment of a large anti-Russian system should the decision be made at a later date to do so.

McNamara's control over the implementation of this decision was simply not great enough to prevent these developments. He was increasingly immersed in Vietnam and clearly on his way out of office. He did not have the support of the President in seeking to limit the system. His principal assistant did not share his desire to reduce the possibility that the system could grow, and the Army, charged with deployment, favored a large anti-Russian system. Thus, despite McNamara's efforts in his statements to distinguish sharply between an anti-Chinese and an anti-Russian system, the Army was able to tell Congress that actual deployment was not different in any significant way from projected first stages of an anti-Russian system and that the system being deployed was expected to grow.

Decisions and Change

The Johnson administration's decision to deploy an ABM system, the way in which it was announced, and the deployment preparations which followed illustrate the policy process described in this book and demonstrate how awareness of politics inside government can help in analyzing a particular decision or action. As is typical, no single actor's views of what should be done dominated, although the President's views played a major role in shaping the general direction in which American actions moved.

Two independent decisions were involved, with different actors influencing the course of each. The first decision was simply whether or not to deploy defensive missiles at all. This was necessarily a presidential decision; there was no end-run around him. As the ABM decision illustrates, the President is qualitatively different—not simply a very powerful participant among less powerful participants.

The second decision related to the timing, substance, and shape of deployment, given the previous decision that there was to be an ABM system of some kind. In this latter decision the President played a much less central role, and other players were more influential. Johnson was both less interested and less in control.

The decision that some sort of deployment would be announced by January of 1968 can thus best be explained by exploring the multiple constituencies and interests that the President had to balance. The foreign policy interests of every postwar President have come to focus on relations with the Soviet Union as they affect the nuclear balance and the need to avoid nuclear war. Although from time to time stimulating interest in arms control, these concerns have mainly led to support for military efforts. At the same time, each President has thought about the image that might be painted of him in the history books and has developed a desire to go down as a man of peace. All of them felt, as Johnson did, the responsibility to avoid a nuclear holocaust that would destroy civilization.

On the other hand, no President can ignore the pressures on him from the bureaucracy, especially the senior military and departmental officers, or the pressures from congressional leaders and the public, when a presidential campaign is around the corner. All these pressures came to bear on Lyndon Johnson as he pondered the ABM question in 1967. Johnson appeared here in the characteristic presidential role of conciliator, a man who attempts to give as much as he can to each of a number of his principal subordinates and the permanent bureaucracies while seeking a position that avoids any conflict between his own various interests and constituencies beyond the government. The limited ABM system which Johnson ultimately directed be deployed could be described by Robert McNamara as anti-Chinese and hence not a danger to Soviet-American relations in general or future arms talks in particular. At the same time, the Joint Chiefs and Senate leaders had their own payoffs. Despite McNamara's statement, they still could describe deployment as a first step toward an anti-Russian system. Moreover, the "small" anti-Chinese system which Johnson approved was much larger than the system the Soviet Union was deploying around Moscow. Given these ambiguities and the simplified view the public takes on such questions, the Republican Party could be denied a missile gap issue. This was the President's payoff.

Johnson was also able to reconcile his own concern to seek an end to the nuclear arms race with the Soviet Union with the need to maintain American military strength. In early 1967, he was prepared to go along with McNamara's proposal that arms talks with the Soviet Union be sought before a firm final decision was made to proceed with an ABM deployment. After talking with Kosygin he concluded that the Soviet Union under the current circumstances would not enter talks. He believed that perhaps the pressure that would be put upon Russia's leaders by the beginnings of an American deployment would move the Russians to agree to talks. In ordering the deployment Johnson was not abandoning his efforts to get arms talks and an arms agreement with the Soviet Union. He thought of himself as structuring the situation to make an American ABM deployment a way to get the very talks that both he and McNamara desired.

If the decision to order a deployment can be most clearly understood in terms of the conflicting pressures on the President, the precise nature of the deployment can be understood largely in terms of pressures within the bureaucracy below the President, constrained by the operating procedures of the Army and of the Pentagon as a whole. Although McNamara himself wanted no deployment or a limited deployment, the staffs on which he had to depend to monitor and implement the President's decision were unanimous in their belief that an ABM system should be built that could grow into a large anti-Russian system. His science adviser John S. Foster, who would have the major role in monitoring both the research on the ABM system and its development and production, believed strongly that the option for a large system should be left open, as did Paul Nitze, McNamara's Deputy Secretary of Defense (following the departure of Cyrus Vance, who more closely shared McNamara's views). The Army itself favored a big system. No imaginative thought had gone into the design of components for a specifically anti-Chinese system. In fact, the implementers were straining as hard as they could to design and later deploy a system that could be expanded. McNamara was stymied. He lacked strong presidential directive to keep the system small; he lacked strong staff support in that direction. He was himself primarily preoccupied with Vietnam, and his days as Secretary of Defense were obviously numbered.

One of the truisms of bureaucracy is that it resists change. In this light, ABM appears to be an anomaly, but it is not. Although McNamara was in one sense a defender of the status quo, he had to take the initiative to try to prevent ABM deployment, since the system seemed to be grinding inevitably toward a deployment. The system was heavily biased toward the deployment of new weapons under certain conditions—ABM deployment was not seen as change. Rules of the game, shared images, and organizational procedures of the American government produced a situation from the time of the Korean War through the end of the 1960s in which the procurement of new weapons was part of the routine.

As noted earlier, the budgetary process itself creates a unique set of pressures. The fact that ABM decisions had to be recorded in the budget meant to proponents that the issue would reach the President without any effort on their part. This was particularly true because of the rule giving the JCS the right to appeal any decision of the Secretary of Defense or the Budget Director to the President. No other career service enjoys this right. Moreover, the President had to make a decision and announce it publicly according to a deadline brought about by the budget. To urge him to delay was to urge him to take a public stand against ABM deployment at that time.

The operating rules of the Joint Chiefs of Staff, as well as their access to powerful senators and congressmen, also biased the system toward deployment of any weapons system favored strongly by one of the services. Given strong Army support for an ABM system and given the judgment of Pentagon scientists that it was technically feasible, unanimous JCS support for the system was forthcoming under the logrolling rules which the Chiefs had begun to use in the McNamara period. The fact that they would report their views to the Congress when asked meant that the President could not keep differences hidden and would have to publicly challenge the JCS in order to prevent a deployment.

The timing of the private negotiations which the President and the Secretary of Defense carried on with the Joint Chiefs in itself biased decisions toward deployment. That is to say, the normal aversion of the Budget Bureau to expensive weapons, the skepticism of the men on the President's Science Advisory Committee, and the opposition of some parts of the State Department to a deployment could not be brought into play early enough in the process to affect the outcome.

Shared images which officials believed dominated American society further pushed the system toward an ABM deployment. There was a widely accepted view that the United States ought to maintain strategic superiority over the Soviet Union and therefore ought to more than match any system the Soviets deployed. The general view was that the United States should deploy any strategic system which worked well and which appeared to have the prospect of reducing damage should war occur. The existence of these shared views made it difficult to put forward arguments within the bureaucracy against an ABM deployment and even more difficult to shape arguments which the President would judge would be effective with Congress and with the public. Given this situation, the President had to be concerned with the domestic political effects, particularly on his re-election prospects in 1968. He did not want to be accused of opening an ABM gap, failing to match the Soviet system, and giving up American nuclear superiority.

The organizational procedures of the Pentagon likewise moved the government in the direction of deployment. Research, both in the Army and in ARPA, was dominated by scientists who believed that any feasible system should be deployed. Moreover, the focus tended to be on the greatest conceivable threat and hence on designing missiles to counter a large Russian attack. A desire to make an effective case for a deployment led to underestimates of cost and overestimates of feasibility.

McNamara seemed to recognize that, because of the constraints within the government, he probably could not stop ABM deployment. Thus his effort had to be directed as much to changing long-standing biases with respect to nuclear strategy as to devising delaying action against deployment. Although he lost the short-run battle to prevent deployment (or else confine deployment to a missile type that could not grow into a large anti-Russian system), his effort to change the terms of the debate as carried on within the bureaucracy, in Congress, and among the public were considerably more successful.

Thus by 1969 President Nixon accepted nuclear sufficiency rather than superiority as the American goal. He also embraced as his own McNamara's arguments against an anti-Russian system. He announced that the United States had no intention of deploying such a system, not only because it was technically infeasible but also because such a system would threaten the Soviet Union's deterrent. He proceeded with a system both against China and in defense of Minuteman, but he directed that the system be designed so that it could not be expanded, or appear to the Russians capable of being expanded, into a large system. In part as a result of the arguments McNamara had made, the attitude of the Senate changed dramatically on this range of issues.

Perhaps the most successful conversion came with the Russians. Kosygin was arguing at Glassboro that ABMs were purely defensive weapons and that the American effort to prevent their deployment was immoral. However, by 1971, at the strategic arms talks, the Russians were pressing for an agreement to limit ABMs. Even the fact that the talks were under way can be attributed to McNamara's efforts to prevent an ABM deployment. The treaty limiting ABMs to very low levels, negotiated in Moscow in May 1972, was a final vindication of McNamara's position.

CHAPTER SEVENTEEN

A Complicated Reality

This book has tried to do two things. At the most general level, it has presented a way of thinking about how governments function in the national security area. It has also provided a good deal of detail about the nature of the American bureaucratic system in the postwar period.

Having concentrated largely on the specifics of the American system in the current period, we wish to pull back briefly to the broader perspective and look at the implications of this approach for an understanding of international politics and of the impact of American actions on the behavior of other nations.

In general, when someone thinks in the conventional way about international politics, the analogy taken for granted is that of two individuals talking clearly and purposefully to each other and reacting in terms of carefully calculated interests. Thus the United States and the Soviet Union are believed each to possess unity of purpose and action in responding to the other's moves.[1]

If, as we believe, all governments are similar to the U.S. government as we have described it here, then the reality is quite different. Understanding of any international event and especially understanding of how American behavior influences the behavior of other countries would be greatly improved if in place of the usual model were substituted a different, more complicated image of what international politics is all about. That image, derived from the discussion of the American government presented here, would reveal the following features.

A government is not, in fact, a single individual with a single purpose and an ability to control completely his actions. Rather each government

1. Graham Allison has presented persuasive evidence of the extent to which this is the dominant way of thinking about international politics. He terms this approach "Model One: The Rational Actor." See Allison, *Essence of Decision*, pp. 10–38.

consists of numerous individuals, many of them working in large organizations. Constrained, to be sure, by the shared images of their society, these individuals nevertheless have very different interests, very different priorities, and are concerned with very different questions. Many of them are preoccupied by events at home and deal with events abroad only as those interact with and affect their ability to pursue their interests at home. Others are concerned directly with what happens abroad but do not agree on what should be done. At any one time a government is concerned with countless issues and problems at home and abroad.

An action by one government, which looks to an outside observer like a deliberate and calculated attempt to influence the behavior of another government, in fact is likely to have emerged from the process of pulling and hauling that we have described above for the American government. One participant's idea of what actions should be taken to influence another government has likely been compromised by other points of view of what will work to influence that government and by still other participants concerned with organizational and domestic interests. Any decision that was taken might well have been adventitious, and what was then done was no doubt influenced by those who had to implement the decision. The implementers are likely not to have fully understood what was decided, and they are constrained by the standard operating procedures of their organization. They also might have the desire and the ability to resist orders and to do something else. Thus actions which appear to be designed to influence another government actually have much more complicated origins.

On the other side, the government toward which the action seems to be directed will not respond according to the common image of two men communicating accurately with each other. For one thing, officials in the second government will not know whether the act that they observe in fact resulted from high-level decisions, more or less faithfully implemented, or resulted from other sources and purposes. In any case they will interpret the action according to the shared images of their own society. They will view the action in light of their own interests within their own bureaucracy and society. Thus the impact of an action by one government on another depends on the nature of the internal debate in that government, on which participants are strengthened or disheartened by the action, and on the common interpretation which comes to be given to it in the second government. How that government in turn responds will be influenced by all of the pulling and hauling discussed above.

Efforts to explain the behavior of two nations in relation to each other are likely to seem less puzzling if such a framework is adopted for purposes of analysis. We would then ask, for example, not why the United States took a certain action and what calculations could have been in "its" mind, but what were the motives, interests, and sources of power of the various participants in the American government which led to the decisions and then to the actions. In seeking to explain the response, we would apply the same analysis, taking account of the great difficulty in perceiving the sources of an action carried on by another government.

This approach also has important implications for policy advice to the American government.

Both inside the government and outside, proposals put forward for actions to influence the behavior of other governments usually are based on the simple model of two individuals communicating accurately with each other. If the approach presented here is applied, then proposals which otherwise would look sensible may appear unwise or even dangerous. What is decided ultimately after a proposal is put forward will almost certainly be a compromise drawn from suggestions by a number of individuals, and what is then done will be heavily influenced by the standard operating procedures and interests of the implementers. How the resulting action affects other governments will depend on their internal situations, their domestic conflicts, and their perceptions of U.S. interests and intentions. Only if one is able to make such an analysis of a policy proposal can we have reasonable confidence that what is being suggested is sensible.

Bibliography

Bibliography

The first section of our bibliography lists the memoirs of men who were involved in the making of U.S. national security policy at one time or another during the postwar period. An attempt has been made to identify and examine every one of these sources—defined as books and articles in which an author describes his involvement in the policy process. Thus Section A is a substantially complete listing of all such memoirs published through early 1973.

A number of interviews conducted and transcribed as part of its Oral History Program by the John F. Kennedy Library likewise contain reminiscences by participants in the policy process. Those Oral History Interviews from which we quote are listed in Section B.

Section C lists all other sources consulted by us. A high proportion are quoted or cited in the text. Some are of special conceptual relevance in the study of bureaucratic politics.

A. Memoirs

Acheson, Dean. *Present at the Creation: My Years in the State Department.* New York: W. W. Norton, 1969.

———. *Sketches from Life of Men I Have Known.* New York: Harper & Brothers, 1959.

Adams, Sherman. *Firsthand Report: The Story of the Eisenhower Administration.* New York: Harper & Brothers, 1961.

Anderson, Clinton P., with Milton Viorst. *Outsider in the Senate.* New York: World, 1970.

Attwood, William. *The Reds and the Blacks: A Personal Adventure.* New York: Harper & Row, 1967.

Ball, George W. *The Discipline of Power: Essentials of a Modern World Structure.* Boston: Little, Brown, 1968.

———. "Top Secret: The Prophecy the President Rejected," *Atlantic Monthly,* Vol. 230 (July 1972).

———. "Vietnam Hindsight." NBC News White Paper, December 1971; processed.

Bingham, Jonathan B. *Shirt-Sleeve Diplomacy*. New York: John Day, 1953.

Blachman, Morris J. "The Stupidity of Intelligence," in Charles Peder and Timothy J. Adams (eds.), *Inside the System: A Washington Monthly Reader*. New York: Praeger, 1970.

Bohlen, Charles E. *Witness to History, 1929–1969*. New York: W. W. Norton, 1973.

Bonal, Philip W. *Cuba, Castro, and the United States*. Pittsburgh: University of Pittsburgh Press, 1971.

Bowles, Chester. *Promises To Keep: My Years in Public Life, 1941–1969*. New York: Harper & Row, 1971.

Briggs, Ellis. *Farewell to Foggy Bottom: The Recollections of a Career Diplomat*. New York: McKay, 1964.

Bucher, Lloyd M., with Mark Rascovich. *Bucher: My Story*. New York: Doubleday, 1970.

Bush, Vannevar. *Pieces of the Action*. New York: Morrow, 1970.

Byrnes, James F. *All in One Lifetime*. New York: Harper & Brothers, 1958.

————. *Speaking Frankly*. New York: Harper & Brothers, 1947.

Christian, George. *The President Steps Down: A Personal Memoir of the Transfer of Power*. New York: Macmillan, 1970.

Clark, Mark W. *From the Danube to the Yalu*. New York: Harper & Brothers, 1954.

Clay, Lucius D. *Decision in Germany*. New York: Doubleday, 1950.

Cleveland, Harlan. *NATO: The Transatlantic Bargain*. New York: Harper & Row, 1970.

Collins, J. Lawton. *War in Peacetime*. Boston: Houghton Mifflin, 1969.

Conant, James B. *My Several Lives: Memoirs of a Social Inventor*. New York: Harper & Row, 1970.

Cooke, Charles. "Organizational Constraints in U.S. Performance in Vietnam." Paper presented at the 66th Annual Meeting of the American Political Science Association, 1970.

Corson, William R. *The Betrayal*. New York: W. W. Norton, 1968.

Cutler, Robert. *No Time for Rest*. Boston: Little, Brown, 1965.

Daniels, Jonathan. *Frontier on the Potomac*. New York: Macmillan, 1946.

Dobney, Frederick J. (ed.). *Selected Papers of Will Clayton*. Baltimore: Johns Hopkins Press, 1971.

Dulles, Allen. *The Craft of Intelligence*. New York: New American Library, 1963.

Dulles, Eleanor Lansing. *American Foreign Policy in the Making*. New York: Harper & Row, 1968.

Eccles, Marriner S. *Beckoning Frontiers*. New York: Knopf, 1951.

Eisenhower, Dwight D. *The White House Years*. Vol. I: *Mandate for Change, 1953–1956*. New York: Doubleday, 1963.

————. *The White House Years*. Vol. II: *Waging Peace, 1956–1961*. New York: Doubleday, 1965.

Eisenhower, Milton S. *The Wine Is Bitter: The United States and Latin America*. New York: Doubleday, 1963.

Enthoven, Alain C., and K. Wayne Smith. *How Much Is Enough? Shaping the Defense Program, 1961–1969*. New York: Harper & Row, 1971.

Fitzgerald, A. Ernest. *The High Priests of Waste*. New York: W. W. Norton, 1972.

Forrestal, James V. *See* Walter Millis.

Frankel, Charles. *High on Foggy Bottom: An Outsider's Inside View of the Government*. New York: Harper & Row, 1968.

Galbraith, John Kenneth. *Ambassador's Journal: A Personal Account of the Kennedy Years*. 3d printing. Boston: Houghton Mifflin, 1969.

Gavin, James M. *War and Peace in the Space Age*. New York: Harper & Brothers, 1958.

Goldman, Eric F. *The Tragedy of Lyndon Johnson*. New York: Knopf, 1969.

Goulding, Philip. *Confirm or Deny: Informing the People on National Security*. New York: Harper & Row, 1970.

Halle, Louis J. *The Society of Man*. New York: Dell, 1969.

Harriman, W. Averell. *America and Russia in a Changing World*. New York: Doubleday, 1971.

Hilsman, Roger. *The Politics of Policy-Making in Defense and Foreign Affairs*. New York: Harper & Row, 1971.

———. *To Move a Nation: The Politics of Foreign Policy in the Administration of John F. Kennedy*. New York: Doubleday, 1967.

Hoopes, Townsend. *The Limits of Intervention: An Inside Account of How the Johnson Policy of Escalation in Vietnam Was Reversed*. New York: McKay, 1969.

Hughes, Emmet John. *The Ordeal of Power: A Political Memoir of the Eisenhower Years*. New York: Atheneum, 1963.

Johnson, Lyndon Baines. *The Vantage Point: Perspectives of the Presidency, 1963–1969*. New York: Holt, Rinehart & Winston, 1971.

Jones, Joseph M. *The Fifteen Weeks: February 21–June 5, 1947*. New York: Viking, 1955.

Kennan, George F. *Memoirs, 1925–1950*. Boston: Little, Brown, 1967.

———. *Memoirs, 1950–1963*. Boston: Little, Brown, 1972.

Kennedy, Robert F. *Thirteen Days: A Memoir of the Cuban Missile Crisis*. New York: W. W. Norton, 1969.

Khrushchev, Nikita. *Khrushchev Remembers*. Boston: Little, Brown, 1970.

Kirkpatrick, Lyman B., Jr. *The Real CIA*. New York: Macmillan, 1968.

Krock, Arthur. *Memoirs: Sixty Years on the Firing Line*. New York: Funk & Wagnalls, 1968.

Lansdale, Edward Geary. *In the Midst of Wars*. New York: Harper & Row, 1972.

Larson, Arthur. *Eisenhower: The President Nobody Knew*. New York: Scribner's, 1968.

LeMay, Curtis E., with MacKinlay Kantor. *Mission with LeMay: My Story*. New York: Doubleday, 1965.

Lilienthal, David E. *The Journals of David E. Lilienthal*. Vol. II: *The Atomic Energy Years, 1945–1950*. New York: Harper & Row, 1964.

Lodge, Henry Cabot. *The Storm Has Many Eyes: A Personal Narrative.* New York: W. W. Norton, 1973.

MacArthur, Douglas. *Reminiscences.* New York: Fawcett, 1964.

McGarvey, Patrick J. *CIA: The Myth and the Madness.* New York: Saturday Review Press, 1972.

McNamara, Robert S. *The Essence of Security: Reflections in Office.* London: Hodder & Stoughton, 1968.

McPherson, Harry. *A Political Education.* Boston: Little, Brown, 1972.

Martin, John Bartlow. *Overtaken By Events: The Dominican Crisis from the Fall of Trujillo to the Civil War.* New York: Doubleday, 1966.

Mecklin, John. *Mission in Torment: An Intimate Account of the U.S. Role in Vietnam.* New York: Doubleday, 1965.

Medaris, John B. *Countdown for Decision.* New York: Putnam's, 1960.

Melby, John. *The Mandate of Heaven: Record of a Civil War, China 1945–49.* New York: Doubleday Anchor, 1972.

Merson, Martin. *The Private Diary of a Public Servant.* New York: Macmillan, 1955.

Millis, Walter (ed.), with E. S. Duffield. *The Forrestal Diaries.* New York: Viking, 1951.

Moyers, Bill. "Bill Moyers Talks about the War and LBJ: An Interview," in Robert Manning and Michael Janeway (eds.), *Who We Are.* Boston: Little, Brown, 1969.

Murphy, Robert. *Diplomat among Warriors.* New York: Doubleday, 1964.

Nixon, Richard M. *Six Crises.* New York: Doubleday, 1962.

O'Donnell, Kenneth. "LBJ and the Kennedys," *Life,* Vol. 69 (August 7, 1970).

Powers, Francis Gary, with Curt Gentry. *Operation Overflight.* New York: Holt, Rinehart & Winston, 1970.

Rankin, Karl Lott. *China Assignment.* Seattle: University of Washington Press, 1964.

Reedy, George E., *The Twilight of the Presidency.* New York: World, 1970.

Ridgway, Matthew B. *The Korean War.* New York: Popular Library, 1967.

———. *Soldier: The Memoirs of Matthew B. Ridgway.* New York: Harper & Brothers, 1956.

Roberts, Chalmers M. *First Rough Draft.* New York: Praeger, 1973.

Rostow, W. W. *The Diffusion of Power, 1957–1972.* New York: Macmillan, 1972.

Rusk, Dean. "Mr. Secretary on the Eve of Emeritus," *Life,* Vol. 66 (January 17, 1969).

Salinger, Pierre. *With Kennedy.* New York: Doubleday, 1966.

Schlesinger, Arthur M., Jr. *A Thousand Days: John F. Kennedy in the White House.* Boston: Houghton Mifflin, 1965.

Sebald, William J., with Russell Brines. *With MacArthur in Japan.* New York: W. W. Norton, 1965.

Smith, Earl E. T. *The Fourth Floor: An Account of the Castro Communist Revolution.* New York. Random House, 1962.

Smith, Walter Bedell. *My Three Years in Moscow*. Philadelphia: Lippincott, 1949.

Sorensen, Theodore C. *Decision-Making in the White House: The Olive Branch or the Arrows*. New York: Columbia University Press, 1963.

———. *Kennedy*. New York: Harper & Row, 1965.

Sorensen, Thomas C. *The Word War: The Story of American Propaganda*. New York: Harper & Row, 1968.

Sparks, Will. *Who Talked to the President Last?* New York: W. W. Norton, 1971.

Strauss, Lewis L. *Men and Decisions*. New York: Doubleday, 1962.

Sulzberger, C. L. *A Long Row of Candles: Memoirs and Diaries, 1934–1954*. New York: Macmillan, 1969.

Taylor, Maxwell D. *Swords and Plowshares*. New York: W. W. Norton, 1972.

———. *The Uncertain Trumpet*. New York: Harper & Brothers, 1959.

Thayer, Charles W. *Diplomat*. New York: Harper & Brothers, 1959.

Trivers, Howard. *Three Crises in American Foreign Affairs and a Continuing Revolution*. Carbondale, Ill.: Southern Illinois University Press, 1972.

Truman, Harry S. *Memoirs*. Vol. I: *Year of Decisions*. New York: Doubleday, 1955.

———. *Memoirs*. Vol. II: *Years of Trial and Hope*. New York: Doubleday, 1956.

Twining, Nathan. *Neither Liberty nor Safety*. New York: Holt, Rinehart & Winston, 1966.

Walt, Lewis W. *Strange War, Strange Strategy: A General's Report on Vietnam*. New York: Funk & Wagnalls, 1970.

Wedemeyer, Albert C. *Wedemeyer Reports!* New York: Holt, 1958.

York, Herbert F. *Race to Oblivion: A Participant's View of the Arms Race*. New York: Simon & Schuster, 1970.

B. Interviews

The following Oral History Interviews, as they are called, conducted, transcribed, and preserved by the John F. Kennedy Library, Cambridge, Massachusetts, have been consulted for the light they throw on the policy process.

Acheson, Dean (interviewed by Lucius Battle), April 27, 1964.

Clay, Lucius (by Richard Scammon), July 1, 1964.

Douglas-Hume, Alex (statement by himself), March 17, 1965.

Farley, Phillip (by Joseph O'Connor), November 1, 1966.

Fisher, Adrian (by Frank Sieberts), May 13, 1964.

Horowitz, Solis (by Joseph O'Connor), March 18, 1966.

Hurwitch, Robert (by John Plank), April 24, 1964.

Johnson, U. Alexis (by William Brubeck), September 13, 1965.

Kennan, George (by Louis Fisher), March 23, 1966.

Reinhardt, Frederick G. (by Joseph O'Connor), October 1, 1966.

Wilson, Donald (by James Greenfield), September 2, 1964.
York, Herbert (by Steven Rivkin), June 16, 1964.

C. Other Sources

Abel, Elie. *The Missile Crisis*. Philadelphia: Lippincott, 1966.
Acheson, Dean. "The President and the Secretary of State," in Price (ed.), *The Secretary of State*, q.v.
Allison, Graham T. "Cool It: The Foreign Policy of Young America," *Foreign Policy*, No. 1 (Winter 1970–71).
———. *Essence of Decision: Explaining the Cuban Missile Crisis*. Boston: Little, Brown, 1971.
Alperovitz, Gar. *Atomic Diplomacy*. New York: Vintage Books, 1965.
Alsop, Stewart. *The Center: People and Power in Political Washington*. New York: Harper & Row, 1968.
Anderson, Patrick. *The Presidents' Men*. New York: Doubleday, 1968.
Argyris, Chris. *Some Causes of Organizational Ineffectiveness within the Department of State*. Occasional Papers, No. 2, Center for International Systems Research, Department of State. Washington: Government Printing Office, 1967.
Armacost, Michael H. *The Politics of Weapons Innovation: The Thor-Jupiter Controversy*. New York: Columbia University Press, 1969.
Aronson, James. "Views of the Press: The Sell-Out of the Pulitzer Prize," *Washington Monthly*, Vol. 2 (October 1970).
Art, Robert J. *The TFX Decision: McNamara and the Military*. Boston: Little, Brown, 1968.
Baar, James, and William E. Howard. *Polaris*. New York: Harcourt, Brace, 1960.
Beal, John Robinson. *Marshall in China*. New York: Doubleday, 1970.
Beichman, Arnold. *The "Other" State Department*. New York: Basic Books, 1967.
Bernstein, Marver H. *The Job of the Federal Executive*. Washington: Brookings Institution, 1958.
Blue Ribbon Defense Panel. *Report to the President and the Secretary of Defense on the Department of Defense by the Blue Ribbon Defense Panel*. Washington: Government Printing Office, 1970.
Bottome, Edgar M. *The Missile Gap: A Study of the Formulation of Military and Political Policy*. Cranbury, N.J.: Fairleigh Dickinson University Press, 1971.
Bowie, Robert R. "The Secretary and the Development and Coordination of Policy," in Price (ed.), *The Secretary of State*, q.v.
Brandon, Henry. *Anatomy of Error*. Boston: Gambit, 1969.
———. "Schlesinger at the White House: An Historian's Inside View of Kennedy at Work," *Harper's*, Vol. 229 (July 1964).
Bundy, McGeorge. "Statement before the Senate Foreign Relations Com-

mittee (March 19, 1971)," in *The Geneva Protocol of 1925.* Hearing. 91 Cong. 2 sess. Washington: Government Printing Office, 1972.

Cahn, Anne Hessing. "Eggheads and Warheads: Scientists and the ABM." Processed. Cambridge, Mass.: M.I.T. Center for International Studies, 1971.

Campbell, Angus, Gerald Gurin, and Warren Miller. *The Voter Decides.* Evanston, Ill.: Row, Peterson, 1954.

Campbell, John Franklin. *The Foreign Affairs Fudge Factory.* New York: Basic Books, 1971.

Caraley, Demetrios. *The Politics of Military Unification: A Study of Conflict and the Policy Process.* New York: Columbia University Press, 1966.

Caridi, Ronald J. *The Korean War and American Politics: The Republican Party as a Case Study.* Philadelphia: University of Pennsylvania Press, 1968.

Cater, Douglass. *The Fourth Branch of Government.* Boston: Houghton Mifflin, 1959.

———. *Power In Washington.* New York: Vintage Books, 1964.

Chester, Lewis, Godfrey Hodgson, and Bruce Page. *An American Melodrama: The Presidential Campaign of 1968.* New York: Viking, 1969.

Clark, Blair. "Westmoreland Appraised: Questions and Answers," *Harper's,* Vol. 241 (November 1970).

Clark, Keith C., and Laurence J. Legere (eds.). *The President and the Management of National Security: A Report by the Institute for Defense Analyses.* New York: Praeger, 1969.

Cohen, Bernard C. *The Political Process and Foreign Policy: The Making of the Japanese Peace Settlement.* Princeton: Princeton University Press, 1957.

———. *The Press and Foreign Policy.* Princeton: Princeton University Press, 1963.

Cornford, F. M. *Microcosmographia Academica, Being a Guide for the Young Academic Politician.* 2d ed. Cambridge: Bowes & Bowes, 1922.

Crozier, Michel. *The Bureaucratic Phenomenon.* Chicago: Phoenix Books, 1964.

Cutler, Robert. "The National Security Council under President Eisenhower," in Jackson (ed.), *The National Security Council,* q.v.

Cyert, Richard, and James March, with contributions by G. P. E. Clarkson and others. *A Behavioral Theory of the Firm.* Englewood Cliffs, N.J.: Prentice-Hall, 1963.

Davis, Arthur K. "Bureaucratic Patterns in the Navy Officer Corps," in Robert K. Merton and others (eds.), *Reader in Bureaucracy.* Glencoe, Ill.: Free Press, 1952.

Davis, Nuel Pharr. *Lawrence & Oppenheimer.* New York: Simon & Schuster, 1968.

Deagle, Edwin Augustus, Jr. "The Agony of Restraint—Korea 1951–1953: A Study of Limited War and Civil-Military Policy Processes." Draft manuscript, 1969. Office of the Chief of Military History, Department of the Army.

deRivera, Joseph. *The Psychological Dimension of Foreign Policy*. Columbus, Ohio: Merrill Publishing Co., 1968.

Destler, I. M. *Presidents, Bureaucrats, and Foreign Policy*. Princeton: Princeton University Press, 1972.

Dommen, Arthur J. *Conflict in Laos: The Politics of Neutralization*. New York: Praeger, 1964.

Donovan, Robert J. *Eisenhower: The Inside Story*. New York: Harper & Brothers, 1956.

Downs, Anthony. *Inside Bureaucracy*. Boston: Little, Brown, 1967.

Draper, Theodore. "The Dominican Crisis: A Case Study in American Policy," *Commentary*, Vol. 41 (April–May 1966).

Drew, Elizabeth B. "Washington," *Atlantic Monthly*, Vol. 225 (June 1970).

Dunn, Frederick S. *Peace-Making and the Settlement with Japan*. Princeton: Princeton University Press, 1963.

Edgerton, Russell. *Sub-Cabinet Politics and Policy Commitment: The Birth of the Development Loan Fund*. Syracuse, N.Y.: The Interuniversity Case Program, Inc., 1970.

Evans, Rowland, and Robert Novak. *Lyndon B. Johnson: The Exercise of Power*. New York: New American Library, 1966.

Flash, Edward S., Jr. *Economic Advice and Presidential Leadership*. New York: Columbia University Press, 1965.

Frankel, Max. Letter to Daniel Patrick Moynihan, March 5, 1971. Privately circulated.

Galbraith, John Kenneth. "Plain Lessons of a Bad Decade," *Foreign Policy*, No. 1 (Winter 1970–71).

Gates, Thomas S., Jr. "The Secretary of Defense," in Jackson (ed.), *The National Security Council*, q.v.

Gawthrop, Louis C. *Bureaucratic Behavior in the Executive Branch*. New York: Free Press, 1969.

Gelb, Leslie H. "Vietnam: The System Worked," *Foreign Policy*, No. 3 (Summer 1971).

George, Alexander L. "American Policy-Making and the North Korean Aggression," *World Politics*, Vol. 7 (January 1955).

———. "The Case for Multiple Advocacy in Making Foreign Policy," *The American Political Science Review*, Vol. 66 (September 1972).

Geyelin, Philip L. *Lyndon B. Johnson and the World*. New York: Praeger, 1966.

Gilpin, Robert, and Christopher Wright (eds.). *Scientists and National Policy Making*. New York: Columbia University Press, 1964.

Graff, Henry F. *The Tuesday Cabinet*. Englewood Cliffs, N.J.: Prentice-Hall, 1970.

Halberstam, David. *The Best and the Brightest*. New York: Random House, 1972.

———. "The Very Expensive Education of McGeorge Bundy," *Harper's*, Vol. 239 (July 1969).

Halperin, Morton H. "The Gaither Committee and the Policy Process," *World Politics*, Vol. 13 (April 1961).

Halperin, Morton H. "The President and the Military," *Foreign Affairs*, Vol. 50 (January 1972).

————, and Arnold Kanter (eds.), *Readings in American Foreign Policy: A Bureaucratic Perspective*. Boston: Little, Brown, 1973.

Hammond, Paul Y. "NSC-68: Prologue to Rearmament," in Schilling, Hammond, and Snyder, *Strategy, Politics, and Defense Budgets*, q.v.

————. *Organizing for Defense*. Princeton: Princeton University Press, 1961.

————. "Super Carriers and B-36 Bombers: Appropriations, Strategy, and Politics," in Stein (ed.), *American Civil-Military Decisions*, q.v.

Harr, John Ensor. *The Professional Diplomat*. Princeton: Princeton University Press, 1969.

Henry, John B., II. "February 1968," *Foreign Policy*, No. 4 (Fall 1971).

Herr, Michael. "Khesanh," *Esquire*, Vol. 72 (September 1969).

Hersh, Seymour M. *My Lai 4: A Report on the Massacre and Its Aftermath*. New York: Random House, 1970.

Hilsman, Roger. *To Move a Nation: The Politics of Foreign Policy in the Administration of John F. Kennedy*. New York: Doubleday, 1967.

Holbrooke, Richard. "The Machine That Fails," *Foreign Policy*, No. 1 (Winter 1970–71).

Howley, Frank L. *Berlin Command*. New York: Putnam's, 1950.

Hoxie, R. Gordon (ed.). *The White House: Organization and Operations*. New York: Center for the Study of the Presidency, 1971.

Huntington, Samuel P. *The Common Defense: Strategic Programs in National Defense*. New York: Columbia University Press, 1961.

Iklé, Fred Charles. *Every War Must End*. New York: Columbia University Press, 1971.

Jackson, Henry M. (ed). *The National Security Council: Jackson Subcommittee Papers on Policy-Making at the Presidential Level*. New York: Praeger, 1965.

(Jackson) Subcommittee on National Security Staffing and Operations of the Senate Committee on Government Operations, *Administration of National Security: Selected Papers*. Hearing. 87 Cong. 2 sess. Washington: Government Printing Office, 1962.

Jayne, Edward Randolph, II. "The ABM Debate. Strategic Defense and National Security." Ph.D. thesis, Massachusetts Institute of Technology, 1969.

Jervis, Robert. "Hypotheses on Misperception," *World Politics*, Vol. 20 (April 1968).

Johnson, Haynes, with Manual Artime and others. *The Bay of Pigs: The Leaders' Story of Brigade 2506*. New York: W. W. Norton, 1964.

Johnson, Lyndon B. "Annual Budget Message to the Congress, Fiscal Year 1968," *Public Papers of the Presidents of the United States 1967*. Washington: Government Printing Office, 1968.

————. "LBJ: The Decision to Halt the Bombing." CBS News Special, February 6, 1970; processed.

Johnson, Richard A. *The Administration of United States Foreign Policy*. Austin: University of Texas Press, 1971.

Johnson, Robert H. "The National Security Council: The Relevance of Its Past to Its Future," *Orbis*, Vol. 13 (Fall 1969).

Kalb, Marvin, and Elie Abel. *Roots of Involvement: The U.S. in Asia, 1784–1971*. New York: W. W. Norton, 1971.

Kennan, George F. "America's Administrative Response to Its World Problems," *Daedalus*, Vol. 87 (Spring 1958).

Khanasch, Robert N. *The Institutional Imperative*. New York: Charterhouse Books, 1973.

Kiker, Douglas. "Washington," in Manning and Janeway (eds.), *Who We Are*, q.v.

King, Edward L. *The Death of the Army: A Pre-Mortem*. New York: Saturday Review Press, 1972.

Kissinger, Henry A. *American Foreign Policy: Three Essays*. New York: W. W. Norton, 1969.

————. Background briefing in *Congressional Record*, Vol. 117, 92 Cong. 1 sess. (1971).

————. "Bureaucracy and Policy Making," in Halperin and Kanter (eds.), *Readings in American Foreign Policy*, q.v.

————. *Nuclear Weapons and Foreign Policy*. New York: Harper & Brothers, 1957.

Korb, Lawrence J. "Budget Strategies of the Joint Chiefs of Staff (Fiscal) 1965–1968: An Examination." Paper presented at the 66th Annual Meeting of the American Political Science Association, 1970.

————. "The Role of the Joint Chiefs of Staff in the Defense Budget Process from 1947 to 1967." Ph.D. thesis. State University of New York at Albany, 1969.

Kraft, Joseph. "After McNamara," in Manning and Janeway (eds.), *Who We Are*, q.v.

————. *Profiles in Power: A Washington Insight*. New York: New American Library, 1966.

————. "Undermining Kissinger," *Washington Post*, January 11, 1972.

Kurzman, Dan. *Genesis 1948: The First Arab-Israeli War*. New York: World, 1970.

Lambright, W. Henry. *Shooting Down the Nuclear Plane*. Indianapolis: Bobbs-Merrill, 1967.

Leacacos, John P. *Fires in the In-Basket: The ABC's of the State Department*. New York: World, 1968.

Lichterman, Martin. "To the Yalu and Back," in Stein (ed.), *American Civil-Military Decisions*, q.v.

Lindblom, Charles. *The Intelligence of Democracy*. New York: Free Press, 1965.

Lovett, Robert A. "Perspective on the Policy Process," in Jackson (ed.), *The National Security Council*, q.v.

Lowenthal, Abraham F. *The Dominican Intervention*. Cambridge, Mass.: Harvard University Press, 1972.

Lowi, Theodore J. "Bases in Spain," in Stein (ed.), *American Civil-Military Decisions*, q.v.

McGarvey, Patrick J. "Army Aviation: After Vietnam, What?" *Government Executive,* Vol. 2 (March 1970).

―――. "The Culture of Bureaucracy: DIA Intelligence To Please," *Washington Monthly,* Vol. 2 (July 1970).

McNamara, Robert S. "The Dynamics of Nuclear Strategy," *Department of State Bulletin* (October 9, 1967).

―――. "Defense Fantasy Now Come True," *Life,* Vol. 63 (September 29, 1967).

―――. "The Secretary of Defense," in Jackson (ed.), *The National Security Council,* q.v.

Macomber, William B., Jr. *Diplomacy for the 70's: A Program of Management Reform for the Department of State.* Washington: Government Printing Office, 1970.

Manning, Robert, and Michael Janeway (eds.). *Who We Are: Chronicle of the United States and Vietnam.* Boston: Little, Brown, 1965.

March, James G., and Herbert A. Simon. *Organizations.* New York: Wiley, 1958.

Martin, Laurence W. "The American Decision To Rearm Germany," in Stein (ed.), *American Civil-Military Decisions,* q.v.

May, Ernest R. "The Nature of Foreign Policy: The Calculated versus the Axiomatic," *Daedalus,* Vol. 91 (Fall 1962).

Merton, Robert K., and others (eds.), *Reader in Bureaucracy.* Glencoe, Ill.: Free Press, 1952.

Millis, Walter, Harvey C. Mansfield, and Harold Stein. *Arms and the State.* New York: Twentieth Century Fund, 1958.

Mosher, Frederick C., and John E. Harr. *Programming Systems and Foreign Affairs Leadership.* New York: Oxford University Press, 1970.

Neustadt, Richard E. *Alliance Politics.* New York: Columbia University Press, 1970.

―――. "Politics and Bureaucrats," in David B. Truman (ed.), *The Congress and America's Future.* Englewood Cliffs, N.J.: Prentice-Hall, 1965.

―――. *Presidential Power: The Politics of Leadership.* New York: Wiley, 1960.

Newhouse, John. *Cold Dawn: The Story of SALT.* New York: Holt, Rinehart & Winston, 1973.

Nixon, Richard M. *U.S. Foreign Policy for the 1970s: Building for Peace.* Washington: Government Printing Office, 1971.

Oberdorfer, Don. *Tet!* New York: Doubleday, 1971.

Paige, Glenn D. *The Korean Decision: June 24–30, 1950.* New York: Free Press, 1968.

Parkinson, C. Northcote. *Parkinson's Law.* Boston: Houghton Mifflin, 1957.

Percy, Charles H. "Paying for NATO," *Washington Monthly,* Vol. 2 (July 1970).

Pett, Saul. "Henry A. Kissinger: Loyal Retainer or Nixon's Svengali?" *Washington Post,* August 23, 1970.

Phillips, Cabell. *The Truman Presidency.* Baltimore: Penguin Books, 1966.

Price, Don K. "The Secretary and Our Unwritten Constitution," in Don K.

Price (ed.), *The Secretary of State*. Englewood Cliffs, N.J.: Prentice-Hall, 1960.

Pyle, Christopher H. "Conus Revisited: The Army Covers Up," *Washington Monthly* (July 1970).

Ransom, Harry Howe. *The Intelligence Establishment*. Cambridge, Mass.: Harvard University Press, 1970.

Reston, James. *The Artillery of the Press: Its Influence on American Foreign Policy*. New York: Harper & Row, 1966.

Roberts, Charles. *LBJ's Inner Circle*. New York: Delacorte, 1965.

Robinson, James A. *The Monroney Resolution: Congressional Initiative in Foreign Policy Making*. New York: Holt, 1959.

Rockefeller, Nelson A. "The Executive Office of the President," in Jackson (ed.), *The National Security Council*, q.v.

Rostow, W. W. "The American Agenda," in Halperin and Kanter (eds.), *Readings in American Foreign Policy*, q.v.

Rourke, Francis E. *Bureaucracy and Foreign Policy*. Baltimore: Johns Hopkins Press, 1972.

————. *Bureaucracy, Politics, and Public Policy*. Boston: Little, Brown, 1969.

Rusk, Dean. "The Secretary of State," in Jackson (ed.), *The National Security Council*, q.v.

Sapin, Burton M. *The Making of United States Foreign Policy*. Washington, D.C.: The Brookings Institution, 1966.

Schilling, Warner R. "The H-Bomb Decision: How To Decide without Actually Choosing," *Political Science Quarterly*, Vol. 76 (March 1961).

————. "The Politics of National Defense: Fiscal 1950," in Schilling, Hammond, and Snyder (eds.), *Strategy, Politics, and Defense Budgets*, q.v.

————. "Scientists, Foreign Policy, and Politics," in Gilpin and Wright (eds.), *Scientists and National Policy Making*, q.v.

————, Paul Y. Hammond, and Glenn H. Snyder (eds.). *Strategy, Politics, and Defense Budgets*. New York: Columbia University Press, 1962.

Schlesinger, Arthur M., Jr. *The Bitter Heritage: Vietnam and American Democracy, 1941–1966*. Boston: Houghton Mifflin, 1967.

Scott, Andrew M. "The Department of State: Formal Organization and Informal Culture," *International Studies Quarterly*, Vol. 13 (March 1969).

————. "Environmental Change and Organizational Adaptation: The Problem of the State Department," *International Studies Quarterly*, Vol. 14 (March 1970).

Scott, Andrew M., and Raymond H. Dawson (eds.). *Readings in the Making of American Foreign Policy*. New York: Macmillan, 1965.

Seidman, Harold. *Politics, Position, and Power: The Dynamics of Federal Organization*. New York: Oxford University Press, 1970.

Sidey, Hugh. "Nixon in a Crisis of Leadership," *Life*, Vol. 68 (May 15, 1970).

————. *A Very Personal Presidency: Lyndon Johnson in the White House*. New York: Atheneum, 1968.

Sigal, Leon V. "Bureaucratic Objectives and Tactical Use of the Press: Why Bureaucrats Leak." Paper presented at the 67th Annual Meeting of the American Political Science Association, 1971.

Sigal, Leon V. *Reporters and Officials: The Organization and Politics of News-making.* Lexington, Mass.: D. C. Heath, 1973.

Simpson, Smith. *Anatomy of the State Department.* Boston: Beacon Press, 1967.

Slater, Jerome. *Negotiation and Intervention: The United States and the Dominican Revolution.* New York: Harper & Row, 1970.

Smith, Beverly. "The White House Story: Why We Went to War in Korea," *Saturday Evening Post,* Vol. 224 (Nov. 10, 1951).

Smith, Bruce L. R. *The Rand Corporation.* Cambridge, Mass.: Harvard University Press, 1966.

Smith, Perry McCoy. *The Air Force Plans for Peace, 1943–1945.* Baltimore: Johns Hopkins Press, 1970.

Snyder, Glenn H. "The 'New Look' of 1953," in Schilling, Hammond, and Snyder (eds.), *Strategy, Politics, and Defense Budgets,* q.v.

————. *Stockpiling Strategic Materials: Politics and National Defense.* San Francisco: Chandler, 1966.

Souers, Sidney W. "The National Security Council under President Truman," in Jackson (ed.), *The National Security Council,* q.v.

Spanier, John W. *The Truman-MacArthur Controversy and the Korean War.* New York: W. W. Norton, 1965.

Stein, Harold (ed.). *American Civil-Military Decisions.* Birmingham, Ala.: University of Alabama Press, 1963.

Steinberg, Alfred. *The Man From Missouri: The Life and Times of Harry S Truman.* New York: Putnam's, 1962.

Steinbruner, John. *Decisions under Complexity* (forthcoming from Princeton University Press).

Stevenson, Chanks. *The End of Nowhere: American Policy toward Laos since 1954.* Boston: Beacon Press, 1972.

Stone, Jeremy J. *Strategic Persuasion.* New York: Columbia University Press, 1967.

Stupak, Ronald J. *The Shaping of Foreign Policy: The Role of the Secretary of State as Seen by Dean Acheson.* New York: Odyssey Press, 1969.

Szilard, Leo. "Reminiscences," in *Perspectives in American History,* Vol. 2 (1968).

Tai-hsun, Tsuan. "An Explanation of the Change in U.S. Policy toward China in 1950." Ph. D. thesis, University of Pennsylvania, 1969.

Thomas, Hugh. *Suez.* New York: Harper & Row, 1966.

Thomson, James C., Jr. "How Could Vietnam Happen?" in Manning and Janeway (eds.), *Who We Are,* q.v.

Tullock, Gordon. *The Politics of Bureaucracy.* Washington: Public Affairs Press, 1965.

United States Congress. Senate. Committee on Foreign Relations. *The Geneva Protocol of 1925.* Hearing. 92 Cong. 1 sess. Washington: Government Printing Office, 1972.

U.S. Congress. Senate. Subcommittee on National Security and International Operations of the Committee on Government Operations. *Conduct of*

National Security Policy. Hearing. 89 Cong. 1 sess., Pt. 3 (June 29 and July 27, 1965). Washington: Government Printing Office, 1965.

U.S. Congress. Senate. Subcommittee on United States Security Agreements and Commitments Abroad of the Committee on Foreign Relations. *United States Security Agreements and Commitments Abroad: Japan and Okinawa.* Hearing. 91 Cong. 2 sess., Pt. 5 (January 26–29, 1970). Washington: Government Printing Office, 1970.

Villard, Henry S. *Affairs of State.* New York: Thomas Y. Crowell, 1965.

———. "How to Save Money: An Open Letter to Congressman John J. Rooney," *Harper's*, Vol. 228 (January 1964).

Waltz, Kenneth N. *Foreign Policy and Democratic Politics: The American and British Experience.* Boston: Little, Brown, 1967.

Weintal, Edward, and Charles Bartlett. *Facing the Brink: An Intimate Study in Crisis Diplomacy.* New York: Scribner's, 1967.

Wicker, Tom. *JFK and LBJ: The Influence of Personality upon Politics.* New York: Morrow, 1968.

Wilensky, Harold L. *Organizational Intelligence.* New York: Basic Books, 1967.

Wills, Garry. *Nixon Agonistes: The Crisis of the Self-Made Man.* Boston: Houghton Mifflin, 1970.

Wise, David, and Thomas B. Ross. *The U-2 Affair.* New York: Random House, 1962.

Wishnatsky, Martin. "Symbolic Politics and the Origins of the Cold War." Paper prepared for the 67th Annual Meeting of the American Political Science Association, 1971.

Wohlstetter, Roberta. *Cuba and Pearl Harbor: Hindsight and Foresight.* Santa Monica, Calif.: Rand Corporation, 1965.

Wolfers, Arnold. *Discord and Collaboration: Essays on International Politics.* Baltimore: Johns Hopkins Press, 1962.

Wriggins, W. Howard. *The Ruler's Imperative: Strategies for Political Survival in Asia and Africa.* New York: Columbia University Press, 1969.

Yarmolinsky, Adam. "Bureaucratic Structures and Political Outcomes," *Journal of International Affairs*, Vol. 23, No. 2 (1969).

———. *The Military Establishment: Its Impacts on American Society.* New York: Harper & Row, 1971.

———. "The Military Establishment," *Foreign Policy*, No. 1 (Winter 1970–71).

Young, Hugo, Bryan Silcock, and Peter Dunn. "Why We Went to the Moon: From the Bay of Pigs to the Sea of Tranquility," *Washington Monthly*, Vol. 2 (April 1970).

Index

DATE DUE			
GAYLORD			PRINTED IN U.S.A.